D0079262

# MODERN
# LATIN AMERICAN
# REVOLUTIONS

# MODERN
# LATIN AMERICAN
# REVOLUTIONS

——————■——————

## Eric Selbin

SOUTHWESTERN UNIVERSITY

Westview Press

BOULDER • SAN FRANCISCO • OXFORD

Copyright © 1993 by Westview Press, Inc.

Published in 1993 in the United States of America by Westview Press, Inc., 5500 Central Avenue, Boulder, Colorado 80301-2877, and in the United Kingdom by Westview Press, 36 Lonsdale Road, Summertown, Oxford OX2 7EW

Library of Congress Cataloging-in-Publication Data
Selbin, Eric
    Modern Latin American revolutions / Eric Selbin.
      p.   cm.
    Includes bibliographical references (p.   ) and index.
    ISBN 0-8133-8461-3. — ISBN 0-8133-8462-1 (pbk. )
      1. Latin America—Politics and government—1948–      . 2. Revolutions—
Latin America—History—20th century.   3. Leadership.   I. Title.
F1414.2.S39   1993
303.4'3'0980904—dc20                                                    93-26055
                                                                                        CIP

Printed and bound in the United States of America

∞ The paper used in this publication meets the requirements of the American National Standard for Permanence of Paper for Printed Library Materials Z39.48-1984.

10     9     8     7     6     5     4     3     2     1

# Contents

CONTENTS

# Acknowledgments

An undertaking such as this relies heavily on the assistance, support, and good graces of a wide array of people. Recognizing them here hardly repays the debt I owe them. (Nor does it implicate them in any way in any errors of omission or commission, which remain solely my responsibility.)

Kathryn Sikkink inspired me throughout the process of writing this book. Her thoughtful and challenging questions and repeated close, critical, and insightful readings served to make this book you hold in your hand far better. I can think of no way to adequately express my appreciation for what she has done.

Brian Job offered consistently helpful criticisms and encouragement. Ron Aminzade, Henry Dietz, Mary Dietz, Raymond Duvall, Cecil Eubanks, John Freeman, Cal Jillson, August Nimtz, Stuart Schwartz, and Gary Wynia have all aided and abetted my interests in revolution and Latin America over the years; each of them has influenced what you will read here.

Kris Thalhammer read the entire manuscript closely and pushed me to be clear and accessible; her optimism and energy were inspirational. Timothy Wickham-Crowley reviewed the manuscript for Westview Press and offered everything one could hope for: a close, careful reading, challenging questions, and compelling arguments.

Leslie Anderson encouraged this project from the start and took the time to read parts; her support and insights were invaluable. Cynthia Kite and Greg McAvoy read bits and pieces, asked tough questions, and provided valuable insights. Kathy Hochstetler shared her knowledge of Latin America with me and, along with Jim Mahoney, Wendy Rahn, and Cynthia Weber, provided thoughtful comments, critical support, and timely enthusiasm. At various stages, Gary Prevost, Harry Vanden, and Thomas Walker all encouraged my work and made helpful suggestions.

In Nicaragua, Ivan Aguilar, Jr., Martha Calderón, Rimer Khordero, and Marvin Ortega all went out of their way for me. Barbara Spencer, coordinator of Project Minnesota-León (PML) during both of my stays in León, was extremely helpful and a great friend. Rosanne Fischer, another PML coordinator, was also a great help. I remain staggered by the warmth and generosity shown me by so many Nicaraguans, particularly the Leónese, who were always willing to take the time to explain the subtle intricacies of daily life in Nicaragua to a less-than-subtle North American.

One of the reasons I chose to work with Westview Press was the opportunity to work with Barbara Ellington; as many people had predicted, it has been a great experience. I also appreciate the efforts on my behalf by others at Westview, including Kathleen McClung, Michelle Murphy, Martha Robbins, Connie Oehring, and Marian Safran, who did a wonderful job copyediting the manuscript.

The research in Nicaragua was funded by grants from the McMillan Travel Fund at the University of Minnesota and a generous Research Abroad Grant from the Graduate School at the University of Minnesota. I greatly appreciate their support.

A special thank-you is owed to my parents, Marion Selbin and Joel Selbin, who instilled in me a commitment to justice, a love of learning, and a fascination with politics large and small and who have always encouraged me to do the things that I wanted to do.

Jesse Cordes Selbin, a truly wonderful child, frequently offered to help with this book and did so far more than she realizes. Besides helping me keep this project in perspective, she proved to have a delightful sense of timing about hugs, smiles, and laughter. Zoe Cordes Selbin cleverly waited until the very last stage of the project to grace us with her delightful presence.

This book is dedicated to the lovely and talented Helen Cordes, an amazing person day in and day out. During the time I was working on what she came to refer to as "our long national nightmare," she did far more than her share of housework, yardwork, and, most important, parenting, all while working more than full time as an editor of the *Utne Reader*. I stand in awe of her love and devotion.

*Eric Selbin*

CHAPTER ONE

■

# Social Revolution and
# the Role of the Individual

Revolution remains endlessly fascinating to scholars and activists alike; it is, H. L. Mencken once suggested, the "sex of politics."[1] However, the concept of revolution has lost much of its utility, rendered by excessive and careless usage into little more than a synonym for "watershed" or "turning point" and invoked as a rhetorical device to lend drama or import to far less dramatic, even mundane, occasions. In addition, the use of the term to connote fundamental societal transformation has recently been challenged by the claim that the triumph of capitalism is contemporaneous with the demise of revolution.

Nonetheless, social scientists who continue to debate exact meanings of revolution remain committed to the importance of the concept and the need to fine-tune it. Revolutions offer us a rare opportunity to glimpse political life in its rawest, most open, and perhaps most revealing form. The drama of revolution lays society bare, providing the opportunity to see the hopes and fears of great numbers of people whose daily struggle is bound up in the mundane questions of where their next meal will come from, how to clothe their children, or how to care for their sick. Suddenly—although in some cases only after an agonizingly long struggle that can last beyond the life of many participants—possibilities seem to abound.

Revolutions thus appear as the most profoundly political moments that occur in any society.[2] Sociologist Michael Kimmel goes as far as to position the concept of revolution as the "centerpiece of all theories about society."[3] Under any set of circumstances, revolution provides an important and critical lens through which to view the world. The human belief in boundless possibilities and the intrinsic ability of people to reshape both the world and themselves present the people involved in the revolutionary process a unique treasure. It is in the revolutionary moment that those people become most accessible to outsiders like us.

1

There is a rich and lengthy tradition of social science research on revolution.[4] Most of this research has been and continues to be based on what are commonly referred to as the "great revolutions": the French, Russian, Chinese, and, occasionally, Mexican. These revolutionary processes were characterized by the societal tensions surrounding the transition from feudalism to capitalism, particularly class struggle; they marked the demise of "ancient, traditional royal, or imperial regimes."[5] As a result, research on these revolutions focused on their causes. Commonly these revolutions were portrayed as evidence of the "grand sweep of history" and the importance of institutions and structures.

The revolutions in France, Russia, China, and Mexico thus may be seen as the "first generation" of social revolutions. These revolutions have served to help social scientists and others define the term *revolution*, and they have fueled research on a "second generation" of revolutions, those in the Third World since World War II.[6] Here again, the focus has largely been on the causes of revolution, particularly the role played by the peasantry.[7] Yet the reference point ultimately seems to remain the first-generation revolutions. The modern Latin American revolutions are related—but distinct from their predecessors.[8] The importance of these differences should not be ignored.

The links between the two generations are not difficult to discern. In both, the social revolutionary process broadly unfolds in the same pattern: insurrection, political victory, and the effort to transform society.[9] Recognition of this connection is important, among other reasons, because it allows us to take advantage of and build on the outstanding work done by several generations of social science theorists of revolution. It also reminds us of the extent to which revolutionaries look to past revolutions for both negative and positive examples. All four revolutions considered here—the Bolivian, Cuban, Nicaraguan, and Grenadian—drew to varying degrees on the experience of the Mexican revolution.[10]

There are, however, important and meaningful differences between the first and second generation of revolutions. At least two of these differences relate to the changes that have occurred in the international system. The modern Latin American revolutions have come of age in a time of economic dependency that contrasts rather sharply with that of the essentially preindustrial first generation.[11] Furthermore, these revolutions have not occurred in "large and predominantly rural nations with long-standing traditional governments," but rather in neocolonial settings that featured relatively modern government institutions.[12] Although these differences are important, it is also the case that they can be readily captured by a structural perspective.

Some differences cannot be easily captured by such a perspective.

The modern Latin American revolutions have been characterized by profoundly multiclass alliances and high degrees of voluntarism: The conscious choices and intentional actions of people have played clearly critical roles in the revolutionary process. Structural theories are poorly equipped to explain the even minor cross-class alliances present in some of these cases and largely deny the importance of leadership in the first-generation revolutions. Such theories are even less useful in helping to understand cases such as Bolivia, Cuba, Nicaragua, and Grenada.

Revolution clearly denotes more than a simple transition. The term implies that in the period after revolutionaries acquire control of the state structures, they will seek to transform fundamentally at least some facet of society. Social revolution describes those relatively rare cases where the revolutionaries seek the profound transformation of the entire society. The failure of most theories to account for these attempts at societal transformation seems problematic.

This failure is exacerbated by the predominance of deterministic or structuralist approaches. Macrolevel structural forces (such as the state, class relations, or the international economic and political arena) are of great use in sketching the conditions present and to be encountered. They are of little use, however, in exploring the essence of the social revolutionary process.[13] Nowhere is this more obvious than the inability of such approaches to explain (or even explore) the often remarkable verve and creativity with which revolutionaries create new societies. It seems clear that what is missing from these conceptualizations is recognition of the central and critical role played by people in the complex process of revolution.[14]

To date, social science researchers have commonly focused on the structural determinants of the breakdown of regimes or the formation of revolutionary vanguards and their ability to cobble together coalitions that succeed in taking power. Given the magnitude implicit in the revolutionary process, this focus is understandable.[15] However, researchers have paid relatively little attention to the revolutionary process as it continues *after* political victory. What attention there has been has focused almost exclusively on institutions and structures. The very aspect that defines the social revolutionary process—the effort at fundamental transformation of society and the people in it—has largely been ignored.

The attention of those scholars who have considered the period that follows political victory has remained focused on various political, economic, or social variables. As a result, social scientists, particularly political scientists and sociologists, have done an excellent job of understanding and explaining the "institutionalization" of revolutions, that is, the reestablishment and reorganization of state structures, including the creation of new institutions.[16] Although the establishment and maintenance of state power is a minimum condition for the success of revolutions, it is only part of the story.

The term *revolution*, as I mentioned, evokes images that include conscious efforts by some of the participants to effect fundamental changes.[17] What defines any list of "great revolutions," as Hobsbawm pointed out, is not acquisition of state power but devotion to the creation of a "new framework," a new orientation for society. A revolution that has not at least attempted to establish such a framework is unlikely to be on the list.[18] Thus revolutions have historically been judged by the people's relationships with the new government and with each other and by how much or how little they embraced the revolutionary process itself, forged in the complex relationship between the revolutionaries and the population in whose name they purport to act.

The quintessence of the social revolutionary process is the transformation of society, more specifically, of citizens. Perhaps the most eloquent and certainly the most compelling explanation of what this means was suggested to me by an older woman in Nicaragua who related with a mix of amusement, disbelief, and disgust how the wealthy in Nicaragua had treated the rest of the population as if it were "cattle." She hastened to assure me: "This could never happen again. We would never allow this. We know now that we are not cattle . . . and we will never be their cattle again."[19] This change in the way citizens view their society and their own roles within it has largely been ignored by political scientists. I will attempt to capture this change by introducing the concept of the *consolidation* of a revolution, as distinct from its institutionalization.

The difference between institutionalization and consolidation is more than a matter of semantics. Although subtle, it is an important, even essential, distinction. Consolidation occurs when a significant majority of the population embraces the core of the social revolutionary project—centered on the creation of a more just and equitable society—and is therefore willing to resist efforts to roll back the gains made through the social revolutionary process.[20] The focus is on people, not structures; choices, not determinism; and transformation, not simply transition. The failure of most social science researchers to adequately incorporate the role played by individuals has rendered their analyses flat, incomplete, and unpersuasive; the omission of human intentions and actions hinders efforts to explain revolutionary processes.

This chapter continues with a brief review of the relevant literature on revolution; I then propose a working definition of revolution. In the next section I introduce the concept of consolidation as a process distinct from institutionalization and as an analytically useful tool in the effort to understand social revolutionary processes as well as other forms of societal change. In a final section, which presages the discussion in Chapter 3, I consider the role of individuals in the social revolutionary process and suggest that they are responsible for the direction the revolutionary process takes after political victory.  □

## THE LITERATURE ON REVOLUTION

*Revolution,* as Finley pointed out, is a term that is used commonly and understood well by academics and nonacademics alike despite a variety of contradictory meanings.[21] This is not to imply that revolution can mean anything at all that one proposes. Indeed, revolution carries with it a common set of implications that distinguish it from other phenomena. Still, there remains a great deal of debate over the meaning and import of *revolution* as a term.[22]

Definitions do not solve problems; the question is whether the chosen definition advances one's understanding of the term.[23] At the same time, as Aya pointed out, confusion arising from the lack of "adequate distinctions may slow solving problems of explanation. Hence, though we need not define, we must often distinguish."[24] Rather than offer yet another "precise" definition of revolution, what I propose here is a working definition that builds directly on preexisting conceptualizations. Other explanations, relying on classic definitions, lack suitable attention to the final, transformative phase of the social revolutionary process and the role of people in that process.

Social scientists, philosophers, and revolutionaries have constructed a wide variety of models of revolution. In the social sciences the current reference points are the people whom Goldstone has designated the "third generation" of revolutionary theorists.[25] The third generation drew in part on the "natural history" of revolutions, cataloged by the first generation of theorists in the 1920s and 1930s.[26] The third generation also built on and reacted against the work of the second generation of theorists, who in the 1960s used social science methodologies to explain revolutions.[27] Most of those social science theories have proven to be poorly conceived, generating analyses based on what Hobsbawm labeled "static dichotomies":[28] simplistic distinctions such as violence/nonviolence[29] or the function/dysfunction of society.[30]

The "third generation" theorists promised more-detailed examinations of a greater variety of revolutions and "holistic" understandings of the revolutionary process.[31] There is little question that these theorists considered a wider array of revolutions than had their predecessors, and they sought broader understandings of the revolutionary process. Their work was marked by important insights as well as Skocpol's paradigmatic definition of revolution.[32] Yet three things that cut across the work of these theorists have remained troubling: Their theories are rooted in the "great revolutions"; their focus is almost solely on causes of revolution; and structural perspectives would appear to be their default position. To the degree that there has been any consideration of the period after the revolutionaries came to power, these scholars continued their predecessors' inclination for positing reestablishment of the state—defined here as institutionalization—as the ultimate goal. None of the third-generation works has held up well as a general theory of revolution.

Although this third generation of theorists holds sway, there remain today in the social sciences three predominant models of revolution.[33] Perhaps the greatest influence on all investigations of revolution continues to be Karl Marx's theory of self-conscious movements rooted in class conflict. A principal alternative to Marx can be found in the "political conflict" approach of Charles Tilly. Finally, the structuralist models of Samuel Huntington and, more recently, Theda Skocpol have been paradigmatic in the social sciences.[34] The conceptualization of social revolution offered here is influenced by and rooted in these perspectives.

## Karl Marx

The massive body of work Karl Marx produced has shaped modern understandings and explanations of revolution more profoundly than any of the other works that undergird social science theorizing.[35] It is not possible in this brief discussion to do justice to Marx's views on revolution, for they permeate virtually everything that Marx wrote. "Marxian historical materialism," Dunn argued, "is above all else a theory of revolution."[36] Even though during the past 140 years Marx's intellectual legacy has been subject to various interpretations, the key components of Marx's views on revolution remain discernible.

Revolutions, for Marx, were not events but processes: class-based movements driven by the inherent contradictions—objective contradictions—in society. Conflict was inevitable given that the relatively small number who owned the means of production extended pervasive control over the lives of those who produced. Socialist revolution was likely to occur when the urban working class, the proletariat, recognized its exploitation at the hands of the wealthy, the bourgeoisie. Marx's perspective was summarized cogently by Skocpol: "Marx understood revolution not as an isolated episode of violence or conflict but as class-based movement growing out of objective structural contradictions within historically developing and inherently conflict-ridden society."[37]

This view of revolution was manifested in several concrete ways throughout Marx's work. The clearest was Marx's focus on economics:

Society's divisions are class-based and classes are determined by one's economic status. Moreover, the "objective structural contradictions," which make conflict inherent in society, are rooted in questions about the ownership of the means of production and the exploitation of the urban working class. Related to this—and at odds with the argument of this book—was his attention to "objective structural conditions" rather than people. Finally, Marx considered the urban workers the revolutionary class. In fact, for Marx: "The lower middle class, the small manufacturer, the shopkeeper, the artisan, the peasant . . . are . . . not revolutionary, but conservative. Nay more, they are reactionary."[38] Yet, as will be seen in the cases considered here—Bolivia, Cuba, Nicaragua, and Grenada— many of these "classes" played important, even leading, roles in revolutionary processes, establishing for themselves impeccable revolutionary credentials.

Most important for my theme is Marx's recognition (or contention) that revolution is fundamentally a process, not simply an event. The idea of revolution as a process seems to have gone in and out of fashion over the years among students of revolution; I will stress it here. Another significant point for my working definition is that Marx's conceptualization of revolution, although definitely structuralist, does not totally preclude human agency. This is perhaps most apparent in the famous dictum from *The Eighteenth Brumaire of Louis Bonaparte:* "Men make their own history, but they do not make it just as they please."[39] Consequently, Marx argued, people can act upon their environment and "objective" conditions, albeit not under conditions of their own choosing. At the risk of sounding trite, one can say that there can be no revolution without the revolutionaries. My proposed theory of social revolution clearly goes beyond Marx to argue that people have and do make choices that overcome structural conditions. The work of Marx, nonetheless, remains an important and influential jumping-off point.

## Charles Tilly

Charles Tilly's work on revolution is, like that of Marx, fundamentally structural. There was, however, clearly an increased role for people to play in Tilly's conceptualization, albeit a role confined well within existing structures.[40] Revolutions defined one end of a continuum of the daily struggle for resources. People's actions were clearly relevant for Tilly at several points. This is most apparent in his notion of "collective action" and his description of the revolutionary process, which he elucidated as a seven-stage sequence.

"Collective action," for Tilly, referred to people acting together with thought and purpose: "joint action in pursuit of common ends."[41]

"Spontaneous, disorganized, random" behavior was excluded.[42] Collective action thus signified conscious and intentional behavior in which people engaged.[43] This behavior in pursuit of change and the subsequent interactions are best understood as a point where the interaction of agency and structure, that is, the relationship between people and institutions, is discernible. People and institutions interact.

According to Tilly, revolution was the mobilization of that discontent into a struggle for political power with those already in power; "revolutionary situations" referred to periods when multiple contenders vied for power.[44] The displacement of those in power by those out of power—the triumph of a single contender—signaled what Tilly referred to as a "revolutionary outcome."[45] Tilly echoed Lenin's maxim that revolutionary situations were no guarantee of revolutionary outcomes.[46] Perhaps as a result, Tilly's points of emphasis generated a theory that lends itself better to investigations of the period prior to political victory than to the process considered here, which unfolds after the transfer of sovereignty from the old regime to the victorious revolutionaries.

A place for people is also evident in Tilly's explication of the revolutionary sequence. He saw the first three stages as (1) the "gradual mobilization of contenders making exclusive claims to governmental control"; (2) a "rapid increase in the number of people accepting those claims"; and (3) "unsuccessful efforts by the government . . . to suppress the alternative coalition." In each stage it is possible to discern people; they are called upon to make conscious choices, perhaps most obviously about whether to accept the claims of the power contenders. People effectively disappear from the next two stages: (4) the "establishment by the alternative coalition of effective control over some part of the government"; and (5) "struggles of the alternative coalition to maintain or expand that control." In the culmination of the revolutionary process, however, people may once again be part of the process. The final two stages are (6) the "reconstruction of a single polity through the victory of the alternative coalition, through its defeat, or through the establishment of a modus vivendi between the alternative coalition and some or all of the old members; fragmentation of the revolutionary coalition"; and (7) the "reimposition of routine governmental control throughout the subject population."[47] Each of those stages incorporates a human element. In these stages the revolutionary leadership is, first, engaged in negotiations and, second, seeking the support of the population.

Of the many implications inherent in the seven-stage progression that Tilly formulated, two merit mention here. The first is that the sequence is overwhelmingly slanted toward the period prior to political victory. Only the final stage—reimposition of routine governmental control—deals with what transpires after the revolutionaries have

achieved political victory. Moreover, the reimposition of routine governmental control focuses explicitly on the institutionalization process.
Structures remain the key.

Nonetheless, Tilly provided some space for people's motivations within the structures. The revolutionary moment arrives "when previously
acquiescent members of that population find themselves confronted with
strictly incompatible demands from the government and from the alternative body claiming control over the government or . . . to be the government."[48] This crisis of multiple sovereignty in Tilly's model is resolved
by the population, or at least a significant segment of it, making
a choice.[49] Voluntary commitment to the new regime would seem to be
human agency in action.

## Samuel Huntington and Theda Skocpol

The conceptualization of revolution that I present here has been influenced by Marx and Tilly. Most directly, however, my understanding of
revolution is rooted in and is a direct reaction to the definitions of revolution and social revolution proposed by, respectively, Samuel Huntington
and Theda Skocpol. Their perspective, like that of Marx and Tilly, may
be referred to as structuralist, that is, the focus remains primarily on
the "objective" dynamic of structures.[50] There is little or no place accorded to agents—people are, quite simply, not relevant to their theories
of revolution.

Huntington's *Political Order in Changing Societies* has, at least in the
study of revolution, been subsumed to some degree by Skocpol's work. It
nonetheless remains an important starting point. From Huntington's perspective, modernization is the cause of revolution. Therefore, the focus is
on political institutions and their ability to meet rising demands. Revolution is brought on by the failure of political institutions to accommodate
new demands and absorb potential challengers that emerge during the
modernization process.[51]

There are two aspects of Huntington's work that are of particular relevance for my conceptualization of revolution. The first is his definition of
revolution as "a rapid, fundamental, and violent domestic change in the
dominant values and myths of a society, in its political institutions, social
structure, leadership, and government activity and policies."[52] The second is his distinction between revolution and related phenomena such as
insurrections, rebellions, coups d'état, or wars of independence.

Huntington's definition is cogent and compelling. Particularly persuasive is his framing of revolution as an *outcome*. At the same time, he construed revolution as little more than an outcome. Although he conceptualized revolution as both "rapid" and "violent," there is little evidence in

his work to suggest that revolution is, in fact, a process rather than an event limited in scope and duration.[53] This rendering is partly a result of the model that Huntington and other structuralists have visualized, according to Kimmel, that of volcanic activity: "Discontent smolders for years, while the pressure below builds and builds, until, unable to contain it any longer, the volcano erupts, destroying the stable mountain underneath and sweeping away all that was beautiful in the traditional landscape."[54] What matters is the outcome; the *process* is essentially absent.[55]

Skocpol's *States and Social Revolution*, published eleven years after Huntington's *Political Order in Changing Societies*, supplanted the latter and emerged as the paradigmatic statement on revolution, the reference point for theorizing on the topic.[56] As we have seen, the essential centerpiece of Huntington's work is modernization, but for Skocpol the state and its relationship with domestic social classes and the international political economy occupy center stage. Revolution, for Skocpol, is basically keyed to the weakening or collapse of the existing state structure.

Most important for the definition of revolution presented here is Skocpol's conceptualization of social revolution as the "rapid, basic transformations of a society's state and class structures; . . . accompanied and in part carried through by class-based revolts from below."[57] There are two critical aspects inherent in this understanding of revolution. First, these "transformations" must be not just political, social, or economic, but all three, in a "mutually reinforcing fashion."[58] In this way Skocpol, having built on Huntington, further distinguished social revolution from related phenomena. Second, social revolutions must include a popular uprising, since they are driven by the presumably disaffected class from below. Although not directly introducing a role for people, Skocpol nonetheless reintroduced the element of *process*, which is missing from the definition proposed by Huntington; consequently revolution was understood as both an outcome and a process.[59]

Consistent with her structural approach, Skocpol explained the social revolutionary process by placing the state in the center of her analysis and avoided voluntarist factors by reference to class relations.[60] This holds up reasonably well for assessments of the so-called great revolutions (those of France, Russia, and China) that she undertook. Skocpol's approach, however, proves much more limited when the cases under investigation are modern social revolutions (Cuba or Nicaragua, for example), which have been fundamentally, in some cases deeply, multiclass in character. They have also been characterized by voluntarism.[61]

Skocpol introduces process in her definition, but she devotes little attention to it. Most notably, she fails to consider the obvious implication: She does not allow a role for people in the revolutionary process.[62] As with Huntington, those who make the revolution are conspicuous by their absence. The failure to include the efforts and intentions of people indicates the belief that structural conditions dictate absolutely what people can do. Skocpol's working assumption, as Kimmel suggested, would appear to be that appropriate and mindless actors are perpetually in place, ready to perform the actions required of them by the structural conditions.[63] This perspective construes people's responses to structural conditions as irrelevant. Consequently, the most basic and most human elements of the social revolutionary process, such as ideology, leadership, and human agency, are ignored.[64] In Skocpol's estimation, "as far as the causes of historical revolutions go, Wendell Phillips was quite correct when he declared: 'Revolutions are not made; they come.'"[65]

Skocpol has provided the paradigmatic definition of social revolution. Moreover, she has presented convincing evidence of the relationship between structural conditions and revolutionary transformations. Yet her analysis is flawed, for it leaves no meaningful role for people to play. People's consciousness and actions are critical variables that cannot be ignored; they are "always part of the story," as Kimmel noted "and sometimes crucial to it."[66] I contend that people are *always* crucial to the story. The question is where and how people enter the revolutionary process.    ☐

## SOCIAL REVOLUTION: A DEFINITION

By now it should be apparent that the central tenet of my working definition of revolution is that revolutions are in large measure the product of and characterized by human action. I compensate for the failure to include people's conscious actions in conceptualizations of the social revolutionary process by introducing the concept of *goal* into the understanding of social revolution.[67] *Goal* implies conscious aspiration and intentional action in pursuit of a final aim. I define social revolution, then, as the successful overthrow of a ruling elite by a revolutionary vanguard that has mobilized broad popular support and undertaken the transformation of a society's political, economic, and social structures in a contemporaneous and mutually reinforcing fashion.

As Huntington did, I distinguish social revolutions from related phenomena by virtue of their outcome. As Skocpol did, I incorporate process because social revolutions are carried forward by popular revolutionary movements. What is now present is the notion of goal; social revolution is understood as an outcome, process, and goal. The range of cases is relatively narrow. It includes only situations where there is an attempt to fundamentally transform society. My definition stresses the importance of the revolutionary leadership's effort to mobilize broad popular support.[68] Finally, the inclusion of transformation as a goal sharpens the distinction between social revolutions and related phenomena that fail to bring about such transformation.

This distinction does not deny the significance of those related phenomena: coups d'état, rebellions, and political revolutions. Trimberger showed that coups d'état in Japan (1868), Turkey (1919), Egypt (1952), and Peru (1968)—which she construed as "revolutions from above"—sought radical transformations.[69] Walton demonstrated that rebellions in the Philippines (1946–1953), Kenya (1952–1956), and Colombia (1946–1958) resulted in significant, if limited, economic and political reforms.[70] Political revolutions in England (1640–1650, 1688–1689) and the United States (1765–1776) profoundly reorganized the state and politics of those countries.

The goals of a coup d'état, rebellion, or political revolution, however, rarely include changing the entire system but rather striking at specific locations within the established system of government or reorganizing the government to address specific grievances. Coups d'état are restricted in both nature and objectives: Power is transferred either within the ruling elite or from one ruling elite to another, but the state, economic, and social structures and relations remain the same.[71] Rebellions are often spontaneous uprisings aimed at changing the leaders, policies, or perhaps even political institutions of the state, but only rarely do they involve efforts to directly affect social structures and values.[72] They are driven by the desire to redress particular grievances or alter specific situations. Political revolutions transform state, but not economic or social, structures. Such government reorganizations may even include class conflict.[73]

Whereas such reforms and political reorganizations may be an antecedent to social revolution (or part of a war of independence/national liberation), these phenomena may be best construed as events because they are limited in time, target, and objective. In other words, they lack the necessary constructive transformative consequences and the fundamental and contemporaneous changes in social and political structure occurring in a "mutually reinforcing fashion" that is the special feature of social revolution.[74]

Social revolution is a dynamic process that encompasses both the destruction of the old regime and the construction of a new society.[75] As a result, the social revolutionary process is most usually thought of as having three phases. The first of these is the *insurrection*, during which political sovereignty is challenged, in some cases by multiple contenders, and may be in doubt.[76] This period is followed by the *political victory*, which is marked by the transition of sovereignty from the old regime to the revolutionary government. This is the most readily discernible phase and the most easily dated—those dates commonly associated with revolutions refer to this phase of the process.

The third and final phase of the social revolutionary process is the *transformation* of society and the people, that is, the institutionalization and consolidation of the revolution: the redistribution of resources, changes in the quality of life, industrialization and urbanization, and moral reconstruction. This last phase, during which the revolutionary leadership undertakes to transform popular attitudes and create a new people and society and the "old" people and society react, is the defining characteristic of social revolution and the focus of this project.[77]

The distinctions between the processes of consolidation and institutionalization, central to the project presented here, are further developed and explored in the next section. Although there is a large literature on institutionalization, few scholars have dealt with the consolidation phase of the social revolutionary process, and little literature exists upon which to base my observations. Consequently, at this point we must explore the differences between institutionalization and consolidation and consider the voluntaristic nature of the consolidation process itself.  □

## PATHS TO SUCCESS:
## THE INSTITUTIONALIZATION AND
## CONSOLIDATION OF SOCIAL REVOLUTION

During the insurrection the revolutionaries must act to mobilize broad popular support and topple the old regime. In the political victory period the leadership's strategy for acquiring power and transferring sovereignty is prominent. As leaders undertake the third and final phase of the social revolutionary process, the transformation of society and the individuals in it—which they inevitably do after taking power—the focus shifts to their strategy for the consolidation of the revolution. In other words, social revolutions are neither haphazard nor spontaneous; rather, "they are led by men, even when they seem most spontaneous. Revolutions occur because men want them to occur."[78] The social revolutionary process requires the conscious effort of people—intentionality is as necessary to the process as are extant structural conditions.

The onset of the final phase of the social revolutionary process represents the moment that Robert Darnton, in seeking to explain what was so revolutionary about the French revolution, referred to as "possibilism."[79] People suddenly find themselves presented with boundless opportunities to reshape themselves and by extension their world. The course of history, Arendt argued, "suddenly begins anew, that an entirely new story, a story never known or told before, is about to unfold."[80] People, she asserted, believe "that they are agents in a process which spells the end of the old order and brings the birth of the new world."[81] If the French revolution remains the primary reference point and the archetype—the leaders sought, after all, to reconceptualize time, measurement, even interpersonal relations—every case of social revolution begins the period of transformation with dramatic visions, which often run headlong into the societal conditions that survived the first two phases of the social revolutionary process.

This final phase is complex and fraught with contradictions. Most immediately, the leaders are faced with two essential tasks. The first is establishment of some sort of at least minimal government that can gain international and domestic acceptance. This is the project of institutionalization; it entails the simultaneous dismantling of whatever institutions remain from the old regime and their replacement or reconfiguration. Central to this project are questions about succession and limitations on personal power.[82]

The second task, achieving consolidation, involves convincing the people that political victory in itself does not signify the success of the revolution. They must embrace the social revolutionary project, its essence or core, which has historically been the promise of health care, education, justice, the rights of the disenfranchised. With political victory, the people win the opportunity to make a better life for themselves and their children.

The success or failure of any particular social revolution lies largely in the paths that the revolutionary process takes. I argue here that the discrete but interrelated tasks of consolidation and institutionalization, which undergird the final phase of the social revolutionary project, represent the primary paths available after the political victory. Whereas the processes of institutionalization and consolidation can be combined in a variety of ways, only when there is attention to both processes is the result a successful social revolution. In other words, when there is a failure either to institutionalize or to consolidate, a social revolution has not occurred. Only those cases where there has been a significant degree of institutionalization and consolidation are successful social revolutions.

## Institutionalization: The Structure of the Social Revolutionary Process

Institutionalization is a critical step in rebuilding a state vacated by the old regime or destroyed by the revolutionaries. Political institutions, which form part of a state apparatus, include government bureaucracies, the military, the executive, the judiciary, and the legislature.[83] A state's claim to political sovereignty must be substantiated via a combination of administrative, legal, policing, and military organizations under the control of an executive authority. As a rule, during the first two phases of the social revolutionary process, the leaders argue that the institutions that constitute the regime in power are corrupt, fundamentally unjust, immoral, and unequal to the task of national development. Presented with the opportunity to create a new society, the revolutionary leadership must either dismantle or reorganize the political, economic, and social institutions inherited from the old regime.

New state institutions are created for a variety of reasons; these institutions can be crudely lumped into two broad categories. The first serves the immediate institutional needs of the nascent government. Attention here, then, is on those institutions related to the state's ability both to defend itself (to maintain its existence) and to require its citizens to obey the laws (to reestablish order in the aftermath of the political victory). This plays itself out in a variety of ways with respect to the components of the government apparatus, but there are certain patterns that have been readily identifiable throughout history. The second category is designed to provide assistance in the drive for consolidation. The focus of these institutions, therefore, is on social services and equitable treatment for the population.

One of the key components in the first category is the justice system. The military and police, or what remains of them, are usually dismantled; the victorious revolutionary army and/or former members of the military or police who were sympathetic to the revolutionary process replace them. The judiciary—often after having served as the legal bulwark in the old regime's repression of the population—must dispense justice in a society in transition, where the very notion of what is just and legal is being hotly contested, sometimes formulated and reformulated on the spot. Therefore, in the early days after political victory, there is usually an abundance of ad hoc tribunals and juries to mete out "revolutionary justice" to those who opposed the social revolutionary process.

The legislative and administrative branches of the government are also key components in the first category, and another set of important changes is effected in them. The legislature, previously a largely irrelevant, privileged arena of the powerful, reflects the whole population, and a large number of laws are passed. Commonly these statutes are aimed at dismantling vestiges of the old regime and legalizing the new. As a rule, wide-ranging guarantees of the new society are passed and provisions made to outlaw the type of excesses that in part served to define the old regime.

Perhaps the most important issues to be resolved in terms of institutionalization of the new government are those of succession and limits on personal power. These matters have often played a role in creating the insurrection, and revolutionaries are quick to try to remedy them.

Historically, however, that has proved difficult: The institutionalization process has rarely succeeded in resolving these problems, and often they have come back to haunt the revolutionary process.

The modern Latin American revolutions have been no exception. Despite occasional forays into electoral democracy, succession in both Bolivia and Cuba had traditionally been via *golpes de estado* (coups d'état). Personal power in both countries had traditionally been limited only by the strictures of the elite and the views of the military. The Bolivian revolutionaries sought to introduce democracy in combination with a system of cogovernment to solve these traditional problems—but for reasons elaborated in the next two chapters, neither worked. The revolutionaries in Cuba took a different tack—no provisions were (or really have been) made for succession, and the limit on personal power was and is considered to be "the people." It is likely that the Cuban population will have to confront the issue of succession within the next decade. The success of the Cuban people in limiting personal power since political victory seems mixed, at best, but bogs down in what may be thought of as definitional questions. It is, however, clear that the personal power of Fidel Castro within Cuba is relatively limitless.

Though Grenada had been independent for only five years at the time of the 1979 revolution, it, like the other Eastern Caribbean states, already had traditions concerning both succession and the limits of personal power. In fact, there were two discordant traditions. These countries have largely retained their colonial legacy of Westminster-style parliamentary democracy, featuring regular, essentially free elections with multiparty participation.[84] In practice, however, some leaders have taken advantage of the "wide latitude allowed to the executive by the Westminster system" and their stature as their country's "founding father."[85] One result of this has been few meaningful restrictions on personal power and in some cases intrafamily succession. As Heine pointed out, in societies where democratic institutions have been imposed by colonial powers, there are rarely "countervailing forces to the unbridled exercise of authority of an all-powerful executive."[86]

By 1979, Grenada had been run by Eric Gairy, under the guise of democracy, for twenty-eight years. Rather than a stereotypical Caribbean dictator, Gairy "was simply the most extreme expression of the peculiar mix of democracy and authoritarianism" endemic to the Eastern Caribbean.[87] Grenadian revolutionaries essentially emulated the Cubans on questions of personal power. Limits on personal power under the revolutionary government appear to have existed as a combination of "the people" à la Cuba and intraparty self-criticism. Also reminiscent of Cuba was the Grenadians' apparent lack of attention to the issue of succession. These issues played a role in the ill-fated 1983 coup, which sealed the fate of the Grenadian revolution. Both are addressed in greater detail in the next two chapters.

Personal power had been unlimited in prerevolutionary Nicaragua; the dictatorship there was a dynastic one in which succession passed from father to son to brother. The Nicaraguan revolutionaries were extremely sensitive to limitations on personal power. As a result they carefully divided up responsibility within the new government and, as is explored more fully in Chapter 3, sought to avoid charismatic leaders. The policy seems to have been successful. In contrast to the other modern Latin American revolutions, personal power in Nicaragua remained limited—some have suggested to the detriment of the revolution—and none of the revolutionary leaders was accused of the sorts of abuses that seemed to occur in the other cases considered here.

The mechanism the Nicaraguan revolutionaries chose to resolve the succession issue was electoral democracy. That was a somewhat controversial choice, in part because it carried with it huge uncertainty: No revolutionary government had ever placed itself before the voting public in free and open elections. The two elections since the Nicaraguan revolution occurred in the midst of a brutal military and economic war. The Sandinista National Liberation Front (FSLN) won the 1984 election, but it lost the one in 1990. The peaceful transfer of power after the 1990 election suggests that alone among the modern Latin American revolutionaries, the Nicaraguans successfully resolved the succession issue.

The first institutions that a revolutionary government must create, as we have seen, are related to the immediate control of state power and its practice. Equally important are those that support and encourage the social revolutionary process. The second category of institutions therefore generates the mechanisms of the consolidation process. Such institutions are supposed to provide at least basic social services and the appearance of just and equitable treatment of the entire population. Social revolutionary governments have typically established institutions concerned with agrarian reform, women's rights, worker's rights, the rights of ethnic or indigenous groups, education, health, children, and employment. The government also encouraged the creation of counterparts to the new institutions among the population. In all modern Latin American revolutions there has been a profusion of such institutions, which enable the government after political victory to shift the focus of society from its elitist exclusionary past to a populist inclusionary present and future.

The creation of government and government-sponsored institutions is intended both to reinforce and to strengthen the break with the past. There seems little question that the Cubans and Nicaraguans were able to use their new institutions in this manner. The Grenadian case is far less clear, although the appropriate institutions were certainly in place. Such

institutions were also created in Bolivia; however, the desire of a significant part of the revolutionary leadership not to effect a break with the
past—a matter explored further in Chapter 2—came back to haunt them
and prevent the success of the revolution.

"Institutionalization" and "revolution" do not always coexist on easy
terms, in large measure, because of the association of institutionalization
with bureaucracy and bureaucratization and, by extension, with a growing inertia and conservatism.[88] The Mexican, Russian, and Chinese revolutions may all be accurately described as institutionalized. What is
more, in each case such institutionalization is associated with negative
results: oppression, conservatism, bureaucracy, inertia, and inefficiency.
The Mexican and Bolivian revolutions in particular came to be seen by
later Latin American revolutionaries as proof of the dangers inherent in
institutionalization.

Some revolutionaries have argued that no revolution should ever
be institutionalized lest it cease to be a creative or progressive force.
Among the modern Latin American revolutions, only the Bolivians enshrined and sought to emulate the Mexican type of institutionalization.
In Grenada, there were sharp divisions among the leadership on this as
on most issues. The leaders in Nicaragua remained leery of institutionalization even as they sought it; they feared that institutionalization would
stultify the social revolutionary process. The Cuban revolutionaries were
the most virulently opposed to institutionalization, often referring to
Mexico and Bolivia as "warnings" of what institutionalization would
lead to. Although the Cubans eventually did begin to institutionalize the
revolution, the "rectification" campaign, which opened in 1986, was in
part an attempt to de-institutionalize the social revolution and regain the
vibrancy, creativity, egalitarianism, and nonexclusivity that were once
distinguishing characteristics of the revolution. Although Cuba's rectification process has met with some success, it has become difficult to discern its status, as the Cubans confront their loss of support from their
former Eastern European allies and particularly the former Soviet Union.
In addition, Cuba is plagued by increasingly uninterested European support, and by growing economic and diplomatic pressure from the United
States.

It falls to the social revolutionary leadership, having seized the institutional structures, to utilize its full resources to reorganize them from the
ground up, based on principles different from and antithetical to those of
the preceding regime. It is this reestablishment of state power, based in
the executive, coercive, and administrative organs, that denotes the
successful institutionalization of a revolution. Two of the revolutions under consideration here—the Bolivian and the Nicaraguan—were successfully institutionalized. One might say that the Cubans have flirted with

institutionalization.[89] Institutionalization, however, provides relatively little evidence about consolidation.

Societies require institutions to deal with the issues inherent to collective existence, but those institutions function only if the population breathes life into them. As we shall see, the government can create and refurbish institutions and encourage people's participation, but it cannot make them work. It is in this way that the government's reorganization of the institutions and structures of society is deftly and profoundly intertwined with the project of consolidation.

Reorganized state structures, particularly the institutions newly created to meet the needs of the population, often provide a basis for consolidating the revolution. Examples include the institutions focused on health, literacy, and agrarian reform in all four of the modern Latin American revolutions. Another tactic, employed in both Cuba and Nicaragua, was the creation of "defense committees," which were organized by neighborhood. In theory, these institutions were charged with the dual responsibilities of promoting and channeling the population's energy and involvement in the transformation of society.[90]

New institutions that are successful in engendering greater participation, furnishing health care, improving the economic lot of the people, providing access to government services, and so on, not only strengthen their own legitimacy but also lay the groundwork for a healthy relationship between the leadership and the population. When such institutions fail, however, they become an obstacle, a barrier, between the government and the population for which the population correctly holds the government responsible. The aforementioned neighborhood defense committees in Cuba and Nicaragua (the Committees for the Defense of the Revolution [CDRs] and the Sandinista Defense Committees [CDSs], respectively) provide instructive examples.

During the first ten years of the Cuban revolution, the CDRs served as the primary revolutionary institution.[91] The CDRs provided contact with and access to government, transmitted propaganda messages, and supported the revolution's commitment to health care, including nutrition, and education. The CDRs also functioned effectively as the eyes and ears of the government in the neighborhoods, which inevitably resulted in some abuses.[92] Nonetheless, from 1960 to 1970, the CDRs were effectively the heart of the revolution, increasing people's commitment to the revolutionary process. In short, the largely popular CDRs served as the integrative and mobilizing arms of the social revolutionary process, driving institutionalization and promoting consolidation at the same time.[93]

Although the CDSs in Nicaragua sought to duplicate the dynamic, positive role played by the CDRs in the first ten years of the Cuban revolution, the contrast between the two was striking. The CDSs had begun as neighborhood support groups during the insurrection; this legacy and people's initial enthusiasm after political victory got them off to a strong start. Yet the CDSs failed to fulfill either the role envisioned for them by the leaders or the concomitant expectations of the population. Rather than being an important component of the social revolutionary process, the CDSs degenerated into what might charitably be described as a conduit for government policy and resources; a more common characterization might be a mechanism of bureaucratic control, mired in petty neighborhood squabbles. This failure led to the CDSs' loss of legitimacy and eventual collapse.[94] The largely unpopular CDSs may have played a role in the process of institutionalization; they appear to have done little to promote consolidation.

The close relationship between institutionalization and consolidation is a recurrent theme throughout this book. Yet these two critical dimensions of the social revolutionary transformation process are most usefully treated as analytically distinct. In practice, as I shall illustrate in Chapter 2, the relationship between the two processes may be characterized as profoundly dialectical in nature.[95]

### Consolidation: The Heart of the Social Revolutionary Process

What little discussion there is about *consolidation* as a term has come largely from those investigating the breakdown of democratic regimes and the transitions to democracy and socialism. Much like their colleagues who study revolution, however, these scholars have largely failed to recognize that consolidation is distinct from the institutionalization process. On other occasions consolidation has been conflated with legitimacy or hegemony.[96] In all these cases, as a rule, institutionalization is considered the ultimate goal, signifying reestablishment of the state, presumably, with democratic or social democratic structures. The result has been a perhaps excessive amount of time and attention paid to the drawing up of new constitutions, enactment of new laws, and the development, construction, and redirection of new and old institutions. Relatively little attention has been paid to questions of deepening democracy, which is where the concept of consolidation that I present would come into play.

Consolidation is often encountered as synonymous to institutionalization, that is, "consolidation" of the state apparatus and state power. This identification is most readily found in three areas of investigation: (1) the study of emergent Third World states;[97] (2) the exploration of the breakdown of authoritarianism and transition to democracy in Southern Europe and Latin America;[98] and (3) the focus on transitions to socialism in the Third World.[99] On the occasions when "consolidation" is discussed, it is usually in terms of the status of the state apparatus and/or power. My contention is that concerns such as the latter are most usefully understood under the designation "institutionalization."[100]

In fairness, we should note that the authors of those studies do not purport to be talking about social revolution, much less the consolidation of social revolution. Social revolution, after all, denotes fundamental transformations, and the focus of much of the work cited above is on transitions. Those interested in the struggles of Third World states have historically focused on their construction; if there is no state, there presumably is nothing to consolidate. For the others, the *transition* to either democracy or socialism, as they understand it, has relatively little in common with the *transformation* that is the hallmark of the social revolutionary process. Nonetheless, this is how consolidation is commonly understood and invoked.[101]

One of the few specific definitions of consolidation was offered by Maravell and Santamaría. Consolidation, they contended,

includes the processes by which the emergent regime eliminates, reduces to a minimum, or incorporates its initial ideological and institutional inconsistencies; establishes autonomy in the face of preexisting established powers within the country, especially the armed forces; mobilizes civil society into political forms of expression; and develops and maintains a structured and relatively stable party system, capable of guaranteeing popularly accountable government.[102]

In practice, consolidation is fundamentally, if not completely, tied to the function, autonomy, and reproduction of the new regime. These are based on "institutionalization of the regime's norms and structures, the expansion of its legitimacy, and the removal of obstacles."[103] Additionally, consolidation's primary value lies in its being "the process that, eventually, leads to political material institutionalization."[104] Although presented as a distinct process, consolidation and its components are rendered suspiciously like those of institutionalization. Consolidation, even in these definitions, remains clearly captive to institutionalization.[105]

Some scholars, particularly those interested in questions about more profound change, have left open the prospect that consolidation denotes possibilities beyond institutionalization. Fagen's focus on the consolidation of state power acknowledged that much more is at stake than institutions: What is up for debate is nothing less than the "real meaning" of things in the new society.[106] His contention that the "politics of transition" must be integrative and patriotic hints at the process of consolidation as defined here.[107] Coraggio, having recognized the limitations of top-down approaches, echoed this notion of consolidation by focusing attention on the population: "Popular power and hegemony are constituent components" that not only compete with but also strengthen "state power within the joint project of revolutionary consolidation."[108] For transitions to occur, the "creative energy" of the population must be utilized. Both these authors touched on elements of what is understood here as consolidation.

### Defining Consolidation

Consolidation is the struggle during which the revolutionaries seek to win what Marchetti described as the people's soul and the people seek to realize the visions that brought many of them to the struggle.[109] Success is measured by the degree to which the population adopts the core of the social revolutionary project not simply in words but in deeds. Consolidation, then, is related to people's perceptions of the conditions of their everyday lives and of their relationships with each other, with the new government, even with the revolutionary process itself. At this stage, the factors central to consolidation are trust, opportunity, and vision of the future, which are bound together by an underlying sense of empowerment. Taken together, these four represent what is referred to here as "popular attitudes."

Trust refers to people's reliance on the character, truth, ability, and strength of the government. It is manifested, in part, by a general acceptance of the new institutions and of the "rules of the game." Presumably, a central reason for this trust, once the initial elation has passed, is the notion of opportunity. Opportunity refers to people's sense of access to what had been the exclusive province of the powerful—education, housing, and the ability to get things done—in other words, efficacy and efficiency. Perhaps opportunity's greatest appeal lies in people's visions of the future. A vision of the future is often rooted in intergenerational justice, that is, the belief that things may be bad now, but with greater opportunity, they will be better for one's children. This notion is critical; people accept present suffering in exchange for a better future. What holds these factors together is the sense of empowerment, that is, people's belief that they can make a difference.

As a component of trust in the government, character relates to perceptions of whether those in government are decent, honorable, and work hard. Truth, quite simply, refers to whether people feel that they are being dealt with honestly and openly. Ability refers to perceptions that those in power possess the skills necessary to run the government. Finally, strength refers to people's sense of whether the government leaders can hold up to the rigors of managing the country—can they continue to function in the face of adversity?—and whether they need outside help, such as foreign support, to do so. These are the core elements in assessing the degree to which people trust the government.

Opportunity is fundamentally about access to goods and services, both public and private, which previously were available only to the elite. Because these goods and services had been unobtainable by most, the notion of equality underlies this concept. Education refers not simply to basic literacy, although that is critical both symbolically and practically—for the creation of a more informed population—but also to higher education, such as training in medicine, agriculture, engineering and electronics, and the law. Housing means access to affordable, adequate housing. The ability to get things done refers to the sense that it is not only possible but also plausible to think that government bureaucrats are accessible and will be honest and able to help. These are the criteria for assessing the degree to which people believe that the government affords them opportunity.

Most people desire a better life for their children or the children of others. A vision of a better future explains people's willingness to suffer and struggle now. This entails the ability to see beyond one's present circumstances and even the immediate future to the long term, a not-too-common trait. People will almost always profess a commitment to their children's having better lives than they do, but most nonetheless lead their own lives with a great deal of immediacy. Since the immediate questions often relate to providing food, clothes, medicine, or shelter to these same children, this is not surprising. Yet the social revolutionary process often demands that the people set aside their more immediate hopes in exchange for a vision of the future.

Empowerment, in this case, refers to efficacy and staying power, that is, giving individuals the sense that their actions will have an effect on the process and that they can defend the gains that they make. This may be seen in a variety of ways: People's involvement in mass organizations and political parties as well as in popular protest and demonstrations are obvious indicators. Empowerment binds these elements together because people do not participate without trust, opportunity increases empowerment, and empowerment is engendered by a vision of the future.

Popular attitudes are like a belief system, albeit one that is less formal and less rigid than that denoted by the term *ideology*. Neither wholly independent sets of ideas nor sets of justifications dependent on the exigencies of political power, popular attitudes form a loose-knit worldview that people bring to bear on the events around them. Such attitudes, composed of a myriad of factors, are best determined by questioning people to reveal their practical political ideology,[110] with which they judge events, and their practical knowledge[111] about day-to-day life. A former political cadre in the Nicaraguan army explained that people approached the vagaries of life in Nicaragua simply: "Listen, capitalism, communism, socialism are all just bullshit—people here just live, they don't care about those things."[112]

I am not suggesting that there is no place for more traditional social science variables. People's economic situation—as they perceive it—and geographic location are two other factors that are useful in explaining the status of consolidation.

The key, however, is popular attitudes; the process of consolidation is not best understood solely by attention to and a reliance on such structural factors as economics and geography. In fact, in the social revolutionary process, ideas can countervail structural factors or at the very least profoundly shape and alter them. As a result, voluntaristic factors, such as popular attitudes, allow us to begin to uncover the process of consolidation. Moreover, economics and geography may be construed as primarily influenced by the institutionalization process; popular attitudes, however, reflect the population's view of its status and are therefore at the center of the government's revolutionary strategy for consolidation.

Given its elusive nature, consolidation is best assessed along a continuum. At one end there is the ideal of consolidation: the complete adoption and incorporation of the social revolutionary process into society so that that process is a seamless, mutually reinforcing, coherent whole. At the other end is breakdown: the complete failure of the government to engender the population's support, much less its commitment to the social revolutionary process. The scale thus runs from support through validation, undermining, and, eventually, breakdown.

Practical indicators of consolidation range from enthusiastic support for the core of the social revolutionary project to the grudging, tacit acceptance of the "new society." The former is enhanced by literacy campaigns, health care and nutrition projects, land redistribution and agrarian reform, income redistribution, and the participation of the population. The latter is demonstrated by the tolerance of unpopular government decisions, for example, not rioting at food price increases, or an unwillingness to take part in behavior that undermines the social revolutionary project.

The dividing line between supporting behavior and validating behavior is permeable. Validation denotes the willingness of people wary or even hostile to the government, such as the "loyal" opposition, to work inside the new structures. Thus a demonstration aimed at specific grievances within the government may serve to strengthen the government both by recognizing its legitimacy and by addressing the new institutions that have been created. This kind of participation indicates at least a tacit acceptance of the rules of the game, further proof of institutionalization, which in turn may be realistically construed as assisting the process of consolidation. However, if the same demonstration were to challenge or deny the legitimacy of the government, it could be construed as undermining behavior. The line between validating behavior and undermining behavior is also permeable. The range of undermining behavior includes the refusal to vote or participate, selling to the black market, trading money on the black market, efforts to create internal disruptions, emigrating, or, ultimately, a decision to join counterrevolutionary forces.

If institutionalization is a familiar concept, consolidation is an elusive one. Institutionalization is a process that may be readily measured by such factors as the status or function of key government structures. Consolidation, which is related to people's perceptions of the material and ideological conditions of their everyday lives and their relationships with each other, with the new government, even with the revolutionary process itself, is not so easily measured. Then how can one identify when the consolidation process is a success, that is, when it is "over"? It is not clear to me that there is a good answer to this question. Revolutions are commonly assigned dates by political victory, for example, October 1917 in Russia or January 1959 in Cuba. Discerning the end of the consolidation process, the conclusion of the revolution, is a much trickier business.[113]

Perhaps the most useful tools for assessing the end of consolidation have been proposed by Hobsbawm. In the period after political victory, he pointed out, there is genuine, if not always universal, "enthusiasm for the construction of a new and better society."[114] At the same time, "the most profound effects of the revolutionary expectation on human personality" rarely occur on a grand scale and generally, he argued, tend to be short-lived.[115] None of this is meant to disparage the real and meaningful changes that occur but rather to remind the reader that transformation is a complex, profound, and difficult process in which to engage.

Reality takes its toll on popular support and the willingness of the people to make sacrifices and continue the struggle. Shortly before the 1990 Nicaraguan elections, a Nicaraguan confided to me that some people were wondering aloud if they should support the FSLN in the upcoming elections and continue the struggle or vote for the National Opposition Union (UNO) and enjoy the roughly one month of luxury they believed the United States would "reward" them with before it turned its traditionally short attention span elsewhere.[116]

Institutionalization may be measured by the stability and functioning of the state structures or assessed when the major social and economic disruptions that commonly accompany the political victory have been overcome.[117] In fact, the reason "over" was placed in quotes in the question, When is a revolution "over"? was to denote that there is a sense in which the consolidation process may in fact never end but, rather, if successful, be simply subsumed into the socialization process that all societies rely on to replicate themselves. So the revolution, in some sense, simply becomes the new framework within which the country's historical evolution henceforth takes place.

Inevitably, inspiration wanes as the distance from political victory grows. Even when the revolutionary spirit holds up in the face of the exigencies of everyday life, Hobsbawm pointed out, its institutionalization inevitably results in routinization and eventually in the rhetoric of anniversaries.[118] The ultimate test of the consolidation project is to determine how far, and to what extent, the changes of values and the capacity of people to mobilize are maintained, especially when many of the revolution's promises—utopian and otherwise—are revealed as impractical.

The question that Hobsbawm posed is this: What remains of the original social revolutions when the transformation that they have brought about has faded from memory or is taken for granted, has become simply an era in a country's history?[119] The range of possibilities is relatively wide, stretching from revolutions that have slipped from public memory, such as those in England or Bolivia, to revolutions that remain either permanent points of reference, as with the Russian, or important elements in current political and ideological debate, as perhaps in the French or the Cuban.[120]

Still, Hobsbawm suggested that there are at least two identifiable reference points. One is when the first adult generation of "children of the revolution" emerges on the public scene.[121] These are the people whose education and careers are based in and therefore entirely belong to the new era. Of course, generational change is an important element in any society, yet revolutions accentuate and depend on it to continue and perhaps expand the social revolutionary project. The new generation often plays an unusually important role in the drive to transform individuals and society. At its earliest, however, this change can only be ascertained after the roughly twenty-five years that conventionally demarcate generations.

The second reference point may take even longer to invoke and, at root, relies largely on hindsight. This point is reached when the social revolutionary government has demonstrated the capacity to resist internal challenges and has not been overthrown for a sufficient period of time. Hobsbawm suggested that we know revolutions are over "when the general pattern or 'framework' set up at one point in history has not been fundamentally altered for a sufficiently long time, though this need not exclude quite significant change within it."[122] Said another way, consolidation is linked to people's long-term and therefore presumably profound embrace of the new society.

Consolidation as it has been conceptualized here is clearly a step beyond any of the ways it is commonly encountered. Is such a new definition justified? To put it more colloquially, what does it buy us? The answer is that it allows us to sketch a more accurate picture of the most important phase of the social revolutionary process, the period that defines the entire process. The task of creating a new world is not one that can be understood solely in terms of structures and institutions, economic statistics and political norms. It requires access to the ways in which people seek to recreate themselves and the material and ideological conditions of their everyday lives. This is the "handle" provided by consolidation.   □

## REVOLUTION AND
## THE ROLE OF THE INDIVIDUAL

The study of social revolution has been dominated by structuralist conceptualizations that fail to recognize that social revolutions are creative acts, concrete episodes in which people pursue goals.[123] I do not deny the general character of social revolutions as macrohistorical phenomena or the conditions that impinge on the process. Yet scholars have largely ignored the strongly voluntarist aspect of social revolutions: People make revolutions. Further, most studies of revolution focus on the causes of revolution and pay virtually no attention to the complex processes that unfold during the transformation of society after the insurrection.

Even those few scholars who do consider separately this final phase of the social revolutionary process do not treat consolidation as distinct from the institutionalization process.[124] They present consolidation as an "outcome" determined by a variety of factors, particularly, structural conditions and events that promote the political victory. The period of transformation they describe, explain, and predict by cataloging and considering structural antecedents, but the latter often ultimately prove to have tenuous relationships to what unfolds.

Revolutionaries have chosen to pursue (or not) the two processes in different ways. As we explore at length in Chapter 3, there are two primary types of social revolutionary leadership: visionary and organizational. Each type deals with consolidation and institutionalization according to its nature. I contend that excessive focus on one comes at the expense of the other.[125]

Let us consider social revolutions with very strong visionary leadership, as in Cuba, which tend toward consolidation, and cases such as Bolivia, with strong organizational leadership, which are prone to institutionalization. In those countries the lack of both types calls into question the success of their social revolutions. Although Grenada appears to have both types of leadership, a disastrous split among the leaders sealed the fate of the revolution. It is only in cases such as Nicaragua, where the social revolutionary leadership achieves some semblance of balance between the two processes and remains united, that the success of the social revolutionary process seems assured.

The debate over the relative weight and dialectical relationship between individual and collective will as opposed to historical circumstances in determining the outcome of a given event or process is important to the argument presented here.[126] Action occurs within a given and defined set of circumstances, and it is the interplay of circumstance and action—neither of which can exist without the other—that creates human history. The importance of voluntarism in the social revolutionary process and the resulting dynamic relationship between structure and agency during the consolidation process fuel the debate over the specific relationship.[127] Resolution of this debate lies in the recognition that the parameters in which human action is possible depend on historically specific conditions.[128] Structuralism and "humanism" (agency) may each, in particular circumstances, be significant.[129]

My argument demands a focus on people's conscious choices and actions and how they shape the world. Structural perspectives provide a framework that may be utilized to evaluate events and processes across time. But it is imperative to recognize that this framework is merely a shell, "determined" by the structure. Predetermination results in a disinclination or inability to estimate the critical voluntarist events and processes that shape reality.

Whereas the relationship between objective conditions and human actors in social history is discernible on a common-sense level, theoretically, matters are less clear. Social revolutions are neither automatic nor inevitable. There is little question that "objective conditions" may set the stage; however, they do not move societies into or through the revolutionary process. I propose that we can understand the transformative period by relating the social, economic, and political structures at the domestic and international levels to purposive, voluntaristic political action. Part of the focus here, then, is on the effort of the revolutionary leadership to consolidate the revolution and the reactions of people in the society in transition.

Voluntaristic events abound during the social revolutionary process, and several scholars have demonstrated the central role people play during both the insurrection and the battle for political power.[130] Yet it is in the incredibly complex and lengthy transformation process after political victory that the efforts and machinations of groups and individuals have their most obvious and dramatic impact. The final phase of the social revolutionary process should be construed as a period of purposeful adaptations to a conglomeration of political circumstances as the social revolutionaries seek to transform the political, economic, and social structures of their society. To omit the element of conscious action and decision from the analysis is a mistake. Options are considered and choices are made: This phenomenon has not been, and cannot be, captured by a structural perspective.

The inadequacy of that perspective can be illustrated by considering two cases where the structural conditions identified by Skocpol do exist but where the results of the revolutions are different. If, as Skocpol argued, only structural conditions are relevant to the social revolutionary process and if they are the same in two cases, the outcomes should be roughly similar. If they are not the same, the question is, what was different about the two cases? My contention is that the difference lies in the role played by individuals—both the revolutionary leadership and the population.

The 1959 Cuban revolution is one of the few cases universally accepted as a successful social revolution. The 1952 revolution in Bolivia, in stark contrast, has been relegated to little more than a historical footnote, a rarely invoked reference point. Therefore, two processes that look remarkably analogous when considered in structural terms result in dramatically different outcomes, outcomes that are not, in fact, persuasively explained by reference to structural factors. The "missing link" is instructive.

For Skocpol, as noted earlier, the state and its relationship with the international political economy and domestic social classes occupy center stage in the social revolutionary process. "Revolutionary crises" occur via "inter- and intranational structural contradictions and conjunctural occurrences beyond the deliberate control of avowed revolutionaries."[131] As a result, investigators require a structural perspective that emphasizes "objective relationships and conflicts among variously situated groups and nations, rather than the interests, outlooks or ideologies of particular actors in revolutions."[132] Specifically, for Skocpol, social revolutions occur in essentially agrarian societies and happen only with the collapse of the administrative-military structure. Critical to the unfolding process is the role played by the peasants as a class either in revolt or mobilized for guerrilla warfare.[133] Therefore, the revolutions in Bolivia and Cuba are casually lumped together by Skocpol as examples of social revolution.[134]

A perspective that equates the Bolivian and Cuban revolutions is missing something, that which would explain the radically different trajectories of the revolutions.[135] What is missing from Skocpol's formulation is a meaningful role for individuals in the social revolutionary process. In fact, it is the inclusion of individuals—both in the social revolutionary leadership and in the population generally—that produces a useful explanation of the dramatic contrast between the two revolutionary processes.

In Bolivia the revolutionary leadership failed to complete the social revolutionary process. There was no real visionary leader, no one to articulate the hopes and dreams of the population and energize them to continue to struggle and participate in the revolutionary process. Moreover, the organizational leaders—those who sought to implement the social revolutionary program—were at odds with each other over the direction of the social revolution.

The Bolivian leaders reached a rough, at times very rough, consensus on the institutionalization of the revolution. Appropriate laws were passed and institutions created and reconfigured. The failure to agree on a strategy for consolidation kept the leaders, however, in contention; the Bolivian revolutionary process unfolded in the "context of bitter ideological conflict and intense factional struggle."[136] As a result, the Bolivian revolution degenerated into a struggle among the leaders, which lasted until those who opposed the core of the social revolutionary project won. The Bolivian people's response to the conflicting signals and messages was to look out for their own, narrower, interests rather than the broader social revolutionary process (see Chapter 2). Thus, Bolivia may be most usefully understood as an incomplete social revolution in which there was a failure of the revolutionaries to consolidate the social revolutionary process.

In Cuba there was an aggressive program of consolidation led by visionary leaders and carefully undergirded by organizational leaders. Eschewing any program of institutionalization, the social revolutionary leadership committed itself to fundamentally transforming the material and ideological conditions of everyday life. The people were mobilized and energized through health and literacy campaigns and empowered to take charge of their lives and "their" revolution.

The success of the consolidation project can be seen in the degree to which the Cuban population, particularly from 1959 to 1969, embraced the core of the social revolutionary project and participated actively in the process. In fact, it is the role of the Cuban people in the process that has led so many to label the revolution a success. Yet the absence of institutionalization during the first decade and its subsequent uneven introduction has created problems for Cuba. In particular, the question of succession and the population's relationship with a popular but aging leadership—both visionary and organizational—may well provide the real test of whether the Cuban revolution has been a success.

The final transformative phase of revolution has commonly been treated by scholars as highly structured, with the primary focus on the structures the nascent governments inherit and the reorganization or creation of institutions. These scholars' premise remains that people are either ineffectual or inconsequential in the face of structures. I contend that although social revolutions will face confining conditions, they are guided by the conscious plans and significant choices made by revolutionaries across the three phases of the social revolutionary process.

Consideration of the processes of institutionalization and consolidation and their possible combinations provides a powerful and useful way to distinguish between and among social revolutions. The failure of social scientists to adequately account for the role of the individual and people's interactions with the structures that surround them has proven limiting. Although from a structuralist perspective, Bolivia, Cuba, Nicaragua, and Grenada may all be cases of social revolution, the perspective introduced here helps draw some meaningful distinctions among them. These distinctions produce both a useful general understanding of the social revolutionary process and worthwhile insights into the respective cases.

In Chapter 2 we will consider the most obvious of the variety of options pursued in the period after political victory: (1) institutionalization without consolidation (Bolivia, 1952–1956); (2) consolidation without institutionalization (Cuba, 1959–1969); (3) institutionalization and consolidation (Nicaragua, 1979–1990); and (4) the absence of institutionalization or consolidation (Grenada, 1979–1983). In Chapter 3 I explore the way in which such paths are chosen—a combination of the nature of the political leadership, the social revolutionary ideology, and the social revolutionary strategy. In Chapter 4 we will return to the Nicaraguan case and consider it in greater degree.

# CHAPTER TWO

■

# Social Revolutionary Paths:
# Bolivia, Cuba, Nicaragua,
# and Grenada

In this chapter I seek to demonstrate the utility of consolidation as an independent analytic concept. Institutionalization and consolidation are the lenses that I use in this section to investigate social revolutionary processes. My approach picks up aspects of the social revolutionary process that previous students of revolution have treated as peripheral, and thus it provides new insights. Specifically, in this section I consider the social revolutionary processes that unfolded in the four modern Latin American revolutions: Bolivia, 1952–1956; Cuba, 1959–1969; Nicaragua, 1979–1990; and Grenada, 1979–1983. These cases are not ideal types; rather, they serve to demonstrate what we might learn by using institutionalization and consolidation as instruments of analysis.

Consolidation and institutionalization are most usefully understood as paths that revolutionaries choose to follow (or not to follow) in the period after political victory. As such, institutionalization and consolidation should be discernible within the social revolutionary process. When we use these processes as analytic tools, we can gain insight into previously murky areas of the social revolutionary process; we can also observe factors and issues that have been marginalized by misunderstanding, inattention, or overly narrow conceptualizations.

Let us briefly consider the four most obvious patterns of institutionalization and consolidation in the context of four specific social revolutionary processes (see Figure 2.1). Bolivia, an example of institutionalization without consolidation, failed as a social revolution and remains little noted. Because of the failure to consolidate, the revolution offered little protection for the gains achieved under the auspices of the revolutionaries. Cuba, the modern-day archetype of social revolution, here serves to illustrate consolidation without institutionalization. Fidel

*Consolidation*

|                       |     | Yes                  | No                  |
| --------------------- | --- | -------------------- | ------------------- |
| *Institutionalization* | Yes | Nicaragua 1979–1990 | Bolivia 1952–1956   |
|                       | No  | Cuba 1959–1969       | Grenada 1979–1983   |

**Figure** 2.1 Institutionalization and consolidation of social revolution in Bolivia, Cuba, Nicaragua, and Grenada

Castro's continued ability to step outside of and alter state institutions as he chooses leaves institutionalization suspect. This phenomenon also means that the ultimate success of the Cuban revolution, its staying power, remains conjecture—What will happen when the immense figure of Fidel Castro departs the scene?

The Grenadian revolution exhibits neither institutionalization nor consolidation. Although Grenada serves as a useful example of this lack, that is not necessarily the best way to understand the Grenadian revolutionary process. Plausible arguments can be made for comparing the Grenadian case to Bolivia, even interpreting it as akin to either Cuba or Nicaragua. Nonetheless, as will be explored below, Grenada is clearly the case in Latin America that most closely fits this category. Nicaragua, in which there was both institutionalization and consolidation, seems to have proved the success of both processes. The successful institutionalization in Nicaragua made it difficult for the FSLN to step outside state institutions to alter the election results, as Castro could in Cuba, where institutions have remained susceptible to his charismatic authority. The strength of consolidation in Nicaragua not only protected the core of the social revolutionary project—in contrast to Bolivia or Grenada—but also forestalled any serious discussion of the rollback of the social revolution, even by a victorious alliance that includes counterrevolutionary factions.

My argument is that in cases where there was a failure either to institutionalize or consolidate, a social revolution has not occurred. Such failure, as in Grenada, 1979–1983, results in a failed social revolution. Institutionalization without consolidation, as in Bolivia, 1952–1956, most likely will also result in an incomplete and therefore failed social revolution. Consolidation without institutionalization, as in Cuba, 1959–1969, is somewhat more difficult—the revolution remains incomplete and therefore both vulnerable and suspect until it has demonstrated the ability to transfer power. Even with the relatively higher degree of institutionalization present in Cuba today, the remarkable staying power of the revolution has yet to face its ultimate test, the loss of the *jefe máximo*, Fidel Castro.

Only when there is both institutionalization and consolidation, as appears to be the case in Nicaragua, is the success of the social revolution likely. Success is most clearly identified when it is clear that the social revolution has not been overthrown and that the tenets of the social revolution have become central to society. Even though under these terms the social revolution in Nicaragua appears to be a success, it merits repeating here that it is difficult to gauge the success of the consolidation process until sufficient time has passed. It is too early to declare the process of consolidation complete in Nicaragua.

If consolidation, institutionalization, or a mix of the two represent the paths available in the post–political victory period, one can ask how a particular path is chosen in a specific case. This question is explored at length in Chapter 3. For the purposes of this chapter, I argue simply that choices are made by the leaders as they appraise the interplay of the population's needs and demands and the domestic and international factors that impinge on their ability to realize the social revolutionary project. The social revolutionary leadership, a small cadre of revolutionaries within the vanguard party, is thus essential to social revolution; the significance of their role is evident in the ensuing discussion.   □

## POPULAR SUPPORT AND CONSOLIDATION

Those most cognizant of the complex, multifaceted nature of consolidation have been revolutionaries who have long recognized that their relationship with "the people" is a complex one, far beyond its obvious instrumental purposes of providing food, shelter, and intelligence.[1] Mao Zedong, Luis Taruc, Ernesto "Che" Guevara, Vo Nguyen Giap, Amilcar Cabral, and other revolutionary thinkers have all discussed this complexity at length and acknowledged the need for the revolutionaries to gain the full support of the people, that is, to win their hearts and minds.[2] To this end, social revolutionaries seek to build and maintain popular support across all the phases of the social revolutionary process.

Given that support prior to political victory is almost always granted at great risk—usually of one's life—the initial relationship between the revolutionaries and the population necessarily involves the murky areas of belief, fear, anger, and commitment on the part of the latter. It is often here that revolutionaries first recognize the complexity of their relationship with the people in whose name they purport to be fighting for state control and for the right to lead in the creation of a new society.

When the revolutionaries do realize that it is the population that is at greatest risk and that is actually bearing the brunt of the fight for political victory, the impact can be both impressive and inspiring. Humberto Ortega, a leader of the Nicaraguan revolution and the country's minister of defense under both the FSLN and the current UNO governments, noted that during the struggle, "we always took the masses into account, but more in terms of them supporting the guerrillas so that the guerrillas could defeat the National Guard. This isn't what actually happened. What actually happened was that it was the guerrillas who provided support for the masses so that they could defeat the enemy by means of insurrection."[3] Such sentiments, taken to heart, can be inspiring; they are doubtless sobering as well.

Political victory, as countless revolutionaries have discovered, does not guarantee people's continued support, much less their commitment to the social revolutionary project: Revolutionary situations do not always beget revolutionary outcomes.[4] Thus, at this critical juncture, the nascent social revolutionary government's primary concern must become the battle for the support of the population. Even though they are confronted with a wide array of confining conditions and threats both internal and external, the revolutionaries must focus on the process of consolidation.

Many revolutionaries have made the mistake of being overly idealistic about the people, presuming that they "understood" the exigencies of the situation; they thought that the people saw the world as the revolutionaries did. To some extent this coincidence of views is certainly the case: People have demonstrated time and time again that they are prepared to make compromises with a new government just as they did with the old. But the people know their wants and needs. To win them to the side of the revolution, to engage them in the revolutionary spirit, it is necessary to involve them in the step beyond the battle for political power, engaging them in the struggle for a new society and for their future and that of their children.

Popular support remains the essential condition for the survival of the social revolutionary process. Only the people can supply the energy, power, and time to create the new society. Persuasion, organization, or coercive measures alone have not been able to create this support. Rather, obtaining popular support is dependent on the package presented by the revolutionaries. This support may be manifested in active participation in the social revolutionary process or in grudging, tacit consent to it, but such support cannot be coerced; it must be voluntary. Whatever its forms, without popular support the revolution cannot be and will not be consolidated. Without popular support the social revolution is unable to transform society and degenerates into simply another in what may be a long line of governments. This can be seen clearly in the case of Bolivia.   □

## BOLIVIA, 1952–1956: INSTITUTIONALIZATION
## WITHOUT CONSOLIDATION

Bolivia's 1952 revolution is often overlooked when social revolutions are discussed.[5] Nevertheless, at one time the 1952 revolution in Bolivia was considered Latin America's second great revolution of the twentieth century, ceding only to Mexico.[6] The most common adjective attached to the Bolivian revolution is "incomplete," although scholars have also used terms such as "unfinished" and "uncompleted" when discussing the Bolivian revolutionary experience. There is unquestionably a consensus that a revolutionary process began to unfold in Bolivia in 1952; there is less agreement about where that process went. Clearly, however, the Bolivian revolution of 1952 has become little more than a historical aside, referenced usually as some sort of revolution—political or social—but most commonly invoked as the modern archetype of an incomplete social revolution.[7]

As I have made clear, I argue that for a revolution to achieve success, the revolutionaries must be able both to institutionalize and to consolidate the social revolutionary process. Institutionalization alone is not enough to ensure success; the "incompleteness" of the Bolivian revolution stemmed from the failure of the revolutionaries to consolidate the revolution. I shall focus on that failure and the unique configuration of Bolivia's revolutionary leadership as factors responsible for the revolution's incompleteness.[8]

As will be explored below, Bolivia's revolutionary leaders were divided prior to achieving political victory; they were never able to overcome this problem. The leaders were able to agree on and impose from above the reforms of many state structures and create new ones to meet the demands and desires of the population. In other words, they institutionalized the revolution. They were unable, however, to convince the majority of the population to embrace the social revolutionary project; therefore, they failed to consolidate the revolution.

In contrast to parties in the other modern Latin American revolutions, the vanguard party in Bolivia was largely moderate, middle-class, and reformist. The National Revolutionary Movement (MNR) was founded in 1941 as a neo-Nazi political party.[9] Its leaders cultivated a populist image while maintaining their essential commitment to a narrow group within Bolivian society, the middle- and upper-middle-class "developmentalists."[10] Just two years later, the MNR was part of the civil-military coup that installed a reformist regime based on "military socialism."[11] When this government collapsed in 1946, the MNR began six years of exile, clandestine activity, and the search for its future in Bolivian politics.

Casting about for a new direction that would return them to power, the MNR leaders lit upon more or less pure nationalism. The party would provide a meeting place of sorts, a pragmatic center, for those shut out and marginalized by the new government. The MNR's premature attempt at a civil coup in 1949 convinced the leadership that the party needed to broaden its base even further before it could return to power. The solution, the leadership decided, was the creation of a broad, multiclass, populist party, which would serve to integrate all the principal elements of society à la Mexico's Institutionalized Revolutionary party (PRI).

By 1951 there were three factions within the MNR. A traditionalist faction remained true to the MNR's rightist roots, offering a rather vague protofascist program built around national dignity, harmony, and anti-Semitism. Another faction, which coalesced around MNR labor leader Juan Lechín Oquendo, proposed a specific labor- or left-oriented program of political, social, and economic change, including universal suffrage, nationalization of the tin industry, and widespread agrarian reform. The third faction was the Centrists, pragmatic nationalists such as Víctor Paz Estenssoro and Hernán Siles Suazo, who articulated "national-developmentalist" values that were "more an attitude than a clear program."[12] These pragmatic nationalists formed the core MNR leadership, playing off the other two factions and manipulating them in their drive for state power.

Seeking to broaden their base with the population, the more pragmatic among the MNR leaders reached out to Bolivia's Left, specifically Bolivian workers. The result was an uneasy and awkward alliance between the traditionalists, the upper-middle-class core MNR leadership, and the more radical working-class leadership of organized labor in Bolivia. Although this fragile alliance was "fraught with mutual distrust and hostility," it enabled the MNR to contest the 1951 elections successfully with a broad-based platform, long on promises and short on specifics. The centerpiece of the platform, in the popular perception, was the adoption of labor/Left's call for universal suffrage, nationalization of the tin industry, and widespread agrarian reform.[13]

In the 1951 election, the MNR ticket of Paz and Siles won a plurality of the votes, falling just short of the absolute majority necessary to win the election outright. The MNR leadership looked forward to their confirmation in the congress, as dictated by the constitution. Before that could happen, however, the military and the elite persuaded Bolivia's president to declare the election results a threat to democracy, outlaw the MNR as communist, and turn the government over to the military for safekeeping until new elections could be held. Thus, in May 1951 the MNR was prevented from taking office.

The MNR began to consider other avenues to power. Despite its election rhetoric, a description of the early MNR remained apt: "an electoral and parliamentary cabal seeking quick access to governmental office through which it intended to impose reform."[14] Not surprisingly, the MNR leadership laid the groundwork for a civil-military coup that would place them in the offices they had won in the election. There is every indication that such a coup had been developed and put in motion, but the MNR's military allies were unable to bring over their colleagues.[15] When the military remained loyal to the government, an armed urban population—quickly joined by the tin miners—stepped into their place. What had begun as a relatively narrow civil-military coup metamorphosed into a broad-based insurrection replete with revolutionary rhetoric.

The history of the MNR and its leadership leaves little doubt that it had neither anticipated nor particularly desired a broad-based revolution from below. Regardless of the MNR's original vision of the process, in April 1952 the country was in the hands, not of the MNR's military coplotters, but of hastily cobbled together militias of workers, party activists, townspeople, and miners. Armed and radicalized, these people demanded more than another coup or rebellion—they wanted a revolution.

After the revolution's unusually brief and relatively bloodless three-day struggle for political power (9–11 April 1952), the MNR was nominally in control and certainly holding the reins of power. By virtue of its role in the 1943–1946 reformist government, its somewhat romanticized history of opposition, its clear victory in the 1951 election, and its initiation of the insurrection, the MNR had immense popular support. Riding the crest of the revolutionary process, the MNR leaders found themselves in what they perceived as their rightful position. Under the aegis of the constitution and Bolivian history, they took office.

The MNR was clearly in control politically. The elite was discredited and the military somewhere between disarray and nonexistence. Neither group was in any position to oppose the changes proposed by the MNR. The changes to be instituted, however, were not immediately clear. The new regime moved cautiously, careful to stress its ties to its predecessors. Its vision and promise were of nationalism and unity; its right to govern was based on *constitutional* grounds.[16] Legitimacy was rooted not in a radical future but in a solid past.

The core MNR leadership thus begin its tenure looking backwards—to the Bolivian constitution and the institutionalization of the Mexican revolution. As a result, the leaders were ill prepared for the strong and radical demands of their partners in revolution, the armed and organized workers, whose expectations and vision went considerably beyond the vague specifics of the MNR's 1951 electoral platform. Having been the driving force, indeed, the fighting force, of the revolution, the workers demanded radical institutional change: nationalization of Bolivia's primary industry, tin mining; a broad program of agrarian reform; the introduction of universal suffrage; and a dramatic curtailment of the army's power.

All these demands except the reduction of the military had been in the MNR's 1951 platform; those whom some have dubbed the "reluctant revolutionaries" acquiesced to demands both to transform the old structures and to create new ones.[17] This also marked the renewal of what would become increasingly bitter internal struggle among the leadership of the revolution. Most dramatically, the MNR's labor/Left and its new rural allies formed the Bolivian Workers Confederation (COB), a powerful, unified labor union, led by Lechín, which successfully demanded a system of cogovernment. In practice, cogovernment meant that COB had veto power over policy decisions, shared in management of the new Bolivian Mining Corporation (COMIBOL), and controlled the Ministries of Mines, Labor, Public Works, and Peasant Affairs. From such a position, COB could maintain "permanent vigilance lest the bourgeois MNR seek to hold back the revolution."[18] The right wing of the MNR responded with accusations that COB was trying to "communize" Bolivia.

In this context, the MNR began to decree changes in structure that were promised in its 1951 platform and that were central to the vision of the population that made the revolution. What is important to recognize here is that these efforts at institutionalization were not part of a broadly based, previously delineated program but instead signified a series of compacts negotiated among the conflicting MNR factions. These compromise agreements were essentially accommodations between the pragmatic nationalists around Paz and between Lechín and his allies from the labor/Left. Universal suffrage was a relatively easy issue to resolve, but nationalization of the tin mines, the dismantling of the military, and agrarian reform—where the MNR and COB eventually accepted what was essentially a fait accompli in the countryside—were trickier.

The implementation of agrarian reform provides an interesting window into the difficulties of the institutionalization process. Bolivia's rural order was firmly rooted in the era of the Spanish Conquest. A relatively small number of people of European descent lived quite well on their haciendas (landed estates), whereas most of the indigenous rural population—a majority of Bolivians—lived lives of abject poverty in near-slavery. In the fall of 1952, emboldened by the revolutionary process, Bolivia's indigenous population—the country's newly enfranchised majority—began to move. In an atmosphere most commonly described as "rural violence," Bolivia's rural inhabitants began to seize the land that they believed rightfully belonged to them.

A hesitant MNR, committed at least in theory to some sort of agrarian reform, debated what to do.[19] The COB, in control of the newly created Ministry of Peasant Affairs, encouraged the radicalization of the rural population. The MNR right wing demanded the suppression of the seizures, lest the indigenous population upset all of Bolivian society. Paz and the centrists initially condemned the land seizures and the violence, then began to hedge on the issue, and finally, grudgingly, got on the bandwagon when the outcome seemed clear. In response, the MNR Right attempted a coup. The failure of the coup strengthened the hand of the Left. A commission was created to study the matter of agrarian reform, which, already a fact in the countryside, was shortly thereafter accepted in theory by those in the capital, La Paz.[20]

As a result, landed *campesinos* organized themselves into *sindicatos*—essentially rural unions—with attendant armed militias. Despite the best efforts of the COBistas to manage and direct the rural population, regional and local leaders quickly emerged and proved impervious to national leaders' efforts to control them. In fact, once their land was assured, most of the campesinos turned inward, seeming no longer to have the interest or ability to act as a national force.[21] The *sindicatos'* focus, rather, became defense of the land they had won. Bolivia's indigenous population became extremely conservative, a conservatism that Paz would later draw on to build the power base he had lacked in the early period following political victory.[22] Most important, however, was that agrarian reform was established; it became an enshrined institution.[23]

In short order, then, the various political institutions were established. Moreover, they appeared to be functioning. The question that remained open was whether, having successfully and rapidly institutionalized, this disparate, multiclass coalition of the urban middle class, the workers, and the peasants could create a new society: Could they consolidate the revolution that was unfolding?

The core MNR leadership took the lessons of the Mexican revolution seriously and was convinced that the strong one-party state that had emerged there would guarantee the success of that process.[24] Therefore, the new government roughly based its political structure on the Mexican model of a formal democratic framework within which the official party controlled all the meaningful levers of power. The MNR, seeking to emulate Mexico's PRI, envisioned itself as the place where all the key groups were to be integrated: workers, peasants, the middle class, and eventually a new civilian-controlled military. Theoretically, then, this inclusive party structure would undergird a strong and autonomous state structure, which would then undertake the creation of the new Bolivian society.

In practice, of course, each faction sought to control the process. The traditionalists resisted most notions of social and political change. The pragmatists recognized that relatively moderate social and political changes might be necessary to achieve the economic development they sought via state capitalism. Regardless of the structural changes that it was overseeing, the core MNR leadership retained its fundamentally reformist character. In the face of rightist and centrist allies, the COB pushed for a quasi-state-socialist system and for further societal changes that would lead to the creation of a new Bolivian society. To this end, the COB became the only faction that sought to mobilize the populace in a systematic fashion.

Tension between the reformists and the COB/Left alliance, however, prevented any coherent effort at creating a new society.[25] In fact there was increasingly little pretense of such an effort, as each group sought to sway the population. The previously mentioned coup attempt from the MNR Right only further exacerbated matters, temporarily strengthening the Left but laying the groundwork for a subsequent rupture between the Left and the Center prior to the 1956 elections. At that time the internal squabbling reached new levels; all sides seem to have surrendered to the notion that they could not fundamentally transform Bolivian society. The watchword of the new Siles administration was the institutionalization of the revolution. To this end, the MNR called on outside help, specifically the United States and the International Monetary Fund.

The failure of the Bolivian revolution to consolidate can be explained fairly simply by considering the main factors of consolidation. Although the revolution clearly created a greater sense of opportunity, it failed to develop trust, build a vision of the future, or ultimately empower the population. The inability of the revolutionary coalition to speak with one voice—in fact its very public squabbling—prevented any coordinated effort to develop trust. The MNR core leadership remained a small group that manipulated the larger factions on the party wings. Such leadership did not inspire trust among the people, and many grew apathetic about the process. The fact that there were three competing factions with different visions of the future was further complicated by the lack of trust in the leadership: It was unclear who was making decisions, how they would be made, and whether they could or would be implemented. Finally, there was little sense of long-term popular empowerment in a situation where control seemed to rest at the top—with those manipulating the competing factions—rather than with the people, who had little input into the social revolutionary process.

Perhaps it is not surprising that the Bolivian revolution remains little more than a footnote in history. "Its own institutionalization," Domínguez and Mitchell argued, "proved to be a hollow accomplishment."[26] Uniquely positioned to aid and abet the consolidation process, the MNR did neither. Lacking a coherent program or accord on an objective, the MNR remained a divided and divisive organization. Ultimately, Malloy suggested, "the MNR became stalemated, with no wing of the party able to impose its concepts on the party organization, let alone the country at large."[27] The legacy of the MNR is top-directed, manipulative intraparty politics, which consequently deteriorated into politics as usual in Bolivia.

The heritage that remains is one of an incomplete revolution, a process begun but never finished. Institutionalization alone is not enough; it lacks the necessary commitment of the population. The Bolivians emulated the Mexicans perhaps far more than they intended to. The failure to consolidate, the inability to protect and extend the gains made by the revolution, is not the only reason that the Bolivian revolution has slipped into obscurity, but it is certainly one of them. The failure of the more radical elements, which constituted a significant portion of the population, to move beyond institutionalization and legitimation so as to consolidate the revolution and create a new Bolivian society was not lost on others seeking to radically alter their societies and create new worlds.  □

## CUBA, 1959–1969: CONSOLIDATION
## WITHOUT INSTITUTIONALIZATION

If the puzzle of Bolivia is in part its obscurity and marginalization, Cuba is intriguing for the position it has come to occupy as the prototype of modern social revolution. Distinguishing characteristics have included the relative lack of internal opposition, the incredible staying power and popularity of Fidel Castro, and, for the first ten years of the revolution, an almost pathological aversion on the part of the leadership to institutionalization; since the mid-1980s the remaining ones of those leaders have been again evincing that attitude in what is called the "rectification" process. But can a revolution that has yet to prove its ability to transfer power be considered a success?

With respect to Cuba, we must ask, What happens when consolidation occurs, but there is no meaningful effort to institutionalize the social revolutionary process? The contention here is that the absence of institutionalization renders the Cuban social revolutionary process suspect, at least until it is clear whether the process can survive the passing of those who have led the revolution since its inception. In other words, in the absence of institutionalization, can the revolutionary process continue without the consolidators?

By most standards there seems little question that the Cuban revolution is the archetype for social revolutionary success. Cuba has handled the social and economic scourges of the less developed world far better than most other countries.[28] Cuba's prodigious successes in the areas of health care, literacy, education, child care, and combating hunger are recognized even by most critics of the revolution.[29] Political rights have been another matter. Despite the introduction of "direct democracy" immediately after political victory and the advent of *poder popular* (people's power) in the mid-1970s, few of the rights and privileges associated with the Western democratic legacy exist in Cuba, and there are no clear lines of succession. These factors imperil the future of the revolution.

The focus in this section is on the decision of the revolutionary leadership not to institutionalize the revolution and the continuing presence—one might say omnipresence—of Cuba's *jefe máximo*, Fidel Castro. As we will see, Cuba's revolutionary leaders were committed from the start to avoid the sort of institutionalization that they believed had derailed the revolutions in Mexico, Russia, China, and, most recently, Bolivia. These revolutionaries were able to convince a majority of the population to embrace the core of the social revolutionary project—the Cuban revolution clearly has been consolidated. The failure to institutionalize, however, has left the revolution vulnerable.

In contrast to the Bolivians, on 1 January 1959 the Cubans stepped into a vacuum, an institutional collapse created by the flight of the elite. During the insurrection the revolutionary 26th of July Movement (M-26-7) focused on the creation of a new society rather than on the destruction of the old one, which seemed to be destroying itself. At the time of the revolution, according to Pérez: "Social structures were in disarray, the political system was in crisis, the economy was in distress. National institutions were in varying degrees of disintegration and disrepute, and because they had not served Cuba well, if at all, they were vulnerable."[30] When the revolutionaries defeated the repressive regime built on the foundations of the old society, those foundations simply crumbled.

The institutions and people that did remain were stained, stigmatized by their complicity in the events that had brought Cuba to this point. Not only the branches of the government but also, by virtue of their association with the discredited regime, Cuba's other important institutions, the old political parties, the press, and the Church, were tainted.[31] There was no institution, for that matter, no individual, in a position to challenge the revolutionaries.

From the time of the political victory and the attendant institutional disintegration, the Cuban revolution has been characterized by ineffectual institutions and the personal leadership of Fidel Castro and a coterie of M-26-7 veterans from the mountains. These were people not inclined to the details of government. The revolution had been won in part by the flexibility with which the revolutionaries confronted specific problems as they arose, according to the demands of the immediate context, and then leading by example. Despite Castro's appointment of Manuel Urrutia to the presidency and José Miró Cardona to the office of prime minister and his own decision to forgo formal office, it was clear by the end of the first month that there were two governments in Cuba: one at the presidential palace, another at the Havana Hilton, where Castro and his lieutenants were ensconced. Two weeks later, six weeks into the post–political victory period, this system of unofficial cogovernment ended: Castro took the recently vacated office of prime minister.

The period after political victory was marked by Castro's adoption of a highly egalitarian, populist style of government that was in effect an extension of the M-26-7 leadership style. An informal band of revolutionaries, led principally by Castro and his chief lieutenant, Ernesto "Ché" Guevara, reasoned that the methods that had brought them to power should work to transform Cuban society. One result of this, according to Fagen, was immense disdain of and disinterest in "the routine processes of public administration."[32]

In fact, the revolutionaries had decided that no institutional framework could possibly provide the flexibility they wanted to move quickly in changing society. Drawing on their experience in the mountains, they desired a form that would provide the arrangements and procedures that would allow for discussion, choice, and flexibility in an extremely dynamic and fluid situation. The population, emboldened by the depth and breadth of the political victory, responded. "Pressure for immediate, deep, sweeping change was building," Pérez argued, and the constituency for radical change was "vast."[33]

What had to be avoided, the revolutionary leadership felt, were the stifling effects of institutionalization. Castro repeatedly denounced bureaucracy as a source of great evil, a scourge that the revolutionaries were determined to eradicate, along with the physical diseases that beset the population.[34] Guevara similarly warned against the spread of "bureaucratism" and called for a "war" against this affliction.[35] True revolutionaries, the leadership stressed, gloried in labor and struggle, not desk work. To prove their point, Castro, Guevara, and the others set the tone by logging long hours not just in their governmental duties but also in voluntary labor: cutting sugarcane, building houses, working in factories.

The absence of strictures and bureaucracy—of even a blueprint beyond the vague promises of the 1956 M-26-7 manifesto[36]—allowed the leaders to continue with the improvisation, flexibility, and sheer will, sacrifice, and determination that had been the hallmarks of the successful insurrection. The revolution was constantly being "invented."[37] Institutions and the attendant bureaucracy could only interfere in the relationship between the revolutionaries and the population. If any institutionalization was taking place, it was the institutionalization of the myth of the Sierra Maestra, the heroic guerrilla fighters and the population who cared for them and on whose behalf they purportedly fought.[38]

Although the new government avoided formal institutionalization, it moved quickly to transform the country's social and political systems and alter patterns of economic development. Clearly, such a task could not be undertaken without some kind of structure. Prior to the political victory, the M-26-7 high command had created "departments," which were charged with administering the "liberated" areas of the Sierra Maestra. These departments of justice, health, social security, agriculture and peasant affairs, construction, industry, social construction, services, education, and finances were, in effect, "embryos of the future ministries."[39] In the period after political victory, these departments quietly became the institutions, the structure, which, regardless of its official status, undergirded the revolutionaries' drive for consolidation.

The formal institutions, rather than being revamped, were to be supplanted by a mix of "direct democracy" and massive mobilization campaigns. Direct democracy was built on face-to-face meetings: Castro, Guevara, and the other leaders traveled throughout the country, talking with people enmeshed in the revolutionary process about their problems, large and small, and trying to solve them. An oft-told tale comes from the experiences of the French philosopher Jean-Paul Sartre, who accompanied Castro on one of his excursions into the countryside in 1960. On this trip Sartre witnessed "direct democracy" firsthand, as he watched Castro tackle problems such as a malfunctioning refrigerator in a bar at a "people's beach," the design of housing being built by rural workers, and deciding which member of an agricultural cooperative should repair the tractors.[40] Whether such questions merited the immediate attention of the country's top leadership is moot: The procedure strengthened a perceived bond between the revolutionaries and the population.

Institutions were thus to be replaced by the deep and abiding personal relationship between the revolutionary leadership and the population, a relationship that the revolutionaries believed would flower. But the leaders could not be everywhere at once, and few created the drama, intensity, and sense of commitment brought by Castro, Guevara, or Camilo Cienfuegos. Beyond the impetus of "direct democracy," then, the people were to be kept energized and involved "through all-inclusive mobilization."[41] Institutionalization was not a priority, and to the degree that it existed or emerged, it was perceived as an obstacle to be overcome and perhaps even counterrevolutionary.

Consequently, the first decade of the revolution was in part characterized by weak and ineffectual institutions. Those institutions that did exist
had little power and served only to increase Castro's power rather than
detract from it; Castro seemed uninterested in the creation of institutions
that could stand on their own. The social landscape in the aftermath of
political victory "had the masses as its foundations, new populists as its
leaders, and a charismatic authority as *jefe máximo*."[42] Unfettered by
"institutional demands, popular pressures, or dissident cliques, Castro's
power was nearly absolute."[43] The key terms here are authority and
power: Both were unquestionably wielded by Castro.

In theory and practice, the Cuban government of this period operated
on the vanguard theory: the assumption that a self-selected core of intel-
lectually and morally superior and proven revolutionaries had to lead
the people. Basic policies, even the most mundane and picayune ones,
were set from above by Fidel and his small circle of advisers, predominantly those who had fought with him in the Sierra Maestra.[44] These decisions were then communicated to the population, which was mobilized
by the regime's revolutionary organizations. Implementation of govern-
ment-planned and -initiated programs maximized support; probably
the most important of these programs were the literacy campaigns, the
health campaigns, the voluntary labor projects, and the neighborhood
committees. These crusades energized and involved the population, but
they did nothing to create or strengthen institutionalization.

There were experiments with institutionalization and institution
building. Probably the most important—and revealing—incident related
to nascent institutionalization was the 1962 ORI/Escalante affair. That
was the attempt of old-line Cuban Communists to take advantage of the
decision to integrate the various revolutionary organizations into a
single, unified vanguard party and to centralize and bureaucratize the
revolutionary process. Although this effort began with the blessings of
Castro, it was perceived by others in the revolutionary leadership as an
attempt to limit creativity, flexibility, and participation.

The ORI/Escalante affair was complex and multifaceted. In theory, it
was an effort to provide the country with a political apparatus, a set of
functional political institutions. In practice, it served to highlight the tension between processes of institutionalization and consolidation. In 1961
a new party was created, a party that was to be the political apparatus
for the country. The Integrated Revolutionary Organization (ORI) combined the M-26-7, the largely student-based Revolutionary Directorate,
and Cuba's old-line, Moscow-oriented, prerevolutionary Communist
party, the Popular Socialist Party (PSP). Because the PSP cadres had extensive organizational experience, construction of the ORI was entrusted
to former PSP executive secretary Aníbal Escalante.[45]

Escalante moved rapidly and effectively to place PSP members in the country's emergent institutions, and he began to have tremendous influence over the most fundamental policies and programs of the revolution. Drawing on Stalin's tactics, Escalante worked to build the institutions into a bulwark against those who had led the revolution and the population in general. He used bureaucratic methods to try to split the revolution's leadership; particularly effective was a purge of army commanders who had led the guerrilla struggle and the defense of the country during the U.S.-sponsored Bay of Pigs invasion. Escalante's heavy-handed tactics, aimed to speed up the agrarian reform process, resulted in the alienation of farmers; that, in turn, created food shortages that began to undermine support for the revolutionary process. In addition, blatant bureaucratic excesses—privilege and corruption reminiscent of the old regime—angered more and more of the population.

Construction of the ORI was "the first major attempt at institutionalization undertaken by the revolution."[46] Castro had apparently envisioned the ORI as a transitional institution that would build a new political apparatus for Cuba. In fact, the ORI simply became the PSP under a new name. As the situation degenerated, Castro first criticized the ORI and removed Escalante and then dismantled the ORI. In effect, Castro stepped outside the embryonic institutional framework to condemn it. The ease with which Escalante was deposed and the ORI "reorganized"—as the United Party of the Socialist Revolution (PURS)—proved the strength of Castro's charismatic authority.

Castro's attack on the ORI and his distancing from the attempt at institutionalization further discredited that process in Cuba. As Castro explained it, the ORI and by extension institutionalization were "a straitjacket, a yoke," binding and limiting the revolution rather than advancing it.[47] The role played by Castro in stepping in, destroying the ORI's influence, and shutting it down, made clear his dominance of the political process; it was clear from his action that any institutionalization that occurred would be of his design and at his discretion.[48]

Apparently Castro feared that the institutionalization and thereby bureaucratization of the revolution would limit his spontaneity of action and power and lay the groundwork for the emergence of a new class governing in its own interests rather than the interests of all Cubans. Castro explained that there had been no rush to set up new institutions because "we would like them to conform to [social] reality and not the other way around."[49] In other words, Castro opted for charisma over bureaucracy in fashioning the daily operation of the government: *Personalismo* was chosen over institution building.[50]

The revolutionary leaders relied on the intense mobilization campaigns to define their socioeconomic and political policies—but the campaigns were not by themselves sufficient to create institutions as long as Castro's charismatic leadership, which could alter any policy, any decision, at any time, existed. Thus, the government's early politics was oriented toward creating new attitudes to meet the dual challenge of ensuring government stability and survival and inaugurating the strategy for creating the new revolutionary society. The leadership did not ignore the political aspects of the country's development; the erosion of the old political culture and the development of a new one, based on the values of the social revolution, were a central concern.

The success of Cuba's consolidation project is readily apparent in terms of the main factors of consolidation. The process of "direct democracy" served to build a high degree of trust and opportunity. The prevalent notion, the perception, if not the reality, was that the leadership was willing to submit itself to the people on a regular basis and live and work among them and like them. This also facilitated the development of a widespread sense of opportunity among the population—clearly, those spheres of Cuban life that had been the purview of society's elite were now accessible to the population, including access to the very top leaders.

The mass mobilization campaigns also contributed to the development of a sense of opportunity. The population was being educated and receiving health care, wealth was being redistributed, and so on. It was clear to the people that they were being afforded opportunities that once were largely beyond their imagination. This, in turn, fueled people's vision of the future. Suddenly the possibilities seemed limitless, and for many there was little question that their children would have greater opportunities and a better future than they had. Underlying all this was a pervasive sense of empowerment—Cubans believed that they had a role to play and that the gains were theirs. What could be more empowering than the belief that an individual could confront the leaders of the government and expect them to respond?

By 1969 government by consolidation—exhortation and mobilization—had become exhausting for both the population and the leadership. There were no permanent, stable institutions of any significance.[51] Moreover, exhortation and mobilization were not proving to be means by which long-term economic and social demands could be met.[52] Faced with a crumbling economy and a revolutionary process that was starting to wear thin, in 1970 the government moved to institutionalize Cuba's governmental processes. For some the move toward institutionalization marked the end of the revolution and the beginning of "the postrevolutionary era."[53] If the goals were depersonalization, diffusion, and democratization or the subordination of individuals to institutions, institutionalization may be adjudged a failure.[54]

The argument that institutionalization has totally failed ignores the fact that since 1970, and especially since the first Communist party conference in 1975, there have been more clearly delineated lines of authority and formalized procedures. Mechanisms were introduced to include more people in decision-making processes, allow at least local leadership to be held accountable, and oversee the day-to-day running of the country.[55] It is probably accurate to suggest that after 1970 the leadership sought to institutionalize a preexisting set of structures and move away from the highly personalistic character of the revolution. The result of this "neoinstitutionalism" is that Cuba's institutions have been rescued from the periphery of Cuban politics and made part of the dynamic.[56]

Such changes were real enough and created more robust institutions, institutions that at least one scholar believed were viable enough to outlast Castro.[57] It is less clear how meaningful these changes were. The late arrival of institutionalization prevented a ready accommodation with consolidation. This may be most directly mirrored in the rectification program undertaken in the mid-1980s (in part as a return to the glories of the first ten years).

The focus of the rectification campaign could not be much clearer.[58] The policies that dominated from 1970 to 1986, which themselves were intended to be a rectification of what Castro considered his own errors of the first decade, were determined to have been a mistake, a deviation from the policies that had begun the revolutionary process. In particular, Castro excoriated the evils of "mechanisms" and "administrators," two of the pitfalls, presumably, of institutionalization.[59] The argument, at least as presented by some reformist politicians, was that the Cuban revolution "copied institutions and norms that did not correspond with our idiosyncrasy, traditions, and style," clearly implying that Cuba had drifted too far under the influence of its Soviet allies.[60] The emotional heart of the rectification process, the attempt to redress this imbalance, was the reintroduction of the Guevarist "moral economy" of the 1960s; the practical centerpiece of the rectification project was the reorganization of the party. Together they also reinforced the prominence of the unique role of Fidel Castro.

More than thirty years after political victory, the Cuban revolution remains overwhelmingly dominated and transfixed by the figure of Fidel Castro. Domínguez and Mitchell were undoubtedly right to warn against the temptation to read the Cuban political system as mere "one-man rule," instead likening Castro to a "laser device, which concentrates focused light waves and emits them in a narrow, very intense beam."[61] Any analysis of Cuba today, however, reveals the extent to which—for better and for worse—the country has been marked by the vision and choices of Fidel Castro. Even the recent rectification campaign designed to remedy the revolution's past errors was inaugurated by Castro, defined by Castro, and would appear to be directed by Castro.[62]

Castro continues to loom larger than life, crisscrossing the island on trips, the primary source of legitimacy of the government and perhaps of the revolution. He remains the "leader towering above all individuals and institutions."[63] In fact, it may be that what has been institutionalized at this point is Fidel Castro.[64] As such, his monopoly on power may well be an obstacle to any further development of Cuba's social, political, or economic processes. At the same time, the consolidation of the revolution has forever changed the people of Cuba; it is hard to imagine that they would ever return to the way things were before. The true test of the revolution will be when Fidel Castro has left the scene.   □

## NICARAGUA, 1979–1990:
## INSTITUTIONALIZATION AND CONSOLIDATION

The Nicaraguan revolution has similarities to both the Bolivian and Cuban experiences. As in Bolivia, competing factions existed within the revolutionary leadership; therefore there was apprehension about the consolidation of the revolution. As in Cuba, the nascent government faced immense pressures, although in Nicaragua these emanated from internal as well as external actors. As a result, there were concerns about institutionalizing the revolution. Yet important differences also existed. Nicaragua's revolutionaries, the Sandinista National Liberation Front (FSLN or Sandinistas), came to power with a commitment to the creation of an inclusive community in Nicaragua predicated on both a mixed economy and a mixed political system. This was indicative of the FSLN's desire to put to use the lessons the leaders believed that they had learned, in part from their interpretations of the Bolivian and Cuban experiences.

The Sandinista revolutionaries, who dominated the new Nicaraguan government, consciously set out to pursue a dual revolutionary project: institutionalization and consolidation. Thus they are unique among the four cases being considered here. Altering the social, political, and economic institutions of the country, the leaders realized, would not be enough to fundamentally transform society: Witness Bolivia. Nor did they want to replicate the Cuban pattern of engaging the population while failing to empower them. The FSLN's commitment was to enable the population: It sought to provide the population with the tools that would "convert them into the active subjects [agents] of their own history."[65]

Nicaragua serves as a useful model for the successful social revolution because of the amount of institutionalization and consolidation there. Yet

Nicaragua also serves as a powerful reminder that a critical international context can shape events and affect processes as they unfold. Social revolutions do not happen in isolation: They are profoundly embedded in the complexities of the international system. Nonetheless, it is the ability to institutionalize and consolidate the revolutionary process internally that denotes success: Consolidation, once achieved, cannot be overthrown.

Chapter 4 is specifically addressed to consolidation in Nicaragua and includes consideration of the 1990 election. Therefore, in this section I will focus on the 1984 electoral process as an exemplar of institutionalization. I make the argument here that the mechanics of the electoral process introduced by the FSLN and its successful implementation on two occasions under adverse conditions indicate that the revolutionary project has been institutionalized in Nicaragua. A brief discussion of consolidation will presage the lengthier discussion in Chapter 4.

On 19 July 1979 the victorious Nicaraguan revolutionaries found themselves in a situation strikingly similar to that of their Cuban predecessors. Although many members of the elite stayed in Nicaragua, in contrast to their Cuban counterparts, the state apparatus, such as it had been under Somoza, departed. Although the FSLN and its allies successfully removed a long-lived dynastic dictatorship, the Junta of the Government of National Reconstruction (JGRN) confronted the collapse of the entire government apparatus, including the army, the congress, the bureaucracy, the courts, and the civil institutions.[66]

The legacy bequeathed to the Nicaraguan revolutionaries was one of antidemocratic, neomilitary, patrimonial politics characterized by massive corruption and pervasive human rights violations. The failure of the previous regime to have made any efforts to build a meaningful state simplified the process. The enactment of new laws, the development and construction of new institutions, and the rehabilitation of some old institutions went relatively smoothly.[67]

The revolutionaries seem to have been conscious of the need to ensure limits on personal power and provide a mechanism for succession. Thus they decided to maintain the collective leadership that had brought them to political victory. In a Nicaraguan variation of Cuba's "direct democracy," public assemblies such as "Face the People," encounter and dialogue sessions between top officials and the population, which served (in theory) to help hold the leadership accountable, were televised.[68] Succession would be handled via the traditional mechanism of the Western democratic systems—elections.

The JGRN quickly installed a legal system, partly as a measure of institutionalization, but also to deal with the crimes of the previous regime, in particular those of the despised National Guard, whose rights were carefully protected.[69] A comprehensive agrarian reform program, which included nationalization and distribution of the substantial land-hold-ings of the former dictator, the formation of thousands of cooperative ag-ricultural enterprises, and the redistribution of hundreds of thousands of acres of other lands to individuals and cooperatives, was enacted. Highly successful and popular mobilization campaigns dramatically reduced adult illiteracy and expanded health services in both curative and pre-ventive medicine. A massive campaign was undertaken to eliminate epi-demic diseases and improve public health, including a highly successful effort to combat diarrhea, the major killer of infants in Latin America. As in Cuba, the implementation of these programs demonstrated to the people the FSLN's commitment to transform their lives and the fabric of society. The resultant underlying base of support and goodwill was a critical component of the government's project to consolidate the revolution.

As a way to assess institutionalization in Nicaragua we shall consider the establishment and functioning of the electoral process there. The 1984 election was the FSLN's most important effort to institutionalize the Nicaraguan revolution. The ratification of the constitution in 1987 and the 1990 election served to codify that institutionalization process.

Since Nicaragua declared its independence in 1821, there have been only two openly contested elections: the first in 1984, the second in 1990.[70] In both cases, the elections were ascertained to be free, open, and fair by significant numbers of international observers.[71] The elections and the peaceful transfer of power to the opposition after the 1990 elec-tion—a unique event in Nicaragua's history—stand as irrefutable evi-dence of the success of the social revolutionary institutionalization project.[72]

There is more democracy in Nicaragua today than there was either under the Somoza dictatorship or in the century of independence that preceded it.[73] The elections of the final member of the Somoza "dynasty," Anastasio Somoza Debayle, "featured translucent ballots, the buying of votes, intimidation, and, when all else failed, stuffed ballot boxes."[74] As a result, the promise of elections or electoral democracy seemed of little importance to the majority of Nicaraguans prior to or during the struggle for power.[75] Nonetheless, elections were part of the FSLN platform well before the defeat of the Somoza regime.[76]

The FSLN's three factions (detailed in Chapter 3) had different ideas on a wide range of topics, not the least of which were elections. The "deep commitment to social justice" shared by all the factions did not mitigate the concern of some "about whether or not that vision was com-patible with pluralist democracy."[77] In particular there was concern that immediate elections risked degenerating "into a sort of directionless populism (à la Mexico in the 1920s and 1930s and Bolivia in the 1950s)."[78]

Nonetheless, the FSLN was the only leftist party in the struggle against Somoza that never called for a "dictatorship of the proletariat" and that defended the notion of a multiparty political system.[79] By the time of the political victory, the FSLN had determined that elections were "not a concession but rather a way to strengthen the revolution."[80]

The revolutionary leaders' commitment to elections was included in the laws presented the day after they achieved political victory.[81] Although various members of the leadership repeated this promise, they often tempered it with the admonition that democracy was more than simply elections.[82] At the huge rally celebrating the end of the successful National Literacy Campaign on 23 August 1980, for example, Humberto Ortega pledged that the electoral law would be in place by 1983 and elections would follow by 1985. In the same speech, however, he warned against equating elections with democracy: "For the Sandinista Front, democracy is not measured only in political terms, nor is it confined merely to participation in elections. It is more, much more. . . . And it must be said once and for all, democracy does not begin and end with elections. It is a myth to want to reduce democracy to that."[83] Still, the revolutionary leaders clearly saw elections as part of the overall democratic package that they were seeking to implement in Nicaragua.[84]

The commitment to elections and to the creation of an equitable electoral process was renewed regularly by the FSLN leadership over the next several years.[85] Delegations were sent to European and Latin American countries as well as the United States to study their political systems. The conclusion was that Nicaragua should marry the best of Western participatory democracy—including regular elections, a parliament, a multiparty system, freedom of the press, separation of powers—with the best of a distributive justice system such as Cuba's, in which medical care, housing, food, and education are assured to all.[86]

Although the opposition and the United States complained about the length of time until the first election, the FSLN argued that under the circumstances, it had to give priority to improving social conditions. There was another factor, however. Nicaragua lacked the technical ability to hold an election. Simply conducting an election in a country that has no meaningful electoral history and no real civil society is a problematic enterprise. How are such things quickly arranged? Although this is what the U.S. government wanted—indeed, demanded—in Nicaragua, the U.S. State Department recognized that a quick election would be at best extremely difficult and more likely impossible to organize.[87] Such an election, they concluded, would simply represent "an absurd projection of North American political culture."[88]

The Council of State—the legislative body that had been established for the period prior to elections—drew up legislation on the elections and on the status of political parties.[89] In September 1983, with considerable opposition input, a political parties law was enacted. Three months later, the government, anxious to capitalize on its popularity and gain the sympathy of the Western democracies in the confrontation with the United States, announced that the elections would be moved up to 1984. In February 1984 an election date of 4 November 1984 was announced. A month later the Electoral Law, modeled on those of the Western European parliamentary democracies, was enacted.[90]

The 1984 Electoral Law established a system "rooted in the classical liberal-democratic concepts of territorial representation and 'one citizen, one vote.'"[91] The law provided for the election of a president, vice president, and a National Assembly of ninety people; all terms would be for six years. There would be a separation of powers between the executive and legislative branches.[92] The voting itself would be direct, popular, and secret, with the electorate composed of all Nicaraguan citizens over the age of sixteen. The presidency would be decided by a simple plurality.[93]

Well before the elections, Ronald Reagan articulated the U.S. view that the elections would be nothing more than a "Soviet-style sham."[94] The United States then began a massive and systematic campaign to discredit the elections, including a program of disinformation and political "dirty tricks" in both Nicaragua and the United States.[95] The center of the U.S. effort to undermine the elections was the candidacy of Arturo Cruz and the coalition that nominated him, the Democratic Coordinating Committee (CD). Cruz, a businessman and former member of the JGRN living in Washington, D.C., was presented by the United States as a moderate who was the only viable opposition candidate. As a result, the United States publicly staked its interpretation of the elections on him.[96]

According to Cruz, he was from the start simply an "electoral teaser," who was never meant to stay in the race.[97] Prior to his return to Nicaragua, Cruz even told a U.S. reporter: "I'm not really going to run. You know that."[98] Mario Rappaccioli, one of the leaders of the CD and a friend of Cruz's, explained to reporters that "Cruz does not intend to run and is interested only in discrediting the election."[99] The FSLN remained overwhelmingly popular with the majority of the people; after all, it had defeated Somoza and introduced extremely popular social programs. The U.S./CD supporters were well aware that they could not defeat the FSLN at the ballot box. The best they could hope for was to use Cruz and the CD itself to delegitimize the elections.[100] This charade, lamented Venezuelan President Carlos Andrés Pérez, allowed the United States to proclaim that there had not been free elections in Nicaragua.[101]

On 4 November 1984, for the first time in its history, Nicaragua held elections that were hailed as free, open, fair, and honest by the six opposition parties that participated and virtually all the international observers not affiliated with the U.S. administration.[102] Of those registered to vote (93.7 percent of eligible voters), 75 percent cast ballots.[103] The FSLN presidential ticket of JGRN members Daniel Ortega and Sergio Ramírez polled 66.7 percent of the vote; the FSLN National Assembly slate received 62.9 percent of the vote (sixty-one seats).[104] The opposition received 33 percent of the vote, mostly split among the three parties that represented the Right and Center, and were awarded thirty-five (36.5 percent) of the ninety-six seats (including seats for the six losing presidential candidates) in the National Assembly.[105]

The 1984 Nicaraguan elections were honestly run and reflected reasonably well the preferences of the Nicaraguan polity. Their primary importance, however, was not technical virtue. The elections provided the country's opposition parties the opportunity to present themselves and their platforms to the public and win places in a legislature where they could seek to implement their program and criticize the government.[106] Thus the elections served to institute these parties as "integral, if subordinate, parts of the polity"; the result was institutionalization of a significant measure of political pluralism.[107] The FSLN became the first revolutionary government to include meaningful, competitive elections in its political repertoire. In so doing, the FSLN became the first "vanguard" party to achieve power through armed struggle and then submit itself to an open electoral contest against as wide a range of opposition parties as chose to compete.

The institutionalization process in Nicaragua has been a success—one all the more significant in view of the legacy of oligarchy and dictatorship that the revolutionaries inherited.[108] The Sandinistas helped the country to overcome that legacy. Although the victory has been uneven, the Sandinistas institutionalized a system that permits debate and criticism at a level "unprecedented in Central American history."[109] That their system allowed the defeat of the social revolutionary forces at the ballot box is unprecedented in the world. The FSLN built the electoral system on a democratic framework that has been widely praised and even proposed as a precedent "for future elections worldwide."[110] Indeed, it would be hard to imagine a stronger claim to the relative success of the institutionalization process in Nicaragua than the successful and peaceful transfer of power that occurred after the 1990 election.

That proof of successful institutionalization would seem to call into question the process of consolidation. After all, this line of argument runs, if the revolution had been consolidated, the FSLN would have won the election. This argument, however, misses the essence of consolidation. Because consolidation is about people's attitudes toward the revolution—it represents the degree to which a significant majority of the population embraces the core of the social revolutionary project—it is not necessarily linked to an exact set of institutions or particular programs or even specific people or parties.

The FSLN quickly moved after political victory to develop and enlarge popular support for the social revolutionary process, that is, to begin the social revolutionary project of consolidation. The project unfolded in two discrete but interrelated parts. One part was the denigration and destruction of privilege, based on the implementation of an array of broadly accessible and popular social programs. Building on this, the second part was the effort to make sure that the population had a *perceived* stake in the process, with the introduction of broadly accessible political structures as well as the aforementioned popular social programs.[111] Throughout, the social revolutionary leadership "championed" the people to bind them to the social revolutionary project.

It required little effort for the new government to denigrate and attack privilege. Nicaragua, at the time of the 1979 revolution, was characterized by the "rancid flavor of the Somoza regime," which had reduced it "even by regional standards, [to] a wretched place."[112] Somoza and his cronies had so alienated the population that even many of those who enjoyed privileges in Nicaraguan society had turned against him. In contrast to Cuba, however, where much of the elite fled with Fulgencio Batista, the FSLN confronted an elite that was not only established but also in fact part of the broad revolutionary coalition that achieved political victory in 1979. As a result, the FSLN leaders had to move carefully. The attack on privilege could not be focused on the wealthy, but rather on the basis of the population's incredible despair and the failure of the Somoza regime to see to minimal standards in areas such as education and health care.

The revolutionary leaders recognized that they had to involve the people and create in them a sense of stake in the project. Praxis was regarded as crucial to the consolidation process; the creative, corrective, and salutary effects of immersion in revolutionary activity in mass organizations, the armed forces, the schools, and for some, the political party were stressed.[113] In this sense, above all, the illusion or perception of participation has been one of the primary vehicles for the social revolutionary transformation of society. I do not say this cynically. Illusion and perception are critical for any government, particularly for those that base their claim to legitimacy on responsiveness to public concerns and demands.[114]

To this end, the FSLN immediately backed the creation of a network of affiliated mass organizations that would debate and vote on issues as well as work collectively to carry out projects important to building the new society. These organizations included labor unions, peasant groups, and associations of women, youth, and small farmers. The effort built on the immense popular support that had been generated during the first two phases of the social revolutionary process. Membership in the mass organizations was actively encouraged among all Nicaraguans, and hundreds of thousands joined.[115] Through such organizations the FSLN was able to complete practical projects, mobilize support, and begin the consolidation process rapidly.

As Chapter 4 is largely devoted to the assessment of consolidation in Nicaragua, I shall not dwell on it here. Suffice it to say that Nicaragua is a society well into the third phase of the social revolutionary process. Institutionalization can hardly seem in doubt after the 1990 election. The FSLN created a mixed economy and a political system that is judged open by any standard. The 1990 election marked not only the first time an opposition party in Nicaragua has ever won an election but also the only case in which a revolutionary government has created an electoral process that it allowed itself to lose. The status of the effort to consolidate the revolution is less clear.

FSLN success at creating opportunity and a vision of the future did not necessarily translate into trust. The failure to build trust or, perhaps more accurately, the loss of trust, is attributable to many factors. Chief among these were serious FSLN mistakes and the massive and systematic efforts of the United States to undermine the government.

One of the FSLN's greatest—if perhaps most bittersweet—successes has been the empowerment of the population, but, overall, empowerment turned out to be a double-edged sword for the revolutionary leadership. Empowerment has resulted in a commitment to the revolution but not to the revolutionaries. The people are convinced that they could realize their revolutionary promise and vision without the social revolutionary leadership.

Powerful elucidation of this point came from an older woman who had raised a large family in León, Nicaragua's second-largest city. In a tone that shifted from amusement to disbelief to disgust, she related:

> For many years here in León the wealthy would hold parties in the park in front of the cathedral. When they had these parties they would rope off the area in front of the cathedral with gold ropes. We would all crowd around to watch them as they were driven up and got out of their cars and had their party and acted as if we were not even there. They danced and ate and drank and it was as if we were their cattle in the field. Cattle. Can you believe that? Is it hard for you to imagine? It never even occurred to us that we could cross the ropes. They would take over this public place for a party and we would just stand there like brutes with our mouths open and stare in awe. Like cattle. Well, this could never happen again. We would never allow this. We know now that we are not cattle . . . and we will never be their cattle again.[116]

The message is clear: People in Nicaragua have been transformed, and it is impossible to take that away; by extension, society has been transformed, and the clock cannot be turned back.

Understanding these fundamental changes is central to any assessment of the consolidation process; and appreciating the attitude articulated by this woman is vital to understanding what consolidation represents. This is what consolidation brings us that is missing from the study of institutionalization: access to the people's attitudes toward the material and ideological conditions of their everyday lives. Access in turn affords us the opportunity to assess the meaning and the impact of the social revolutionary process.  ☐

## GRENADA, 1979–1983:
## THE REVOLUTION THAT NEVER WAS

The Grenadian revolution represents an anomaly. One scholar likened it in stature to the revolt that culminated in the creation of the Haitian Republic in 1804 and to the 1959 revolution in Cuba.[117] Another important Caribbean scholar thought that the Grenadian revolution represented, in some sense, the "intrusion" of Latin American revolutionary processes into the largely conservative, English-speaking, Anglophile Eastern Caribbean.[118] Castro hailed it as "a big revolution in a small country."[119] The United States was so concerned that it worked almost from the start to destabilize the revolution and developed military plans to overthrow it, one of which was implemented in 1983. Certainly the process in Grenada was dramatically new to the Eastern Caribbean.

Yet when the topic is revolution, Grenada does not even rate the footnote customarily accorded Bolivia: Most recent work on revolution in general or on revolution in the Third World simply omits mention of Grenada.[120] Although the U.S. invasion of Grenada seems to have assured the country a measure of fame—at least in discussions of the numerous U.S. interventions in the Third World—especially in Latin America and the Caribbean, Grenada does not even appear on most lists of failed revolutions. Given the scholarly attention commonly visited upon most revolutionary processes, this omission is rather striking.

The question is, What happened? According to the model presented here, a successful revolution is one in which both institutionalization and consolidation are attained. The Grenadian revolution's failure either to institutionalize or to consolidate has apparently served to relegate it beyond the margins of consideration as a revolution—particularly as a social revolution.

If the Bolivian revolution was "incomplete" and the Cuban revolution remains in some sense vulnerable, the Grenadian revolution has been aptly described by one of its leading students as "aborted."[121] The question, however, is whether the termination of the revolution was a result of the U.S. invasion or of the inability of the revolutionary leadership to find common ground on which to pursue the social revolutionary process. The U.S. effort to destabilize the revolution should not be discounted, but the consensus among scholars of the Grenadian revolution is that by the time of the U.S. invasion, the revolution had self-destructed. No less an authority than Fidel Castro declared the Grenadian revolution a suicide.[122]

Of the explanations that have been proffered for the collapse of the Grenadian revolution, most are based on one of two theories. The first, and by far most common, focuses on the disintegration of the relationship between the primary leaders of the revolution, Maurice Bishop and Bernard Coard.[123] A second explanation concerns internal party divisions over questions of socialism versus democracy, the pace of the revolutionary process, politics versus culture, and political legitimacy.[124] These explanations nonetheless often devolve to questions surrounding the Bishop Coard split. A third set of scholars effectively merges these two perspectives.[125]

We may analyze the failure of the revolution by looking at the attempts of the Grenadian leaders to institutionalize and consolidate the revolutionary process. One intriguing aspect of the Grenadian case is that there were clearly conscious efforts at institutionalization and consolidation—efforts that mirrored to varying degrees the processes in Bolivia, Cuba, and Nicaragua. Although the Grenadian revolutionary leaders pursued more or less the same self-conscious processes as the Nicaraguans, the Grenadian leaders were unable to stay unified and became dramatically—and for Bishop and some of his close associates, fatally—split.

Maurice Bishop was clearly Grenada's visionary leader—often likened to Cuba's Castro in terms of charisma and style.[126] Bernard Coard is best understood as an organizational leader—often described as a classic bureaucrat, born to organize. In Nicaragua, as we shall see in Chapter 3, the revolutionary leaders were careful to make sure that those with different leadership styles could work together. In Grenada the consolidation process seems to have been largely in the hands of Bishop and the institutionalization project guided primarily by Coard; although shortly before the end, they found these positions ironically somewhat reversed. Their differing leadership styles led them to act at cross-purposes, so that neither process got the necessary attention.[127]

The former "Commonwealth Caribbean" nations that make up the Eastern Caribbean began to gain their independence from Britain in the early 1960s. The British had left superficial democratic institutions behind, but the people actually had relatively little meaningful experience with democracy.[128] The Eastern Caribbean states were all led to independence by powerful, charismatic figures such as Vere Bird, Sr., in Antigua, Grantley Adams in Barbados, Norman Manley in Jamaica, and Eric Williams in Trinidad. Whereas the Westminster system remained intact throughout most of the Eastern Caribbean, some of these leaders discovered that it was possible to adhere to the letter of the system while enjoying near-dictatorial powers.[129] No one more nearly approached the dictatorial status than Grenada's Eric Gairy.

Sir Eric Gairy may not have been a Latin American dictator in the classic mold; however, "Gairyism," in the view of noted Caribbean scholar Gordon Lewis, "marked the intrusion into the region of the habits of Latin American *caudillismo*."[130] As leader on Grenada's long trek to independence, Gairy attained greater and greater stature; he was Grenada's "hero."[131] Correspondingly, he became more corrupt and less interested in democracy and the complexities and complications it entailed. During the five years after Grenada received its formal independence from Britain, Gairy's delusions of grandeur and international significance increased. He not only monopolized power but also manipulated the parliamentary system to legislate abuses. In a further parallel with Latin American traditions, Gairy reached new heights of brutality in attacks on his perceived enemies.

Gairy, moreover, courted notorious dictators such as South Korea's General Pak Chung Hee, the Duvaliers in Haiti, and Somoza in Nicaragua.[132] Perhaps most chilling, however, was his increasingly close tie with the new dictator of Chile, General Augusto Pinochet.[133] Gairy's personal bodyguard, the nefarious Mongoose Gang, and its Night Ambush Squad auxiliary operated as instruments of terror.[134] Their primary targets were opponents of Gairy and those who displeased him, particularly any women who spurned his advances. There may be no greater indication of the influence of South America's repressive military dictators than Gairy's emulation of the practice of "disappearing" their political opponents.[135]

Such an atmosphere contributed to the further erosion of Grenada's already suspect democratic institutions. Moreover, independent Grenada was faring little better economically or socially than had colonial Grenada. Despite some half-hearted and ineffectual efforts by Gairy to encourage economic development, the country remained mired in the classic counterproductive spiral endemic to the developing world, selling agricultural products cheaply for export to world markets while paying outrageously inflated prices for imported goods.[136] The social services that existed were "backward, inefficient, and operating with a dilapidated infrastructure."[137] With illiteracy high by Eastern Caribbean standards and education lagging relative to previous Grenadian standards and those of the other Eastern Caribbean states, the school buildings themselves fell increasingly into disrepair. Health standards were low; real medical or dental care required off-island trips, usually to Barbados or Trinidad, for those able to finance them. Five years after becoming the first of the Windward Islands to gain independence, Grenada was, by Eastern Caribbean standards, struggling politically, economically, and socially.

The first meaningful opposition to Gairy emerged in 1970, after a number of Caribbean leftists, galvanized by the populist black power movement sweeping the region, met at Rat Island (St. Lucia).[138] The guiding spirit of the meeting has been described as reformist rather than revolutionary, and no broad strategies were planned; the commitment of the participants was to raise popular consciousness and to confront and challenge the region's continued state of dependence.[139] These populist and anti-imperialist sentiments resonated with the Grenadians, particularly with one young lawyer, Maurice Bishop, who returned determined to challenge Gairy's control and "politics as usual."

Several years of this small, informal organizing yielded few results. By 1972 two groups had emerged: the Movement for the Assemblies of the People (MAP), led by Bishop, and the Joint Endeavour for Welfare, Education, and Liberation (JEWEL).[140] Neither MAP nor JEWEL was long on specifics, but both were inspired by Tanzania's *ujamaa* experiment, where power was vested in citizen's communal villages. Both groups called for popular participation in the country's decision-making process via participatory democracy and people's assemblies, and both stressed national consciousness and pride.[141]

MAP, located in, and largely limited to, the capital city of St. George, was characterized by its urban focus, intellectual concerns, and inability to reach a large segment of the population.[142] JEWEL, working in the countryside to revitalize Grenada's farmers and peasants, paid particular attention to the development of agricultural cooperatives; an unsuccessful 1972 electoral alliance with the Grenada National party (GNP) raised questions about JEWEL's leadership ability. Recognizing the need for a more broadly based organization with both urban and rural components, MAP and JEWEL merged in 1973 to form the New Jewel Movement (NJM).

Despite the clearly radical orientation of the NJM and the abundance of radical rhetoric, the "1973 Manifesto of the New Jewel Movement for Power to the People and for Achieving Real Independence for Grenada, Carriacou, Petit Martinique, and the Grenadian Grenadines" was essentially a reformist document. The primary themes of the NJM manifesto were "genuine independence," "self-reliance," "anti-Gairyism," and "anti-imperialism." Overall, the manifesto reflects radical democracy, which may well have been inspired in part by Manley's democratic socialist experiment that had begun in Jamaica just the year before.[143] This radical slant fits as well with the NJM's decision to join with a variety of groups in seeking to force Gairy out of office before Grenada received its independence in 1974; in the estimation of one scholar, the NJM became "the driving force behind a growing coalition of anti-Gairy forces."[144]

Gairy was rescued by independence. Neither Britain nor the United States was interested in an unsettled situation in the Caribbean's newest state; both moved to prop up Gairy. The anti-Gairy opposition, still hopeful that the 1976 election would remove him from office, joined together in the People's Alliance as a vehicle to contest the parliamentary elections. Led by the NJM, the People's Alliance received 48 percent of the vote and six of the fifteen parliament seats—despite evidence that the Gairy regime had tampered with the election results. With the NJM winning three of the six seats (two went to the GNP, one to the United People's party, a GNP splinter group), NJM leader Bishop became the official leader of the opposition. Gairy responded by running roughshod over the parliament and reducing its meetings to the minimum mandated by law. There was a corresponding increase in censorship, curtailment of civil rights, and prohibition of strikes. Most dramatic, however, was the brutality aimed at the NJM.

The 1976 election clarified what everyone on the island already knew, that the leader of the opposition to Gairy and probably the country's most popular politician was Maurice Bishop. The year 1976 also saw the return to Grenada of Bernard Coard. Coard, a lecturer at the University of West Indies campus in Trinidad, had supported the NJM from its inception and helped draft the NJM manifesto.[145] In contrast to Bishop, who had evolved into the leader of the anti-Gairy struggle through his experiences in "the streets," Coard attained his position via negotiation: He joined the NJM in 1974 on the condition that he be appointed to a leadership position, and he demanded and received the safest parliamentary district for the 1976 election.[146]

During this period the NJM gravitated toward a more conventionally socialist perspective, a move many scholars ascribed to Coard and his Organization for Research, Education, and Liberation (OREL).[147] The members of OREL, which had once attacked the NJM as "a petit-bourgeois party," became a party within the party, setting themselves up as "revolutionary socialists" who formed the "Marxist-Leninist component" of the NJM.[148] Although OREL was forced to disband formally in 1978, it continued informally and was to play a divisive and decisive role in the fate of Grenada's revolutionary process. Coard's impressive command of theory, his tirelessness, and his outstanding organizational skills combined to propel him, by 1979, to an unquestioned status as the number-two person in the NJM leadership.

It was in this context that the Latin American revolutionary tradition arrived in the Eastern Caribbean. As the NJM gained stature, it became more and more a threat to the increasingly repressive Gairy. In March 1979 Gairy apparently ordered the assassination of the NJM leadership while he was scheduled to be out of the country.[149] Informed by friends, the NJM leaders went into hiding and decided to send into action its armed wing, which totaled fewer than fifty people.

At approximately 4 A.M. on March 13, forty-six people, of whom only eighteen were armed and those poorly, attacked the main army barracks at True Blue. The troops fled; then the NJM forces went to take control of Radio Grenada, where all guards but one had fled. He was waiting to surrender the station to the NJM forces. They seized all the island's police stations, encountering only token resistance at the main police headquarters, Fort George. When the Fort George resisters surrendered at 4 P.M., twelve hours after the initial attack at True Blue, the NJM held total control of the island. The death toll was three. Thus the Eastern Caribbean had had its first extraconstitutional change of power; a Latin American–style solution to a Latin American–style problem.

Although the exact nature of the political victory may be debatable—coup, revolution, or something in between[150]—there is little question that the population reacted with great glee to news of Gairy's overthrow and to the establishment of a Provisional Revolutionary Government (PRG). The response of the population "was astonishing and fully justified the PRG's claim that the revolution was legitimized by the clearly expressed will of the people."[151] Undoubtedly the NJM was celebrating as much as any group; its leaders, however, now found themselves faced with the rather unexpected and daunting task of running the country.

Five days later the PRG, renamed the People's Revolutionary Government, was officially proclaimed. The PRG was broad based: It included trade union leaders, professionals, and business leaders. In contrast to Nicaragua, however, and akin to Cuba, there was little doubt as to who was in control: the NJM and the new prime minister, Maurice Bishop. Bernard Coard, soon to be deputy prime minister, was named minister of finance. The situation inherited by the PRG could not be compared to the destruction confronted by the revolutionaries in Cuba or Nicaragua. Nevertheless, the revolutionaries found a country in which the political institutions were discredited. The economy was weak, and the country poor even by Eastern Caribbean standards. The social system was a "shambles."[152]

The PRG moved quickly, pursuing a strategy of measured reforms and broad, popular support built around the gradual introduction of populist politics, social improvement, and economic change. The government promised elections, and most Grenadians apparently expected the "revo," as they called it, to introduce its reforms and then pass quickly back to the Westminster system with which they were familiar.[153] It was a situation reminiscent of Bolivia in 1952, but this time the population was more conservative than the revolutionary leadership.

We can now turn our attention to the efforts of the Grenadian social revolutionary leadership to institutionalize and consolidate the revolution. These efforts resembled what we have seen in each of the three other cases considered here. The government structures were partly reconfigured, new programs designed to mobilize the population were introduced, and the people of Grenada were invited to take part in running the country. This was the initial, public face of the revolutionary process.

Yet as suggested earlier, there was also a private side to the social revolutionary process, one that many islanders were, despite rumors, apparently unaware of until the end. Any consideration of public efforts to institutionalize and consolidate the process must be paralleled with exploration of the internal dynamics of the revolutionary process, for it is there that the seeds of the revolution's destruction were sown by the revolutionaries themselves. It almost seems that the demise of the revolution was fixed at the same time it was getting off the ground.

The PRG, building on its apparent revolutionary legitimacy, moved to institutionalize the revolutionary process within days of political victory. Before the end of the month, the PRG had replaced the suspended constitution with an initial package of ten fundamental "people's laws," which were followed by a number of others, including some clauses from the previous constitution. The structure of the provisional government was also outlined, including the resurrection of parish councils as forums for popular participation.

Popular participation was, in fact, one of the hallmarks of the Grenadian social revolutionary process. The island's relatively small size and population made feasible the type of participatory democracy that had been discussed elsewhere in the abstract. Organizations such as the National Women's Organization (NWO) and the National Youth Organization (NYO), the trade unions, and "popular assemblies" would represent popular sentiment.[154] The initial popularity of this political process is not disputed: There was a high degree of participation across the island.[155] At least in theory, the Grenadian people would hold the country's leadership accountable. No plans were announced for succession.

The government also began to lay the groundwork for the tangible benefits that, along with the charisma and magnetism of the prime minister, were central to the support for the social revolutionary process. Medical care was improved, made free, and more doctors and nurses were hired. School lunches were provided, and school capacity was increased at the same time that fees were drastically cut. Milk was made available to mothers and infants, major housing projects were undertaken, and access to piped water was provided. A literacy campaign effectively wiped out illiteracy. As in the other cases considered, these efforts clearly enabled the consolidation process. However, they did not help with the process of institutionalization nearly so dramatically as similar efforts had in Bolivia and Nicaragua.

Despite the popularity of the new participatory politics and the success of the social programs, the institutionalization process has been considered a failure.[156] As it became apparent that decisions were being made by the leadership regardless of the popular will, participatory democracy lost its luster and the popular organizations began to wane. Of particular concern to many Grenadians were the lack of means to hold their leadership accountable and the PRG's continued failure to make provisions for succession. Specifically, the citizens wanted to reinstitute the electoral process with which they were familiar. Shortly before the end of the revolution the PRG moved to convene a constitutional convention charged with, among other things, setting up elections. This seems to indicate a belated recognition of popular sentiment by at least some within the leadership; many claim that it was Bishop. At least one scholar has suggested that Coard, the consummate bureaucrat, felt that the consolidation process had played to Bishop's advantage and feared that institutionalization would ensure Bishop's continued status.[157]

As is so often the case with the Grenadian revolutionary process, appearances were deceiving. The projects and programs noted above and the PRG's attention to the "people's laws," which had effectively replaced the constitution, seem evidence of institutionalization. This appearance was supported by the emergent, if not entirely welcome, bureaucratization. Yet at least two factors actively undercut the success of the institutionalization process. The first, Thorndike suggested, was the piecemeal fashion in which the PRG continued to implement the programs and run the government itself.[158] Institutionalization followed no coherent, logical pattern; matters were often dealt with simply as they arose, as in the early days of the revolution in Cuba.

Perhaps more destructive, however, was the failure to adopt any measure of accountability: Lines of responsibility were no clearer within the PRG than they were to the population at large. Simultaneous with the population's appreciation of the improved health care, new educational opportunities, and the increased sense of community was its resentment over the lack of accountability. As a result, the public perceived the PRG—and specifically the NJM—as a new ruling class. Moreover, it soon became evident that neither the popular organizations nor the assemblies would be able to alter the leadership; the lack of an electoral process reinforced the lack of a successionary mechanism. The PRG's failure to create the political mechanisms necessary to sustain the revolutionary process doomed that process.[159]

The consolidation process fared a bit better—largely because of the charismatic figure of Maurice Bishop. The spirit, one scholar argued, not the structure, made the revolution.[160] Others, noting the essentially reformist character of the process in Grenada, suggested that the most revolutionary aspect of the Grenadian experience was "the widespread challenge to psychological dependency."[161] Initially the revolution enjoyed a great deal of popular support, although it is difficult to discern how much of that was for the social revolutionary process, for the ouster of Gairy, or for the leadership of Bishop. It is clear that people trusted the PRG—they believed that they were involved in the process, that the PRG would well represent their interests, and that increased opportunity was likely. People also felt that in Bishop they heard a voice of the future, a person articulating their hopes and vision.

In 1983, Bishop told an audience in the United States that the Grenadian people were "always at the center and heart and focus" of all revolutionary activities.[162] If the population was in fact always the center of PRG attention, however, it was as the object of what Mandle described as a largely "paternalistic" approach.[163] "Paternalistic socialism," according to Mandle, assumes that the population cedes governance to the ruling party (in this case the NJM), and in return, the government implements benevolent programs, which benefit the population. Key here for the question of consolidation is the set of assumptions made about the population: They are not equals with the leadership, they may not organize to make demands, they must mobilize to support the decisions the government makes on their behalf. Mandle was undoubtedly correct in his estimation that paternalism, under stress, "can turn quite ugly. . . . Benevolent paternalism is no less authoritarian for being benevolent in its intentions."[164]

There was never a program in Grenada designed to win the hearts and minds of the population.[165] In fact, there are indications that some elements of the revolutionary leadership held the majority of the population in contempt; others looked upon the population more favorably but nonetheless considered the citizens to be underdeveloped, undereducated, and unsophisticated. The revolution's populism, then, was simultaneously its area of greatest strength and greatest contradiction.[166] This can be seen in the position of the NJM and its internal dynamic, specifically the complex relationship between the two leading figures of the Grenadian revolution, Maurice Bishop and Bernard Coard.

Scholars of the Grenadian revolution agreed that one of its defining characteristics was the NJM leadership's desire to control every aspect of the social and political process in the country. The party leaders appeared to have been much less concerned with the status of the economic system, since they understood themselves to be in the national-democratic stage of socialist revolution.[167] In practice, this translated into an extraordinary pragmatism. Cognizant of the position of capitalism in Grenadian society and the importance of private property, the NJM nationalized only Gairy's holdings, introduced a mild land reform two years after political victory, and made little effort at rural collectivization.[168] The results of these policies were high growth rates and an economy that was widely hailed as a success and even was lauded by the World Bank and the IMF.[169]

Although the PRG allowed the economy to go its own way, it turned its attention closely to politics and society. In the view of the NJM leadership—a view that predated political victory—Grenadian society and by extension its political institutions were "backward."[170] Therefore, the leaders decided to monopolize power while they gradually led the population toward a new society. For four and a half years, the NJM totally dominated politics in Grenada in pursuit of its vision—no other organization was allowed to operate. Decisions were made and then implemented by the NJM.[171] This is not to suggest that there was not a commitment within the NJM to develop popular participation. However, the leaders were not convinced that the people were ready to control their own destiny.

The problems with the institutionalization process may have occurred because of rifts in the NJM. There is little question that there were disagreements over specific policies and ideological differences within the leadership and, for that matter, within the NJM's strikingly small membership: There were only seventy-two members when the revolution disintegrated.[172] Perhaps the most important conflict was between Bishop's vision of a more open, broadly based party and government with greater popular accountability and Coard's adherence to a Leninist vanguard party structure that would speed socialist transition. It seems clear that the specifics of this and other areas of contention increasingly became secondary to the discord between the unquestioned leader of the revolution, Maurice Bishop, and the person who emerged as his primary challenger, his friend and deputy, Bernard Coard.

Every work on the Grenadian revolution since the coup d'état wrestles with Bishop and Coard's complex relationship and the respective roles they played in the social revolutionary process. It is agreed that Bishop was a charismatic, visionary figure who was popularly acclaimed the leader of the social revolutionary process. A widely reported graffito around the island after Coard and his old OREL clique staged their coup d'état was, "No Bishop, no revo."[173] Yet the fact that Bishop was more than simply a charismatic figure is indicated by his efforts shortly before he was overthrown to institutionalize the revolution. Scholars seem equally in accord that Coard was a natural bureaucrat who believed not in the individual but in immutable structures. Coard, however, was conscious of the importance of retaining popular support and recognized, at least to some extent, the importance of consolidation. Nonetheless, although both individuals clearly felt that the Grenadian population had to be led, Coard seems to have been generally contemptuous of the Grenadian people.[174]

Through much of the post–political victory process in Grenada, the revolution was organized—some would say managed—by Coard. He was the detail man, the bureaucrat, who thrived on interparty debates and the minutia of decision-making. He also apparently craved the position of prime minister, to which he felt entitled. Although Coard and Bishop may have agreed on many details, Coard lacked Bishop's touch with people, in fact, any connection with the population and their feelings. Bishop, in contrast, seems to have been Grenada's Castro: a man who could do little or no wrong in the eyes of the people, the person they trusted, the person who offered them opportunity, the person who articulated for them a vision of the future.

It may never be clear what prompted Coard and his followers to depose and then murder Bishop in 1983. Some attributed it to differences over policy; others, to ideological splits. A common reference point among both sets of scholars was Coard's Stalinist proclivities.[175] Perhaps the most compelling argument was made by Heine, who suggested that the real issue was personality.[176] It is impossible here to do justice to the complexities of Heine's analysis. However, the puzzle, for him, is why Coard, seemingly at the pinnacle of the power that he had been aspiring to all his life, would "risk it all for an endeavor so dubious as trying to de facto unseat the revolution's maximum leader."[177] Bishop, after all, was Coard's friend, mentor, and staunchest defender. Moreover, Heine argued, their policy disagreements were slight, and their ideological differences have been exaggerated.[178] Heine therefore turned to a psychoanalytic analysis of Bishop and Coard and concluded that Coard's need for power and prestige, his compulsive behavior, and ultimately his capacity for self-delusion forced him to remove the obstacle in his path— Maurice Bishop.[179]

The Grenadian revolution led to the most serious attempt to introduce socialism into the Eastern Caribbean; this is perhaps the final sense in which the social revolutionary process represented the intrusion of Latin America.[180] This effort alone brought Grenada closer to countries like Cuba and Nicaragua, which traditionally had relatively little (in the case of Cuba) or no (in the case of Nicaragua) contact with the states of the Eastern Caribbean. One scholar of the Caribbean, however, suggested another reason that the Grenadian revolutionary process garnered such attention. Gordon K. Lewis argued that "Grenada, of all the islands of the archipelago, was chosen to become the rendezvous of new elements."[181] Still, Lewis noted, the Grenadian revolution was too brief to establish anything new; as a result its importance may be primarily symbolic[182]—if any one remembers it at all.

Grenada is important for this study because it was a social revolution that failed either to institutionalize or to consolidate. In that sense, it offers us the opportunity to assess the relative importance of these factors. It seems clear that despite the four years of constant U.S. hostility, the revolutionaries might have survived the internal strife if at least institutionalization had occurred. By the same token, consolidation might have created a more committed population, willing to fight for the gains of the social revolutionary process. Although in both cases the revolution would likely have ultimately failed, it probably would not have simply disintegrated. ☐

## CONCLUSION:
## THE IMPORTANCE OF CONSOLIDATION

I have argued in this chapter that consolidation is a useful analytic concept that merits attention by those interested in exploring the social revolutionary process. As the four brief case studies here demonstrate, consolidation provides another approach to understanding how and why the processes unfolded as they did. By avoiding an overemphasis on state structures, we are able to consider revolutionary processes in a fuller and more meaningful way. After all, consolidation—the project of social transformation—is the ultimate goal of social revolution. As Darnton suggested, social revolutions are inherently dramatic and hopeful processes.[183] Yet, it is difficult to assess the realization of these promises and visions. The notion of consolidation provides a vantage point from which to make such assessments.

The Bolivian revolution, which institutionalized but failed to consolidate, faded into obscurity, leaving little behind to commemorate its occurrence. Thirty-three years after the Cuban revolution, the level of institutionalization remains an open question, as the degree of consolidation is so intimately tied to the figure of Fidel Castro that only his demise will allow an accurate assessment of a revolution that clearly has left its mark on Cuba and the world. Grenada's failure either to institutionalize or to consolidate seems to have left little, if any, mark on Grenada or the world.[184]

After thirteen years the fate of the revolution in Nicaragua has remained unclear. The 1990 election seemed to indicate a triumph for institutionalization. What the election suggested about consolidation was less clear. The fact that the Sandinistas received 41 percent of the vote in the face of the dire economic situation and the opposition's care not to threaten the revolution's core agenda suggested that a significant degree of consolidation had occurred and that life was unlikely to return to the prerevolutionary patterns.

There is little question that there are discernible connections among the four cases. Some of these linkages are obvious; others are not so readily apparent. A focus on institutionalization and consolidation serves to reinforce what we already know and illuminate previously marginalized or omitted aspects. The invocation of consolidation clarifies the degree to which the conscious, intentional choices and actions of individuals make an impact on the social revolutionary process. That is the focus of Chapter 3, specifically the role played by social revolutionary leadership in the transformation process.

# CHAPTER THREE

■

# Social Revolutionary Leadership: Ideology and Strategy

Revolutions do not happen but are *made*, guided by the conscious plans and significant choices of revolutionary leaders throughout the three phases of the social revolutionary process. Social revolution in particular—defined as it is by the effort to transform society—is largely the result of, composed of, and driven by human action, not simply structural phenomena. The process is overall neither mindless nor aimless, although both of these elements may be evident in specific instances. It is, rather, predominantly purposive, goal-directed behavior. If this is the case, a set of questions follows: Who directs the revolution? For what purpose? To what goal? These questions point to the importance of leadership and of social revolutionary ideology and strategy.

The third phase of the social revolutionary process, which follows political victory, is the defining phase. It is during the implausibly complex and protracted process of societal transformation that the efforts of groups and individuals have their most obvious and dramatic impact: People act, make strategic choices, and influence one another. As a result, this phase of the social revolutionary process is best understood as a period of purposeful adaptations to a variety of political circumstances, as the revolutionaries seek to transform the political, economic, and social structures of their society. Leaders must bargain, compromise, and negotiate in an effort to institutionalize and consolidate the revolution—both among themselves and with the population. They consider options and make choices. Omitting the element of conscious action and decision from the analysis of social revolutionary processes, as structuralist or deterministic perspectives do, is a mistake.

If we agree that consolidation, institutionalization, or a mix of the two represents the paths available in the post–political victory period, we should ask how such paths are chosen. To the degree that structural explanations might recognize the existence of such paths, they would be presented as determined—perhaps even predetermined—or severely constrained; in either case the working presumption/assumption is that choice is largely irrelevant. My contention is that such choices are made by the social revolutionary leadership. On occasion, as perhaps in the Grenadian case, such decisions are made in isolation. As a rule, however, the revolutionary leaders consider the interplay of the wants and needs of the population in whose name the revolution has been made, their own vision, and the domestic and international factors that impinge on their ability to realize the social revolutionary project.

This is not to deny or denigrate the importance of structures or the reality that there are conditions that may confine the range of options available either to the leadership or the population. "Objective" conditions undoubtedly create an atmosphere that may be conducive to insurrection, political victory, or transformation. What is not at all clear is that such conditions in and of themselves have moved any society into or through revolution.[1] Therefore, the focus of this chapter is on the social revolutionary leadership in the post–political victory period, those elements that constitute the leadership, and their implication for the social revolutionary project.

Leadership—particularly political leadership—has received a great deal of attention in oral and written history. Rejai and Phillips pointed out that over the centuries, philosophers and social theorists have proffered differing concepts of political leadership. Some of the better known include Plato's "philosopher kings," Machiavelli's "prince," Carlyle's "great man," Nietzsche's "superman," Freud's "primal father," and Lasswell's "political man."[2] Since World War II, social scientists have built on such notions and looked at questions of and about leadership in a variety of ways.[3] These studies are broadly of two types: speculative analyses focused on archetypes of leaders and their functions[4] and empirical analyses of characteristics, social backgrounds, education, and occupation.[5]

Although political scientists were part of this movement, the increasing attention to analytical models in the 1960s brought on by the so-called behavioral revolution in the social sciences often ignored leaders. Only recently has the importance of leadership in society been "rediscovered" by most political scientists.[6] But they largely continue to neglect such questions as why people opt for revolution in general and noticeably avoid the challenging and enigmatic question of revolutionary leadership specifically.[7]

Social revolutionary leadership has received surprisingly little attention from political scientists; the few studies done have focused almost exclusively on psychological factors.[8] There are a number of problems with such studies, two of which merit mention here. The first is that the organization of revolutionary behavior, that is, the constitution of revolutionary activity, cannot be explained by analyzing personality traits of revolutionaries.[9] The second is that the examination of revolutionary personalities is not helpful in explaining the emergence—where or when—of revolutionary activity. Psychological explanations, unless they can establish a link between individuals' specific experiences as they are socialized into society and as their personality develops and their subsequent political behavior, seem problematic. Many people share the experiences that supposedly shape those who are most often identified as revolutionary leaders. Yet remarkably few people, even by the most generous of definitions, engage in revolutionary or quasi-revolutionary activity, much less become revolutionary leaders. Until this mystery can be solved, it would seem that psychological explanations remain suspect.

Still, psychological studies of revolutionary leaders may offer important insights into the dynamics of revolutionary leadership across the three phases of the social revolutionary process.[10] Perhaps of greatest use have been the efforts to categorize revolutionary leadership. In particular, scholars have discerned different categories of leadership.

Brinton's typology identified the roles of revolutionary leaders according to their skills as idealists, formulators, propagandists, agitators, and organizers.[11] Hopper cataloged leaders for each of the four revolutionary stages he distinguished: the agitator, in the preliminary stage; the prophet and the reformer, in the popular stage; the "statesman," in the formal stage; and the administrator-executive, in the final, institutional stage of the revolutionary process.[12] Hoffer reduced the number of types of leaders in mass movements to three, drawing distinctions among the "men of words," fanatics, and the "practical men of action."[13] Eckstein discerned leaders as ideologues, organizers, experts in violence, demagogues, and administrators.[14] Rejai and Phillips differentiated among founders, agitators, generals, scholars, and professional revolutionaries in the process of political revolution.[15]

I put forward two specific propositions in this chapter. The first is that there are two distinct types of leaders critical to the social revolutionary process, visionary and organizational. Visionary leaders generate the social revolutionary ideology, which combines a critique of the previous regime and society with a compelling vision of the future. Organizational leaders work with the visionary leaders to create the social revolutionary strategy and to implement it.

The second proposition is that these two types of leaders may be associated with the strategies of institutionalization and consolidation. Whereas both types are critical during all three phases of the social revolutionary process, this connection is clearest after political victory when the leaders seek to transform society. As a rule, visionary leaders are most readily identified with the consolidation process: They energize the population, present the social revolutionary ideology, and articulate a vision of the future. Institutionalization is the province of the organizational leaders: They work to create the structures that undergird the social revolutionary process. Excessive dominance by one type of leader or leaders and the resultant preponderance of either institutionalization or consolidation, as the Bolivian and Cuban cases suggest, comes at the expense of the other. A leadership that finds itself locked in a struggle over the appropriate path, as arguably happened in Grenada, is likely to self-destruct. A more balanced leadership, such as that evinced in Nicaragua, appears to allow the revolutionaries to pursue institutionalization and consolidation in a roughly simultaneous and mutually reinforcing fashion. In each case these leaders—visionary and organizational—confront not just the exigencies of the domestic situation but the inescapable complexities of the international situation as well. □

## VISIONARY AND
## ORGANIZATIONAL LEADERSHIP

The proposition that revolutions do not succeed without accomplished and able leadership is, as Greene suggested, self-evident and perhaps tautological.[16] Nonetheless, the point is important. Spontaneous uprisings are by definition unorganized; potentially strong movements can be undermined by leadership problems. Historically, vision and ideology without coherent organization and strategy have not succeeded; organization and strategy without a guiding vision and ideology have degenerated into stultifying bureaucracy.

Vision and the organization to realize that vision are the hallmarks of social revolutionary leadership. Visionary leaders, who articulate the social revolutionary ideology, are verbal and dynamic people with broad, popular, often charismatic appeal.[17] Organizational leaders, who seek to translate the social revolutionary ideology into reality, are often taciturn and methodical people who work behind the scenes.[18] Both types of leader may be quixotic idealists, hesitant to make concessions, or pragmatic realists, willing to maneuver and compromise as they seek to maximize popular support; but idealists tend to be visionary leaders, whereas realists are more likely to be organizational leaders.[19]

Most of the familiar Latin American revolutionary leaders demonstrate characteristics of both visionary and organizational leadership. I contend, nonetheless, that it is worthwhile to categorize them. Ernesto "Ché" Guevara (Cuba), Tomás Borge (Nicaragua), and Maurice Bishop

(Grenada) all had or have formidable organizational skills, but they are most usefully understood as visionary leaders whose greatest skill lay in their ability to articulate the social revolutionary ideology and arouse support for it. Conversely, whereas Juan Lechín, Víctor Paz, and Hernán Siles (Bolivia), Raúl Castro (Cuba), Daniel Ortega (Nicaragua), and Bernard Coard (Grenada) all have or had demonstrated skills as visionary leaders, they are more productively regarded as people whose primary talent lay in organizational leadership.

It is important to note that these categories are not mutually exclusive: Some visionary leaders have been as much organizers as orators or vice versa. In fact, visionary and organizational leadership may be found equally in the same person. V. I. Lenin and Leon Trotsky in Russia, Mao Zedong in China, Ho Chi Minh in Vietnam, and Fidel Castro in Cuba all resist categorization—they filled both roles, often simultaneously.[20] It is almost certainly no coincidence that these five people would likely top any list of "great" revolutionary leaders. Just as a social revolution must have both institutionalization and consolidation to succeed, revolutionary leaders need both vision and organization. When these elements are embodied in one person, the task of balancing the strengths of one leader with those of another is simplified or eliminated.[21]

As has been suggested throughout, the three phases of the social revolutionary process are distinct, yet intimately bound to each other: Social revolution is a process. In the broadest sense the phases are tied together by their part in the larger historical struggle within a specific society and, in the increasingly complex modern world, between societies. At another level the phases are linked in their dependence on each other and on the visions and people that may, but do not necessarily, carry over. Yet each of these periods is at least partly defined by its particular reality and is populated with people suited to the demands of that phase. Some leaders flourish during the insurrection, able to rally people to the process or organize the groundwork for the process; others thrive during the battle for political victory. What is clear is that not all leaders can lead across all three stages of the social revolutionary process.[22]

## Vanguard Parties

The place where the visionary and organizational leaders meet is in the vanguard party. The vanguard is, in theory, a self-selected, self-abnegating, and disciplined revolutionary elite, which seeks to lead a mass-based transformation of society. In practice, however, the vanguard often becomes an institution. The vanguard may be distinguished from other elitist conceptions of leadership by the emphasis on mobilization and transformation of the people rather than their marginalization and disempowerment.[23] Inherent in the vanguard concept, Gilbert pointed out, is immense ideological tension: The vanguard seeks to liberate and empower the people and at the same time to control and transform them.[24]

The concept of the vanguard political party was most explicitly advanced by Lenin, who, drawing on Karl Marx, argued that revolutions were made by a small cadre of professional revolutionaries and that revolutionary "indoctrination" of the population was not possible; people had to be brought to consciousness, guided much as a bricklayer uses a guideline to keep the wall being built straight.[25] In another analogy, Lenin assumed that the revolution would be propelled by popular discontent but that the population could not steer. Thus the vanguard party existed to give bearings to the revolution. To attain this position, however, the party must appeal to the values and interests of the people, albeit carefully. Popular participation that was out of control, undirected, was a risk to the revolutionary project.

Others discerned a more complex relationship, a critical dialectic between the vanguard party and the population. Trotsky, for example, argued that "without a guiding organization the energy of the mass would dissipate like steam not enclosed in a piston-box. But nevertheless what moves things is not the piston or the box, but the steam."[26] Gramsci emphasized that intellectual skills and theoretical knowledge could be acquired and developed by workers, arguing that neither politics nor history could be made without "this sentimental connection," which must be "provided by an organic cohesion in which feeling-passion becomes understanding and thence knowledge."[27]

This is clearly the point from which the FSLN began in Nicaragua. Omar Cabezas, revolutionary hero and former CDC director, explained that the Nicaraguan vanguard never sought to impose structure "top down" on the population. Specifically, according to Cabezas: "We want the people to organize for what they want to do . . . to work for the things they want. We seek to stimulate people to resolve their own problems. We tell the people that they can transform their own reality if they organize."[28] Dora María Téllez, a hero of the revolution and holder of various important posts including minister of health, had insight into the complex relationship between the vanguard and the population: "There are a few men and women who at a given moment in history seem to contain within themselves the dignity of all the people. They are examples to all of us. And then, through the struggle, the people as a whole reclaim the strength and dignity shown by a few."[29] Although the vanguard party leads, it does so as the people's representative.

The concept of the vanguard party coincides neatly with an increased recognition of the role played by people. For Lenin the population had to be appealed to and manipulated by *people*. Trotsky clearly implied that people taking action was the key, and Gramsci argued that politics and history were made by people. Cabezas and Téllez plainly acknowledged that people were central to the social revolutionary process. The people who constitute the vanguard party, then, operate as both a catalyst and a guide for the population. The people should be aroused to organize in pursuit of their interests, and then, with the social revolutionary leadership as models, individuals (it is assumed) will choose "correctly" from the options they created for themselves. Stimulation of the population— via the cultivation of revolutionary values, consciousness-raising, and education—and setting an example to the people are profoundly bound up in and reliant on visionary and organizational leadership.

### Visionary Leadership

Vision here refers to the rare capacity to consider "existing realities as transformed possibilities" and to inspire a collective image of a better future.[30] Prior to political victory, the visionary leadership is engaged in two intimately related projects. First, it draws attention to popular grievances and discontent with the status quo and its maintenance. Second, and more important, the leaders propose a vision of the future in which these grievances and discontent are rectified. Thus the social revolutionaries seek both to undermine the regime in power and to rally the population to the social revolutionary project and elicit from them the commitment and devotion necessary for the struggle.

The outcome of the period of institutionalization and consolidation that follows political victory depends on visionary leadership. The revolutionary society's institutions have been undermined, and people's traditional consciousness about their lives has been challenged. Thus visionary leadership is not simply "functionally useful" but necessary during this period.[31] The transformation of society requires daring, commitment, creativity, adaptability, and vision. The visionary leaders must provide both inspiration and direction to the people mobilized on behalf of the social revolutionary project and attract others to the struggle. As a result they are at the forefront of the consolidation process, exhorting and energizing members of the population to take control of their own lives and determine their destiny.

Critical to the social revolutionary project are the tasks of promoting new values, mobilizing people, and pursuing the reconstruction of the social consensus, often rent during the insurrection and/or the political victory. Visionary leaders, then, articulate, promote, and in some sense sell the social revolutionary project. Therefore, they seek to articulate and justify the desires of the population, kindle dramatic visions of the future to justify the sacrifices of the present, and evoke the fervor of community—the sense of liberation from the alienated and atomistic past.

Visionary leadership is virtually always charismatic in nature. In the social revolutionary context, charismatic leaders call for the rejection of societal convention and the established political order and, in their place, propose new and different forms of societal organization. With respect to societies where institutions are weak to begin with (such as those considered here), Heine suggested that "charismatic leadership can be a precious, vital resource."[32] Charismatic leaders promote, advance, and facilitate the social revolutionary process by their ability to give voice to people's needs and aspirations as part of the vision of the future that the revolutionary leaders propose.[33] Hence charisma can be a critical ingredient for transformative leadership, particularly when the collective leadership is supplemented by a charismatic figure who has heroic qualities and appeals strongly to the people.

What does this mean in practice? According to Max Weber's work on charisma, one function of leadership is to bring society to at least accept and perhaps adopt new moral principles because new conditions or newly organized groups cannot be absorbed under the old morality.[34] In the absence of a cultural doctrine legitimizing and institutionalizing new social activities, charismatic leaders intervene in order to institute new moral principles. Charismatic figures raise the promise, the potential, of rejecting convention and creating possibilities for the people. The period during which authority is transferred from the existing order to the alternative vision espoused by the charismatic or visionary leader is one characterized by revolutionary potential.

It is hard to capture the essence of visionary or charismatic leadership on paper or even on film—it is best witnessed. Such leadership varies dramatically from one individual to another and is often manifest in elusive factors: tone of voice, gestures, a pattern of call and response, a relationship to the population rooted in its knowledge of the particular leader, a shared pain and suffering, a shared joy, and an association of citizens' lives with the life of the particular leader. Although the contribution of these or other factors may be difficult to assess, the impact is undeniably real.

There are two cases of charismatic leadership particularly relevant for our purposes. The first illustrates charismatic leadership primarily by example; the second combines example with speech making. Both brief profiles may offer some insight into the compelling character of charismatic leaders.

Ernesto "Ché" Guevara is a compelling figure in history. An Argentinean physician who suffered from asthma, Guevara was radicalized by his firsthand experiences of the Bolivian revolutionary process and the invasion and overthrow of the democratically elected government of Guatemala in 1954, which was orchestrated by the United States. By 1955 he was in Mexico City, committed to assist Fidel Castro, who was preparing to return to Cuba and pursue the revolution. Once in Cuba, Guevara quickly rose to the position of Castro's chief lieutenant: He became an important military and political leader and the revolution's primary ideologue.

A measure of Guevara's stature can be seen in Castro's astute pairing of him with another chief lieutenant and outstanding organizational leader, Camilo Cienfuegos, in perhaps the most important military and psychological campaign of the revolution. Guevara and Cienfuegos were sent to replicate the famous "incendiary" march of the Cuban War of Independence when national heroes Antonio Maceo and General Máximo Gómez lit up the sugarcane fields.[35] This replication was hugely successful, evoking the link with Cuba's independence war and capturing the popular imagination. Moreover, the ability of Guevara and Cienfuegos to rally the population to the revolutionary cause and their military skill have become important elements in Cuban revolutionary mythology as well as in the enshrinement of both Guevara and Cienfuegos as national heroes.[36]

What the population found so appealing in this instance and many others was the message Guevara brought, the ideology he proclaimed or—more accurately—practiced. "A neat swing of the machete," according to Guevara, "cutting the stalks like a pro, will do more than a long speech."[37] Guevara believed strongly that people were conscious actors who could create their own reality. The ideology he articulated, as a result, was focused on the emergence of a "new person" who valued moral rather than material incentives as the standard of success. This revolutionary individual would transcend personal ambition and work for the greater good of all. Guevara's vision inspired a social doctrine that redefined relations between people and the state. Personal worth would be measured in terms of devotion to the revolutionary struggle rather than by the accumulation of money and power.

It is important to recognize that Guevarism emerged as a coherent ideology largely in retrospect. Guevara essentially mixed idealism and pragmatism with a heavy dose of voluntarism and action. The revolution "must have a great deal of humanity and a strong sense of justice and truth in order not to fall into extreme dogmatism and cold scholasticism, into an isolation from the masses. We must strive every day so that this love of living humanity will be transformed into actual deeds, into acts that serve as examples, as a moving force."[38] The "true revolutionary is guided by a great feeling of love";[39] his or her most "beautiful quality" is the capability "of feeling any injustice committed against anyone, anywhere in the world."[40]

People were made to feel that they could change themselves and their world and that all they had to do was do it; theory would follow. Talk was less important then action—Guevara reportedly liked to quote the maxim of Cuban hero José Martí: "The best way to speak is to act." Castro, who, as Hodges pointed out, shared "the same fundamental premises," summarized this perspective as "the duty of every revolutionary is to make the revolution" and "many times practice comes first and then the theory."[41] For Guevara the emphasis was on revolutionary attitudes and new sensibilities that would develop along the way, as the social revolutionary process unfolded. People would learn by doing in Guevara's view: "We walk by walking."[42]

The charisma of "Ché" ("his bohemian getup," one Cuban revolutionary wrote, "and his air of a revolutionary prophet"[43]) transcended the Cuban revolution. The ideology Guevara articulated continues to be a significant force among a wide assortment of revolutionaries throughout the world. Radicals from Africa, Asia, Europe, Latin America, the Middle East, North America, and Oceania have enshrined Guevara's commitment to action and declaration of revolutionary love as the core of their social revolutionary ideology. The "myth of Ché" looms large and has unquestionably played a profound role in the development of the Nicaraguan social revolutionary ideology. Guevara's vision has been at least equal to that of Sandino and more important than that of Marx or Lenin in the formation of Nicaragua's social revolutionary ideology.[44]

In fact, it is interesting to note that the FSLN has a pantheon of deceased charismatic figures: Sandino, Guevara, and the party's original visionary leader, Carlos Fonseca. The FSLN's propensity for enlisting the images of dead men is almost certainly no accident. Live charismatic figures can be divisive, often developing cults of personality and perhaps pursuing their own agendas, which may differ from that advocated by the collective leadership.[45] The FSLN chose to pursue "an organizational ideology that rejects the personalistic leadership of the *caudillo*."[46] Accordingly, it established a model of collective leadership within the vanguard that proved practical and popular across all three phases of the social revolutionary process.[47]

The apparent lack of a charismatic figure within the FSLN vanguard does not mean that there were no leaders with charisma, no one to fill the visionary role. Tomás Borge, the only surviving founder of the FSLN, emerged as just such a figure in the post–political victory period. Borge is not in the pantheon with Sandino, Guevara, and his former colleague Fonseca, nor is he likely to be. For some Nicaraguans he is the epitome of the revolution's extremes. Nonetheless, for many others he represents a link with those charismatic figures; his own charisma is evident. Although Borge is small in stature, his voice is powerful and poetic; his rousing speeches, as Gilbert pointed out, frequently told of a future free from greed, need, oppression, and exploitation, relying on "simple, unpretentious language" and frequent invocations of the Bible.[48]

A particularly powerful example of Borge's masterful style can be found in his stirring 1982 May Day speech in Managua's Carlos Fonseca Plaza of the Revolution. Borge told the crowd:

> Here, near the tomb of Carlos Fonseca, we should like to speak a little with our brother and tell him . . . the anger, the tenderness, the burning coals, the hopes belong to you . . . your dreams have come true! Here is your working class, our working class with its calloused hands and its shining eyes . . . standing at attention, which will be faithful to you until victory, until blood, until death. . . . We are the gatherers of your resurrection. We are not frightened by phantoms . . . by mummies . . . by imperialism, nor are we afraid of Cains. . . . Once we said to you . . . "Free homeland or death!" But today we say to you, we are moving toward a new society, we are moving toward development and consolidation of a revolutionary party, the Sandinista National Liberation Front, as the party of the workers and peasants, of the intellectuals and the Nicaraguan patriots, we are moving toward the total elimination of the exploitation of man by man, and we say to you, regarding the belief and thoughts of our people: Free homeland or death![49]

The hallmarks of Borge's rhetorical style, his invocation of patriotism, his involvement of the population, his evocative religious imagery, and the promise of a better future are all in evidence.

Borge's speeches are made more compelling by the story of his life, which the people know well. He spent years in struggle and isolation in the jungle, experienced brutal attacks on his family, and endured cruel torture at the hands of the Somoza regime.[50] Borge can speak of pain and suffering, grief and deprivation, from firsthand experience. Although few Nicaraguans can match his harsh experiences, Borge is well aware that almost all have known hunger and hardship, denial and distress.[51] Whatever they may think of him, and Borge is certainly not the most popular of the revolutionary leaders, Nicaraguans are aware that he knows of what he speaks. Furthermore, Borge's broadly populist style served to identify him as "the FSLN's most charismatic leader."[52] And this, Gilbert suggested, was the primary reason that Borge, the FSLN's "most compelling leader," was passed over when the party selected its 1984 presidential candidate.[53] Although he commands a devout following among a significant segment of the population, Borge has not been the revolution's central figure.

The commitment to collective leadership among Nicaragua's revolutionary leadership was undeniably profound, a commitment dramatically reinforced by what they came to see as the "lesson of Grenada": If the leadership splits, the United States sends in the Marines.[54] Borge's charisma stands in marked contrast to the resolutely uncharismatic Daniel Ortega, masterful pragmatist and coalition builder, who has been one of the revolution's preeminent organizational leaders. And from the nine-member National Directorate, which included Borge, it was clearly Daniel Ortega who emerged as first among equals.[55]

This is an important reminder that charisma alone is not sufficient to account for the transformation process. An overemphasis on the potency and ability of visionary leadership results in the "great person of history" fallacy. Charismatic figures cannot by themselves move a society into revolution and on occasion may in fact find themselves rushing frantically (as in 1917, when the Bolshevik leadership was caught unprepared by the spontaneous uprising) not to be left behind by events.[56] What is critical is the social revolutionary ideology that is articulated: It is the visionary leaders' primary tool in the pursuit of consolidation.

## Social Revolutionary Ideology

In our context, ideology is "a value or belief system accepted as fact or truth by some group."[57] Ideologies are intimately related to people's material conditions: They neither exist in a vacuum nor appear out of thin air. Rather, an ideology is composed of sets of attitudes toward the institutions and processes of society, providing the believer with a picture of the world both as it is and as it should be. An ideology thus organizes the tremendous complexity of the world into something fairly simple and understandable, something that guides behavior.

A social revolutionary ideology is a strong critique of the previous regime and society; it provides a framework for both the articulation of social ills and obstacles and the creation of the new society. As a result, it rationalizes, legitimizes, and justifies the demands that the social revolutionary leadership places on the people and supplies dignity to their actions. Ideally, the leadership articulates a vision of the new society and thereby promotes a sense of unity, solidarity, cohesion, commitment, devotion, and sacrifice among the people; the ideology is vital to the all-important task of mobilization.

The French revolution remains a touchstone of sorts for this ability to articulate a vision, with the focus on liberty, equality, and humanity. In modern Latin America—and elsewhere—these values are often attendant to some sort of grand myth (such as the international revolution, the workers' paradise, a classless society), which becomes a rallying cry for the population. The social revolutionary ideology, building on the mobilization that occurred in the earlier phases, reorients the population and taps its energies for the realization of social revolutionary objectives.[58] After political victory in Bolivia there was no clear social revolutionary ideology; rather, there were competing ideologies of varying stripes, few of which would qualify as social revolutionary. In Cuba the focus was on the creation of "the new person" and what came to be referred to as Guevarism. Grenada seems to have lacked any coherent social revolutionary ideology and, like Bolivia, was beset by competing perspectives, specifically Bishop's broad-based, if vague, socialist populism and Coard's Stalinist vanguardism. Nicaragua has had probably the most compelling, if not necessarily the most coherent, social revolutionary ideology: Sandinismo.

Sandinismo is not the thought of its namesake, though elements of Augusto César Sandino's views are incorporated into it. Sandino, an immensely popular nationalist and populist guerrilla leader in the 1920s and 1930s, successfully fought to oust the U.S. Marines, who had been occupying Nicaragua almost continuously since 1912.[59] The United States left behind in Nicaragua Anastasio Somoza García, "El Yanqui," as the head of the National Guard, paving the way for a forty-five-year dynastic dictatorship.[60] Shortly after the Marines withdrew, Somoza ordered the assassination of Sandino and the massacre of approximately 300 of his followers.

There is a very real sense in which the ensuing history of Nicaragua may be understood as a continuing tension between the rule of the Somoza family, or Somocismo, and Sandinismo, at least to the degree that Sandinismo came to represent the alternative. The Somoza family symbolized the continuation of U.S. domination and attention to the needs of the country's elite at the expense of the majority of the population. Sandino in martyrdom served as an enduring catalyst of what became a lengthy struggle and a reminder of the aspirations of much of the population.

Although Sandino's personal ideology was undoubtedly complex, the ideology that he articulated to the population and thereby passed on to history was marked by impassioned nationalism, resistance to foreigners, and hostility for imperialism and the abusive aspects of capitalism; it offered a populist perspective on collective welfare.[61] This simplified rendition of Sandino's thought was articulated by one of the FSLN's founders, Carlos Fonseca, who emphasized Sandino's revolutionary behavior and anti-imperialism. Although Fonseca interpreted Sandino through Marxism, he felt that Sandino helped him interpret Marxism for the specifics of Nicaraguan reality.[62] As a result, Sandinismo, according to former vice president Sergio Ramírez, represented "the expression of our deepest identity. It is the defense of the nation, of its political, social, and cultural values."[63]

Perhaps the most succinct and most often quoted depiction of Sandinismo was provided by Thomas Walker, one of the premier scholars of Nicaragua: Sandinismo is "a blend of nationalism, pragmatic Marxism, and Catholic Humanism."[64] As such, Sandinismo clearly exists as a meeting place for many different perspectives, including some that are frequently considered contradictory. Drawing on such diverse traditions in constructing their unique ideology has required pragmatism and resulted in a lack of dogmatism on the part of the Sandinistas.[65]

The FSLN's espousing an ideology as eclectic as Sandinismo has a number of implications, not least of which is a commitment to political pluralism, a commitment that, in this case, derived from three sources.[66] The first was the nature of the ideology itself, drawn from a broad, and not historically intuitive, spectrum. The second was the conditions confronted by the revolutionaries after the political victory. The new government inherited a country whose capital city had not been rebuilt after a devastating 1972 earthquake, a country that was plagued by underdevelopment and poverty and that had seen destruction of some parts during the civil war. Under the circumstances, the FSLN needed to maintain its broad-based, multiclass coalition to undertake the crucial program of national reconstruction.[67]

The third source of the commitment to political pluralism was the internal pluralism of the FSLN itself. The FSLN has a long pluralist history; its early activists reflected various radical perspectives.[68] By 1974 the FSLN was actively recruiting all across the country's political spectrum, including the Democratic Conservative party (PCD), the Liberal Independent party (PLI), the Chamber of Commerce, the Nicaraguan Institute of Development, the Nicaraguan Democratic Movement (MDN), and the university faculty.[69] This flexibility and tolerance received its greatest test in the 1970s when the FSLN was reemerging in the national consciousness and gaining in popularity: At that point the party split into factions over disagreements about Marxist theory and the strategy for victory.

The Prolonged Popular War tendency (GPP) hewed most closely to the FSLN's earlier strategy of emphasizing a slow, patient, cautious "accumulation of forces" and campesino support in the rural areas, with logistical backing from urban areas.[70] A more "traditional" Marxist line was advocated by the Proletarian tendency, which argued that Nicaragua had evolved and that the workers rather than the campesinos were the hope for revolution.[71] In the aftermath of the GPP-Proletarian split, a third faction emerged: the Insurrectional tendency (popularly known as Terceristas, or the Third Force), distinguished from the other tendencies by its pragmatism.[72] The Terceristas advocated a policy of creating a broad, multiclass alliance and staging bold military action to overthrow Somoza, and its members were willing to make the compromises necessary to do so.[73] With the Proletarian leaders marginalized and the GPP leadership largely out of action, the Tercerista faction took control of the FSLN and began to implement its ultimately successful strategy.[74]

In 1978 the three factions reunited and agreed to a system of collective leadership. To attain this, the integrity of each tendency was respected and a nine-person National Directorate was established. The latter consisted of three members of each group: Borge, Henry Ruíz, and Bayardo Arce from the GPP; Jaime Wheelock, Carlos Núñez, and Luis Carrión represented the Proletarian tendency; and Daniel and Humberto Ortega and Victor Tirado were the Tercerista emissaries. In the directorate, each faction brought its social revolutionary ideology and its social revolutionary strategy together under the rubric of Sandinismo.[75]

Beyond pluralism, Sandinismo also advocated participatory democracy and foreign policy nonalignment, both rooted in national self-determination, national and international dignity, and a more just, or humane, social order—all of which were realized. Another ramification of this ideology is a mixed economy, composed of a private sector—individual and cooperative ownership—and a state sector; this has also been established.[76] The FSLN's flexible perspective on capitalism drew more from Sandino than from Marx. Sandino, although he regarded "Wall St. bankers" as implacable foes,[77] had no fundamental objection to capitalism. He wrote, "Capital can play its part and grow; but the workers should not be humiliated or exploited."[78] Undoubtedly the conditions that argued for political pluralism also encouraged pursuit of a mixed economy.[79]

Specifically, the FSLN characterized the revolution as "a popular, democratic and anti-imperialist revolutionary struggle that is based on a political project of national unity and an economic project of a mixed economy."[80] Taken together, these elements add up to a vision of a dramatically new society unlike any other in Central America or Nicaragua. Whereas the leaders' choices unquestionably were made with an eye to the international audience, the envisioned new society faithfully reflected the ideology. Clearly, such a new society would require the population to change many if not all of its basic conceptions about society and its operation. Thus, the final implication of the ideology of Sandinismo was the creation of a new person: a new Nicaraguan.

The popular sentiment in Nicaragua, according to one Nicaraguan lawyer and leader of opposition to the FSLN, is that Sandinismo represents a "correction" to Somocismo.[81] Specifically, former vice president Ramírez argued that Sandinismo in practice represents for most Nicaraguans a way of acting, a political and cultural behavior . . . more than anything it is a conviction, an idea, an attitude to life. We have taken responsibility for the fact that we were born here, that we live here, that we must defend what we have, the unity and independence of our territory. . . . This is beyond any ideological tendency. It is what mobilizes people, whether they have Marxist ideas or not. It is a powerful force for unity. Respect for the country, for its integrity and independence.[82]

Sandinismo, then, is a mechanism through which the population has been able to redress the political, social, and economic inequities and injustices that made up Nicaraguan history. This ideology made possible the retention of a vanguard party and a commitment to profound socioeconomic transformation even as political opposition was being institutionalized, the private sector was largely being preserved, and traditional civil liberties established.

Most social revolutionary leaders bring with them a new political and cultural system with an elaborate ideology entailing a new institutional order. Of the cases considered here, only the Bolivian leadership appears not to have brought such an ideology with it. It is a serious mistake, however, to suggest that where a social revolutionary ideology is present, it is necessarily imposed upon the population. Individuals have their own sets of feelings, ideas, and expectations, some of which are distinctly antisystemic and even perhaps revolutionary, but which do not necessarily correspond to the vision of the vanguard. Popular attitudes have played roles in both limiting and extending various decisions made by the leadership in all the cases considered here.

Rudé argued that these attitudes represent a "popular" ideology, which "is not a purely internal affair and the sole property of a single class or group."[83] Rather, it is a mix of two distinct parts. *Inherent* ideology is "a sort of 'mother's milk' ideology based on direct experience, oral tradition or folk-memory and not learned by listening to sermons or reading books." *Derived* ideology is "borrowed from others, often taking the form of a more structured system . . . such as the Rights of Man, Popular Sovereignty, *Laissez-faire* and the Sacred Right of Property, Nationalism, Socialism, or the various versions of justification by Faith." There is not, Rudé continued, a "Wall of Babylon" between these two types of ideology, and in fact there may be a great deal of overlap.[84]

As a result, social revolutionaries *seek* to transfer or transmit their ideology via the agents of political socialization. The resulting ideology will differ from that held by the social revolutionaries, which may have been cobbled together from among various factions, as in Bolivia and Nicaragua, because the social revolutionaries' ideology inevitably either blends or clashes with elements of the preexisting culture to produce a new ideology. This is where the vanguard party (composed of both the visionary and organizational leadership of the social revolution) must mediate the relationship between the population and the revolutionaries.

## The Link Between Ideology and Action: Organizational Leadership

Visionary leaders engage and mobilize the population; organizational leaders draw on the talents and vigor of the population in an attempt to make concrete the promise of the social revolutionary ideology. During the first two stages of the social revolutionary process, the organizational leadership must arrange for food, arms, and other necessities, coordinate military actions, maintain communication, and provide internal discipline and justice. As a result, at the point of political victory (the transfer of sovereignty from the old regime to the revolutionaries) organizers are usually the leaders responsible for the all-important process of institutionalization.

During the final, defining phase of the social revolutionary process, organization is the link between ideology and action. The social revolutionary leadership must have the capacity not only to devise, spread, and inculcate its vision of radical change but also to create and maintain the necessary institutional apparatus for the realization of that change. Organizational leadership, therefore, focuses on the reestablishment and reorganization of the state structures. In the drive to legitimate the social revolution's status and increase popular allegiance, the leaders pay particular attention to making such institutions more accessible to the population. These factors—reestablishment and reorganization of the state structures to make them functional and accessible to the majority of the population—define the process of institutionalization.

Organization represents the "road to political power," Huntington argued, and those who organize politics control the future.[85] It is the organizational leadership that provides the political infrastructure for the new society. It is no coincidence that just five months after the political victory in Nicaragua, a front-page editorial in the FSLN newspaper *Barricada* by directorate member Carlos Núñez was headlined, "La consigna es: organización, organización, y más organización" (The [guiding principle] is organization, organization, and more organization).[86]

All revolutionaries suppose themselves engaged in creating a better future: That is the fundamental premise of social revolution.[87] In seeking to institutionalize the social revolution, the organizational leadership confronts three critical issues. The first is that the revolutionaries must take into consideration the sensibilities of the people or risk alienating and turning them away from the social revolutionary process. In other words, the new organizational norms and practices that the revolutionaries propose must be at least broadly consistent with those prevalent in society at large. The second issue is accessibility: Organizational leaders must overcome the popular conviction that the state is no friend of the general population. In other words, the institutions must be (re)conceived in ways that convince citizens that they can trust the government and have something to gain by interacting with it. Related to this is the third issue: commitment. In any social revolution a significant part of the population is committed to the revolution: These people will remain with the process in the face of the worst conditions. The reasons for this vary, but people often act this way because of the conditions under which they had been living or the life they envision in the future. There is a larger segment of the population, however, that simply conforms to the process: Those people may defect under stress. The revolutionary leaders must attempt to reach them; in fact, their loss is likely to signal the failure of the social revolutionary process.

The revolutionary leadership confronts these three problems together. In practice, however, the first two fall to the organizational leaders; only the element of commitment is really shared equally. Thus organizational leaders may be most usefully thought of as either "practical men of action"[88] or "administrator-executives"[89] who create the new arrangements that enable the realization of social revolutionary goals. The problem is that there may be a significant gap between the skills needed to acquire government power and those necessary to exercise it.

In Bolivia the MNR began as a highly organized political party and retained its organizing abilities throughout much of its existence. MNR leaders Juan Lechín, Víctor Paz, and Hernán Siles are all best understood as organizational leaders.[90] Lechín was perhaps the closest to a charismatic figure, a labor movement leader and organizer uncomfortable with theory but adept at negotiations. Paz was a professor; he held various posts in the finance ministry, including a brief stint as minister of economics, and was a longtime deputy in the parliament; he was regarded as very articulate, and his skills as a power broker were legendary. Siles was a founder of the MNR and son of a former Bolivian president; he served in parliament several times and was considered the driving force of the internal sector of the party, where he proved his competence at adroit political maneuvering. The MNR, with such outstanding organizational leadership and a reliance on its legacy as a political party and as victor of the 1951 election, moved quickly and confidently to institutionalize the revolution (see Chapter 2). Although proving proficient at the establishment of institutions consistent with societal norms and the creation of a sense of accessibility, the MNR had far less success generating commitment rather than conformity from the population. The revolutionaries failed to dramatically change Bolivian society or the daily life of much of the population.[91]

Raúl Castro, an avid proponent of administration and efficiency, was almost certainly the greatest organizational leader in the Cuban revolution. Raúl made up for his brother's aversion to institutionalization (see Chapter 2) with minute attention to detail. Raúl first demonstrated his organizational prowess as the revolutionaries expanded in their Sierra Maestra stronghold. His style was particularly evident, however, when he was sent in 1958 by his brother to open a "second front." After securing the area militarily, Raúl moved quickly to set up a structure for the region. Whereas Fidel and Guevara referred to organization in their exhortations, Raúl introduced literacy programs, health programs, education programs, union organization, civic administration, peasant militia, and agrarian reform in the area under his control.[92] These institutions were consistent with societal norms, accessible, and created a high degree of commitment from the population. After political victory, Raúl and his people proved adept at creating a "hidden" infrastructure that aided in the consolidation process.

As suggested in Chapter 2, Grenada's Bernard Coard proved to be one of the revolution's premier organizers. Although Coard was a relative latecomer to the NJM, his status as an effective organizer was evident, in part, when he was appointed head of the party's "organizing committee" a year before the political victory. Heine described Coard's "unquestioned ability as an organizer" and referred to him as "a first rate organizer."[93] Although Bishop may have brought Grenada to the attention of the world's "political donors," as Heine pointed out, "Coard's thorough follow-up work ensured that feasible project proposals were prepared and submitted, thus leading to the Eastern Caribbean's most ambitious development projects of the early eighties."[94] Coard's inclination and fondness for planning paid dividends with the Grenadian economy, widely hailed as one of the success stories of the brief PRG tenure in office. Ultimately, however, as discussed in Chapter 2, Coard's obsession with organization played a critical role in the self-destruction of the Grenadian revolution. His conviction that only an improved organization under the guidance of an efficient manager—such as himself—could save Grenada's revolutionary process fueled the other problems confronting the increasingly divided revolutionary leadership.

Perhaps the most highly successful organizational leadership has been demonstrated in Nicaragua, particularly by Daniel Ortega. As was noted earlier, the FSLN had decided to follow an organizational ideology rather than one reliant on visionary or charismatic leadership. Ortega positioned himself as a calm, cool bureaucrat amidst more colorful personalities, even allowing his younger brother, Humberto, to do much of the writing and talking for the Terceristas.[95] Thus Daniel Ortega was able to emerge as the "leader of the pragmatists."[96] The collective leadership model proved realistic and popular, particularly in the final phases of the social revolutionary process, when there was widespread recognition among the leaders that the pragmatists were the glue holding the group together. In the period after political victory, Daniel Ortega was the one official member of the FSLN selected to serve in the initial Government of National Reconstruction. He focused specifically on the administrative/executive branch and the armed forces. Basically copying Raúl Castro's program from Cuba, with allowances made for Nicaraguan sensibilities, Ortega oversaw the quick establishment of institutions that were consistent with societal norms, open and accessible to the population, and, most important, engendered commitment to the social revolutionary process on the part of the population.

In all four cases, the organizational leadership took its cues from the social revolutionary ideology. Having achieved political victory, the vanguard party must implement the promises made and visions extolled. This is where the organizational leaders turn ideology into action; their plan to do so is the social revolutionary strategy.

### Mobilizing the Population: Social Revolutionary Strategy

Every social revolution has a revolutionary strategy that emerges from the social revolutionary ideology. For the purposes of this book, I define revolutionary strategy as the social revolutionaries' plans in the post–political victory period for the operationalization, implementation, direction, and coordination of the constructive transformation of society. Thus the revolutionary strategy is, in fact, composed of a variety of strategies for dealing with the issues that arise and are bound together by ideology.

The social revolutionary strategy evolves from the idealistic visions of the transformation process that the revolutionaries had before attaining power. Prior to political victory, revolutionaries often espouse broadly popular programs, which may be neither coherent nor realistic. Furthermore, the conditions may either facilitate or constrain the revolutionary strategy they seek to develop.[97] Even when they are able to "test" their strategy in "liberated" areas, revolutionary leaders are often forced to adopt more pragmatic strategies after they win political power. Moreover, revolutionary leadership, particularly of the vanguard type, may evolve during the often lengthy social revolutionary process.

There are certain broad variables that are present after political victory. They may be grouped as the economic, political, and social structures that confront the revolutionaries and the skill, commitment, and creativity the leaders demonstrate in fashioning the tools and undertaking activities to realize their objectives.[98] It is not just the contemporaneous value of these variables that must be considered. Past legacies have profound repercussions on contemporary processes.

The organizational leadership creates all the actions, policies, instruments, and apparatuses necessary for the constructive transformation of society. This entails the deployment of people, material, ideas, symbols, and force in the pursuit of the social revolutionary objectives. Specifically, the revolutionary strategy has as its principal component the mobilization and socialization of the population. The reasons for this are perhaps most clearly seen in the case of Nicaragua.

Let us review the history of the FSLN.[99] The party was founded as a vanguardist revolutionary organization in 1961, and during most of the ensuing eighteen years it was a small underground movement struggling to bring about a social revolution—at one point membership fell into the dozens. FSLN members survived torture, jail, the death of important leaders, and infighting that split the organization into factions. It led the population in July 1979 to overthrow one of Latin America's most firmly entrenched dynastic dictatorships. All these factors—the laborious struggle, the intraparty turmoil, and the eventual success—are important to understanding the FSLN's social revolutionary strategy.

The character of the FSLN leadership was forged during the long and arduous struggle against Somoza. The early years of the revolutionary process, during the insurrection, saw the emergence of a distinctly Christian martyr—like ethos of self-sacrifice, discipline, modesty, and collective spirit.[100] Sergio Ramírez, Nicaragua's former vice president, likened membership in the FSLN to a "monastic order [in which members] take a vow of silence, suffer great privations, make sacrifices, and take a Christian-like vow to the death—as we say, *patria o muerte.*"[101] It is perhaps then not surprising that like the Church, the FSLN would evolve a top-down, hierarchical, system of internal government: Issues were debated, the leadership chose a position, and everyone was expected to implement and defend it without question. That approach was well suited for the struggle against the Somoza regime, a struggle where "you don't carry on a debate in the middle of a battle."[102]

Although the FSLN developed the democratic centralization and vertical lines of command characteristic of a vanguard party, it did not fit neatly with conventional notions of such a party. Because of the peculiar nature of the Nicaraguan revolution, particularly the historically unusual role of the bourgeoisie, the FSLN represented the broad popular majority rather than any single class. As the behavior of the Somoza regime became more and more excessive, a variety of opposition groups turned to the FSLN as the only organization capable of ousting Somoza.[103] The result was that the Nicaraguan revolution developed a multiclass nature. It is significant that the FSLN, rather than propagating a stereotypical "dictatorship of the proletariat," sought to combine vanguardism and pluralism.[104]

The FSLN emerged from the political victory as Nicaragua's dominant political force, a status underscored by the adulation that the majority of the population accorded to *los muchachos* (the boys). To the Nicaraguans, the victorious FSLN "in their ragged uniforms . . . appeared scrawny, heroic, unbelievably young. They embodied the best of everything that three and a half million people who were used to seeing their nation treated as a fourth-rate banana republic might dream of."[105]

By virtue of its stature, the FSLN was sufficiently strong—and popular—to set itself up as the government; however, the FSLN resisted the temptation to do so.[106] Instead, one of the FSLN's priorities was the establishment of state institutions that were distinct from the party. This served a dual purpose: aiding the creation of strong institutions (perhaps the leaders had Cuba in mind) and freeing the FSLN from specific responsibility for "simply" the government. In fact, it quickly became clear that the FSLN had almost as many permutations as there were possibilities. As the vanguard of the revolution and in response to the almost total collapse of Nicaragua's civil society, the FSLN saw its primary task as providing guidance in all situations. The result was such deep involvement in such a wide variety of groups that at times it became difficult to discern where the FSLN left off and certain organizations began.

The initial FSLN strategy called for pragmatism in the pursuit of socialist-style redistributive projects and democratic pluralism. At the same time, the contra war and U.S. economic embargo absorbed the energies of the FSLN and distorted the debates over social revolutionary strategy. In particular, debate focused on the FSLN's role in the creation of the new Nicaraguan society. The leadership continued to reflect the tripartite split that had emerged during the mid-1970s, a division codified in the careful distribution of the various government ministries; according to Gilbert, however, two factions evolved: the ideologues and the pragmatists.[107]

The differences centered on a variety of issues such as the role of the private sector, support for revolutionaries in neighboring countries, and relations with the United States and the Soviet Union.[108] The ideologues in the leadership, Borge, Arce, and Ruíz (the three representatives of the Prolonged Popular War tendency), pushed a more radical vision of the revolution.[109] Since pragmatism was the hallmark of the Terceristas, it is no surprise that the pragmatists included their three representatives—the Ortega brothers and Tirado.[110] But Wheelock, leader of the more radical Proletarian tendency, was an important ally in pushing the pragmatist's agenda, and the other two Proletarian tendency representatives, Carrión and Núñez, supported this position as well.[111]

The two groups respected each other and worked closely together, but each pursued its vision of the new Nicaragua. The resultant strategy was appropriately vague and highlighted by a program of political pluralism, a mixed economy, and a nonaligned foreign policy, mixed with the mobilization and socialization of the population.

The social revolutionary strategy had as its principal component a commitment to the participation of the Nicaraguan people. Participation refers to people's willingness to involve themselves in the process of the revolution. The support of the population and the ability to mobilize them in large numbers are central to sustaining the social revolution, as it inevitably encounters obstacles and opposition both internally and externally. In Nicaragua there was a particular commitment to and attention paid to the popular organizations. The conviction was that such groups would empower and link the population to the social revolutionary process.

Participation may be engendered in a variety of ways, but it is not easily accomplished. As we shall see in Chapter 4, leaders are not able to dictate the process without regard to the population; the ability to elicit support and maintain progress cannot be directed from above. It was the failure to remember and appreciate this point, according to Omar Cabezas, the charismatic hero whom the FSLN charged with resurrecting, reorganizing, and directing the ailing Sandinista Defense Committees (CDSs), that was instrumental in their downfall: "In the past errors were committed in telling people how to organize and what to organize for. They are adults, not children, they know what they want and what they need."[112] If Cabezas's proposition is accepted, it is important to look at how and where people choose to expend their energies beyond their daily struggle for subsistence.

The lengthy and exacting revolutionary struggle, the party splits, the political victory, and subsequent differences within the leadership all shaped the social revolutionary strategy that the FSLN pursued. The struggle fostered hierarchical and centralist tendencies that were to some extent mitigated by a growing recognition of the importance of pluralism.[113] This recognition was thrown into high relief by the FSLN's victory in July 1979. The transformation of society was no longer a theoretical discussion—opportunity lay before the leaders. By building on the very real threats to Nicaragua's sovereignty and invoking themes of struggle, sacrifice, and patriotism, the government was able to move along the consolidation process and convince a significant majority of the population that they had a profound stake in the social revolutionary process.  □

## ANTIPATHY FOR THE REVOLUTION:
## THE INTERNATIONAL SITUATION

As we have seen, the social revolutionary leadership must bargain, compromise, and negotiate in an effort to institutionalize and consolidate the revolution. Those tasks are complicated by the leaders' need to address both domestic conditions and the international situation. Within the country they must move quickly to instantiate the social revolutionary ideology and to devise an effective program for the promotion of the social revolutionary project. Such efforts are equally critical internationally: The leaders must seek, at the very least, to neutralize potentially and historically intrusive international forces or, if possible, to get them to support the revolution.

Because social revolutions influence and are in turn influenced by the international system and the actors in it, manipulation of the international situation is an important component of revolutionary strategy across all three phases. There are certain dynamics inherent in social revolutions that conspire to "internationalize" it.[114] Virtually all the power contenders during the revolutionary situation vie for international support. The weaker insurgents seek such support to neutralize the power wielded by the government and, if necessary, compete with other factions. The government, for this reason, opposes such assistance and often seeks international support for its position. As a result, revolutions are often internationalized well before the achievement of political victory.

This has particularly been the case in Latin America, where standard U.S. operating procedure has been to intervene against any perceived revolutions, often prior to political victory. The Nicaraguan revolution is the prime example of early internationalization. Besides the extensive U.S. connections with the Somoza regime, other countries, primarily Latin American, were heavily involved on both sides. During the insurrection, the Somoza regime received support from Argentina, El Salvador, Guatemala, Israel, and South Africa. The FSLN received support from Costa Rica, Cuba, Mexico, and Venezuela. Unofficial aid to both sides came from other countries and organizations.

After political victory, social revolutionaries may be confronted by another dynamic if an attitude toward revolution different from that of the social revolutionaries prevails in the international system. Further, specific actors may act regardless of the dominant "climate of opinion" in the system.[115] Those who are friendly to the nascent social revolutionary government may provide economic or military assistance, facilitate the flow of supplies and funds, and boost morale and hopes. Those who oppose the new government are likely to seek to isolate the social revolution and support its foes, perhaps to the point of participating in destabilizing activities or the overthrow of the new government.

The fate of the social revolution, then, depends in part on attitudes in the international system and agendas of other actors in the system at the time it occurs. As a result it is incumbent upon the revolutionary leadership to accurately gauge these variables and to manipulate them with the maximum possible efficiency. Such manipulations are not easy, but every effort must be made to capture international support and, if possible, money and material. The key issue is to ensure the survival of the social revolution without jeopardizing its independence. This may be accomplished in a variety of ways, including adopting a pragmatic approach or one designed to appeal to other key state or nonstate actors in the international system.

In fact, the threat or reality of international opposition, particularly invasions, can either galvanize the population (thereby strengthening the revolution) or fatally cripple it. Migdal argued that external threats to the survival of the leadership or the sovereignty of the state require the leaders to move boldly and quickly toward institutionalization and consolidation.[116] Success will be affected by the degree to which the international system allows the leaders to avoid or cope with the problems that confront them.[117]

Manipulation of international support lays the groundwork for the project of consolidation, which is the heart of the constructive transformation program. Active international opposition creates an atmosphere in which it is difficult to implement any social transformation. This can be seen clearly in the final phase of the social revolutionary process in Russia, which was invaded by Allied troops from 1917 to 1921. Certainly this has also been a major factor in Nicaragua, which was besieged by U.S.-sponsored forces from 1981 to 1990.[118] The social revolutionaries, as a result, must move rapidly to consolidate their international support.

Although the international situation may affect the social revolutionary ideology, its greatest ramifications are for the social revolutionary strategy. Visionary leaders, after all, not only critique the former government but also articulate a vision of the future, ideally taking into account the realities of the international situation. This almost certainly contributed, for example, to the ascendancy of the more pragmatic ideology put forth by the Terceristas in Nicaragua.

It is, however, entirely possible for visionary leaders to ignore the demands of the international situation and advocate social revolutionary ideologies that not only fly in the face of international convention—which is not unusual for a social revolutionary ideology—but are considered abhorrent by most people. The radical egalitarian visions of Pol Pot and the Khmer Rouge (Cambodia) and Abimael Guzmán's Peruvian Communist party (the Shining Path), for example, have engendered very little international support.

Organizational leaders, however, are charged with realizing the social revolutionary ideology. As a result, the exigencies of the international situation represent a critical dimension for them. The organizational leaders must seek to counter those in the international system most opposed to the revolution and appeal to those most inclined to support them.

The Nicaraguans, for example, developed an international strategy that combined a variety of approaches (see Chapter 4 for a more extensive discussion). In essence the social revolutionary government sought to combine a package of moderate and mixed reforms, designed to disarm critics in the United States and Latin America, with social democratic and socialist transformations, designed to garner support from other socialist states and revolutionary regimes.

Although Nicaragua's international machinations almost certainly contributed to the revolution's initial success, they could not overcome the animosity of the United States, animosity that grew first into hostility and then obsession. The international strategy did not succeed in maintaining the FSLN in power, but it does seem to have protected the revolution.  □

## LEADERSHIP AND THE
## TRANSFORMATION OF SOCIETY

Revolutions fundamentally concern people—they are created by people, led by people, and fought and died for by people. To show how people make revolutions, I focused on the two types of social revolutionary leadership, the visionary and the organizational.

As we have seen, in Bolivia the revolution was dominated by organizational leaders who implemented a program of institutionalization. At the same time, the absence of any real visionary leaders left the social revolutionary ideology unarticulated. The leaders' failure to generate the support of the population was central to their inability to consolidate the revolution.

In Cuba the situation was somewhat different—there was an abundance of both visionary and organizational leadership. Fidel Castro combines both qualities. Raúl Castro is an organizational leader of great ability. Camilo Cienfuegos's skills as an organizer were prodigious, but his stature as a visionary cannot be ignored. Conversely, Ché Guevara—one of the best examples of a visionary leader—had strong organizational skills.

In Cuba, however, the decision was made to actively avoid institution-alization and focus on the process of consolidation. The Cuban revolutionaries were convinced that in Russia, China, Mexico, and Bolivia, institutionalization had derailed, distorted, even destroyed the social revolutionary process. Guevara explained that the Cuban revolutionaries' aversion to institutionalization came from "our fear lest any appearance of formality might separate us from the masses and from the individual, might make us lose sight of the ultimate and most important revolutionary aspiration, which is to see man lifted from his alienation."[119] The Cuban leadership was committed to learning from what they perceived to be the mistakes of their revolutionary predecessors.

The apparent conflict between organization and vision in Grenada seems to have helped doom the social revolutionary process. As in Cuba, there were leaders of both types—Maurice Bishop, the charismatic visionary, and Bernard Coard, the committed organizational genius. In contrast to Cuba, however, where the organizers were relegated to a behind-the-scenes role, Coard's apparent desire to be out in front precipitated the collapse of the revolutionary process.

Nicaragua also benefited from a combination of visionary and organizational leaders. In contrast to the Cubans, however, the Nicaraguans sought a balance between the two types of leadership; in contrast to the Grenadians, there were no power grabs. Leery of the power of personal leadership and concerned with the mechanics of succession, the Nicaraguans created a collective leadership. In opting for balance, the nine members of the National Directorate divided the responsibilities in the state and party among themselves in a careful, calculated manner.

It was no accident, as Gilbert pointed out, that both the security forces and the economic decision-making powers were divided among the three factions.[120] It was hardly a coincidence that the security forces were split not only between the two most powerful factions but also between a visionary leader and an organizational one. Tercerista Humberto Ortega, a masterful organizer, was minister of defense, with control of the military. The revolution's greatest living visionary leader,[121] GPP leader Tomás Borge, became the interior minister, with control over both the police and the state security forces. A similar situation existed with respect to the economy. The key post of minister of agriculture went to Jaime Wheelock, leader of the Proletarian tendency and a visionary leader. The Ministry of Planning, however, was entrusted to Henry Ruíz of the GPP, a talented organizer, who was popularly known in Nicaragua as "Modesto" for his low-key and humble manner.

From the earliest days of the political victory it was clear that the compelling, visionary leadership of Borge would be balanced by the pragmatism and organizational leadership talent of Daniel Ortega. Thus, although Borge spoke for the government on several key issues related to the consolidation of the revolution—justice and human rights, women's and children's issues, literacy, freedom of the press, and the role of the popular church—Ortega was the directorate's choice to be the FSLN's 1984 presidential candidate.

Across the social revolutionary processes in Bolivia, Cuba, Nicaragua, and Grenada, it is possible to discern the individuals who were or are organizational or visionary leaders and the role they played in the final, transformative period. The point is that revolutionary leaders learn and make choices. The paths that they choose—or avoid—are based on their understanding of the past and their sense of the population. The choices that they make are central to the process that unfolds and can in fact mitigate the structures and conditions that confront the revolutionary process. Nowhere has this been more apparent than in the Nicaraguan revolution.

■

## CHAPTER FOUR

# Making the Revolution Reality:
# The Nicaraguan Revolution,
# 1979–1990

Is the Nicaraguan revolution "over"? Did the 1990 election consign the Nicaraguan revolution to the obscurity of the Grenadian revolution or force it to join the Bolivian revolution as little more than a historical reference point? For many people who perceived of the election as a referendum on the revolution, the results raised just such questions. These questions lead to the ones I deal with in this chapter: If the Nicaraguan revolution was successfully institutionalized and a significant degree of consolidation was achieved (as I have argued), how did the Sandinista National Liberation Front—the vanguard of the revolution—lose the election? Does this loss represent a repudiation of the revolution?

There is clearly something different about the revolution in Nicaragua. The program of Sandinismo—pluralism, a mixed economy, a nonaligned foreign policy—seems closest to Scandinavian social democracy. Fourteen years into the revolution the degree of economic and political pluralism far exceeds that of any comparable social revolution. Nicaragua is well into the third phase of the social revolutionary process, the transformation of society. Despite overwhelming odds, the program of institutionalization has been completed. The contra war left more than 30,000 Nicaraguans dead and tens of thousands of other citizens wounded, orphaned, or homeless.[1] To put this number in some perspective, as Cooper pointed out, these 30,000+ deaths mean that nearly twice as many Nicaraguans per capita were killed in the contra war as were U.S. soldiers in both world wars, Korea, and Vietnam combined.[2] Nicaragua's economy was also devastated and its infrastructure destroyed.[3] The psychological and emotional damage wrought by the war and economic privation is immeasurable. Despite this, the Sandinistas created a mixed economy and a political system that is remarkably open by any standard. The

101

Nicaraguan government has confronted a unique set of problems and has overcome many of them.

The status of the effort to consolidate the revolution is not so clear-cut, in part, because of the more elusive nature of consolidation. Judgment is further nuanced because consolidation has to do with the way that people look at and go about living their lives on a day-to-day basis: It is by nature not a rapid process.[4] Nonetheless, it is possible to assess the status of consolidation by investigating its indicators: economics, geography, and popular attitudes.

The purpose of this chapter, then, is threefold. First, it offers a preliminary assessment of consolidation, based on a small-scale investigation of consolidation in Nicaragua during 1988–1989.[5] I thus begin with a discussion of the primary indicators of consolidation—trust, opportunity, and a vision of the future, bound together by a sense of empowerment. Second, I return to a discussion of institutionalization in Nicaragua, paying specific attention to the international and domestic context of the 1990 election. In the third and final part of this chapter I explore the juncture between institutionalization and consolidation in terms of the 1990 Nicaragua election. ☐

## CONSOLIDATION IN
## THE NICARAGUAN REVOLUTION

In the preceding chapters I argued that consolidation is an independent concept worthy of being explored, and I discussed the importance of individual actors and the role of leaders. Now I shift the focus directly to the process of consolidation in Nicaragua. In Chapter 2 I demonstrated the utility, viability, and importance of distinguishing between the consolidation and the institutionalization processes in the final phase of social revolution. The critical role of consolidation in the social revolutionary process helped explain the failure of the Bolivian revolution. Exploring consolidation during the Cuban revolutionary process helped explain the unusual relationship between Fidel Castro, the population, the government, and the revolution; recognition of the importance of consolidation may also prove useful in ascertaining what unfolds after Castro's eventual demise. A focus on consolidation shed light on the degeneration and collapse of the Grenadian social revolutionary project. The utility of consolidation as an analytical tool can perhaps be most neatly demonstrated in explaining the unusual success of the Nicaraguan revolution.

The issue of the success or failure of the consolidation process, however, is complicated by its elusive nature. Unlike institutionalization, which may be assessed by considering institutions created by new governments, consolidation is primarily evaluated via an understanding of people's attitudes, or "popular attitudes." Measurements of institutionalization have long been one of the criteria used by social scientists to investigate the status of a state and its various components; by focusing on a set of structural characteristics, social scientists have been able to achieve a relatively high degree of precision in their assessments. Consolidation, in contrast, is decidedly noninstitutional and nonstructural in character. It is obviously more difficult to be precise with a concept that is based on people's attitudes; the payoff, however, more than makes up for the loss of precision.

The process of consolidation cannot be fully understood by paying sole attention to "objective" indicators of such structural factors as economics and geography. In fact, the Nicaraguan case seems to suggest that ideas can countervail structural factors or, at the very least, shape and profoundly alter them. As a result, understanding voluntaristic factors, such as popular attitudes, is key to grasping the support for the social revolutionary process in Nicaragua. Popular attitudes indicate the population's view of and relations with the government and the revolutionary process.

This is not to say that there is no place for more traditional social science variables. People's economic situation—as they perceive it—and geographical location are two other factors that would seem to be of use in assessing the status of consolidation, although, at least in my research, the geographic factor has proven inconclusive. In sum, a consideration of the variables of economics, geography, and popular attitudes provides indicators as to the status of consolidation.[6]

### "A Roof for My Children Is a Wonderful Thing": After Political Victory

Economic adversity, in some form, is always present after the transition of political power in a revolutionary situation. Often, there is the flight of domestic and international capital either prior to the revolutionaries' political victory or at the onset of the transformative period. Complications may also arise if the battle for political power entailed destruction of the physical infrastructure, for example, plants or farms. Furthermore, past legacies of development and dependency often have a profound impact on contemporary processes. It is not easy to alter conditions that may be centuries old and reinforced or "propped up" as much by external forces as internal ones. Any or all of these factors can constrain the economic programs undertaken by the new government and make rectification of past inequities difficult. Some economic factors, however, may facilitate the planning and introduction of changes. A tradition of strong, centralized government may be useful if the new goal is centralized planning, although this advantage may be undermined by a legacy of centralization that was harmful to the population—a difficult factor to overcome. Another possible benefit would be the availability of previously unobtainable foreign investment and economic assistance. Historically, however, social revolutions have rarely if ever seen such benefits.

Failure to expand the economic pie is assumed, at least in theory, to undermine the ability of a government to maintain or gain broad popular support. In social revolutionary processes, for example, most people expect the rectification of their economic grievances. Reflecting on this, Fidel Castro once noted that after the revolutionaries had achieved political victory in Cuba, "many people thought they had stepped into a world of riches. What they had really done was to win the opportunity to start creating—in the midst of underdevelopment, poverty, ignorance, and misery—the wealth and well-being of the future."[7] To date no social revolutionary government has been able to realize fully the popular expectations.

The economic situation in which the Nicaraguans found themselves in the mid-1980s was disastrous. A combination of revolutionary exhaustion, government mistakes, the U.S. trade embargo and pressure on international lending institutions, the contra war, and natural disasters had left almost all Nicaraguans in dire straits. By any measure the economy was a complete catastrophe: Urban wages had fallen drastically—to perhaps only 5–10 percent of 1980 levels,[8] basic commodities were scarce, unemployment was endemic, government services had been reduced, and the currency was constantly losing its value. Per capita income fell every year after 1984, and inflation in 1988 peaked at the astounding rate of 33,600 percent.[9] In the aftermath of that staggering inflation rate, the government undertook massive economic restructuring, adopting IMF-style austerity measures—an amalgam of currency devaluations, massive cutbacks in government spending (the cessation of most government subsidies and the end or cutback of many social programs, especially in the areas of health and education), wage controls, and significant public-sector layoffs.[10] Taken together, these measures added up to "severe (and distinctly orthodox) austerity measures."[11] The IMF told the Nicaraguan government that the measures adopted were harsher than those that it would have recommended and strongly suggested that the government reconsider them.[12] The UN Economic Commission on Latin America assessed the measures as "Draconian."[13]

It is not surprising, therefore, that forty-nine of the fifty people interviewed indicated displeasure with the economy.[14] Such figures normally coincide with a dramatic loss of support for the government. Indeed, a widespread perception of economic disaster should place a damper on the ability of the government to inculcate a new ideology. In fact, the reverse seems to have been true: Some degree of consolidation was achieved even in the face of these terrible economic conditions. This finding seems to support the argument that structural economic reality can be mitigated by social revolutionary ideology.

The question is *how*. Central to the answer is the fact that most people use their own relative economic position before and after the beginning of the revolutionary process as their measurement, rather than basing their judgment on their level of absolute wealth.[15] It is striking that in the face of a catastrophic economic situation, when individuals were asked to relate their previous situation to their current lot, the majority responded that even though they personally might have less now, overall things were better.[16]

Of the people interviewed, 42 percent identified themselves as being better off than before, albeit in some cases only marginally so. Many cited the free health care and education, two of the cornerstones of the government's social revolutionary project. One young man provided the example of his sister in rural León, not far from the town of La Paz Centro: "Before she had nothing and to me now she still has nothing . . . but her children can get medical help, go to school, get clothes. To her this is a lot!"[17] A tailor who lived in a housing project in León explained that before the revolution, he had no house: "Houses were started after the Triumph . . . it is very empowering to have a house. It is a big change for me. I had four kids and no house. Having this house is like a fortune. Having a roof for my children is a wonderful thing."[18] A young woman who worked as a maid summed it up this way: "It's better now. Not economically, but in all ways."[19]

Twenty-six percent of the people interviewed described themselves as being in more or less the same economic situation as before the political victory. Whereas most of these people simply said that things were roughly the same, a few mentioned that things were harder for everyone or that their economic situation had not changed for reasons unrelated to the economy. One young man who was on his second tour with the Popular Military Service (SMP) compared the economic situation before and after the political victory by noting: "I could say that it is relatively similar, but there are other factors now to take into account. For example the war we are in. The war has made it bad, there are terrible economic problems. . . . The economic problems we face now are at the general level. Before it was all on the poor. Now everyone's biting the bullet."[20] A woman who cooked at a restaurant said, "It's hard for everyone, but I think that it's better now."[21] An older woman who worked washing clothes echoed this and pointed out: "It's hard for everyone. Money is worthless and no one has enough."[22]

Sentiments similar to these cropped up among the 32 percent of those interviewed who identified themselves as having been better off before the revolution.[23] These people mentioned prices having risen, less economic stability, and low wages. Here, too, people noted (often at length), the impact of the contra war on their standard of living.

Several critical factors emerged from these interviews. The first is that individuals' perception of their relative economic status (were they better off than they were ten years ago?) played a significant role in their acceptance of Nicaragua's profound economic difficulties. People seemed to feel that if things were better, the struggle and difficulties had been worthwhile. Also important is their perception of where they were relative to their fellow citizens (did they have more or less than those who were their relevant reference group?). Finally, they asked themselves, Were things harder for everyone?

Of those who indicated that their relative economic situation had remained more or less the same, 62 percent pointed out that things were harder for everyone and 23 percent related that they were currently better off than their peers. Among those who identified their economic situation as having been relatively better before the revolution, all acknowledged that today they were still better off than most of their fellow Nicaraguans and only two people felt they were not better off than their peers. The few wealthy Nicaraguans interviewed did not particularly envy their friends and colleagues who had "taken their wallets" and left the country. Several pointed out that those who had left, particularly, for the United States, had not found the business climate congenial or their skills and backgrounds helpful.

It is important to note the role people assign to their own government in all this: Do they see their economic well-being, or lack thereof, as the result of the government or blame other factors?[24] Of the people interviewed, 80 percent mentioned economic mistakes made by the government. Yet only 20 percent partially blamed the government for their economic situation, and only 6 percent placed the blame totally on the government. Most people expressed the view that the U.S. embargo and the contra war were such drains on the economy that they outweighed the government's mistakes. Further, even those who held the government partially responsible gave it high marks for being willing to admit its mistakes in the economic arena. This led to many people's perception that steps would be or had been taken to remedy these errors.

Among those interviewed were two people who argued that the country's current economic problems stemmed largely from the government's having "spoiled" the population in the period immediately after the revolutionary triumph. A government agronomist from Bluefields explained: "At first the government spoiled the people like a parent spoils a child. . . . What happens when you stop spoiling a child? She gets mad, she pouts. That's how Nicaraguans are behaving today. They want the government to give them everything, do everything, make this place a heaven for them."[25] This view was echoed by an older businessman who said: "I think the revolution has made some mistakes. For example, they set price controls and subsidized food, gas, fertilizer, all types of things. There was no way the government could maintain this. So now that the government cannot continue this, people don't thank them for the years they did and instead just complain that prices are at actual cost."[26] From this perspective, then, the government was to blame for having promised too much and thereby failing to make clear, as Castro suggested, that citizens had won the right to struggle for a new future, not simply to expect it.

Among those who assigned complete blame to the government, many focused on what they perceived as the government's anticapitalist, anti-U.S. stance.[27] These people all dismissed the notion that there was any meaningful "mixed economy" in Nicaragua, arguing that it was simply on a fast track to communism. A young architect trying to explain his outlook finally said, "The Front [the FSLN] is too radical for Nicaragua and has failed the people."[28]

In contrast, 94 percent blamed the United States partly or fully for their economic situation, focusing particularly on the costs of fighting the contra war and the deprivations owing to the economic blockade. Even those who blamed the government for all of Nicaragua's economic problems mentioned the difficulties created by the war and the economic blockade. An older man who sold newspapers in one of León's markets believed that the government was to blame because so many mistakes had been made with the economy but allowed that "the war has hurt us and the economic blockade too."[29] A young government worker who felt the government was partially to blame summed up the sentiment of many, pointing out with resignation, "We can't say . . . [what] could have been achieved in economic development if not for the economic blockade and the war imposed on our country."[30] Given the overwhelming impression that Somoza had had the country in an economic stranglehold, the "lost chance" for economic development in the aftermath of Somoza's fall—regardless of where people assign the blame—is a strong and recurrent theme.

People's perception of their economic situation, both individual and collective, appears to have played a consequential but not pivotal role in government's ability to consolidate the revolution. Nicaragua's economic condition should have profoundly shaken Nicaraguan society. It does not seem to have done so. Economic conditions not nearly so severe as those in Nicaragua have resulted in massive demonstrations, paralyzing strikes, coups d'état, or rebellions in other Latin American countries, most recently Venezuela, and in countries around the world. Historically, the reality reflected by numbers such as those mentioned earlier has even been a precursor to revolution. Yet none of these phenomena occurred in Nicaragua. The economic disaster did profoundly shake people's faith in the talents and decision-making abilities of the leadership of the revolution; but the people's responses were peaceful, democratic, and powerful. There seems no doubt that economics played an important role in the outcome of the 1990 election, but it also seems clear that the economic disaster was not sufficient to overcome the overall faith that people had developed in the new system.

The failure of the economy, although it has undoubtedly slowed the consolidation process, has not stopped it. As we have seen, the Nicaraguan government under the FSLN implemented an austerity program. It included: dramatic currency devaluations, a drastic cutting of the social programs that had been the heart of the social revolution, a 44 percent reduction of the budget and the elimination of 34,000–35,000 government jobs.[31] These actions were considerably more severe than those that sparked violent popular reactions in the Dominican Republic, Brazil, and Venezuela in the early 1990s. The population's apparent equanimous acceptance of this massive economic restructuring demonstrates at least in part how effective the consolidation process has been. Perhaps the strongest indicator, however, which will be explored later, was the peaceful transfer of power after the 1990 election.

### Where You Live and Where You Stand:
### After Political Victory

Where an individual lived before and after the revolution at first appeared to be a potentially useful tool in assessing whether she supported the social revolutionary process. It seemed common sense that those in the forefront of the contra war were likely to be politicized. Moreover, much has been made, particularly with reference to revolutionary situations, of urban-rural distinctions. Finally, many people inside and outside of Nicaragua make reference to people's location as an explanation for an individual's support (or lack of support) for the social revolutionary process.[32]

Specifically, two interrelated geographic dimensions appeared relevant. First in importance is whether people lived in the midst of the areas where the government and the contras were fighting. The "contra front" comprised smaller cities such as Esteli, Matagalpa, Ocotal, Bocoa, and Jinotega and the rural areas near the borders. The war forced many people to move from these areas into the major cities; the presence of those who stayed in or in some cases moved to the contra front was construed as an act in support of the revolution. These people, Slater suggested, were in a very real sense the frontline troops in the government's battle to control and defend Nicaraguan territory and sovereignty.[33] Not surprisingly, the contra front is also where many people perceived the revolution to have been strongest, that is, where it enjoyed the greatest commitment among the population. The second dimension is whether people lived in the urban areas such as León, Managua, Masaya, Esteli, and Matagalpa, which were the heart of the final struggle for political victory during 1978–1979.[34]

As noted earlier, both revolutionaries and scholars of revolution generally draw a crude distinction between urban and rural populations. The common wisdom is that people in rural areas are less engaged in the process of institutionalization than are those who live in urban centers; presumably the same would hold true for consolidation. This should be even more the case when, revolutionary romanticism and mythology aside, political victory was largely achieved in neither the mountains nor the countryside but in the poorer barrios (neighborhoods) of Masaya, León, and Managua. Yet in the late 1980s what one encountered in Nicaragua was a rural population that was engaged and active, particularly in contrast to the more disillusioned urban population.[35]

Beyond respondents' vague comments and asides, the interviews turned up little to support either of the first two distinctions.[36] This may have been a result of the geographic location in which the interviews took place and the relatively small number of interviewees. Although responses offered somewhat greater support for the urban-rural distinction, this too may have been more conclusively tested had there been more interviews with people in rural areas. As it was, those respondents from rural backgrounds were, proportionally, far more engaged in and supportive of the revolution than those from urban backgrounds. This, however, may be explained by their comparative youth and status as students. Overall, geography did not prove to be a particularly useful factor for assessing support for the revolution or for determining the consolidation of the social revolutionary process in Nicaragua.

### Empowerment After Political Victory: Popular Attitudes in Society

Popular attitudes (as we saw in Chapter 1) represent a belief system. To explore popular attitudes about consolidation, I focused on the indicators of consolidation first mentioned in Chapter 1: trust, opportunity, and a vision of the future, bound together by a sense of empowerment. It is important not to lose sight of how intimately these are linked.

*Trust.* Of the people interviewed, 54 percent clearly indicated that they trusted the government. Many of these people had a deep conviction that society had changed and that things were different from the Somoza era. Several factors appeared central to their perception that things were different; important among them was the perception that the government was willing to admit its mistakes. Related to this was the widely held perception that "unlike any other government in our history . . . [this one] treats people like adults."[37] Finally, with reference to both these points—and in dramatic contrast to their treatment by the country's previous governments—these people were convinced that the government was making a good-faith effort to report its activities consistently and honestly to the population. This was neatly summarized in the reaction of one worker, who had just watched President Ortega's 1989 New Year's Message: "Did you see Danielito tell us the mistakes that had been made? He trusts us. He knows that if he tells the people that they tried and failed or that they chose wrong they will understand. Listen, in how many countries do the leaders say 'we made a mistake' or 'we were wrong'? It is a sign of respect."[38] For a population long marginalized, even brutalized, and denied basic rights, the receipt of respect from its government is significant.

Things were equally clear for the 26 percent that did not trust the government. Asked about trust, a travel agent in León simply dismissed the government as "totalitarians."[39] One regional opposition leader explained his distrust with the contention that it was impossible to trust a "government [that] has carefully not defined itself."[40] One of his colleagues concurred, charging "We can not figure out what they are—communists, Marxist-Leninists, capitalists."[41] A woman who made her living washing clothes argued that the government was simply not to be trusted: "No good can come of them. They are destroying the country. They talk about development and take away land, they talk about freedom and force people to move. They have no respect."[42] Many of these people felt that the new government was simply more of the same.

Not surprisingly, 20 percent of those interviewed could be best characterized as unsure. This was particularly apparent with regard to the government's ability to manage the country. There was, for example, some concern that the government would not know how to deal with peace. One older man, echoing the fears of several people, pointed out rather ruefully that "you do not learn about peace fighting in the mountains."[43] One unique explanation was offered by a young woman who said that she trusted the government's economic decisions but feared its political stance: "Politics is the problem, it is terrible. I am not with the government in that respect."[44]

Others were concerned less with ability than with strength. A surprising number of people claimed that Nicaraguans required strong and forceful leadership because of their Latin or Indian "natures." This perspective was well articulated by an older construction worker who explained that his concern was not with the government's ability to govern per se but with the manner in which it had chosen to govern. Specifically, he expressed his skepticism about the strength of those individuals running the government. According to him: "The Sandinistas have good ideas, but they don't know how to run a government. When Daniel and Sergio were elected, they should have taken power. They were elected by the people to take power. You can not have a country run by nine men— sometimes it even seems like more than nine. People want to know who is in charge." Until those "at the top" would take charge, he continued, the government would not be sufficiently strong to run Nicaragua.[45]

Even though a majority of those interviewed indicated trust for the government, it was clear that there was some wariness, and over a quarter were outrightly distrustful. This spilled over into people's perceptions in interesting ways. Although the interviews did not capture this nuance well, I found that people distinguished between the FSLN, which they seemed to trust more (actually, they trusted specific party leaders), and the government, which they seemed to trust less. It is also interesting to note that whereas it was unclear whether responsibility for the honesty of the elections was assigned to the FSLN or the government, there was a palpable sense of trust (perhaps faith would be a better word) that the 1990 election would be run fairly and that the results would be respected.[46]

*Opportunity.* Seventy percent of the people interviewed believed that the government had afforded Nicaraguans more opportunity and greater equality. All these people, as well as some others, mentioned the access to education and the government's efforts to provide housing. Many noted their newfound ability to get things accomplished. One woman who worked as a maid epitomized this view: "I can go to a government office, see someone without paying for it and something may be done. I never thought I would see this . . . and I know from others that you do not see this in, say, Mexico or in Honduras."[47] For people whose basic notion of government had long been that it was something that was best avoided, such changes were significant.

Some people did add interesting caveats. When asked whether greater opportunities and equality existed, one man responded: "Politically, yes. Morally, yes. Economically, no . . . but that is because of the war."[48] One woman pointed out that although there was greater opportunity and equality overall, "there are problems for women."[49] Another woman, who was a strong supporter of the government, elaborated on this idea.

The revolution, according to her, had won rights for women, but primarily the "right to work two jobs. The right to have children, keep the house and go out and work."[50]

Of those interviewed, 18 percent felt that the government had not provided greater opportunity or equality. Most of them felt strongly that access to higher education and housing was dependent on one's standing with the FSLN. This was less the case with the access to government bureaucracy, although all of these people were dismissive of the notion that the Nicaraguan government was any more efficient than it had ever been. One man argued: "So you can go in to see them, and most will not take anything, but they are helpless, so it is a waste of everybody's time. They are there for the government to pay them and for us to go get pieces of paper from."[51] The notion of efficacy and efficiency in Nicaragua, according to a young architect, is a smoke screen.[52] As far as equality, one man who believed that there was more opportunity qualified equality by saying that it existed "in studying, yes, but in work and politics, no."[53] An older woman snorted derisively when we talked about opportunity and equality and said simply, "They hate anyone with money. Understand?"[54]

Twelve percent of those interviewed were unsure whether the government had provided more opportunity or greater equality. The overriding attitude among these people seemed to be that it was difficult to say, given the conditions in Nicaragua. Interestingly, they split evenly on whether it was the fault of the government or of what one woman described as "our unfortunate international situation."[55] The other common theme here was that time would tell—it was simply too early to say.

With the central place accorded education and housing, along with health care issues, as the core of the social revolutionary project, it is perhaps not surprising that there would have been such a strong perception that the government had provided both greater opportunity and equality. Somewhat more surprising was the degree to which people felt that they could accomplish their goals. As with the earlier discussion of respect, the sense that government offices were open and relatively responsive to them was powerful and real. The amount of service these offices actually provided was clearly secondary to the powerful message of access that was sent.

*Vision of the Future.* The overwhelming majority of those interviewed were eager to discuss their visions of the future. Moreover, their discussions were animated and positive. Only a few people declined to discuss the future or were pessimistic about it. It was particularly interesting that there was a clear difference in how people discussed their vision and that the difference was related to the individual's age.

There was a wellspring of positive feelings for the Sandinistas among people over thirty. These are the people who were most directly affected by the excesses of the Somoza years, and their memories of that period are strong and clear; there is no interest, even among those critical of the government, in returning to that era or way of doing things. This resolution is a powerful indicator that consolidation has occurred.

At the same time, many of these people were weary, and their support for the government and the social revolutionary process had been tempered by ten years of government mistakes, the contra war, and the U.S. economic embargo. Because many of these people no longer expected to see in their lifetime the things they believed that they had fought for, they felt some frustration and even bitterness. A relatively young government agronomist who had returned to Nicaragua from Mexico to fight in the revolution explained with a world-weary sigh: "I think we expected too much, too soon. Things will be better for my children. Of that I have no doubt. In many ways it is better for them already. But it is too late for me."[56] Another man, with some exasperation, expressed his frustration by asking: "So they beat Somoza, they got rid of the National Guard. Great. And since then?"[57]

In contrast, those who came of age since the revolution were not as harsh. In talking with a group of young women at one of León's religious high schools, I asked four students to respond with the first thing they thought of when they heard a certain name. First I mentioned the pope. With very serious faces they responded slowly and thoughtfully: "a lot of luxury," "strong tradition, hard on those who don't agree," "a formidable man, but he needs to change," and "a man who does not understand us."[58] When I asked about President Ortega, smiles broke out and the answers came fast: "future," "development," "possibilities," and "realizing prospects for peace."[59] At the very least, this says something about the success of the social revolutionary strategy in terms of the project of political socialization.

This generational difference is also mirrored in the very way that people talked about their visions of the future. Older people (a relative term in the Nicaraguan context) talked about how great their hopes were for their children's future—seemingly conceding that their own prospects were somewhat dim. In dramatic contrast, the youth often talked eloquently, at length, and almost cockily about the future they envisioned for themselves and their cohorts even in the face of incredible obstacles that lay in their path.

A majority of the people interviewed rated high in all three of the indicators used to ascertain popular attitudes about the government. Trust was the weakest category: This is probably not surprising given the economic situation in the country, government admissions of mistakes and mismanagement, and traditional Nicaraguan attitudes toward government. What did seem surprising was the strength of people's belief that opportunities and equality had been so much greater in the ten years since the revolution. Although Nicaragua's disastrous economic situation had curtailed opportunities, the leadership had clearly created a perception that such opportunities were available and that there were a number of possibilities. As a result, very few people doubted that a better future lay down the road; their vision of the future was strong. Of at least equal importance, as will be seen in Chapter 5, was the powerful sense of empowerment generated by all these factors combined.

### Conclusion: Consolidation in Nicaragua

The process of consolidation—the project of social transformation—is in a very real sense the ultimate goal of social revolution. Historically, social revolutions offer grand promises and dramatic visions. To date, they have fulfilled neither.

As we saw in Chapter 3, although the leadership makes the decisions and seeks to dictate the timing of the consolidation process, it is the people who must tolerate, accept, or (ideally for the revolutionaries) reconceive their belief systems to accept the social revolutionary ideology and reorder their lives accordingly in the service of the revolution.[60] Without the participation of the population there can be no successful changes in the economic, political, or social spheres of society. Therefore, there is a continuous and pervasive effort to mobilize the people and enlist their energies, loyalties, and skills in creating the new society.

The Nicaraguan government after the political victory expended great energy in pursuit of these goals. The fate of the revolution in Nicaragua remains—at this writing, in 1993—unclear. This is evident in the description of the FSLN leadership offered by one older man: "In my heart I love them like I love my sons. In my head I think they have made many mistakes. Maybe too many."[61] This stands as a succinct summation of much of what was discussed in the interviews. What was clear—and explored more fully in the final section of this chapter—is that many people continued to believe that the promises and vision of 1979 would be fulfilled, with or without the FSLN. This conviction, as we shall see, drew sustenance from the success of the institutionalization process.   □

### INSTITUTIONALIZATION REDUX:
### THE INTERNATIONAL AND DOMESTIC CONTEXT
### OF THE 1990 ELECTION

The 1984 elections and the 1987 ratification of the constitution were two shining jewels in the FSLN's effort to institutionalize the Nicaraguan revolution. The final jewel in the crown was to be the 1990 election. The election, however, represented far more than the closure of the institutionalization process. It was also imbued with great promise by the social revolutionary leadership and heralded as the commencement of a historic new era of peace and economic growth. Thus there existed the perception that both the present and the future were hanging on this one election—an extraordinary burden to place on a single event among the myriad that have occurred throughout Nicaragua's history and within the process of the revolution.

To deny the complexity of Nicaragua's 1990 election would be disingenuous, yet its multiple levels, subtlety, and degrees of intrigue are largely beyond the scope of this section. It is not the nuances and intricacies of this election that interest most people. Rather, the spotlight is on why the FSLN lost and the implications of that loss for the social revolutionary process. To answer those questions, it is necessary to return to the institutionalization process, specifically the international and domestic situation in Nicaragua leading up to the election.

### The World Comes to Call:
### The International Context

The international context of the Nicaraguan revolution—even before political victory—was overwhelming and profoundly conditioned by the international context. The role of the international system and the need for leaders capable of dealing with it were discussed in Chapter 3. What merits some attention here is the degree to which attacks on and support for the Nicaraguan institutionalization process produce repercussions for the consolidation process. Specifically, I shall focus on U.S. efforts to overthrow the government of Nicaragua and on the support for the Nicaraguan government that was derived from the various regional peace processes.

*The United States, 1984–1988.* Perhaps the single most remarkable aspect of the institutionalization process—the 1984 election, the constitutional process, and the 1990 election—was that each phase occurred while Nicaragua was under a large-scale direct and indirect attack from the United States.[62] On 9 March 1981, six weeks after taking office, Ronald Reagan approved a "presidential finding" to provide $19.5 million to the people that would become known as the "contras" (short for *contrarevolucionarios*).[63] For four years, the Reagan administration took great pains to deny one of the world's worst-kept secrets, U.S. efforts to overthrow the government of Nicaragua.[64] In fact, the overthrow of the Nicaraguan government became a *primary* goal of the Reagan administration; by 1986 the pretense had been dropped entirely.[65] U.S. policy was to overthrow the Nicaraguan government; if that could not be achieved, the policy sought to destroy the Nicaraguan economy, discredit the government, and so thoroughly exhaust the population that the "Nicaraguan example" would exist solely as a negative one for those in the Third World.[66]

The United States approached the destruction of the Nicaraguan economy at a variety of levels: in international, regional, and local boardrooms and on the ground. The United States introduced a sweeping trade embargo, devastating for a country long dependent on U.S. markets for export and on U.S. products, notably machinery, for import. To intensify the pressure of the embargo, the United States intervened to block loans from private and international lending agencies as well as allies in Western Europe. On the ground, the contra war proved to be "a frighteningly effective instrument of economic aggression."[67] Attacks were designed to displace people and force meager public funds away from popular social programs—with the added "bonus" of sharply reducing agricultural production and further destroying Nicaragua's ravaged infrastructure.

In its continuing drive to discredit the Nicaraguan government, the United States adopted a political-ideological campaign to delegitimize, subvert, and sabotage the efforts aimed at the institutionalization of the democratic process.[68] By 1984 the issue of Nicaragua and the FSLN had became a U.S. policy obsession, one that eventually overwhelmed the entire foreign policy decision-making process and culminated in the Iran-Contra debacle.[69] Despite the best efforts of the Reagan administration and its allies—efforts that included serious violations of domestic and international law—U.S. policy began to unravel in 1987. When Ronald Reagan left office in January 1989, he had not fulfilled his commitment to overthrow the Nicaraguan government. Many Nicaraguans celebrated Reagan's exit—the popular slogan was "¡Reagan se va, la revolucíon se queda!" (Reagan is going, the revolution remains). Nicaragua was, however, far from free of the United States, and the legacy of the Reagan administration continued.

In the United States the Iran-Contra Affair raised concerns that the president of the United States and his staff had sought to subvert the Constitution in their support of the contra policy: The domestic and international reverberations of the failed contra policy were substantial.[70] Central America was on the brink of a regional war; tensions between the military and civilians in El Salvador, Guatemala, and Honduras were higher than at any time since the 1930s. Although many Nicaraguans were undoubtedly buoyed up by having outlasted Ronald Reagan, they had precious little else to raise their spirits. One Nicaraguan, with a hopeful smile and a wistful tone, thought that with Reagan out of office and his country at rock bottom, there seemed nowhere to go but up.[71] U.S. policy had proven highly successful in wreaking havoc throughout the country and exhausting the population.

*Latin America, the Esquipulas Accords, and the 1990 Elections.* The Nicaraguan revolution might never have occurred had it not been for the support of other Latin American countries, particularly Costa Rica, Cuba, Mexico, Panama, and Venezuela. These countries also played central roles in helping Nicaragua in the early years of the revolution, and in 1983 three of them—Mexico, Panama, and Venezuela—were joined by Colombia in the Contadora process. Focused largely on issues of security between the United States and Nicaragua, this collective effort to stem direct U.S. intervention set the stage for a regional peace initiative, which included provisions for internationally observed elections throughout Central America.

The draft treaty that was produced through the Contadora process called for limiting arms acquisitions, renouncing support for insurgent groups, eliminating foreign military personnel and bases, and holding open elections. Initially Nicaragua was the only one of the Central American countries unwilling to agree to the treaty draft—a public relations opportunity not lost on the United States. When Nicaragua reversed its position, however, the Reagan administration was caught off guard and moved quickly to pressure its allies—Honduras, Costa Rica, and El Salvador—to find fault with the draft.[72] When, as a result, the plan fell through, there was great glee in the Reagan administration.[73] The heavy-handed tactics of the United States, however, proved to be an embarrassment to some U.S. allies in Central America.

By mid-1987 the U.S. behavior toward the Contadora process and the disintegration of U.S. policy toward Nicaragua had presented an opening for regional negotiations without outside support. The Central American states—including those that were pro-U.S.—saw the opening and stepped in. The breakthrough occurred in August when the Central American presidents met in Esquipulas, Guatemala, and signed "The Procedure for the Establishment of a Strong and Lasting Peace in Central America" (known variously as the Central American Peace Accords, the Arias Peace Plan, or, most commonly, the Esquipulas Accords).

Guided by Costa Rican President Oscar Arias—who was awarded the Nobel Peace Prize for his efforts—the Esquipulas Accords were designed to bring peace and democracy to Central America. Specific provisions banned international support for insurgencies—including the use of national territory as staging areas—called for the release of all political prisoners, provided for the complete restoration of civil rights, and outlined a framework for open electoral processes in all the countries.

Enforcement would be by the International Commission of Verification and Security (CIVS) comprising representatives from the UN, the OAS, and the Group of Eight—the Contadora countries plus "the Support Group"—Argentina, Brazil, Peru, and Uruguay.

The Esquipulas Accords proved to be much easier to sign than to implement. This situation was further exacerbated by the decision of the five Central American countries to reserve for themselves the right to veto any part of the CIVS reports that they found problematic. The draft of the first report was highly critical of the United States and its four Central American allies—particularly El Salvador, Guatemala, and Honduras—and praised the efforts of Nicaragua.[74] This served to embarrass the other Central American governments and infuriate the Reagan administration.[75] El Salvador and Honduras, under heavy U.S. pressure, demanded the elimination of the CIVS as the price for continuation of the Esquipulas Accords. The offending draft report was withdrawn and a new version considerably more favorable to the United States and its Central American allies—and correspondingly less favorable to Nicaragua—was circulated.[76]

Problems aside, the Esquipulas Accords were a positive step for Nicaragua. By far the greatest benefit for the Nicaraguan government was the recognition of the legitimacy and permanence of the revolution: Nicaragua's neighbors were prepared to acknowledge at least the *institutionalization* of the Nicaraguan revolution. This, coupled with the apparent military defeat of the contras and the call by the other countries for the disbanding of the contras and an end to U.S. aid for them, was perhaps the major reason for the eagerness with which the Nicaraguan government embraced the peace process.[77]

### The Domestic Context, 1988–1990

Given the overwhelmingly positive aspects of the Esquipulas Accords for Nicaragua, it is perhaps not surprising that the government moved faster and farther than any of its neighbors in implementing the changes called for.[78] The Nicaraguan government opened talks with the contras in March 1988 in the Nicaraguan town of Sapoá, near the Costa Rican border, although the Esquipulas Accords did not obligate the government to do so.[79] These talks resulted in agreement on a sixty-day cease-fire, acceptance of "interim" nonmilitary aid for the contras, and the release of half the contra prisoners held by the government when the contras moved into designated zones inside of Nicaragua.[80]

Eerily reminiscent of its responses to the Contadora and Esquipulas agreements, the United States reacted quickly to pressure its allies, the civilian contra leaders who had signed the accords, to back out. When the latter refused to do so, the contra leaders who had agreed to the deal were berated by their CIA supporters and hundreds were removed from contra leadership and staff positions worldwide.[81] By June these recalcitrants were replaced with contra hard-liners, who were placed under the nominal direction of Somoza-favorite and long-time contra military leader Colonel Enrique Bermúdez. The new leadership immediately issued demands that it anticipated to be completely unacceptable to the government. As a result, the negotiations collapsed and contra activity, which had never ceased completely, rapidly increased.

As we have seen, by early 1988 the economic situation in Nicaragua had deteriorated disastrously from that of the first years of the revolution. The government introduced austerity measures in early 1988 in an attempt to regain some control of an economy run wild. The brunt of those measures fell directly on the people least equipped to deal with them, and some Nicaraguans felt that the FSLN was abandoning those in whose name the revolution had been made and they purported to rule.[82] Making matters worse, at the same time that the FSLN's constituency of poor farmers, the popular urban sectors, and new professionals (state employees, teachers, and health care workers) felt themselves under attack, the government was reaching out to those most opposed to the revolutionary project.[83] The program dubbed *concertación* (working together) was designed to promote unity and win over landlords and the bourgeoisie by offering production incentives and promising an end to confiscations. To many FSLN supporters it seemed all too apparent that concessions were being made to the wealthy while they were being told to tighten their belts yet again in defense of the revolution.[84] As Vilas pointed out, "The Sandinistas' program of structural adjustment was no different from anyone else's: It favored the rich and hurt the poor."[85]

Furthermore, the government failed to include or at least consult the popular organizations in the decision-making process; this meant that there was relatively little public explanation of the new policies. Many Nicaraguans apparently interpreted such behavior as arrogant or indicative of the FSLN's increasing inability to deal with bad news.[86] There seems little question that people were no longer willing to accept the contra war and U.S. economic pressure as the primary explanations for their economic circumstances.

Responding to this, President Ortega acknowledged in June 1988 that the measures appeared contradictory to the direction of the revolution. He went on, however, to explain that "this must be understood as a necessary step to prevent the economy from collapsing and to create the conditions so it will recover and become stronger."[87] Still, efforts were undertaken to increase the level of information available to the population and increase popular participation in the decision-making process.

The challenge for the FSLN in the period prior to the election was to rec-oncile the discrepancy between those who were bearing the burden of the austerity program and those whom the government assumed would support it in the election. In many ways the economy would prove to be a pivotal issue in the election, as the government sought to rectify the situ-ation while balancing the demands of the business community, which the government hoped could help rescue the economy, with those of the gen-eral population.

By the time the election campaign began, the economic situation had rebounded a bit from its low point.[88] By the second half of 1989, inflation was down to 10 percent per month, and there had been a dramatic in-crease in the goods available in the marketplaces. But the economic "pan-orama" remained bleak, particularly in the street, and few could afford to partake of this relative abundance of goods. Moreover, in an ugly re-minder of the years prior to political victory, access to these goods was rationed strictly by income—the government subsidies and redistribu-tion programs that had, as the Latin American Studies Association (LASA) pointed out, long mitigated inequalities had been canceled be-cause of the austerity program.[89] Whatever positive results were being achieved by the austerity program did not filter down to the day-to-day life of the vast majority of the population.[90]

At the same time that the domestic economic situation was a disaster, Nicaragua's political situation was wide open. None of the U.S. "demo-cratic allies" in Central America complied so thoroughly with either the spirit or the letter of the Esquipulas Accords as Nicaragua.[91] Moreover, in January 1988, the Nicaraguan government accepted amendments to these accords that lifted media censorship, further reduced restrictions on political party activities, and led to the previously mentioned negotia-tions with the contras at Sapoá. A further outgrowth of these amend-ments was that the electoral law and laws governing political parties were once again brought up and debated in the National Assembly.

The 1984 electoral law, with modifications, had been codified by the 1987 constitution. Further liberalization of the electoral laws was man-dated by the Esquipulas Accords and its subsequent amendments; the National Assembly responded in October 1988 with the enactment of a new electoral law. This law set up the rules for municipal elections, pro-vided constitutional guarantees to political parties, and addressed the rules on the requirements for establishing and registering political parties.[92]

In February 1989 Nicaragua agreed to move the 1990 elections ahead from November—as mandated by the constitution—to February[93] and to again open a dialogue on electoral reforms. Chief among the additional reforms that resulted from these negotiations were the composition of the Electoral Council, the promise of free media time with guarantees of no censorship, the suspension of the rules favoring larger parties, rules for the electoral police, the suspension of military recruitment until after the elections, the cessation of the wartime internal security laws, and the financing of political parties.[94] In return, all the parties agreed to participate in the elections and signed an accord calling for contra demobilization by 5 December.[95]

Of particular interest was the reform that dealt with the financing of political parties. The 1988 Nicaraguan Electoral Law, drawing on those of Costa Rica, Venezuela, El Salvador, Guatemala, Honduras, and Spain, had provided for state funding of political parties based on the proportion of votes received in the preceding election.[96] The reform drew in equal parts from the 1988 law and the U.S./opposition demands. Half of the public funding would be divided according the proportion of votes received in the previous election. The other half would be divided equally between all parties or coalitions that chose to field a presidential ticket. The result is more generous funding for minority parties than that found in the other Central American states, Mexico, Spain, Venezuela, or the United States.[97] Perhaps most remarkable was the concession that allowed for the unlimited amount of foreign campaign financing.[98]

The U.S. funding of its chosen ally for the 1990 elections, the UNO, was massive by any standard. On 24 October 1989, the U.S. Congress voted to provide $9 million in overt assistance, primarily through the National Endowment for Democracy (NED), to the UNO and its affiliated groups.[99] Although not all the money reached the UNO in time for the campaign, largely for bureaucratic reasons, almost $3.5 million in cash and roughly $200,000 in material aid did.[100] A further $5–$12 million was provided to the UNO covertly through the CIA.[101]

Although the amount of money donated by the United States and the extensive U.S. involvement were clearly significant, the role they played in the campaign is less clear. In fact, the FSLN ran the more visibly expensive campaign. Although the FSLN's foreign cash contributions totaled only slightly over $400,000, the funds were bolstered by over $3 million in material aid from abroad.[102] This tactic may have been a strategic blunder, however, and ultimately contributed to the government's defeat. As some U.S. citizens living in Nicaragua pointed out, it seems not to have occurred to anyone that "the lavish campaign could actually alienate voters," whose own economic privations made them "loath to see such conspicuous spending in times of enforced austerity for the popular sectors."[103]

In this section I have presented an overview of the playing field on which the parties would compete in 1990. Not surprisingly, the situation did not remain static. As in any election campaign, shifting and jockeying continued until the very end—with parties switching in and out of alliances and/or splitting, the sway of international events, such as the U.S. invasion of Panama, and domestic events, such as demonstrations—but the basic parameters were those outlined above. What merits our attention before we continue, however, is what this suggests about the status of institutionalization in Nicaragua.

These basic parameters indicate that an essentially democratic and pluralist political system had been established in Nicaragua and thus provide evidence of the institutionalization of the Nicaraguan revolution. In July 1979 very few envisioned that the revolutionaries who had achieved the political victory would work to build democratic institutions in a country with no meaningful history of them. Yet ten years after that political victory, the process of institutionalization was so deep and so strong that the government—dominated by the social revolutionary leadership and acting against the advice of, among others, Fidel Castro—felt obligated by the system it had created to hold elections. It lost and it left.

As much as the 1990 election offers evidence of the success of the institutionalization process, it also provides an important way to gauge the consolidation process. It is, therefore, useful as we examine the participants in the 1990 election and their campaign strategies, to shift the focus slightly. Reflecting on the campaign strategies of the FSLN and the UNO brings us into the realm of consolidation. As a result, many of the elements in the next section are central to the exploration of the significance of the 1990 election and the insights it provides us into the consolidation of the revolution.   □

## THE NEXUS OF INSTITUTIONALIZATION AND CONSOLIDATION: THE 1990 ELECTION PARTICIPANTS AND STRATEGIES

If institutionalization is fundamentally about political structures and consolidation about the degree to which the population embraces the core of the social revolutionary project, then the 1990 election campaign presents an obvious meeting place. Not even those campaigning from the ultraright suggested any desire to return to the Somoza era or dismantle most of the new institutions created by the government since political victory. If one accepts the thesis that politicians of various stripes provide insight into the mindset of the general population, this clearly suggests a widespread recognition among Nicaraguans that the revolution has in fact been institutionalized.

With institutionalization accepted, the focal point of the election—debated vigorously and emotionally—was what the 1979 revolution had meant, that is, how it should be interpreted and who rightfully could make such interpretations. Almost every party proclaimed itself the rightful and proper heir to the process begun by the political victory over Somoza. Several, most notably the Movement for Revolutionary Unity (MUR) and the UNO, made being the heir the centerpiece of their campaigns. When the debate shifts to who has the right to continue the revolutionary process, the question then squarely becomes one of consolidation: Has the revolution reached a stage at which it is sacrosanct, accepted and respected by all, simply a part of their everyday life?

One way to assess the degree to which consolidation of the social revolutionary project has been obtained is by considering the strategies employed by Nicaragua's political parties as they sought office in the 1990 election. A low level of consolidation, perhaps even no consolidation, would presumably result in parties running against the social revolutionary process in general or at least its most obvious manifestations (the highest-profile programs of the social revolutionary project). A higher degree of consolidation, in contrast, would be indicated by the greater extent to which the political parties focused on the achievements of the revolution and promised to protect and even extend those gains.

The 1990 election campaign has largely been treated as a contest between the incumbent FSLN and the UNO coalition. This does capture the heart of what transpired, but it misses one aspect that is important in regard to both institutionalization and consolidation. In point of fact, the 1990 election included eight parties besides the FSLN and the UNO—all ten ran presidential tickets and several ran full or large slates for the National Assembly. Although my primary focus must be on the two major contenders, the strategies of the other opposition parties merit at least brief consideration here for three reasons. First, they indicate the range of ideological diversity available to Nicaraguan voters—a spectrum much greater than is available anywhere else in the Americas. Second, the wide-open nature of the 1990 election campaign is another sign of the institutionalization of the social revolutionary process. Third, and most important for our purposes, their strategies speak to the status of consolidation.

## The Third Path: The Non-UNO Opposition

Shortly before the 1990 election, the presidential candidate of the Movement for Revolutionary Unity (MUR), Moisés Hassán—a popular former Sandinista member of the JGRN and FSLN mayor of Managua—explained to one writer that choosing between the FSLN and the UNO was like choosing between hanging yourself and shooting yourself.[104] At least eight political parties seemed to agree and sought to provide the voters of Nicaragua with less dramatic alternatives. Four of these parties presented centrist/reformist platforms, one presented an ultraright perspective, Hassán's MUR offered "the true spirit" of the Sandinista revolution, and two staked out the territory to the left of the FSLN.

What merits attention is that all the parties except the tiny, ultraright Social Conservatism party (PSOC) respected, embraced, or sought to build on the social revolutionary process.[105] The four centrist/reformist parties drew on their respective Christian Democratic and Social Democratic backgrounds to provide a "third path" for Nicaragua, a path that would simultaneously honor and moderate the gains of the social revolutionary process.[106] The MUR was drawn from Nicaragua's various leftist parties, though mostly the FSLN, and identified itself as the true representatives of the revolution "shorn of bureaucratism and corruption."[107] The Revolutionary Workers party (PRT) and the Marxist-Leninist Popular Action Movement (MAP-ML) sought to radicalize the social revolutionary process, specifically to push it farther faster.[108]

Not many Nicaraguans, apparently, shared Hassán's perspective on the choice between the UNO and the FSLN. In 1984 the opposition parties had polled roughly one-third of the vote.[109] In 1990 opposition voters overwhelmingly supported the UNO slate. The eight non-UNO opposition parties garnered only 4.7 percent of the presidential vote and 5.1 percent of the National Assembly vote.[110] The small percentage reflected the degree to which the electorate was polarized; the choice over the course of the campaign was effectively narrowed to pro-FSLN versus anti-FSLN. The UNO's broad political spectrum, its anointment as the sole recipient of the massive U.S. funding,[111] and its unexpectedly shrewd choice of presidential candidate—all factors to be explored at length below—made it the logical choice as an alternative to the FSLN.

The preponderance of support for the UNO, which encompassed a wide range of views, does not negate the fact that an equally wide array of views was available among the non-UNO opposition. As LASA pointed out, "There was a considerable and broad spectrum of political options during the period of jockeying for position prior to the election."[112] The variety of parties as well as their ability to mount campaigns serves as further evidence of the depth of institutionalization. That all but one of the parties espoused a deep commitment to the continuation of the social revolutionary process in some form suggests consolidation.

### "Everything Will Be Better": The FSLN's 1990 Election Strategy

The FSLN slate for the 1990 election featured the same ticket as in 1984: Daniel Ortega for president and Sergio Ramírez for vice president.

Both men had been part of the five-member JGRN, which had been named prior to the defeat of Somoza and had governed Nicaragua until the 1984 elections. In 1984, Ortega and Ramírez were elected easily at the head of the FSLN ticket. Thus both men had been intimately involved in running the country since the political victory—which fit with the notion of a vanguard party. The FSLN's decision nonetheless raised two unfortunate specters: It suggested that the party did not want to rock the boat, and it raised the prospect of *continuismo* in a revolutionary society.[113]

It seems plausible that the voters feared *continuismo* by either Ortega or the FSLN after eleven years in power. *Continuismo* has been a common practice throughout Latin America, and as an appropriate description of the Somoza dynasty, it is a ready reference point for the Nicaraguan population. The decision to run the Ortega/Ramírez ticket, then, may well have raised some suspicions that the FSLN was engaging in *continuismo*. Such concerns would have resonated poorly with many in Nicaragua for whom the possibility "violated a deep Nicaraguan sentiment against re-election, which grew out of the inveterate electoral practices of Anastasio Somoza and his son."[114] The FSLN seemed to be changing from an unusually conceived type of political party to a political party of the type that was all too familiar to many Nicaraguans. This also reflects a picture of the FSLN as somewhat distant, perhaps even estranged, from the population.

If the FSLN was not estranged from the general population, the campaign that Ortega and Ramírez chose to run highlighted the degree to which they were out of touch with the people. As LASA pointed out, the "campaign was highly personalistic, focusing on the characteristics and attributes of the candidates."[115] Having produced a vague platform short on specifics, the FSLN sought to "focus attention on the personality and attributes of President Ortega. They focused upon his experience, close relationship to the people, family bonds, and broad support from a wide range of people, including sports figures and other personalities."[116] Rather than dealing with the substantive issues confronting the people, the contra war and the military draft, as well as the economy, the FSLN slogan was the glib "Todos ser mejor" (Everything will be better).

The strategy was reminiscent of the very worst sort of content-empty, U.S.-style incumbent campaign. A band and fireworks would announce Ortega's arrival on horseback (or in the "Dannymobile" in urban areas). "El gallo" (Ortega's FSLN-supplied nickname—"the cock") would be rigged out in blue jeans, bright shirt, and cowboy boots to convey a lively, youthful, macho, debonair image meant to contrast with his older, female opponent. Popular songs rewritten to emphasize Ortega's virtues would be sung, local groups would perform, beauty queens crowned, and gifts doled out.[117] A vague, positive speech, with group cheerleading led by the president, would follow. Finally, photos would be taken with supporters, and more fireworks and music would send off the president.[118] The message was simple: Thanks to the FSLN, life was good; with the FSLN, life would get better.

At a time when the overwhelming daily reality for the vast majority of Nicaraguans was austerity and poverty, the FSLN's expensive makeover of Ortega and Ramírez as patronage-dispensing, gift-giving, baby-kissing, glad-handing cheerleaders seems quite curious. Equally strange to many Nicaraguans must have been the FSLN's candidates' public rediscovery of their Catholicism—invoking "the Lord" in speeches and attending mass. Finally, no one could blame the weary and worn people if they found the promises of a better world after the election suspect.

The intent of the FSLN strategy—developed in consultation with media and public relations specialists from other Latin American countries, France, and West Germany, and a private Managua-based polling firm[119]—was to isolate Ortega from "negative opinions associated with specific problems" and present the president as a "warm but commanding figure, with roots among the people, but tested, experienced, and capable of leading the nation to a better future."[120] To many Nicaraguans, however, it must have appeared an effort to ignore the economic devastation and the war—perhaps even the revolution itself. The FSLN appears to have assumed that it would benefit from some fundamental bond with the population.[121] In fact, the expense of the FSLN campaign, the assumption that the victories of the past could be trumpeted and the failures disregarded, and the conviction that the opposition would be "tainted" by its link to the United States or the contras served to highlight the estrangement of the FSLN from the Nicaraguan population. As one observer noted, the FSLN basically ran the campaign as if the people had no memory and no interest in the past.[122]

One implication of this is that on the one hand, the FSLN had failed to transcend its character as a vanguard party, and on the other, the population had transcended the need for the vanguard.[123] As will be explored more fully below, the population "grew" faster than the party. As with Humberto Ortega's conviction that it was the population that led the FSLN during the revolution, it would seem that it once again was the population that took the lead. Nicaraguans apparently felt confident that they could protect the hard-won achievements of their revolution—perhaps even protect them better—without the people who had led them to these gains. The feelings of many were undoubtedly summed up in the thoughts of the Managua taxi driver who told a reporter: "The *muchachos* [boys], they had good intentions. They've done their best. But it's time for a change."[124] Such confidence goes beyond the reality of institutionalization to suggest a relatively high degree of consolidation.

In the process of successfully institutionalizing the revolution, the FSLN provided the population with the very tools necessary to turn them out of office. That the FSLN leadership had the confidence to do so says a great deal about its faith in the process of consolidation; the leaders were apparently confident that the gains of the social revolution would not and could not be reversed. The population was apparently similarly confident and was therefore prepared to trust the government to those not in the vanguard—but to others, who in a very real and meaningful sense carried with them the FSLN's and the revolution's seal of approval. This brings us to the saga of the UNO and the candidacy and campaign of Violeta Chamorro.

### Doña Violeta: The National Opposition Union and Its 1990 Election Strategy

The National Opposition Union (UNO) brought together a broad alliance, which ranged from the farthest right of Nicaragua's political spectrum to the farthest left. This confederation seems to have been bound by a common antipathy for the FSLN, a mutual desire for power, and a healthy appreciation for U.S. financial incentives. Wracked by internal bickering, pushed and pulled—much of the time willingly—by U.S. desires, this unlikely coalition not only won the 1990 elections but also held together surprisingly well in the critical first months after that victory and has remained a vaguely coherent organization. Because the UNO's existence has been largely defined by its Byzantine political intrigues, extreme ideological vagaries, and intense personal rivalries, its maintenance of such a coalition has required strenuous efforts and adroit maneuvering that has not always been entirely successful. Early on, these efforts brought compromises such as those on who would be the coalition's presidential and vice-presidential candidates, deals on the candidates on the slate for the National Assembly, and the modification of and eventual general retreat from the UNO platform.

*The UNO's Factions.* Prior to 1979, there was no meaningful political space in Nicaragua in which parties could develop and grow. This stunted political development resulted in parties (like those in most of Latin America) that were little more than personalistic vehicles, often with no real apparatus or public following. Another consequence is that interpersonal or familial relationships were often a more reliable indicator of which parties might line up together or reach accommodations than similar political perspectives. This explains why the parties that made up the UNO have tended not to create within the alliance new factions that reflected their political stances.[125]

There were three clear factions in the UNO from its inception. One group of five parties embraced the four far-right microparties affiliated with COSEP and one of the rightist parties.[126] Another faction consisted of the three leftist parties and the coalition's largest party, the center-right Liberal Independent party (PLI); this faction was dubbed "The 4 from '84," a reference to their participation in the 1984 election.[127] A disparate set of five small parties, which nearly replicated the UNO's breadth of political perspectives in miniature, constituted the third faction.[128]

The COSEP faction collected elites that had been heavily involved in the domestic opposition since 1979.[129] For the 1990 election, COSEP and its affiliates put forth the "Blue and White Plan for National Salvation," which promised a drastic curtailment of the revolution and evoked notions of "Somocismo sin Somoza."[130] To guide the country, this faction proposed far-right former COSEP president Enrique Bolaños, who was not affiliated with any political party.

"The 4 from '84" brought together the most established parties in the UNO[131] and the only parties that at various times since 1979 had supported the social revolutionary process. Because of ideological differences, this faction proposed no coherent program akin to the "Blue and White Plan." Rather, its message was built around the belief that the FSLN had had its chance and now it was someone else's turn—specifically, professional politicians such as PLI's Virgilio Godoy, former JGRN minister of labor (1979–1984) and one of the leaders of opposition in the National Assembly.[132] In fact, it was this image of themselves as the established class of old-time politicians that further bound together this faction.

The third faction was the most ideologically diverse, ranging from the far right through the right to the center. Commonalities in this faction were not readily apparent, but it did seem held together by a combination of personal ties and the fact that members were not welcome in the other factions.[133] This faction emerged as the standard bearer for the preferred candidate of the United States, the former JGRN member Violeta Chamorro. Like Bolaños, Chamorro was not identified with any political party.

The working assumption, according to most scholars and observers, was that COSEP's high profile and power would allow it to place Bolaños in the presidential slot and that Godoy would receive the vice-presidential position as a sop to "The 4." In the face of fairly serious divisions, however, and under U.S. pressure,[134] the factions united behind Chamorro as the coalition's presidential candidate. Godoy rather than Bolaños got the vice-presidential slot.[135] The choice was tactically clever—the PLI's credentials were solid and Godoy fit easily with the notion of "the revolution betrayed"—and represented a further setback for COSEP.[136]

*1990 Election Strategy.* With the ticket of Chamorro and Godoy and a COSEP-heavy National Assembly slate, the UNO seemed to offer the people exactly what it purported to be, a broad umbrella that all Nicaraguans could gather under. Perhaps most important, a ticket topped by a former JGRN member and the former JGRN minister of labor had undeniable revolutionary credentials; and UNO candidates could argue that the FSLN had betrayed the 1979 revolution, forgetting the needs of the very people that it had fought for. But what was the UNO's program? How would it articulate its vision of Nicaragua? Disputes centering on this—the party platform and the direction of the campaign—continued throughout the campaign.

Creation of the UNO platform, not surprisingly, entailed a great deal of negotiation. COSEP's efforts to force the adoption of its "Blue and White Plan" came to naught, although elements of it found their way into the platform. Ultimately, the document produced was suitably vague, moderate, and—not unlike that produced by the FSLN—short on specifics. Although the platform did call for a review of many of the government's core programs, Chamorro led many of the UNO assembly candidates in assuring the voters that the UNO proposed no rollback of the gains made under the revolution. The UNO positioned itself as "the true follower of Sandino," dedicated to "carry out the true revolution."[137]

The UNO's campaign strategy, then, echoed that of the FSLN—an almost exclusive focus on the presidential candidate. Yet there was a critical difference. Many observers suggested that the UNO had selected Chamorro for the same reason that many assumed that she was part of the JGRN in 1979–1980: her symbolic value. It would be disingenuous to suggest that Chamorro was initially selected for other reasons—she herself embraced the designation on occasion.[138] This perception was underscored by the UNO's creation of a Political Council, composed of one representative from each member party and presided over by Godoy, that was meant to make the coalition's strategic decisions. Both the UNO's Political Council and the FSLN mistakenly assumed that a symbolic figure was necessarily an insubstantial one.

Shortly after her nomination, Chamorro demanded respect from a reporter who insisted on referring to her as "a symbol" that was being "manipulated." Such contempt would result in her victory, she warned. She further reminded people that the FSLN leaders were the ones who had first asked her to participate in politics when they invited her to join the JGRN.[139] These were not empty words, and she moved quickly to ensure she would be more than the UNO's front person.

Chamorro surrounded herself with a campaign team led by her son-in-law Antonio Lacayo and Lacayo's two brothers-in-law, Alfredo César and Chamorro's son Pedro Joaquín, Jr. She and her team quickly established that they had their own technocratic and pragmatic agenda and little time for the concerns of the UNO's Political Council and the old-line politicians who dominated it. COSEP fared little better: Chamorro's advisers were also the founders of the Commission on the Recuperation and Development of Nicaragua (CORDENIC), a moderate, technocratically oriented alternative to the COSEP's old guard. Neither group was pleased.[140]

In the ensuing squabbling, which lasted throughout the campaign and was highlighted by a public fistfight between PLI's Political Council representative Jaime Bonilla and Lacayo, Chamorro stayed above the fray and emerged as the only person providing coherence to the UNO coalition. Chamorro made no pretense about her background or her abilities, making it abundantly clear that she considered herself neither a politician nor an expert but rather "a bond of unity and a bridge between a team of experts, the people, and the politicians who have gathered around me."[141] How long she can serve this role for the country remains to be seen; it is evident that she did serve in such a capacity for the UNO and has done so for Nicaragua so far.

While the FSLN scrambled to remake Ortega's image, the UNO quickly discovered it could just let "Doña Violeta," as she was popularly referred to, be herself. Everyone in the country knew her story: wife of revolutionary martyr Pedro Joaquín Chamorro, member of the JGRN from 1979 to 1980, owner of the opposition paper La Prensa, and matriarch of a family divided among the FSLN, the domestic opposition, and the contras. Chamorro stressed the tradition of her martyred husband, her own nationalism and service to the revolution, her motherhood, and her Catholicism. The UNO campaign picked up on these themes of national reconciliation, family, and religion, and presented Chamorro as a living icon, a revolutionary version of the Virgin Mary.[142]

The UNO had no need to exaggerate in its presentation of Chamorro as a revolutionary—her credentials as widow of a martyr of the revolution were impeccable. She liked to point out that "if [her husband, Pedro Joaquín] had not died, those boys, the Sandinistas, would still be in the mountains today."[143] As for her progressive sensibilities, Chamorro charged the FSLN with exploiting the workers and peasants and making a mockery of the revolutionary slogan "Workers and Peasants Toward Power!"[144] Her final campaign speech included the assurance that "the workers" would always take part "in all things related to their jobs and lives."[145] These hardly seemed the words of a counterrevolutionary.

Even the FSLN recognized her revolutionary credibility. On the tenth anniversary of the revolution, Ortega praised her "firm and courageous position when we negotiated with the Yankees . . . she would not accept the Yankee's impositions."[146] Moreover, Ortega said, Chamorro had behaved patriotically and remained true to her convictions, not betraying anyone. People's knowledge of her very public life and praise such as Ortega's made later FSLN attempts to paint Chamorro as a contra or little more than a U.S. puppet seem peculiar at best. It also enhanced her ability to claim that the revolution that her husband had helped bring about and that she had served had been betrayed by the FSLN.

Faced with attempting to reconcile coalition partners whose politics ranged from the far right to the far left, the UNO ultimately ran on little more than its anti-FSLN character and a surprisingly charismatic presidential candidate whose energy, sincerity, and moral authority took her "symbolic" role far beyond what anyone in or out of Nicaragua had anticipated. In many cases, Nicaraguans supporting the UNO confessed to knowing little about the alliance's platform. What they knew was that the UNO, specifically Doña Violeta, offered an alternative to the FSLN that also promised to remain true to the vision of the 1979 revolution, which they continued to cherish.

### Who Won? The Outcome of the 1990 Election

In 1990, 86 percent of the eligible voters in Nicaragua went to the polls and delivered a result that stunned nearly everyone. The UNO received approximately 55 percent of the vote, compared to roughly 41 percent for the FSLN. In the National Assembly this translated into fifty-one seats for the UNO and thirty-nine for the FSLN. The UNO domination was total: The FSLN won only two electoral regions—one by a handful of votes—and lost badly in many of the places it was considered strong, including Managua. Moreover, the UNO won 99 of the 131 municipalities, including Managua and the country's third- and fourth-largest cities, Granada and Matagalpa. It also won in 28 of the other larger cities (20,000+) and 71 of the smaller cities (under 20,000). The UNO victory was clearly impressive by any standard.

The meaning of these results, however, remains considerably less clear and continues to be debated. There are three themes that have dominated the interpretations of the 1990 elections. The first is repudiation, although who or what is being repudiated varies: the revolution, the revolutionary process, the FSLN, or even, in an interesting twist, the U.S./contra forces. The second theme is exhaustion: The population was, for a wide array of reasons, simply too tired to continue with the social revolutionary process. A third theme is that the Nicaraguan population was essentially blackmailed by the United States.

These and similar analyses are flawed by a basic misreading of both the outcome and the implication of the election. In fact, the 1990 election and subsequent peaceful transfer of power indicated the success of the institutionalization process and a significant degree of consolidation. It is a mistake to construe the electoral failure of the FSLN as a failure of either institutionalization or consolidation. It is an equally serious error to read it as a repudiation of either the social revolution or the social revolutionary process.

The mechanics of the electoral process introduced by the FSLN and implemented twice despite inauspicious circumstances demonstrates the success of institutionalization in Nicaragua. It is hard to imagine more convincing proof of that than the peaceful transfer of power to an opposition aligned with the country's worst enemy. But what of consolidation? If a significant degree of consolidation has been achieved, how did the FSLN, the vanguard of the revolution, lose the election?

The 1990 election provides ample evidence of the extent to which consolidation has been realized. The essential quality of consolidation is an unwillingness to accept a return to the way things once were; the majority of the Nicaraguan population would never allow their lives or the conditions they live in to return to their pre-1979 status. Rather than repudiating the revolution, Violeta Chamorro embraced it, promising a return to the glories of the first few years after the political victory. The UNO's posture as the genuine voice of the revolution is indicative of the degree of consolidation achieved.

The UNO did not run a particularly positive campaign or offer any meaningful program to improve the lot of the population beyond promising to end the contra war and the economic embargo; instead, it simply ran against the FSLN. Specifically, the UNO's appeal to the population was based on the charge that the FSLN could no longer advance the process of the social revolution, whereas it, the UNO, could. That is indicative of a profound degree of consolidation.

Prior to 1979 few people anywhere had ever been concerned with whether there were elections in Nicaragua. It was only in the aftermath of the 1979 revolution that such concern began to be articulated; and the institutions created by the revolution made elections possible.[147] The day after the 1990 election, Senator David Durenberger (R-Minn.) told his colleagues on the Senate floor that it had been

> the Ortega brothers, and others who really began the revolution to democracy in Central America. It was not the president of the United States. It was not the CIA. It was not any of the so-called democratic institutions of this country. It began with the people who took to the hills in the sixties and seventies against the Somoza regime. It is these people who began the revolution to democracy when they went to the hills. Few people endorsed their tactics. No one today endorses their tactics. But the results are in that election.[148]

This election, moreover, was hailed widely as a model of fairness and probity.[149]

There were people, however, who recognized the success of the election-day process while questioning the atmosphere that surrounded the entire process from start to finish. Sklar, for example, likened the overall process to the 1980 "electoral coup" engineered by the United States in Jamaica, where the combination of "economic boycott, decapitalization, austerity (in which the International Monetary Fund played a critical role), media manipulation, sabotage, murder, bombings, and other violence rolled back the Manley government's social programs, eroded its credibility and popular support and resulted in its electoral loss to the U.S.-backed party of Edward Seaga."[150] Sklar argued that although she had not thought such a fate would befall Nicaragua, this is in fact what happened.

A more common contention has been that the people of Nicaragua were blackmailed in a sense, forced to vote with a gun held to their head by the United States, which offered an implicit ultimatum: Unseat the FSLN or the contra war and the economic embargo/ pressure will continue.[151] Alejandro Martinez, a former Nicaraguan official, explained:

> The election was a nearly perfect process—not because we lost, but because the mechanisms that we set up worked technically . . . and still we must say that the election was unfair and undemocratic. A detailed analysis shows that the election was unfair and undemocratic not because the government made it that way but because the people faced unfair conditions in which to vote that were created by people outside of Nicaragua. People were forced to vote with a pistol to their head.[152]

Therefore, Martinez contended, the majority of the population chose the only "rational" route and voted for the UNO.

Such interpretations of the situation do not seem unreasonable and, in fact, would be hard to deny per se. At the same time, they address only a part of the Nicaraguan reality. However dramatic a role the U.S. pressures played—and it would be foolish to deny their impact or import—it is also true that there was a great deal of popular sentiment against the FSLN. In fact, as a number of people have pointed out, considering the circumstances, the FSLN's receiving almost 41 percent of the vote is astounding. Nonetheless, as in 1984, the election occurred under extraordinary conditions. Moreover, as in 1984, the citizens expressed their preference.

Nicaragua's 1984 and 1990 elections marked the only two times in history that a group of revolutionaries was willing to risk its power and test its popularity at the polls—actions long characterized as impossible.[153] The 1990 election led to the first time in history that revolutionaries walked away from power when they were voted out.

### A Victory for the Revolution,
### A Defeat for the Revolutionaries:
### The 1990 Elections and Consolidation

Consolidation, as we have seen, refers to the embrace of the core of the social revolutionary project by a significant majority of the population. Successful consolidation is characterized by the willingness of the population to defend the gains made through the social revolutionary process. It seems clear that this is what the FSLN brought to the Nicaraguan population.

There is enormous tension latent in the concept of the vanguard party. The vanguard seeks to liberate and empower the brutalized and disenfranchised. Empowerment, however, like democracy, entails risks for leaders. Having given people power over their own lives, the vanguard must be prepared to adapt to the new situation or lose its place of prominence. Its time, at least as the vanguard, has passed.

The tension between the vanguard and the population first manifests itself after political victory, when the vanguard tries to direct the transformation of the population, and it peaks when the revolutionaries have succeeded at their self-appointed task, that is, when the people discover their voice and take control over their lives. They have been empowered. In Nicaragua the sense of empowerment among those who had been brutalized into indifference was and is palpably clear. Along with this empowerment is a fortitude to resist any threat to the gains they have realized or the power they now know they have.

Arturo Cruz, former JGRN member and pseudocandidate for the 1984 presidential elections, recognized this in the aftermath of the 1984 presidential noncampaign.

> It is now clear that the revolutionary process is somehow irreversible—that Nicaragua will not return to its former feudalistic status which prevailed prior to July 1979. . . . Revolutionary social transformation is not questioned. Even the staunchest adversary of the Sandinistas—the Nicaraguan Democratic Force (FDN)—pretends to justify its military stand on the ground that the revolution has been betrayed by the FSLN.[154]

Cruz's comment suggests that as early as 1984 the consolidation of the revolution was well under way and, at least from his perspective, already "irreversible."

There is, in fact, a very real sense in which the UNO's 1990 campaign strategy reflects the same conviction: that consolidation of the revolution is well under way. From the selection of the candidates to the speeches made, great efforts were made to assure people that there would be no rollback of the revolutionary gains and that the UNO would respect not just the laws but the norms and mores of the Nicaraguan revolution as well. In much the same way that the Esquipulas Accords represented recognition by the other Central American countries that the Nicaraguan revolution had been institutionalized, the UNO's decision to present itself as the authentic voice of the revolution acknowledged the consolidation of the social revolution.

Although Nicaraguan voters undoubtedly heard and were perhaps even reassured by the UNO's promises, they also demonstrated a degree of sophistication and confidence. They understood that the hard-won gains of the social revolutionary process were not tied to one organization, one program, or one person. Rather, the gains of the revolution were based in them, the people. Moreover, they clearly felt that they could protect the gains they had made if those gains were threatened by the UNO or any other segment of the population.[155] The FSLN had given them the tools, teaching them how to mobilize and organize to accomplish what they wanted and defend their interests. As Cruz recognized, things had changed—the revolution could not be taken away.

The degree of consolidation achieved in Nicaragua so far suggests that nothing could return matters to their former state. It remains too soon to state definitively that the Nicaraguan revolution is consolidated. But the 1990 election process suggests that the fundamental changes in Nicaraguan society are not in immediate jeopardy because they are now part of both the material and ideological conditions of people's everyday lives.

The period examined here ends with the 1990 elections: however, circumstances since then tend to confirm my conclusions. Several events in particular stand out. The first is Chamorro's retention of much of the FSLN bureaucracy, including Humberto Ortega as head of the armed forces. Although there has been speculation in the United States that this reflected some sort of deal, it is more plausible to credit the promise that Chamorro made all along: that her primary commitment was to the continuation of the revolutionary process.

This same commitment has fueled a split in the UNO coalition that has been present from the start. Essentially the division is between Chamorro and the technocrats whom she appointed to run the country on the one hand, and those who in fact did envision either rolling back some aspects of the social revolution (COSEP and others on the right) or reshaping it in their image (the old-time PSN and PCdeN politicians) on the other. These groups control the majority of the UNO's assembly seats and have rallied around Vice President Godoy.[156]

The Godoy supporters charge that Chamorro is "protecting" the revolution and have even alleged that she is a closet Sandinista. As proof they cite several of her actions, including her settling two major strikes by agreeing to defend the gains of the revolution, her failure to integrate the contras into the armed forces and the police, and her moves to stop the UNO mayor of Managua from removing the symbols of the revolution.

Moreover, there is the issue of the retention of not only most of the former government's employees but also the attendant policies.

Ironically, the FSLN pragmatists have been Chamorro's most significant supporters and the key to the implementation of her government's programs. Their view is that Chamorro and her technocrats share a commitment to the revolution and that by working with them, they will assure the continuation of the revolution. Popular speculation is that the FSLN pragmatists and Chamorro's wing of the UNO, which have been successfully cooperating in the National Assembly, will form a new coalition to run in the 1996 elections.

Nicaraguan society today looks unlike anything Sandino, Fonseca, or even those "ragged heroes" of 1979 anticipated. This is in large part because each failed to recognize the dialectical relationship that exists between those who seek to rule in the name of the people and the people in whose name they seek to rule. This relationship constructs the new society and therefore sets the stage for consolidation. Although this relationship does not fit neatly with Leninist theory, it is, perhaps, the point at which the vanguard, having accomplished its historical task of guiding the population to social revolution, withers away.

The consolidation of the social revolution represents a permanent mark on every facet of society. Institutionalization can be undone (as in Bolivia) or stifling (as in Mexico). But the success of consolidation means that, even in the face of setbacks, nothing reverts to what it was before. The tenets of the revolution become central to the society. A change of government would not, could not, signify a return to the past. It is for this reason that a case like Cuba's—consolidation with no institutionalization—remains an open issue.

The day after the elections, Dora María Téllez, the Nicaraguan minister of health and one of the heroes of the revolution, told a reporter that "if all we did was to make Nicaragua into a nation, that was still the most extraordinary thing we could have achieved."[157] The contention here is that the FSLN did far more than that. It showed a brutalized and disenfranchised population the limitless possibilities inherent in the social revolutionary promise and worked with them to make some of those possibilities real.

It would be disingenuous to look at the circumstances in which the vast majority of Nicaraguans find themselves today and claim complete success for the Nicaraguan revolution. It is too early to tell whether the Nicaraguan revolution is fully consolidated; as was made clear in Chapter 1, only time will tell. The fact, however, that the central item of debate in the 1990 election was who would best be able to realize the promises of the 1979 revolution is a powerful indicator that the consolidation process remains well under way.

■

## CHAPTER FIVE

# Bringing People Back In: Exploring Revolutionary Processes

I will begin this chapter by reviewing the theoretical approach advocated in this book. In particular, I will reemphasize some of what may be gained by the use of consolidation as a distinct analytic tool, concentrating on the roles played by individuals and their ideas, ideals, and learning in the social revolutionary process and the continuing puzzle presented by change. Then I will consider the practical utility of the approach: how useful the concepts of institutionalization and consolidation are for investigating other phenomena related to transition and transformation, especially transitions to socialism and revolutions in progress.  □

## THE THEORETICAL THEMES

In light of the theory I proposed and the cases I analyzed, what insights into theorizing about the social revolutionary process have I offered? Three merit mention here: first, the need to reincorporate individuals as conscious, intentional, powerful actors; second, the need to recognize that ideas carry weight and that they carry across time and state boundaries; and third, that change remains an enigma, rarely understood and always open to interpretation.

### Individuals

The historical world, that is, the world's past as we understand it, is fundamentally the world of human action. Structures are significant; there seems little question that they can serve to constrain people's choices and actions. Whereas the interaction between people's conscious and intentional actions and structures defines the limits of decision and action, it is primarily the actions of people that define the possibilities of action. Thus people hold the key to moving beyond the largely structural and in some cases deterministic explanations that characterize most social science theorizing about sociopolitical change.

Social scientists, in their efforts to understand and explain the world, have tended to marginalize individuals or omit them altogether. Institutions and structures, although they undeniably acquire a momentum, an existence that at times may appear to be their own, are constructions, artifacts created and populated by people. Yet the exploration of the role played by individuals is absent from most social science theorizing about change and revolution. The central assumption has been that people do not "make" revolutions; rather, because of the configurations of structures or the confluence of classes or other social groups, revolutions "happen." Never, in the view of those social scientists, has a revolutionary movement, mass movement, or vanguard party created a revolutionary situation that brought it to political power. The situation, instead, is structural, and the behavior of people or groups can be understood only in those terms.

This is a serious mistake. Such a perspective ignores the fact that people's thoughts and actions—however haphazard or spontaneous—are the mediating link between structural conditions and social outcomes. Structural conditions, moreover, do not unconditionally dictate what people do; instead, they place certain limits on people's actions or demarcate a certain range of possibilities. Within the revolutionary process, there is more than one potential outcome. Structural conditions may define the possibilities for revolutionary insurrections or the options available after political power has been seized, but they do not explain how specific groups or individuals act, what options they pursue, or what possibilities they may realize.

There is thus a significant omission in the social science literature on revolutions in general and social revolutions in particular: people. At the same time, it seems increasingly apparent that revolutions are human creations rather than inevitable natural processes—revolution, as Dunn pointed out, is fundamentally an actor's concept.[1] Therefore, one should invoke theories that can take agents and structures, both with meaningful roles, into account. However, it seems ironic that the most dramatic and purposive of human actions has been reduced to an essentially structural process, with people consigned to little more than functional, robotic roles. I argue that there are two moments when the critical role of individuals is discernible in the social revolutionary process. Leaders play a unique role in the social revolution, organizing the population and, perhaps most important, articulating the vision—the ideas and ideals—around which they rally. The core of consolidation is the population's response to these efforts, the degree to which the individuals who constitute the broader population accept the efforts of the leaders and shape them to their reality. I argue that we need to refocus the discussion of profound change or transformation on the power and possibility of individuals to control their destiny.

## Ideas, Ideals, and Learning

Besides recognizing the power and purpose of people, social science theorists should evaluate the power and promise of ideas and ideals by studying the manner in which social revolutionary leaders invoke, manipulate, and build on timeless conceptions to arouse and mobilize the population. The ideals of justice, liberty, equality, democracy, opportunity, and freedom (from fear, from hunger, from disease; of assembly, of speech, of religion) remain powerful and compelling in a world where many people's daily lives reflect none of these. These ideals become, in a very real sense, the touchstone of the revolution, and they carry the revolutionaries and the population through the arduous struggle. Idea streams, historically connected, transcendent ideas, are powerful, pervasive, and timeless.

This is not to ignore the fact that in practice many, perhaps most, of the ideals may be betrayed once political victory has been achieved. Historically, the achievement of political victory has not been sufficient to guarantee that the visions of the revolutionaries or the population—which are not necessarily, in fact, may rarely be, the same—will be realized. Nonetheless, slogans predicated on trust, opportunity, and a vision of the future abound and reflect the prowess of ideas and ideals.

Ideas—transmitted via people—travel across time and space. Moreover, people learn, taking into account past experiences and factoring in new information. Although it would be disingenuous to suggest that social revolutions somehow constitute an unbroken process, it is evident that modern revolutions have to some degree imitated (or, as Dunn suggested, attempted to imitate) the "classic" revolutions of France, Russia, Mexico, and China. Beyond these historical connections between earlier and later revolutions, there are strong historical and current connections among the modern revolutions. Both types of connections are discernible in the modern Latin American revolutions considered here. The revolutionaries in Bolivia looked back explicitly to Mexico; Cuban revolutionaries drew on a wide array of sources, including their own struggle for independence, Mexico, Sandino in Nicaragua, the incomplete revolution in Bolivia, even the destruction of democracy in Spain (1936–1939) and Guatemala (1954);[2] Nicaraguan revolutionaries were inspired and influenced by Mexico, their own past, and the Cubans. The Grenadians drew on the Eastern Caribbean's anticolonial and socialist legacy, the Cubans, the contemporaneous Nicaraguan revolution, and the various socialist experiments in Guyana, Jamaica, and Suriname. The connections are across time and within time, across cultural bounds and within them. The transmission of revolutionary ideas, ideals, and learning merits far more attention than it has received in traditional approaches to the study of revolution.

## Change

It is impossible to gauge with any precision the ramifications or implications of change as it unfolds. The relevance of the myriad facets of change is variable, and some factors may not make their presence felt for years. Moreover, change differs in degree from level to level, from the life of an individual to the status of the international system. It is in some sense an enormous continuum, perhaps even a Möbius strip: one seamless, infinite process in which the medium is ideas and the currency is learning. Only time and distance make possible plausible efforts to assess societal change comprehensively. Even then, the perspective invoked will inevitably color the picture painted.

Finally, a note of warning. The exploration of the processes of institutionalization and consolidation serves as a powerful reminder that change is no panacea. This does not mean people should accept or tolerate bad situations; in many such cases, almost any change, any action, is better than inaction. Rather, it reflects the recognition that however easy it may be to discuss change in the abstract, in the practical world it is an intricate, perplexing, and protracted process. Despite the dramatic visions and promises inherent in the social revolutionary process, the pace of change (particularly after the most easily resolved issues are dealt with) may not be dramatic. This is the sentiment captured in Castro's comment cited in Chapter 4, that despite the understandable assumptions and presumable intentions of both the revolutionaries and the population, what political victory obtains is the *opportunity* for people to change their world for the better: Change is neither automatic nor inevitable. In many cases social revolutions have simply replaced the dominance of the traditional elite with an equally powerful and pervasive bureaucratic party elite. The profoundly voluntaristic nature of social revolutions means that the process is often marked by the flaws of their creators; brutality, corruption, and incompetence all may be present in varying degrees. But there are tangible and extraordinary differences that cannot and should not be ignored.

## The Practical Contribution

Although the distinction between institutionalization and consolidation is subtle, it is significant. An important contribution can be made by

treating consolidation as a distinct concept and pairing it with institutionalization as dual analytical lenses. None of the points made in this
chapter regarding the importance of individuals, the power of ideas and
their circulation, and the multifarious and enigmatic character of change
are new; in fact they have been around for as long as people have wres-
tled with notions of metamorphoses of various types. By focusing on
consolidation we are reminded of the importance of such issues and
forced, despite their difficult nature as concepts, to include them in discussions of change, especially social revolutionary change, that purport
to offer a plausible scenario of the processes that are involved.   □

## THE PRACTICAL UTILITY

The analytical lenses of institutionalization and consolidation bring
into focus and render problematic previously undervalued or omitted
facets of the social revolutionary process. Having proposed a new set of
tools with which to think about social revolutionary processes, I used
those tools to analyze the four modern Latin American revolutions. An
obvious question, however, is whether such a perspective has any utility
beyond the study of social revolutionary processes. What advantages
might this approach lend to the study of transitions to socialism, which
have traditionally been rendered in almost purely institutional terms?
Might such a perspective be useful in assessing revolutions that have not
yet achieved political victory? The next section begins with a recapitula-
tion of the revolutions explored earlier and is followed by brief discussions of how institutionalization and consolidation might be useful in
the investigations of transitions to socialism. In a final section I consider
the utility of my approach for assessing the revolutions in El Salvador
and Peru, which have not yet achieved political victory—at least as political victory is conventionally defined.

### The Latin American Revolutions Considered Here

We have considered four cases of modern Latin American revolutions:
Bolivia, Cuba, Nicaragua, and Grenada. I argued that the failure of the
Bolivian social revolutionary leadership to consolidate the social revolution is central to understanding the historical stature, or lack thereof, of
the Bolivian revolution. The failure to institutionalize the social revolution in Cuba leaves questions about the fate of Cuba after Castro, whereas the success of the consolidation process there helps explain the staying
power of the social revolutionary process and why the revolution in
some form will likely survive Castro's eventual demise. By considering
Grenada as a case in which neither institutionalization nor consolidation
occurred, I provided a framework that can encompass the clash between

revolutionary leaders (as well as the impact such conflict has on society) and the result of the alienation of the leadership from the population. Finally, the case of Nicaragua, in which I contend that both institutionalization and some degree of consolidation took place, helps explain the continuance of the social revolutionary process in the face of a variety of obstacles and the unprecedented electoral defeat of the revolutionary leadership.

## Transitions to Socialism in Latin America and the Caribbean

Nonrevolutionary transitions to socialism,[3] such as those in Chile (1970–1973), Guyana (1970–1985), Jamaica (1972–1980), and Suriname (1980–1983), lend themselves to institutional explanations for several reasons, two of which stand out. The first is that leaders in these countries faced trying to install new systems while the existing systems were still viable and various groups in society were battling for their control. The second is that the interaction between the states and the international system played a significant role. A focus on structures thus offers plausible and powerful explanations for the failure of socialism in those countries. Given that failure (as well as the apparent collapse of socialism in Eastern Europe, the former Soviet Union, and some of the African revolutions such as Angola and Mozambique), one may ask whether transitions to socialism remain a fruitful reference point for social science investigations.

The structural, or perhaps, more narrowly, institutional, response to this would seem to be no. Yet a consideration of these same four cases from the perspective of consolidation suggests otherwise. In practice, Latin American socialism has never been akin to the doctrinaire socialism that existed in Eastern Europe or the Soviet Union; typical descriptions have ranged from "tropical socialism" to "seat of the pants socialism" to "bourgeois-democratic socialism."[4] In fact, socialism in Chile and Jamaica was largely marked by the attention to the social concerns of the population and the redistribution of wealth; in both cases the democratic electoral systems that brought the socialists to office were scrupulously respected.[5] Thus socialism and democracy were profoundly linked.

Latin American socialism, in practice, may be best understood as an effort to provide the social component absent from U.S. conceptions of Western democracy, which has traditionally been focused on "respect for rights and the rule of law, freedom of speech, institutionalizing of electoral procedure and separation of powers, checks and balances, etc."[6] In Latin America the commitment to opportunity and a vision of the future retains great appeal, especially when contrasted to the "liberation" offered by market economies. The obligation to end poverty, feed people, and improve health and educational opportunities is inherent in the regional conception of socialism. This helps explain why the socialist legacy in Chile remains a vibrant element of the effort to reconstruct democracy despite the best efforts of the Pinochet dictatorship to eradicate memories of the socialists' short time in office.[7] It also helps explain why the Jamaicans returned the socialists to office in 1989.

The Jamaicans' reelection of Michael Manley, a vice president of the Socialist International, says a great deal about the continuing power and promise of the socialist vision. Although Manley has abandoned his high-profile if mild confrontations with the United States, which sought and got his ouster, and with the International Monetary Fund, he remains committed to the gains made and maintained through almost a decade of opposition rule. He explained to two scholars: "We sowed the seeds of social revolution. . . . We altered class relations. Household helpers now enter by the front door, and poor Jamaicans have an unconscious reflex assumption about their rights. The poor used to say 'Do I have rights?' Now they know they do, and he who has rights forgets the time when he didn't have them."[8] This indicates consolidation as it has been defined here. The focus rendered via consolidation helps to explain why socialism continues to appeal to many people in Latin America and the Caribbean.[9]

### Modern Latin American Revolutions-in-Progress: El Salvador and Peru

The focus on institutionalization and consolidation, particularly the latter, is integrally tied to what I have described as the third and final phase of the social revolutionary process: the effort to fundamentally transform society once the revolutionaries have achieved political victory. The processes that are central to this effort (to institutionalize and consolidate the revolution) are also rooted in and related to those that predate the political victory. Nevertheless, there is an important distinction to be drawn between the period prior to political victory and in the one that follows it. For example, prior to political victory, revolutionary leaders concentrate on garnering support for the revolutionary organization rather than for the revolutionary process; after political victory, the leaders' failure to move beyond the organization to develop support for the process is likely to doom that process. This suggests that the concept of consolidation draws attention to the vital role of the mobilization of the population. One implication of this focus is that consolidation should prove a valuable conceptual tool for inquiring into revolutionary processes that have not yet achieved political victory (the transition of sovereignty to the revolutionary leadership).

Although considerably fewer than during the 1960s and 1970s, a variety of revolutionary movements remain throughout Latin America and the Caribbean. The two with the highest profiles, in fact, the only two in the past ten years considered viable contenders for power in their respective countries, have been El Salvador's Farabundo Martí National Liberation Front (FMLN) and the Peruvian Communist party (PCP or PCP-SL), popularly known as Sendero Luminoso (the Shining Path).[10] Similarities between the two are, however, limited. The FMLN and its political wing, the Revolutionary Democratic Front (FDR), are the latest in the line of modern Latin American revolutionary movements distinguished by broad-based, multi-class coalitions. Perhaps as a result, the FMLN has become the first such organization to reach an accommodation with the very government it was trying to overthrow. Sendero Luminoso, in contrast, is substantially different from the four cases considered here. Rather than seeking accommodation with the government—or even with potentially like-minded allies—Sendero has chosen the route of "purifying violence," in a total war against all.

Can institutionalization and consolidation, and particularly the notion of consolidation, offer insight into either of these processes—which have yet to achieve political victory? In other words, what might these concepts tell us about revolutionary processes such as El Salvador's, quiescent at this writing, or Peru's, which at this writing seems to be on the verge of new extremes of struggle?

### El Salvador: A Second-Generation Revolution
### Reaches an Accommodation

The revolutionary process in El Salvador has attracted a great deal of attention from scholars since the early 1980s.[11] There would seem to be two primary reasons for this. The first is the role played by the United States, whose involvement in El Salvador has been its most overt, extensive, and long-lasting intervention in Latin America since the introduction of the Good Neighbor Policy in the 1930s. The second factor seems to have been the massive, systematic violence employed by the Salvadoran government against the population: In eleven years approximately 75,000 people were killed. According to Booth and Walker, "Virtually all objective observers blame at least 80 percent of these deaths" on the Salvadoran government and its affiliated death squads.[12] In early 1992, however, El Salvador's revolutionary movement and government reached an accord that ended the fighting and outlined a plan for the reintegration of the revolutionaries into the government and society.

The Salvadorans can trace their revolutionary struggle to the ill-fated indigenous and peasant uprisings of 1932, remembered as *la Matanza* (the Slaughter). More immediately, however, the revolutionary situation evolved in the early 1970s and was fueled by massive government terror and brutality; by 1979 the government was murdering over a thousand people a month.[13] In late 1979 there was an allegedly "reformist" civil-military coup d'état. Within the next year some of the moderate and leftist civil and popular organizations banded together as the Revolutionary Democratic Front (FDR), and the country's five guerrilla groups of various Marxist stripes united as the Farabundo Martí National Liberation Front (FMLN); shortly thereafter, these two groups fused into one organization, the FMLN-FDR, with a political wing (FDR) and a military wing (FMLN). The FMLN-FDR received international recognition as a legitimate opposition force.[14]

The FMLN-FDR thus resembles the other social revolutionary movements we have been assessing. It is most similar to the FSLN in Nicaragua, but clear and meaningful comparisons can also be made with Bolivia's MNR, M-26-7 in Cuba, and the NJM in Grenada.[15] What all share, albeit to varying degrees, is a broad-based, multiclass character conducive to coalition politics. Moreover, the FMLN-FDR has linkages to the Mexican revolution and to figures such as Sandino, whom Martí briefly joined in Nicaragua, as well as strong bonds with both the Cubans and the Nicaraguans. The FMLN-FDR situates itself, according to one observer, "in the democratic revolutionary tradition of the Western Hemisphere, which encompasses such diverse experiences as the American, Mexican, and Cuban revolutions, as well as myriad 'liberal' or nationalist revolutions and guerrilla movements over the past two hundred years."[16]

Just as the Cuban revolutionaries had, the FMLN-FDR was able to control significant parts of El Salvador; at times as much as a third of the country was "liberated territory." In these areas, the FMLN-FDR effectively operated as a government seeking to introduce its social revolutionary project. During the decade-long struggle, the FMLN-FDR established schools, hospitals, a justice system, social welfare programs, and accountable local governments. Partially reflecting these accomplishments, the FMLN-FDR by the mid-1980s had shifted from a more radical project focused on nationalization, economic planning, and agrarian reform to one of meeting socioeconomic needs, demanding respect for human rights, and renewing notions of Salvadoran nationalism.[17] The impressive degree of institutionalization that occurred within the FMLN-FDR–dominated areas indicates that some degree of consolidation was reached. Despite its best military and political efforts, however, the FMLN-FDR was unable to establish itself beyond its rural strongholds.

Between 1981 and 1989 the FMLN-FDR launched several "final offensives," substantial military efforts intended to oust the Salvadoran government; they did not result in the military defeat of the government or the demise of the FMLN-FDR.[18] A stalemate lingered while talks between the government and the FMLN-FDR sputtered off and on between 1984 and 1989. When the FMLN-FDR's 1989 offensive highlighted the continuing political-military impasse, the talks were pursued with a new intensity; they culminated in the 1992 agreement on a wide-ranging plan that brought an end to the war and laid the groundwork for the "reincorporation" of the revolutionaries into "civilian, political, and institutional life."[19]

Like the Nicaraguan elections, the Salvadoran peace accords raise the question of where this leaves the revolutionary process. The glib response is that the revolution is over. Yet that is not entirely clear. The revolutionaries were not militarily defeated and were able to negotiate a political and social accord with the government as equals. Although the primary focus of the accord was on the military and the security forces, implicit in the agreement reached was acceptance of some core elements of the revolutionary project. FMLN leader Shafik Handal pointed out that there was a basic agreement on "socioeconomic matters," including such critical issues as "the just distribution of land, the elimination of huge farms, the financing of farm credits, the expropriation of haciendas and farms which are larger than 245 hectares [an area larger than 500 football fields]."[20] Some observers cautioned that these represent only minor socioeconomic reforms, but most observers agreed that they nonetheless signal the beginning of a new process.[21] It is thus plausible to argue that the FMLN-FDR, despite its failing to achieve a political victory analogous to the four cases considered here, did achieve some degree of consolidation. Of course, we must construe consolidation somewhat differently than we have been, positing consolidation as predicated upon political victory. At the same time, the concept of consolidation draws attention to the attitudes of and the role played by people, two useful components for explaining the unprecedented negotiated resolution of revolutionary conflict in El Salvador.

The success of the FMLN-FDR in presenting its revolutionary project to the population and convincing people to embrace it served it well in bringing the government to the negotiating table. If core elements of the revolutionary project are integrated into El Salvador's social, political, military, and economic structures as well, it is not implausible to argue that the revolutionary process, in some sense, continues. This is even more the case if, as has been suggested, the Salvadoran government respects the institutions and structures that the FMLN-FDR created and maintained in the country's "liberated territories." It is far too soon to say with any certainty that the war in El Salvador is over; at the same time, recent events suggest that revolutionary organizations similar to the FMLN-FDR may achieve political victories of a different sort and consolidate the process in new ways. A "negotiated revolution," saving "a lot of blood, a lot of human lives, and a lot of destruction" is a compelling and powerful concept.[22]

## Peru: A New Generation of Revolution in the Andes?

The Peruvian Communist Party–Shining Path (PCP-SL), commonly referred to as Sendero Luminoso (the Shining Path), made its first public appearance in 1980.[23] In the twelve years since, academics and other observers have struggled to understand and explain Sendero Luminoso. There are, however, some areas of consensus, chief among them that it is unlike any other revolutionary movement witnessed in Latin America. Particularly notable have been Sendero's disdain for either allies or compromise and its enshrinement of violence.

If interpretations of Sendero Luminoso are somewhat controversial, its history is well documented: The outlines are reasonably clear, and the imminent translation of works by leading Peruvian scholars will further enhance our knowledge.[24] Sendero originated out of a series of splits within the Peruvian Communist party between 1964 and 1970. Under the leadership of Abimael Guzmán, a philosophy professor from one of Peru's regional universities, the Senderistas spent the 1970s developing and refining their perspective and their plans. Peruvian anthropologist Carlos Iván Degregori, one of the leading scholars of Sendero, pointed out that this strategy was the opposite of what most of the Peruvian Left were doing at the same time. The result of Sendero's inward turn and isolation was "ideological rigidity and organic cohesiveness, until it became a sort of dwarf star—the kind in which matter gets so compressed it acquires a specific weight, disproportionate to its size."[25] In 1980, as Peru returned to democracy, Sendero Luminoso emerged publicly to denounce the election. Since then, Sendero has managed to control parts of rural Peru, black out the capital of Lima at will, and maintain its relatively isolated status—it seems to have made no more than the occasional, transitory alliance in order to reach a particular objective and continues to brutally attack all those not affiliated with it.

Sendero Luminoso's antipathy for allies—internal or external—does not fit with the cases considered here: Even the closet Stalinists in Grenada's NJM sought allies and forged alliances. Sendero's only connection to Peru's rich revolutionary heritage (which ranges from Túpac Amaru in the sixteenth century, Túpac Amaru II in the eighteenth century, Víctor Haya de la Torre's American Popular Alliance party in the 1920s, 1930s, and 1940s, Hugo Blanco in the 1960s, and even the first years of the late 1960s revolutionary military government) is its vague invocation of the founder of the Peruvian Communist party, José Carlos

Mariátegui.[26] Sendero has brutally attacked all of Peru's progressive forces as well as the other major—and more traditionally Latin American—revolutionary movement.[27] A recent spate of particularly brutal murders of progressive leaders of the poor illustrates their consistent determination to leave no middle ground in Sendero's drive to heighten the contradictions.[28] Scholars and observers concurred that Sendero forges alliances only with those that it can control; as a result it has at times made strategic choices to reach its objectives.[29]

If Sendero Luminoso's internal linkages are few, its external connections are nonexistent. According to Henry Dietz, a leading Sendero scholar in the United States, Sendero receives "virtually nothing from outside sources. . . . Moreover, this absence of material support is by intent."[30] Some of Sendero's earliest public activities (in 1980–1981) included attacks on the Soviet, Chinese, Cuban, and Nicaraguan embassies in Lima.[31] In its perception, the Soviets had betrayed the people's interests and the Chinese were "capitalist-imperialist dogs," in part, the Sendero claimed, because Mao failed to go far enough with the Cultural Revolution.[32] Other Latin American revolutionaries, notably the Cubans and the FSLN in Nicaragua, have been "excoriated . . . as 'petty bourgeois reformists.'"[33] Castro is a "traitor," simply a "revisionist servant of the United States," and Guevara was a "chorus girl."[34] The failure of the Nicaraguans as revolutionaries was most evident in their willingness to turn over power after losing the 1990 election.[35]

There are a few external reference points that Sendero Luminoso both invokes and evokes: One is Mao's Cultural Revolution, although Sendero's reverence for it is tempered.[36] The other common reference point is "the specter of Cambodia's Pol Pot and the Khmer Rouge.[37] In both cases, the ideas that were appropriated connect violence with success. In spite of Latin America's long tradition of revolutionary activity, the discussions of Sendero Luminoso do not cite to the region's old quasi-revolutionary movements, the broad-based, multiclass Latin American revolutionary movements considered here, or even the region's narrower, more violent urban revolutionaries of the 1960s and 1970s. According to Gustavo Gorriti, another of Peru's premier "Senderologists," Sendero is "wholly unrelated to other Latin rebellions."[38] Moreover, he contended that "in Latin America's violent milieu, the Shining Path insurgency stands out."[39]

Along with its self-imposed isolation, perhaps the defining characteristic of Sendero Luminoso is its glorification of violence. This is where Sendero relates most directly to the Khmer Rouge and Mao's Cultural Revolution; for that matter, it is perhaps where they have a connection to the French revolution, in which terror became an instrument of the revolutionary process. Sendero has, according to Degregori, "maximized and lionized violence"; another observer contended that its message "is that terror, not broad support" will bring power.[40] Peruvian researcher Nelson Manrique concurred, adding that what "matters is not so much that adversaries are being eliminated in ever increasing numbers, but how the killing is done—with fury and an orgy of extreme cruelty."[41] Sendero's favorite words, according to Americas Watch, "are *destroy, eradicate, erase,* and *dismantle*"; Americas Watch concluded that there "can be no question that murder of the defenseless, often in grotesque fashion, is Sendero policy."[42] In the estimation of Sendero's leader, Guzmán, "Violence is a universal law ... without revolutionary violence, one class cannot be substituted for another, an old order cannot be overthrown to create a new one."[43] As a result, Starn argued, for the Senderistas, to "kill is to contribute to the forging of 'La Nueva Democracia.' To die is to become a martyr."[44]

Sendero Luminoso has been able to control parts of Peru, including some of the shantytowns around Lima, and is particularly strong in its home base in the department of Ayacucho. In the areas that Sendero does control or influence, there has been some attempt to institutionalize a system of government. Gorriti described Sendero control as reflecting its policies in "communal affairs, including education, security, and taxes."[45] Sendero's control, however, is ultimately predicated on a brutal system of justice, often summarily carried out according to its precepts.[46] There has been no real effort to "win the hearts and minds" of the population, except perhaps through terror against those Sendero has determined are the "enemies" of the population—increasingly often people who seek to organize and lead the population in the struggle for their rights. Sendero appears to believe in the salutary effect of heightened contradictions and immersion in the revolutionary struggle. It has made no discernible attempts to create trust or develop a sense of opportunity; the vision of the future it offers is vague, perhaps intentionally so:[47] Empowerment is attainable only through the party. Consolidation, to the degree that any effort has been made at it, appears to be rooted in a brutal application of revolutionary justice that grows out of Sendero's defining theory, the power, promise, and purification inherent in violence.

In some ways Peru's situation does resemble that of El Salvador. Sendero Luminoso's violence, for example, has not occurred in a vacuum. The Peruvian military has matched the Senderistas' brutality with brutality and far surpassed their record of killing. Most scholars and observers agreed that Peru's military are responsible for the deaths of most of the 20,000 people killed since 1980.[48] Another similarity with El Salvador is the apparent stalemate between the government and Sendero Luminoso. Unlike the case with El Salvador's FMLN-FDR, however, this has not prompted Sendero Luminoso to consider negotiations. If anything, the recent coup should strengthen Sendero's effort to "heighten the contradictions" of Peruvian society and bring the country further into crisis. This is also, therefore, a critical juncture for the revolutionary process. Having sought to bring Peru to crisis, Sendero finds its predictions confirmed by the coup; the destruction of democracy seems unlikely to halt the revolutionaries' activities and bodes ill for the future. Sendero Luminoso has made itself ubiquitous in Peruvian society—the working assumption is that it has infiltrated virtually every level of society.[49] Most observers believe that Sendero, at least as it is currently configured, cannot win, but they have little confidence that the government can defeat Sendero.[50] President Alberto Fujimori's early 1992 *autogolpe* (self-coup) has created a situation that makes destitute the state and legitimates Sendero Luminoso; one observer pointed out that the Peruvian constitution guarantees the population the "'right to rebel in defense of constitutional order' when the Constitution has been violated by government officials. The Shining Path will surely present Fujimori's suspension of the Constitution as an open invitation to do just that."[51]

### The Institutionalization and Consolidation of Revolutions-in-Progress

Institutionalization as it has been conceptualized here—rooted in the state structures—would of course have to be reconfigured to be of much use in analyzing revolutions-in-progress. Domínguez and Mitchell's work on the role of revolutionary parties suggested one approach that would likely prove fruitful; Wickham-Crowley's analysis of the rise and fall of what he referred to as "guerrilla governments" might be another.[52] There is undoubtedly some utility in considering institutionalization within territory controlled by revolutionaries, but it is unclear what is gained by doing so. Consolidation would also have to reconceptualized, but less dramatically so, and the payoff may be greater. If the relationship between the revolutionaries and the population is important—most revolutionaries see it as central—then a focus on the elements that I have proposed as constituting consolidation would seem extremely useful. The same factors that enable consolidation—trust, sense of opportunity, and a vision of the future, all undergirded with the perception of empowerment—should be useful in assessing the status of the revolutionary process prior to political victory.  □

### THE CONSOLIDATION OF SOCIAL REVOLUTION

The brief discussion in this chapter highlights the two most critical aspects of social revolution. The power of social revolution may lie in its promise of possibilities, but the reality lies in reconciliation and the adaptations necessary to keep the hope alive. The project of social revolution is to transform society and the individuals who constitute it, that is, to take people beyond politics so that they live the revolution. In practice such a program confronts very real limits. The economic and political vagaries of the international system, domestic pressures, even natural disasters, all combine to present the social revolution with a constant challenge.

As Robert Darnton suggested about the people of France at the time of the French revolution, the people in social revolutionary societies are not extraordinary: They are unexceptional people who find themselves in exceptional circumstances.[53] Determined to build a better life, they find the promises of the social revolution battered as the social revolutionary process unfolds. The immense majority of humanity live in fear for themselves and their children—fear of hunger, of disease, of ignorance, of abuse. As long as people are forced to live like this, they will seek both freedom from such a life and their dignity as human beings. The challenge thus becomes not only to reach the vision of the social revolutionary project but also to continue the process.

---
■
---

# Notes

## CHAPTER ONE

1. As quoted in M. Kimmel, *Revolution: A Sociological Interpretation* (Philadelphia: Temple University Press, 1990), p. 1.

2. J. Dunn, *Modern Revolutions*, 2d ed. (Cambridge: Cambridge University Press), p. xvi.

3. Kimmel, *Revolution*, p. 2. Revolutions, Kimmel suggested, "provide a lens through which to view the everyday organization of society" (p. 1).

4. Useful overviews include R. Aya, "Theories of Revolution Reconsidered," *Theory and Society*, vol. 8, no. 1 (1979), and J. Goldstone, "Theories of Revolution: The Third Generation," *World Politics*, vol. 23, no. 3 (1980).

5. J. Goldstone, "Introduction," in J. Goldstone, T. R. Gurr, and F. Moshiri, eds., *Revolutions of the Late Twentieth Century* (Boulder: Westview, 1991), p. 2.

6. The distinction between the two generations is one of the themes of the recent volume by Goldstone, Gurr, and Moshiri, *Revolutions of the Late Twentieth Century*. A. Knight, "Social Revolution: A Latin American Perspective," *Bulletin of Latin American Research*, vol. 9, no. 2 (1990), recently made a compelling argument that such "rigid and somewhat arbitrary" (p. 191) chronological (as well as geographical) distinctions are often misleading and should be "broken down" (p. 175). He contended that "the concepts of 'bourgeois' and 'socialist' revolutions still offer the best global categories for making sense of . . . revolutionary phenomena" (p. 183).

7. The most important of the studies that pose the question, What makes peasants revolutionary? (to borrow from T. Skocpol's review "What Makes Peasants Revolutionary?" *Comparative Politics*, vol. 14, no. 3, 1982), are E. Wolf, *Peasant Wars of the Twentieth Century* (New York: Harper and Row, 1969); J. Migdal, *Peasants, Politics, and Revolution: Pressures Toward Political and Social Change in the Third World* (Princeton: Princeton University Press, 1974); J. Paige, *Agrarian Revolution: Social Movements and Export Agriculture in the Underdeveloped World* (New York: Free Press, 1975); and J. Scott, *The Moral Economy of the Peasant* (New Haven: Yale University Press, 1976).

8. Although they are beyond the scope of this book, one might include here the revolutionary processes in Algeria, Vietnam, Cambodia, Angola, Guinea-Bissau/Cape Verde, Mozambique, and Iran.

9. Goldstone argued that as long as the focus is on processes (and, I suspect, structures), "the basic patterns of state breakdown, the nature of revolutionary contention, and the challenges of state building remain largely the same": J. Goldstone, "An Analytical Framework," in Goldstone, Gurr, and Moshiri, *Revolutions of the Late Twentieth Century*, p. 37.

10. Walker pointed out that "both revolutionaries and counterrevolutionaries learn from history and from each other. In the twentieth century, from the Mexican revolution through the Nicaraguan revolution, the tactics and strategies of both sides evolved considerably": T. Walker, "Introduction," in T. Walker, ed., *Revolution and Counterrevolution in Nicaragua* (Boulder: Westview, 1991), pp. 2–3. Not surprisingly, time takes its toll. The Bolivians, with the Mexican revolution relatively close, explicitly sought to emulate many aspects of the Mexican process, particularly the creation of a single, inclusive ruling party. The Cubans explicitly sought to avoid certain aspects of both the Mexican and Bolivian models, chiefly what they perceived as the inhibition of institutionalization. For the Nicaraguans and, even more, the (non-Latin) Grenadians, the Mexican and Bolivian revolutions stood more as distant reference points from which some lessons could be gleaned; in both processes the influence of the Cuban revolution was much greater.

11. Goldstone, "An Analytical Framework," p. 37, made a similar point and included "superpower competition" as a factor. Because France, Russia, and China all suffered to varying degrees from international intervention—rather substantial intervention in the Russian case—I find this a far less compelling distinction.

12. T. R. Gurr and J. Goldstone, "Comparisons and Policy Implications," in Goldstone, Gurr, and Moshiri, *Revolutions of the Late Twentieth Century*, p. 325. Most of the cases cited in note 8 happened in colonial settings. I find less compelling Gurr and Goldstone's contention that modern revolutionaries have been less concerned with "universal ideals" than their predecessors (ibid.).

13. Twenty years ago in the introduction to a special issue of *Comparative Politics* devoted to the study of revolution, Kochanek noted that "somehow the present social science literature has failed to capture the essence of revolution": S. Kochanek, "Perspectives on the Study of Revolution and Social Change," *Comparative Politics*, vol. 5, no. 3 (1973), p. 318. See also Knight, "Social Revolution," who argued that "statist" approaches do not "necessarily get to the heart of the revolutionary experience and outcome" (p. 176).

14. Probably the most notable exceptions to this have been Wolf, *Peasant Wars of the Twentieth Century*, and Scott, *The Moral Economy of the Peasant*, for whom people are clearly relevant. Wickham-Crowley recently suggested that Wolf, *Peasant Wars of the Twentieth Century*; Paige, *Agrarian Revolution;* and C. Tilly, *From Mobilization to Revolution* (New York: Random House, 1978), all agreed that "movements make revolutions": T. Wickham-Crowley, *Guerrillas and Revolution in Latin America: A Comparative Study of Insurgents and Regimes Since 1956* (Princeton: Princeton University Press, 1992), pp. 5–6. It is certainly the case that Paige and Tilly, who will be discussed here, provided space for people, particularly in contrast to structuralists represented by work such as T. Skocpol, *States and Social Revolution* (Cambridge: Cambridge University Press, 1979). The contention here, however, is that in both cases people remain at the mercy of what are understood here as structures.

15. See Hobsbawm, who argued that "comparative students of revolution in the past generation have concentrated their attention overwhelmingly on its causes and the circumstances determining its outbreak or success": E. Hobsbawm, "Revolution," in R. Porter and M. Teich, eds., *Revolution in History* (Cambridge: Cambridge University Press, 1986), p. 15.

16. As Wickham-Crowley pointed out to me, institutionalization has some broader implications in the social sciences. In sociology, for example, "it refers to the creation of 'worlds taken for granted,' with their accompanying values and norms, in the key institutional areas of family, religion, political life, economic life, etc." In political science,

however, the term *institutionalization* has largely become conflated with state-building and/or the maintenance of state structures. Since part of the argument here is that institutionalization and consolidation are profoundly and intimately related, this duality, or perhaps, possibility, is exactly the reason that I have chosen to use the word *institutionalization*.

17. This is not to deny the obvious profusion of concomitant unintended consequences as well.

18. Hobsbawm, "Revolution," p. 21. Such frameworks, for Hobsbawm, appeared to be institutionally based. Walker similarly argued that if revolutions are in fact to be revolutionary, they "must immediately embark on social programs designed to improve the human condition of the previously exploited majority. . . . Such programs are important not only for their intrinsic human impact but also because they provide opportunities for popular participation and tend to build a social base for the revolution": Walker, "Introduction," p. 4. As with Hobsbawm, however, the programs and legislation that Walker listed are largely institutional in character and objective.

19. Interview. León, Nicaragua (1989).

20. See also Knight, who suggested that a successful revolution is denoted by "substantial and irreversible socio-political change": Knight, "Social Revolution," p. 181.

21. M. I. Finley, "Revolution in Antiquity," in R. Porter and M. Teich, eds., *Revolution in History* (Cambridge: Cambridge University Press, 1986), p. 47.

22. Some feel the term has so lost its utility that social scientists should dispense with it entirely. Perhaps the strongest case made for this can be found in J. Walton, *Reluctant Rebels: Comparative Studies of Revolution and Underdevelopment* (New York: Columbia University Press, 1984).

23. Finley, "Revolution in Antiquity," p. 47.

24. R. Aya, "Popular Intervention in Revolutionary Situations," in C. Bright and S. Harding, eds., *Statemaking and Social Movements: Essays in History and Theory* (Ann Arbor: University of Michigan Press, 1984), p. 323. Aya prefaced this with a point similar to Finley's, noting that there is "no such thing" as a "correct" definition since "definitions are neither right nor wrong" (p. 322).

25. Goldstone, "Theories of Revolution." Goldstone considerd Paige, *Agrarian Revolution;* S. N. Eisenstadt, *Revolutions and the Transformation of Societies* (New York: Free Press, 1978); E. K. Trimberger, *Revolution from Above* (New Brunswick: Transaction, 1978); and Skocpol, *States and Social Revolution,* as the "third generation" theorists. I would add Goldstone himself to this list; see J. Goldstone, *Revolution and Rebellion in the Early Modern World* (Berkeley: University of California Press, 1991). A good brief overview of Goldstone's contribution is F. Moshiri, "Revolutionary Conflict Theory in an Evolutionary Perspective," in Goldstone, Gurr, and Moshiri, *Revolutions of the Late Twentieth Century,* pp. 29–35.

26. This "first generation," according to Goldstone, "Theories of Revolution," p. 425, includes P. Sorokin, *The Sociology of Revolution* (Philadelphia: Lippincott, 1925); L. Edwards, *The Natural History of Revolution* (Chicago: University of Chicago Press, 1927); G. Pettee, *The Process of Revolution* (New York: Harper, 1938); and C. Brinton, *Anatomy of Revolution* (New York: Vintage, 1965).

27. The "second generation" theorists listed by Goldstone, "Theories of Revolution," p. 425, include J. Davies, "Toward a Theory of Revolution," *American Sociological Review,* vol. 27, no. 1 (1962); C. Johnson, *Revolutionary Change* (Boston: Little, Brown, 1966); S. Huntington, *Political Order in Changing Societies* (New Haven: Yale University Press, 1968); T. R. Gurr, *Why Men Rebel* (Princeton: Princeton University Press, 1970); and Tilly, *From Mobilization to Revolution.*

28. Hobsbawm, "Revolution," p. 10.

29. Davies, "Toward a Theory of Revolution"; Gurr, *Why Men Rebel;* M. Rejai, *The Comparative Study of Revolutionary Strategy* (New York: McKay, 1977).

30. Brinton, *The Anatomy of Revolution;* Johnson, *Revolutionary Change.*

31. Goldstone, "Theories of Revolution," p. 426.

32. Skocpol, *States and Social Revolution.*

33. See also T. Boswell, "World Revolutions and Revolutions in the World System," in T. Boswell, ed., *Revolution in the World System* (New York: Greenwood, 1989), p. 5. Boswell suggested that "three theories dominate the literature on revolution: Marxist class analysis, relative deprivation, and resource mobilization." Relative deprivation theory, represented by the work of Davies, "Toward a Theory of Revolution," and Gurr, *Why Men Rebel,* is not considered here and has faded in prominence. Resource mobilization theory refers to the work of Tilly, *From Mobilization to Revolution,* which is called here the political conflict model.

34. Although I agree with Goldstone's placement of Tilly and Huntington with the second generation of theorists, their works remain important and highly influential reference points.

35. This brief overview benefited greatly from discussions with August Nimtz. For an excellent concise overview of Marx's thought, see A. Nimtz, "Marxism: An Interpretative Essay," in *The Oxford Companion to Politics of the World* (Oxford: Oxford University Press, 1992).

36. Dunn, *Modern Revolutions,* p. 9. See also Kimmel, *Revolution,* p. 16, where he invoked the contention of Marx scholar Robert Tucker that the concept of revolution is the "theoretical axis" of Marx's early work, "the master theme of Marx's thought." Kimmel was quoting R. Tucker, "The Marxian Revolutionary Idea," in C. Friedrich, ed., *Revolution* (New York: Atherton, 1966), pp. 218–219.

37. Skocpol, *States and Social Revolution,* p. 7.

38. K. Marx and F. Engels, "The Communist Manifesto," in R. Tucker, ed., *The Marx-Engels Reader,* 2d ed. (New York: Norton, 1978), p. 482. The entire quote reads: "Today the proletariat alone is a really revolutionary class. The other classes decay and finally disappear in the face of modern industry. The proletariat is its special and essential product. The lower middle class, the small manufacturer, the shopkeeper, the artisan, the peasant, all these fight against the bourgeoisie to save from extinction their existence as fractions of the middle class—they are therefore not revolutionary, but conservative. Nay more, they are reactionary, for they try to roll back the wheel of history."

39. K. Marx, "The Eighteenth Brumaire of Louis Bonaparte," in Tucker, *The Marx-Engels Reader,* p. 595.

40. Tilly, *From Mobilization to Revolution.* Kimmel, *Revolution,* pp. 206–215, took this a step further and argued that Tilly in fact provided a synthesis of agency and structure.

41. Tilly, *From Mobilization to Revolution,* p. 84. See also C. Tilly, "Revolutions and Collective Violence," in F. Greenstein and N. Polsby, eds., *The Handbook of Political Science* (Reading: Addison-Wesley, 1975), pp. 506–508.

42. Tilly, "Revolutions and Collective Violence," p. 508.

43. In fact, Tilly warned of the problems posed in analyzing collective action because "people vary continuously from intensive involvement to passive compliance, interests vary from quite individual to nearly universal": Tilly, *From Mobilization to Revolution,* p. 7. Although Tilly argued that "real people do not get together to Act Collectively" (p. 143), it seems clear that real people make real choices in the real world.

44. Ibid., p. 191. "Revolutionary situations" are distinguished by "multiple sovereignty" where the government is in competition with competing blocs for "control of a single sovereign polity" (ibid.).

45. Tilly, *From Mobilization to Revolution*, p. 193. A "revolutionary outcome" occurs "when a single sovereign polity regains control over the government" (p. 191).

46. Tilly (ibid., p. 199), noted that "extremely revolutionary situations do not necessarily produce extremely revolutionary outcomes." Lenin, seeking to explain why World War I was not sparking the anticipated revolutions, argued that there was no guarantee "that today's revolutionary situation . . . will produce a revolution": V. I. Lenin, "The Collapse of the Second International," *Collected Works*, vol. 21 (Moscow: Progress Publishers, 1964), p. 214. Dix similarly noted that "many revolutions are begun, but few are brought to fruition": R. Dix, "Why Revolutions Succeed and Fail," *Polity*, vol. 16, no. 3 (1984), p. 423.

47. Tilly, *From Mobilization to Revolution*, pp. 216–217.

48. Ibid., p. 192.

49. Kimmel, *Revolution*, p. 215.

50. A structural perspective, according to Skocpol, stresses "objective relationships and conflicts among variously situated groups and nations, rather than the interests, outlooks, or ideologies of particular actors in revolution": Skocpol, *States and Social Revolution*, p. 291.

51. Huntington, *Political Order in Changing Societies*, p. 266.

52. Ibid., p. 264.

53. See also Tilly, who argued that "Huntington's definition stresses *outcomes*, not the political process that leads to these outcomes": Tilly, *From Mobilization to Revolution*, p. 193.

54. Kimmel, *Revolution*, p. 65. Aya also invoked the volcano metaphor to describe the structuralists. See Aya, "Theories of Revolution Reconsidered," pp. 40, 49–50, and "Popular Intervention in Revolutionary Situations," pp. 323–325.

55. The failure of social scientists to construe revolutions as processes was noted as early as 1965 by H. Eckstein, "On the Etiology of Internal Wars," *History and Theory*, vol. 4, no. 2 (1965), pp. 136–137.

56. Skocpol, *States and Social Revolution*.

57. Ibid., p. 4.

58. Ibid., p. 5.

59. This is reiterated by the three stages of revolution that Skocpol identified: (1) the collapse of the old regime state; (2) the mass mobilization of the peasantry into class-based uprisings; and (3) the reconsolidation of state power by a new elite. Kimmel, *Revolution*, p. 185, however, suggested that Skocpol's formulation remains essentially tied to outcomes and lacks "process," which he defined as "how human beings actually make a revolution."

60. Skocpol's "three major principles of analysis" are a "non-voluntarist, structural perspective" on the causes and process of revolution; a "systematic reference to international structures and world-historical developments"; and a conception of states "as administrative and coercive organizations . . . that are potentially autonomous from (though conditioned by) socio-economic interests and structures": Skocpol, *States and Social Revolution*, p. 14.

61. Skocpol subsequently applied her methodology to modern social revolutions. In the article "Rentier State and Shi'a Islam in the Iranian Revolution," *Theory and Society*, vol. 11, no. 3 (1982), Skocpol specifically considered the case of Iran, which she suggested as an excellent test of her argument. In another article, "Social Revolutions and

Mass Military Mobilizations," *World Politics,* vol. 42, no. 2 (1988), Skocpol was concerned with mass military mobilization and included brief consideration of Bolivia, Cuba, Iran, Mexico, Nicaragua, and Iran. Finally, J. Goodwin and Skocpol dealt broadly with revolution in the Third World in "Explaining Revolutions in the Third World," *Politics and Society,* vol. 17, no. 4 (1989).

62. In one response, Skocpol contended that she had simply been "misunderstood" and "never meant to read intentional group action out of revolution": T. Skocpol, "Cultural Idioms and Political Ideologues in the Revolutionary Reconstruction of State Power: A Rejoinder to Sewell," *Journal of Modern History,* vol. 57, no. 1 (1985), pp. 86–87. Although her subsequent work on revolution has continued to be heavily structural, people have crept in. This is most apparent in Skocpol, "Social Revolutions and Mass Military Mobilizations," and Goodwin and Skocpol, "Explaining Revolutions in the Third World," where there is even a question posed about "how professional revolutionaries put together broadly based coalitions" (p. 493).

63. Kimmel, *Revolution,* p. 186.

64. See also Kimmel, who argued that Skocpol "systematically undervalues the role of ideology, political organization, and self-conscious social action": Kimmel, *Revolution,* p. 186.

65. Skocpol, *States and Social Revolution,* p. 17.

66. Kimmel, *Revolution,* p. 186.

67. Kimmel suggested that this problem might be remedied via the concept of "process," and invoked the work of Charles Tilly to do so (ibid., p. 185).

68. Greene noted that "when we talk about the mobilization for revolution of workers, peasants, or the middle class, we are talking about a small minority of activists within each of those categories": T. Greene, *Comparative Revolutionary Movements,* 3d ed. (Englewood Cliffs: Prentice-Hall, 1990), p. 75.

69. Trimberger, *Revolution from Above.* Skocpol, *States and Social Revolution,* pp. 100–104, described Japan's Meiji Restoration as a political revolution.

70. Walton, *Reluctant Rebels.* Walton believed that the term *revolution* had lost its utility for social scientists and proposed *revolt* in its place. I am inclined toward the view of Bell, who argued that "a revolt is a quite different matter, and a much less complex one. A revolt is narrower than a revolution": J. B. Bell, *On Revolt: Strategies of National Liberation* (Cambridge: Harvard University Press, 1976), p. 5.

71. M. Hagopian, *The Phenomena of Revolution* (New York: Dodd, Mead, 1974), p. 39.

72. Huntington, *Political Order in Changing Societies,* p. 264. Rebellions may, however, be precursors to revolutions. Persuasive evidence for this can be found, among other places, in Wolf, *Peasant Wars of the Twentieth Century.*

73. Skocpol, *States and Social Revolution,* p. 4.

74. Ibid., p. 5.

75. The relationship between which, Dunn pointed out, proves to be "contingent and elusive": Dunn, *Modern Revolutions,* p. xvi.

76. Although the insurrection emerges from the conditions that precede what is defined here as social revolution, I chose to begin with insurrection because it is a far more readily identifiable period than the one that precedes it.

77. Most definitions of revolution explicitly or implicitly suggest that decisive changes happen rather suddenly. Although there is indisputably an identifiable break when the revolutionaries take power from the "old regime," the transformative period is a lengthy process fraught with complexity and contradictions.

78. Kochanek, "Perspectives on the Study of Revolution and Social Change," p. 319.

79. R. Darnton, "What Was Revolutionary About the French Revolution?" *New York Review of Books,* vol. 35 (19 January 1989), p. 17.

80. H. Arendt, *On Revolution* (New York: Penguin, 1965), p. 28.

81. Ibid., p. 42.

82. See also J. Domínguez and C. Mitchell, "The Roads Not Taken: Institutionalization and Political Participation in Cuba and Bolivia," *Comparative Politics*, vol. 9, no. 2 (1977), p. 173. In their discussion of the institutionalization of revolutionary political parties in Bolivia and Cuba they defined institutionalization as "the process by which organizations and procedures acquire value and stability."

83. See Skocpol, *States and Social Revolution*, p. 29. Such a narrow definition of the state as a specifically political set of institutions is analytically useful. This definition makes it easier to explore the relationship between the state and other spheres, such as the economy or, in the case of this project, society.

84. An excellent source on the difference between majoritarian democracies such as the Westminster model predominant among the former (and current) British colonies in the Eastern Caribbean and consociational (or consensual) democracies such as Switzerland is A. Lijphart, *Democracies: Patterns of Majoritarian and Consensual Government in Twenty-One Countries* (New Haven: Yale University Press, 1984). Lijphart has also specifically considered the case of Grenada and other Eastern Caribbean states. See A. Lijphart, "Size, Pluralism and the Westminster Model of Democracy: Implications for the Eastern Caribbean," in J. Heine, ed., *A Revolution Aborted: The Lessons of Grenada* (Pittsburgh: University of Pittsburgh Press, 1990). Not everyone agreed that the British legacy is one of democracy. Kurlansky suggested that this is "one of the great British myths." The British, he argued, "did not bring democracy to their colonies. The colonial system was a plantocracy": M. Kurlansky, *A Continent of Islands: Searching for the Caribbean Destiny* (Reading: Addison-Wesley, 1992), p. 290.

85. J. Heine, "Introduction: *A Revolution Aborted*," in J. Heine, ed., *A Revolution Aborted: The Lessons of Grenada* (Pittsburgh: University of Pittsburgh Press, 1990), p. 8. Lijphart, "Size, Pluralism and the Westminster Model of Democracy," p. 321, pointed out that newer democracies lack not only strong democratic traditions but also strong informal constraints on government power. Without such restraints, he argued, "the Westminster model easily spells excesses of majority power and of *the power of popular leaders*" (ibid. [emphasis added]). The authority of some chief executives in the Eastern Caribbean has been greatly enhanced by the role they (or their fathers) played in leading their country to independence.

86. Heine, "Introduction: *A Revolution Aborted*," p. 8.

87. Ibid.

88. This was called to my attention by Leslie Anderson.

89. One can say that some form of institutionalization has occurred in Cuba, especially if one considers Fidel Castro an institution—which might not be as inappropriate as it sounds. See, for example, Habel, who referred to the "institution of Fidel": J. Habel, *Cuba: The Revolution in Peril* (London: Verso, 1991), p. 150.

90. This includes both the promotion of the "party line," that is, the government's version of reality, and the prevention of acts of violence and sabotage aimed at the revolution. These elements have made these committees "notorious" in the eyes of some who regard them as little more than propagandistic surveillance instruments. Most critics, however, will concede that they have served to bring a formerly distant and disinterested government into the neighborhoods and thereby have enabled the provision of previously unobtainable social and medical services and economic assistance.

91. By 1970 a number of other revolutionary institutions had come into their own, in terms of membership and activities, and the system of revolutionary instruction begun in 1960 was reaching fruition.

92. However, the CDRs served the Cubans well during the 1961 U.S.-sponsored invasion.

93. In the 1970s, perhaps because of the emergence of other institutions and a highly successful socialization process, the CDRs moved away from their innovative and progressive tradition and degenerated into little more than the administrative and vigilance organizations they are most commonly caricatured as.

94. In what amounted to a last-ditch effort to revitalize them, the CDSs were reconfigured into Community Development Committees (CDCs), under the leadership of revolutionary hero Omar Cabezas. According to Williams, Cabezas's "efforts to depoliticize the CDSs (including changing their name to Community Development Committees) revitalized and broadened participation": H. Williams, "The Social Programs," in Walker, *Revolution and Counterrevolution in Nicaragua,* p. 201. One of the best discussions of the transformation of the CDSs is P. La Ramée and E. Polakoff, "Transformation of the CDSs and the Breakdown of Grassroots Democracy in Revolutionary Nicaragua," *New Political Science,* no. 18/19 (1990). An excellent general discussion of the grass-roots organizations in Nicaragua as they move into the 1990s is L. Haugaard, "In and Out of Power: Dilemmas for Grassroots Organizing in Nicaragua," *Socialism and Democracy,* vol. 7, no. 3 (1991).

95. "Dialectical" here refers to the process in which a concept or its realization is preserved and fulfilled, that is, made complete, by its opposite.

96. The relationship between legitimacy and consolidation is relatively weak. (The two are equated by J. Domínguez, "Political Change: Central America, South America, and the Caribbean," in M. Weiner and S. Huntington, eds., *Understanding Development* [Boston: Little, Brown, 1987], p. 76). Legitimacy is generally used with specific reference to politics and the political system (see, e.g., M. Weiner, "Matching Peoples, Territories, and States: Post-Ottoman Irredentism in the Balkans and the Middle East," in D. Elazar, ed., *Governing Peoples and Territories* [Philadelphia: ISHI, 1982], p. 131) and is inherently about acceptance of the rules of the game (Skocpol, *States and Social Revolution,* p. 25). Consolidation, in contrast, refers more broadly to society and its varied aspects. Still, there may be some overlap. See, for example, Migdal's conceptualization of legitimacy as the popular acknowledgment of a particular social order (J. Migdal, "A Model of State-Society Relations," in H. Wiarda, ed., *New Directions in Comparative Politics* [Boulder: Westview Press, 1985], p. 50).

The relationship between consolidation and hegemony is more complex. It is impossible to do justice to the richness and complexity of hegemony in this brief space. Fundamentally, however, according to Gramsci's understanding—the most famous and common delineation—hegemony refers to the manner in which the bourgeoisie, the economically dominant class in a society, establishes and maintains its rule, that is, domination. See A. Gramsci, *Selections from the Prison Notebooks,* Q. Hoare and G. N. Smith, eds. (New York: International Publishers, 1971). There is a consensual element to this domination: Directions from the top are willingly followed by the rest of society. Dominance is maintained through pragmatic intellectual and moral leadership by those Gramsci referred to as "intellectuals," who play an organizational role in society, who formulate and constantly revise a lattice of institutions, social relations, and ideas, which convinces people to submit to conditions when it is not in their best interests to do so. Hegemony is ultimately about the manufacture of consent and the creation of accommodation by those who govern society.

Hegemony is commonly conceived of as intimately related to the cultural and intellectual spheres of society, areas critical to the process of consolidation. The push for hegemony undoubtedly contributes to the generation of a popular ideology, thereby assisting in the production of the more complex web of beliefs, behavior, and relations that constitutes the popular attitudes that people bring to their everyday lives and characterizes consolidation.

Conventional conceptualizations of hegemony ignore the extent to which "subordinate" classes can infiltrate the ideology of the dominant class; the focus is on consent and compliance (J. Scott, *Weapons of the Weak: Everyday Forms of Peasant Resistance* [New Haven: Yale University Press, 1985], p. 317). Some interpretations of Gramsci explore this, e.g., C. Mouffe, "Hegemony and Ideology in Gramsci," in C. Mouffe, ed., *Gramsci and Marxist Theory* (Boston: Routledge and Kegan Paul, 1979).

Consolidation, reflecting the multiclass character of most post–World War II revolutions, does not presume a dominant class. In addition, an integral assumption of consolidation is that the organization of society emerges from the confluence of the social revolutionary leadership and the population, which have made the revolution together. Whereas institutionalization may be imposed from the top down, consolidation cannot be. Hegemony may be consensual, but power resides at the top.

Overlap would be most evident in an argument such as that in D. Brown, "Sandinismo and the Problem of Democratic Hegemony," *Latin American Perspectives*, vol. 17, no. 2 (1990). Brown distinguished between "authoritarian hegemony," where power resides at the top, and "democratic hegemony," which "involves the construction of a new unity through the acceptance of various social groups' divergent interests" (p. 44). Brown's subsequent discussion of democratic hegemony in Nicaragua is compelling, indicating where hegemony and consolidation may overlap.

97. A. Stepan, *The State and Society: Peru in Comparative Perspective* (Princeton: Princeton University Press, 1978); C. Clapham, *Third World Politics* (Madison: University of Wisconsin Press, 1985); Domínguez, "Political Change: Central America, South America, and the Caribbean."

98. D. Levine, "Venezuela Since 1958: The Consolidation of Democracy," in J. Linz and A. Stepan, eds., *The Breakdown of Democratic Regimes: Latin America* (Baltimore: Johns Hopkins University Press, 1978); J. Linz, *The Breakdown of Democratic Regimes: Crisis, Breakdown and Equilibrium* (Baltimore: Johns Hopkins University Press, 1978); R. Kaufman, "Liberalism and Democracy in South America: Perspectives from the 1970s," in G. O'Donnell, P. C. Schmitter, and L. Whitehead, eds., *Transitions from Authoritarian Rule: Comparative Perspectives* (Baltimore: Johns Hopkins University Press, 1986); G. O'Donnell, P. Schmitter, and L. Whitehead, *Transitions from Authoritarian Rule: Prospects for Democracy* (Baltimore: Johns Hopkins University Press, 1986); S. Jonas, "Elections and Transition: The Nicaraguan and Guatemalan Cases," in J. Booth and M. Seligson, eds., *Elections and Democracy in Central America* (Chapel Hill: University of North Carolina Press, 1989); H.E. Sergio Lacayo, "Consolidating Democracy Under Fire," in J. M. Kirk and G. W. Schuyler, eds., *Central America: Democracy, Development, and Change* (New York: Praeger, 1989); J. Peeler, "Democracy and Elections in Central America: Autumn of the Oligarchs?" in Booth and Seligson, *Elections and Democracy in Central America.*

99. Probably the most important examples of this work can be found in R. Fagen, C. D. Deere, and J. L. Coraggio, eds., *Transition and Development: Problems of Third World Socialism* (New York: Monthly Review Press, 1986). See, in particular, J. L. Coraggio, "Economics and Politics in the Transition to Socialism: Reflections on the Nicaraguan Experience"; R. Fagen, "The Politics of Transition"; and P. Marchetti, "War, Popular Participation, and Transition to Socialism: The Case of Nicaragua." Another example is J. Petras and F. Fitzgerald, "Authoritarianism and Democracy in the Transition to Socialism," *Latin American Perspectives*, vol. 15, no. 1 (1988).

100. The tendency to simply equate institutionalization and consolidation is common. Stepan, for example, argued that institutionalization denotes, among other things,

"that a regime has consolidated the new political patterns of succession, control, and participation" (*The State and Society*, p. 292). In a similar vein, Clapham equated consolidation with the role played by political parties and administration and maintains that "much of the process . . . [represents] a return to the authoritarianism of colonial rule" (*Third World Politics*, pp. 66–68). Taking Clapham's perspective to its logical extreme, Lamounier directly defined institutionalization as consolidation. See B. Lamounier, "Brazil: Inequality Against Democracy," in L. Diamond, J. Linz, and S. M. Lipset, eds., *Democracy in Developing Countries*, Vol. 4: *Latin America* (Boulder: Lynne Rienner, 1989), p. 44. Initially, it would appear that Diamond, Linz, and Lipset took issue with such perspectives, suggesting that stability rests on both institutionalization and consolidation (p. xviii). Yet just a few pages later, Diamond and Linz proposed that the sole distinction between institutionalization and consolidation rests on the extension of suffrage to nonelites in the consolidation phase. (L. Diamond and J. Linz, "Introduction: Politics, Society and Democracy in Latin America," in Diamond, Linz, and Lipset, *Democracy in Developing Countries*, p. 8). This distinction echoes O'Donnell and Schmitter's contention that the "most visible and noisy manifestation" of consolidation occurs via the extension of the franchise. G. O'Donnell and P. C. Schmitter, *Transitions from Authoritarian Rule: Tentative Conclusions About Uncertain Democracies* (Baltimore: Johns Hopkins University Press, 1986), p. 43. O'Donnell and Schmitter did mention two other elements: "historic compromise" and discrete reforms. The former refers to bringing "long-excluded participants into partial governing responsibility"; the latter to such relatively low-level changes as "changes in the electoral code and party finance statutes; more effective voter registration; more equal legislative apportionment; more transparent public information acts; greater administrative decentralization; lower barriers to party formation and parliamentary representation; dissolution of corporatist monopolies and obligatory associations; easing of citizenship requirements; and so forth." In Latin America, to date, most efforts at "historic compromise" have in practice been inter- or even intra-elite pacts concerning the rules of the game, that is, institutionalization. The discrete reforms listed quite clearly fall in the arena that has been defined here as institutionalization. I agree with O'Donnell and Schmitter's assessment that, particularly as a package, these reforms can significantly promote democratization and are important as such. Here as well, to date, such discrete reforms represent negotiating points among and between elite groups in society. Consolidation, in all of these conceptualizations, is rooted in the expansion of voting rights among the population.

101. Further, the evidence suggests that few scholars have considered the implications of simply subsuming consolidation into institutionalization. For example, when pressed on consolidation as an independent concept, Schmitter argued that democracy should not be consolidated but rather simply chosen by the majority (P. Schmitter, public presentation, May 1988, University of Minnesota, Minneapolis). While allowing that consolidation may somehow reduce uncertainty (which corresponds in general terms with the position adopted here), he likened it to the Gramscian notion of "war of position" and tied it to the reemergence of structures. Because this reemergence revolves around labor codes, party codes, and so forth (à la Southern Europe), democratic consolidation is ultimately evident when internal regulations and external status are established. This perspective accords at least in part with the position that Whitehead has taken, suggesting that consolidation is substantively signified by the ability of the government to engage in external activities, such as the pursuit of foreign policy goals. See L. Whitehead, "International Aspects of Democratization," in O'Donnell, Schmittera, and Whitehead, *Transitions from Authoritarian Rule: Comparative Perspectives*, p. 18.

102. J. M. Maravell and J. Santamaría, "Political Change in Spain and the Prospects for Democracy," in G. O'Donnell, P. C. Schmitter, and L. Whitehead, eds., *Transitions*

*from Authoritarian Rule: Southern Europe* (Baltimore: Johns Hopkins University Press, 1986), p. 73.

103. Ibid., p. 89.

104. Ibid., p. 73.

105. A similar result occurs with one of the only explicit definitions of consolidation offered by a scholar of revolutions. Calvert divided revolutions into three stages: "preparation, action, and consolidation": Peter Calvert, *Revolution and International Politics* (New York: St. Martin's Press, 1984), p. 4. It is ironic, Calvert lamented, that "the key to the relationship between the act of a political revolution and the aspiration to social change" remains "the part of the revolutionary process most lacking in a theoretical framework." Perhaps equally ironic is that all the elements that, according to Calvert, produce consolidation across two stages are unquestionably institutional in character (pp. 22–23).

106. Fagen, "The Politics of Transition," pp. 251–252.

107. Ibid., p. 259. "Integrative" refers to people of diverse backgrounds and beliefs coming to see themselves as one. "Patriotism" refers to identification with the "patria" and connotes far more in Latin America than is commonly suggested by the term *patriotism* in North America.

108. Coraggio, "Economics and Politics in the Transition to Socialism," pp. 155–156.

109. Marchetti, "War, Popular Participation, and Transition to Socialism," pp. 309–310.

110. H. Vanden, "Ideology of the Nicaraguan Revolution," *Monthly Review*, vol. 34, no. 2 (1982).

111. C. Geertz, *The Interpretation of Cultures* (New York: Basic Books, 1973).

112. Interview. Léon, Nicaragua (1989).

113. Hobsbawm argued that revolutions cannot be said to "conclude" until they have either been overthrown or are sufficiently safe from overthrow. See E. Hobsbawm, "Revolution," in Porter and Teich, *Revolution in History*, pp. 23–24.

114. Ibid., p. 35.

115. Ibid.

116. M. Gabaldon, interview. Minneapolis, Minnesota (1989).

117. Hobsbawm, "Revolution," p. 32.

118. Ibid., p. 35.

119. Ibid.

120. Ibid.

121. Ibid., p. 33.

122. Ibid.

123. Hobsbawm (ibid., p. 12) argued that this nature of social revolutions as creative acts is true regardless of the causes or motives that make people act or the inevitable differences between their intentions and the results of their actions.

124. Besides Huntington, *Political Order in Changing Societies*, and Skocpol, *States and Social Revolution*, see S. Eckstein, "The Impact of Revolution on Social Welfare in Latin America," *Theory and Society*, vol. 11, no. 1 (1982); Eisenstadt, *Revolutions and the Transformation of Societies*; B. Moore, *Social Origins of Dictatorship and Democracy* (Boston: Beacon Press, 1966); and Trimberger, *Revolution from Above*.

125. See also Domínguez and Mitchell, "The Roads Not Taken," p. 174, where they argued "that a stress on institutionalization of a ruling revolutionary party will tend to lead to less mobilization. . . . Conversely, an emphasis on mobilization is likely to curb institutionalization." Domínguez and Mitchell's definition of mobilization as an increase in political participation and focused on social reorganization resonates with what I refer to as consolidation (pp. 173–174). Mobilization, for them, nonetheless, seems to remain an essentially structural phenomena.

126. This brief discussion draws on discussions with Alex Wendt. See also A. Wendt, "The Agent-Structure Problem in International Relations Theory," *International Organization*, vol. 41, no. 3 (1987).

127. It is also central to the thought of revolutionary thinkers such as Antonio Gramsci, José Carlos Mariátegui, and Ernesto "Ché" Guevara.

128. P. Anderson, *Arguments Within English Marxism* (London: Verso, 1980), p. 21.

129. A. Callinicos, *Making History: Agency, Structure and Change in Social Theory* (Ithaca: Cornell University Press, 1988), p. 10. One of the strongest statements for the role and importance of agency is E. P. Thompson, *The Poverty of Theory* (New York: Monthly Review Press, 1978).

130. J. DeNardo, *Power in Numbers* (Princeton: Princeton University Press, 1985); Tilly, *From Mobilization to Revolution*; Rejai, *The Comparative Study of Revolutionary Strategy*.

131. Skocpol, *States and Social Revolution*, p. 291.

132. Ibid.

133. Ibid., p. 287.

134. Ibid. In a later article, Skocpol recognized some difference between the processes in Bolivia and Cuba, most notably the different role played by the United States in the respective cases. Skocpol, "Social Revolutions and Mass Military Mobilizations."

135. Other perspectives on the difference between the two can be found in Domínguez and Mitchell, "The Roads Not Taken," where the focus is on the role of the revolutionary party, and Knight, "Social Revolution," where the focus is on the difference between "bourgeois" and "socialist" revolutions.

136. J. Malloy, "Revolutionary Politics," in J. Malloy and R. Thorn, eds., *Beyond the Revolution: Bolivia Since 1952* (Pittsburgh: University of Pittsburgh Press, 1971), p. 120.

## CHAPTER TWO

1. Not that such assistance is ever treated as unimportant or taken for granted. Only the population can furnish the vital supplies, recruits, and intelligence necessary for the revolutionaries to survive and succeed. The longer the battle, the more important such assistance becomes to offset the superiority of the government forces in resources and numbers.

2. I would be remiss not to comment on the use of the phrase "win their hearts and minds." Long identified with the endeavor of counterrevolution, according to Stubbs, the phrase was coined by British High Commissioner General Sir Gerald Templer during the 1948–1960 guerrilla war in Malaya (he is later said to have referred to it as "that nauseating phrase I think I invented"). See R. Stubbs, *Hearts and Minds in Guerrilla Warfare: The Malayan Emergency 1948–1960* (Oxford: Oxford University Press, 1989), p. 1. The revolutionaries made clear their belief that their victory would be tied to obtaining and maintaining popular support, and the British responded with the concept of WHAM, Winning the Hearts and Minds of the Masses. Although I am uncomfortable with the use of counterrevolutionary terminology to describe or discuss revolutionary behavior, the notion of "winning hearts and minds" can be a useful and simple shorthand for describing the consolidation process undertaken by the social revolutionaries.

3. H. Ortega, "Nicaragua—The Strategy of Political Victory," in T. Borge et al., *Sandinistas Speak* (New York: Pathfinder Press, 1982), p. 58.

4. This point has been made by, among others, V. I. Lenin, "The Collapse of the Second International," *Collected Works,* vol. 21 (Moscow: Progress Publishers, 1964), p. 214; C. Tilly, *From Mobilization to Revolution* (New York: Random House, 1978), p. 199; and

R. Dix, "Why Revolutions Succeed and Fail," *Polity*, vol. 16, no. 3 (1984), p. 423. For their specific quotes, see Chapter 1, note 44.

5. Dunkerley pointed out the paucity of books in English that consider the revolution "with more than passing reference" and noted that "even in Spanish [the revolution's] bibliography cannot compare with that of the revolutions in Mexico, Cuba, Nicaragua, or even El Salvador": J. Dunkerley, *Rebellion in the Veins: Political Struggle in Bolivia 1952–1982* (London: Verso, 1984), p. xiii. Notable exceptions have been J. Domínguez and C. Mitchell, "The Roads Not Taken: Institutionalization and Political Participation in Cuba and Bolivia," *Comparative Politics*, vol. 9, no. 2 (1977); A. Knight, "Social Revolution: A Latin American Perspective," *Bulletin of Latin American Research*, vol. 9, no. 2 (1990); and the excellent body of work by Susan Eckstein: "The Impact of Revolution on Social Welfare in Latin America," *Theory and Society*, vol. 11, no 1 (1982); "Transformation of a 'Revolution from Below': Bolivia and International Capital," *Comparative Studies in Society and History*, vol. 25, no. 1 (1983); "Revolution and Redistribution in Latin America," in C. McClintock and A. F. Lowenthal, eds., *The Peruvian Experiment Reconsidered* (Princeton: Princeton University Press, 1983); "Revolutions and the Restructuring of National Economies," *Comparative Politics*, vol. 17, no. 4 (1985).

6. Dunkerley, *Rebellion in the Veins*, p. xiii; J. Malloy and E. Gamarra, *Revolution and Reaction: Bolivia 1964–1985* (New Brunswick: Transaction Press, 1988), p. 2.

7. Dunkerley, described it as a "political revolution": Dunkerley, *Rebellion in the Veins*, p. xiii. Several scholars clearly considered Bolivia as a social revolution: S. Huntington, *Political Order in Changing Societies* (New Haven: Yale University Press, 1968), p. 275; J. Kelly and H. Klein, *Revolution and the Rebirth of Inequality: A Theory Applied to the National Revolution in Bolivia* (Berkeley: University of California Press, 1982), p. 3; T. Skocpol, *States and Social Revolution* (Cambridge: Cambridge University Press, 1979), p. 287; E. Hobsbawm, "Revolution," in R. Porter and M. Teich, *Revolution in History* (Cambridge: Cambridge University Press, 1986), p. 23; and Knight, "Social Revolution," p. 182. Huntington's subsequent description of Bolivia as a *failed* social revolution (*Political Order in Changing Societies*, pp. 326–334), however, is indicative of the standard interpretation. Most common are descriptions that focus on this failure, such as Malloy's phrase "uncomplete revolution" (J. Malloy, *Bolivia: The Uncompleted Revolution* [Pittsburgh: University of Pittsburgh Press, 1970]), or Hobsbawm, who argued that although "the Bolivian revolution of 1952 was undoubtedly a major and successful social revolution," it was "incomplete" because no "post-revolutionary force has been able to establish unquestioned control": Hobsbawm, "Revolution," p. 23. (What Hobsbawm referred to as "post-revolutionary" is, I suspect, what is referred to here as the post–political victory period.) Knight concurred, arguing that the "Bolivian revolution made for a fundamental transformation in Bolivian society, which subsequent regime changes did not and could not reverse." The revolution failed, he contended, because of the inability of the MNR to "maintain post-revolutionary hegemony": Knight, "Social Revolution," p. 182.

8. It is interesting that Huntington put primary blame for the revolution's deterioration on the failure to *institutionalize* the revolution, contrasting Bolivia's failure with Mexico's "success": Huntington, *Political Order in Changing Societies*, p. 326. Knight seemed in accord with this when he suggested that the failure in Bolivia was due to the inability of the MNR to "maintain post-revolutionary hegemony": Knight, "Social Revolution," p. 182.

9. The character of the MNR's 1941 program had distinct similarities to the Nazi's program in Germany, not the least of which was a virulent anti-Semitism. At the same time, the MNR's most immediate reference point was Argentine populist and crypto-fascist Juan Perón.

10. Domínguez and Mitchell, "The Roads Not Taken," p. 186.

11. It is probably a mistake to construe "military socialism" as a Bolivian variant of the Nazi's "national socialism." "Military socialism," according to Klein, was "essentially a populist and reformist administration to be led by the newly aware officer caste." The main civilian groups in the coalition, however, were "more closely tied to a modified fascist position": H. Klein, *Bolivia: Evolution of a Multi-Ethnic Society* (New York: Oxford University Press, 1982), p. 201.

12. Malloy, *Bolivia*, p. 162.

13. J. Malloy, "Revolutionary Politics," in J. Malloy and R. Thorn, eds., *Beyond the Revolution: Bolivia Since 1952* (Pittsburgh: University of Pittsburgh Press, 1971), p. 117. With reference to this platform, Malloy suggested that "a number of the original MNR leaders either viewed this program as tactical rhetoric or had limited conceptions as to what these measures would entail" (ibid.).

14. Ibid., p. 115.

15. For a succinct description of these events, see Dunkerley, *Rebellion in the Veins*, pp. 1–4.

16. Malloy opined that "it is more than coincidental that the revolutionary government did not draft a new constitution until 1961." The MNR government's claims to legitimacy, he contended, were built on the past. See Malloy, *Bolivia*, pp. 168–169.

17. There appears to be general agreement among scholars of Bolivia that the nationalization of the tin mines was, in Malloy's phrase, "not a socialistic measure": Malloy, "Revolutionary Politics," p. 121. See also the descriptions of the handling of tin mine nationalization in R. Thorn, "The Economic Transformation," in Malloy and Thorn, *Beyond the Revolution*, pp. 186–212; Klein, *Bolivia*, p. 233; and Dunkerley, *Rebellion in the Veins*, pp. 54–65.

18. Malloy, "Revolutionary Politics," p. 119.

19. The reasons for such hesitation, according to Malloy (ibid., pp. 124–125), were manifold. At base, he argued, "to threaten the agrarian structure was to threaten a complex system of values and a way of life traceable to colonial times" (p. 124). Moreover, "the issue of agrarian reform awakened fears that ran deep in Spanish-speaking Bolivia. The relationship between the Spanish-speaking culture and the suppressed Indian culture was pervaded with mutual hate, distrust and fear" (p. 125).

20. Klein pointed out that "however reluctant the new regime may have been to attack the hacienda problem seriously, the massive mobilization of the peasants, now the majority of the electorate, and the systematic destruction of the land tenure system forced the regime to act": Klein, *Bolivia*, p. 234.

21. Malloy, *Bolivia*, p. 209.

22. Klein, *Bolivia*, pp. 235–236. Although it is somewhat unusual in Latin America, governments in the developing world have often played on the innate conservatism of the rural population. Land reform has been used not only as a progovernment strategy but even as a counterrevolutionary tactic. See, in particular, A. McCoy, "Land Reform as Counter-Revolution: U.S. Foreign Policy and the Tenant Farmers of Asia," *Bulletin of Concerned Asian Scholars*, vol. 3, no. 1 (1971).

23. And, arguably, it was one that was consolidated: Agrarian reform seems to be the only revolutionary gain that survived. This raises the possibility that particular aspects of a revolutionary project may be consolidated. More likely, however, it reflects the transformation of the indigenous population into a bulwark against the revolutionary process, a status reflected in Roxborough's description of the Bolivian peasants as "beneficiaries and counterrevolutionaries": I. Roxborough, "Theories of Revolution: The Evidence From Latin America," *LSE Quarterly*, vol. 3, no. 2 (1989), p. 105. Some

scholars speculated that the success of agrarian reform in Bolivia contributed to Guevara's 1967 failure in creating a revolutionary situation.

24. To take but one example, Malloy cited the remark of Walter Guevara Arze, a major MNR leader, that the Bolivians set out "to make a Mexican Revolution, but without ten years of Pancho Villa": Malloy, *Bolivia*, p. 235. See also E. Gamarra and J. Malloy, "Bolivia: Revolution and Reaction," in H. Wiarda and H. Kline, eds., *Latin American Politics and Development*, 3d ed. (Boulder: Westview, 1990), p. 367.

25. Domínguez and Mitchell, "The Roads Not Taken," p. 193, n. 2, described the MNR as "complex and adaptable, relatively autonomous, but very seldom coherent."

26. Ibid., p. 192.

27. Malloy, *Bolivia*, p. 171.

28. This is one of the primary reasons that the Cuban revolution has been enshrined throughout much of the less developed world. As Wright pointed out, "The Cuban Revolution owes its vast influence in Latin America to the fact that . . . it embodied the aspirations and captured the imaginations of Latin America's masses as no other political movement had ever done": T. Wright, *Latin America in the Era of the Cuban Revolution* (New York: Praeger, 1991), p. xi.

29. Good brief overviews of Cuba's success in these areas can be found in M. Azicri, *Cuba: Politics, Economics, and Society* (London: Pinter, 1988), pp. 46–69; J. del Aguila, *Cuba: Dilemmas of a Revolution* (Boulder: Westview, 1988), pp. 80–86; or L. Pérez, Jr., *Cuba: Between Reform and Revolution* (New York: Oxford University Press, 1988), pp. 358–374. A recent example of those critical of the revolution who nonetheless acknowledged its success in social issues was R. Rabkin, *Cuban Politics: The Revolutionary Experiment* (New York: Praeger, 1991), pp. 53–55. She was also representative of such scholars in her admonishment that the improvements are not as dramatic as they appear because Cuba was one of Latin America's more developed countries at the time of political victory. Kirk provided an interesting counterpoint to this view, exploring how Cuba's social policies have fared vis-à-vis Venezuela—a roughly parallel case—over the same time. See J. Kirk, "Cuba at 30: How Fares the Revolution," *Canadian Dimension*, no. 7/8 (1989), pp. 13–15. In a purely critical review, Eberstadt complained that even critics of Cuba such as "President Reagan's Commerce Department" and the Organization of American States recognized Cuba's claims: "Irrespective of their political inclinations, it seems, the consensus of virtually all informed observers is that Cuba has made model progress against disease and ignorance, those two basic scourges of low-income nations": N. Eberstadt, "Did Fidel Fudge the Figures? Literacy and Health: The Cuban Model," *Caribbean Review*, vol. 15, no. 2 (1986), p. 5. Eberstadt contended that such views were "fundamentally unsound" (ibid.). Far more common, however, remain critiques that accept the successes in the social arena while decrying Cuba's domestic political structure. See, e.g., T. Szulc, "Fidelismo," *Wilson Quarterly*, vol. 12, no. 5 (1988), p. 57, or H. Thomas, G. Fauriol, and J. C. Weiss, *The Cuban Revolution, 25 Years Later* (Boulder: Westview, 1984), p. 56; the latter conceded in a highly critical assessment that it "would be churlish not to recognize some social changes in Cuba since 1959 which must be said to be positive. . . . Some Cuban medical and educational achievements have been quite impressive."

30. L. Pérez, Jr., *Cuba and the United States: Ties of Singular Intimacy* (Athens: University of Georgia Press, 1990), p. 239.

31. Ibid., p. 314.

32. R. Fagen, "Charismatic Authority and the Leadership of Fidel Castro," *Western Political Quarterly*, vol. 18 (1964), p. 282.

33. Pérez, *Cuba*, p. 238.

34. M. Halperin, *The Taming of Fidel Castro* (Berkeley: University of California Press, 1981), p. 87; W. LeoGrande, "Party Development in Revolutionary Cuba," *Journal of Interamerican Studies and World Affairs*, vol. 21, no. 4 (1979), p. 469. According to Halperin, who lived in Cuba from 1962–1968, Castro "set himself up as a model nonbureaucrat . . . he even appeared to be outside the government, and, like his listeners, a victim of its myriad of dull, parasitic, paper-pushing and paper-storing officials": Halperin, *The Taming of Fidel Castro*, p. 87. He cultivated the image that the revolution was "not the idiotic creatures who filled the ministries and messed everything up" (ibid.).

35. E. Guevara, *Venceremos: The Speeches and Writings of Che Guevara* (New York: Simon and Schuster, 1968), pp. 220–225.

36. "The Program Manifesto of the 26th of July Movement (November 1956)" had ten points: national sovereignty, economic independence, work for all, social justice, education for all, political democracy, civil authority, freedom of conscience, public morality, and constructive friendship with all countries. A copy in English can be found in R. Bonachea and N. Valdés, eds., *Cuba in Revolution* (New York: Anchor Books, 1972).

37. R. Fagen, "Continuities in Cuban Revolutionary Politics," *Monthly Review*, vol. 23, no. 11 (1972), p. 35.

38. On this point, see, e.g., ibid., pp. 26–27.

39. J. Habel, *Cuba: The Revolution in Peril* (London: Verso, 1991), p. 92.

40. J. P. Sartre, *Sartre on Cuba* (New York: Ballentine Books, 1961), pp. 122–127. There seems little question about the "direct" component. As LeoGrande pointed out: "In his travels, Castro gave the ordinary Cuban direct access to the center of governmental power—himself. He would often spend hours with small groups of people discussing local problems, ordering action to solve problems, or explaining why the problems were unsolvable": W. LeoGrande, "Mass Political Participation in Socialist Cuba," in J. Booth and M. Seligson, eds., *Political Participation in Latin America*, Vol. 1: *Citizen and State* (New York: Holmes and Meier, 1978), p. 118. The "democratic" component was less immediately obvious, although it referred at least in part to the accessibility of the leadership. This does not, as Rabkin emphasized, translate into accountability. In fact, Rabkin suggested that in practice "direct democracy" resembled the old paternalism of the *patrón* for his employees. Rabkin, *Cuban Politics*, p. 56. Although the imputation of such an atmosphere is plausible, at least as related by Sartre, these "employees" certainly do not appear to be constrained by the traditional bounds of such a relationship in their questions, statements, and demands.

41. M. Azicri, "Twenty-six Years of Cuban Revolutionary Politics: An Appraisal," in S. Jonas and N. Stein, eds., *Democracy in Latin America: Visions and Reality* (New York: Bergin and Garvey, 1990), p. 164.

42. Pérez, *Cuba: Between Reform and Revolution*, p. 319.

43. del Aguila, *Cuba*, p. 159.

44. By most accounts, Castro's closest advisers besides Guevara appear to have been his younger brother, Raúl, and Celia Sánchez.

45. Castro's turn to the PSP has been described by del Aguila, *Cuba*, p. 55, as "tactical." The PSP, according to Pérez, *Cuba: Between Reform and Revolution*, p. 323, was an organization of "singular discipline and preparation, with historic ties to mass organizations and political connections to the socialist bloc." Pérez quoted Castro to the effect that the PSP "had men who were truly revolutionary, loyal, honest, and trained. I needed them" (ibid.). This view was supported by others, e.g., LeoGrande, "Party Development in Revolutionary Cuba," p. 458; Rabkin, *Cuban Politics*, p. 48.

46. LeoGrande, "Party Development in Revolutionary Cuba," p. 462.

47. Ibid., p. 463.

48. The ORI/Escalante affair proved not to be unique. The tension between the old-line Communists of the PSP and Castro's guerrilla coterie has surfaced and resurfaced throughout the thirty-plus years of the revolutionary process, often around issues that reflected the tension between the PSPistas' desires to institutionalize the revolutionary process and the *fidelistas'* reaction against such efforts.

49. Cited in Azicri, *Cuba*, p. 39.

50. del Aguila, *Cuba*, p. 77. The "absence of mediating institutions or rules of political behavior," del Aguila argued, "reinforced Castro's special relationship with the masses" (p. 68). See also Pérez, *Cuba: Between Reform and Revolution*, p. 319.

51. LeoGrande, "Party Development in Revolutionary Cuba," p. 478; del Aguila, *Cuba*, p. 68.

52. del Aguila, *Cuba*, p. 74.

53. Halperin, *The Taming of Fidel Castro*, p. ix.

54. The former three goals were suggested by Rabkin, *Cuban Politics*, p. 67, the latter by Thomas, Fauriol, and Weiss, *The Cuban Revolution*, p. 16.

55. Excellent discussions of how such efforts at democratization have played out in Cuba in terms of democratic norms and procedures are C. Bengelsdorf, "The Matter of Democracy in Cuba: Snapshots of 3 Moments," in S. Halebsky and J. Kirk, eds., *Transformation and Struggle: Cuba Faces the 1990s* (New York: Praeger, 1990), and M. Pérez-Stable, "Socialism and Democracy: Some Thoughts After 30 Years of Revolution in Cuba," in Halebsky and Kirk, *Transformation and Struggle.*

56. The term *neo-institutional* here is borrowed from del Aguila, *Cuba*, p. 157, who used it to characterize Cuba in the 1980s. Azicri, "Twenty-six Years of Cuban Revolutionary Politics," p. 145, characterized this same period as "postinstitutional." The point about the country's institutions being brought in from the periphery is from LeoGrande, "Party Development in Revolutionary Cuba," p. 457.

57. Wayne Smith, Public presentation, Latin American Studies Spring Lecture Series, "Cuba Since the Revolution: An Assessment," University of Minnesota, Minneapolis (1987). See also W. Smith, "Commentary," in J. Suchlicki, ed., *Problems of Succession in Cuba* (Coral Gables: University of Miami, North-South Center for the Institute of Interamerican Studies, 1985), p. 82.

58. An excellent overview piece on the rectification process is M. Azicri, "The Cuban Rectification: Safeguarding the Revolution While Building the Future" in Halebsky and Kirk, *Transformation and Struggle.*

59. F. Castro, "Important Problems for the Whole of International Revolutionary Thought," *New International*, no. 6 (1987).

60. These anonymous Cuban politicians are cited in *Latin American Regional Report: Caribbean Report*, 7 November 1991 (RC–91–09).

61. Domínguez and Mitchell, "The Roads Not Taken," p. 176.

62. See also Bengelsdorf, "The Matter of Democracy in Cuba," p. 51. According to Martínez Heredia, a Cuban academic: "The process of rectification was initiated by Fidel Castro, and he has been the principal force and protagonist behind it. The question of leadership emerges clearly here. Fidel has fulfilled fundamental roles at every phase of the revolution. The great majority credit him for his role in its inception, the history of the process, the present-day society, and above all, the goals and plans to which it aspires. The people see in him the dialectic of their own power and the power of the revolution which is fundamental to their political life. As trustee of the spiritual unity of the country, it is natural that it would be Fidel who would denounce contradictions, make the harshest criticism of past mistakes, give direction to the rectifying course, and assure the fraternal relations of all those who support the revolutionary cause":

F. Martínez Heredia, "Cuban Socialism: Prospects and Challenge," *Latin American Perspectives,* vol. 18, no 2 (1991), p. 29. Martínez Heredia added that "by power of his vast moral authority, Fidel's leadership in the present process offers confidence in the permanent revolutionary principles, experienced leadership for directing tactics and strategy, expresses cohesion and unity, provides clarification and conscientiousness at a pedagogical level, and denounces the shortcomings of the people and the system" (p. 36, n. 1).

   63. Azicri, *Cuba,* p. 70.

   64. See also Habel, *Cuba,* p. 150), who referred to the "institution of Fidel." Castro would undoubtedly reject that such a thing was possible. He told one interviewer: "I am neither pragmatic nor dogmatic. I am dialectical. Nothing is permanent, everything changes" (cited in Habel, p. 107).

   65. FSLN–Secretariata Nacional de Propagada y Educacíon Politica, cited in D. Gilbert, *Sandinistas: The Party and the Revolution* (New York: Basil Blackwell, 1988), p. 37. Parenthetical term inserted by Gilbert.

   66. Many have catalogued the situation. Prevost, for example, described the destruction of the Somoza regime as "total: The National Guard collapsed, as did Somoza's ruling Liberal National party (PLI). . . . The task the . . . [FSLN] faced was enormous: the organization of an entirely new state and military apparatus": G. Prevost, "The FSLN as Ruling Party," in T. Walker, ed., *Revolution and Counterrevolution in Nicaragua* (Boulder: Westview, 1991), p. 107. See also A. Reding, "The Evolution of Governmental Institutions," in Walker, *Revolution and Counterrevolution in Nicaragua,* p. 15. Reding suggested that "popular revulsion" with Nicaragua's discredited and disgraced institutions was so intense that "even the buildings in which the institutions had been housed—most notably the National Palace—had to be converted to other uses" (ibid.). Reding also made an important point about the name of the new government: "The JGRN was commonly referred to as the *junta,* a term that in English has come to be associated with dictatorships by cliques of Latin American generals" (p. 23). The inspiration, Reding argued, was not the South American military *juntas,* but the "all-but-forgotten precedent in neighboring Costa Rica, where another civilian *junta* ruled for eighteen months in 1948–1949" (ibid.). This was in the aftermath of the Costa Rican civil war.

   67. There is a wealth of good material on the institutionalization process undertaken by Nicaragua's social revolutionary government in the post–political victory period. Especially useful are a number of the chapters in the volumes edited by T. Walker: *Nicaragua in Revolution* (New York: Praeger, 1982); *Nicaragua: The First Five Years* (New York: Praeger, 1985); *Revolution and Counterrevolution in Nicaragua;* in the latter, see in particular the chapter by Reding, "The Evolution of Governmental Institutions." Also helpful are J. Booth, *The End and the Beginning: The Nicaraguan Revolution,* 2d ed. (Boulder: Westview, 1985); Gilbert, *Sandinistas;* and T. Walker, *Nicaragua: The Land of Sandino,* 3d ed. (Boulder: Westview, 1991). Good brief overviews that discuss the post–political victory institutionalization process include J. Booth and T. Walker, *Understanding Central America* (Boulder: Westview, 1989), pp. 66–70; D. Grynspan, "Nicaragua: A New Model for Popular Revolution in Latin America," in J. Goldstone, T. R. Gurr, and F. Moshiri, eds., *Revolutions of the Late Twentieth Century* (Boulder: Westview, 1991); S. Jonas, "Elections and Transition: The Nicaraguan and Guatemalan Cases," in J. Booth and M. Seligson, eds., *Elections and Democracy in Central America* (Chapel Hill: University of North Carolina Press, 1989); and S. Jonas and N. Stein, "The Construction of Democracy in Nicaragua," *Latin American Perspectives,* vol. 17, no. 3 (1990).

   68. A transcript of one such *"Cara al Pueblo"* can be found in M. Dixon, ed., *Nicaragua Under Siege* (San Francisco: Synthesis, 1985), pp. 157–168. In practice, Serra pointed

out, such exercises had their liabilities: "Though complaints and demands that the authorities resolve existing problems abounded, there was frequently a lack of follow-up on the accords and promises made at the meetings": L. Serra, "The Grass-Roots Organizations," in Walker, *Revolution and Counterrevolution in Nicaragua*, p. 52. Beyond such assemblies, Serra noted, there were also media outlets, specifically radio shows and letters columns in the newspapers.

69. Reding noted that "for the first time in the history of major social revolutions, the ancien régime was spared violent retribution": Reding, "The Evolution of Governmental Institutions," p. 18. For more on the FSLN's notion of retribution, see the discussion on Tomás Borge in Chapter 3. The only significant government crackdown after political victory was on some of the radicals who had fought alongside the FSLN during the final struggle and considered the new economic, political, and justice systems as abandonment of the social revolutionary project they had envisioned during the insurrection. The Marxist-Leninist Popular Action Movement (MAP-ML) was the only other organized group to take part in the fighting during the final struggle. According to LASA, the MAP-ML leaders "were jailed by the Sandinistas in 1980 when they pressed too hard for an acceleration of the revolutionary process": LASA, "The Electoral Process in Nicaragua: Domestic and International Influences," Report of the Latin American Studies Association Delegation to Observe the Nicaraguan General Election of November 4, 1984 (Austin: LASA, 1984), p. 9. According to Black, members of the Workers Front (who may have been connected to MAP-ML) and the Communist Party of Nicaragua (PCdeN) were also jailed. See G. Black, *Triumph of the People: The Sandinista Revolution in Nicaragua* (London: Zed, 1981), p. 234.

70. Actually, the first post–political victory elections, according to LASA, were the local elections for the Municipal Governments of Reconstruction in 1979 shortly after political victory. See LASA, "Electoral Democracy Under International Pressure," Report of the Latin America Studies Association Commission to Observe the 1990 Election (Pittsburgh: LASA, 1990), p. 13. Booth and Walker also made note of these local elections in *Understanding Central America*, p. 67. T. Wickham-Crowley pointed out that there were a number of "contested elections" in the nineteenth and early twentieth century, albeit with "severely restricted franchise."

71. In 1990 the number of these observers was unprecedented. For more on the views of the observers, see note 102 below.

72. There are those who disagree that these events are unique. T. Wickham-Crowley noted that in 1893 there was a peaceful transfer of power from the Conservatives to the Liberals. Pastor, however, argued that "on November 4 1928, the United States supervised the first 'free' Presidential election in Nicaraguan history. . . . On January 1, 1929, for the first and only time in Nicaraguan history, power was transferred peacefully": R. Pastor, *Condemned to Repetition: The United States and Nicaragua* (Princeton: Princeton University Press, 1987), p. 25. This received some support from LASA, which stated that "the presidential elections of 1928 and 1932, *organized and supervised by the United States*, are generally accepted as having been free of fraudulent vote counting" (emphasis added): LASA, "The Electoral Process in Nicaragua," p. 4. LASA pointed out, however, that the leading candidate was not permitted to run, that there had been an almost constant U.S. occupation since 1912, and that a U.S. Marine was posted at every polling place (ibid.). I concur with Theodore Wright, whom Pastor cited in a note to his claim. Wright contended elections cannot be construed as "free" when supervised by what Pastor disingenuously referred to as a "a foreign military presence" (Pastor, *Condemned to Repetition*, p. 326, n. 31). Most people, I believe, would agree that the over 5,000 U.S. Marines, supported by eleven cruisers and destroyers that oversaw this election and transfer of power were by any reasonable definition an occupation force.

73. Prerevolutionary Nicaragua, Close argued, "knew neither liberal democracy nor even constitutional government": D. Close, *Nicaragua: Politics, Economics, and Society* (London: Pinter, 1988), p. 107. Stahler-Sholk pointed out that "formal institutions of democracy had lost their substantive meaning under the Somoza regime, as constitutions were rewritten and elections manipulated to legitimize the dictatorship": R. Stahler-Sholk, "Building Democracy in Nicaragua," in G. Lopez and M. Sthol, eds., *Liberalization and Redemocratization in Latin America* (New York: Greenwood, 1987), p. 61. To the degree that there may have been a tradition of electoral democracy, LASA described it as "thin and discredited." LASA, "Electoral Democracy Under International Pressure," p. 7.

74. LASA, "Electoral Democracy Under International Pressure," p. 7. Somoza's cynical manipulation of elections staged for his benefactors in the United States was hardly original but simply followed in the footsteps of those who had preceded him, his older brother Luis and their father, Anastasio Somoza García. Elections, for most Nicaraguans, according to LASA, "meant little more than automatic ratification of candidates chosen by the incumbent party and the U.S. government": LASA, "The Electoral Process in Nicaragua," p. 4.

75. The novelist Graham Greene, in his book about Panama's General Omar Torrijos, noted that "Somoza had frequently called elections and, thus, had legitimized his dictatorship, if only in the eyes of the United States, by winning all of them with huge majorities. So 'election' for most people in the crowd was a word which meant trickery. 'No election' was a promise to them of no trickery": G. Greene, *Getting to Know the General* (New York: Simon and Schuster, 1984), p. 187. Although most Nicaraguans may have been wary of any promises of elections, some Nicaraguans were calling for them. Pedro Joaquín Chamorro's Democratic Union of Liberation (UDEL)—a multiclass coalition of workers, small business people, and traditional elites—demanded free elections when it was formed in 1974. The UDEL collapsed in the wake of Chamorro's 1978 assassination, widely attributed to Somoza and his cronies. The assassination was a key event—perhaps the catalyst—in setting the stage for the final popular insurrection against the Somoza regime. Chamorro was enshrined as a "Hero and Martyr of the Revolution." Current president Violeta Chamorro was married to him.

76. "The Historic Program of the FSLN," first released in 1969, does not mention elections per se. However, the first section of the document, which outlines the formation of the revolutionary government, lists as its first measure of political character the creation of a political structure "that allows the full participation of the entire people, on the national as well as the local level (departmental, municipal, neighborhood)": FSLN, "The Historic Program of the FSLN," in Borge et al., *Sandinistas Speak*, p. 14. The FSLN's perspective on democracy and commitment to the development of a democratic framework evolved into a commitment to political pluralism that Jonas and Stein argued was related to four factors: (1) the FSLN's desire to overcome Nicaragua's lack of democratic traditions; (2) the pluralistic nature of the FSLN itself; (3) the ideological pluralism that has undergirded the social revolution; and (4) the FSLN's interest in maintaining a broad-based, multiclass coalition. See Jonas and Stein, "The Construction of Democracy in Nicaragua," pp. 13–14.

77. W. LeoGrande, "Who Lost Nicaragua? Was the Left Wrong About Nicaragua?" *Tikkun*, vol. 5, no. 3 (1990), p. 15.

78. L. Serra, "The Sandinista Mass Organizations," in Walker, *Nicaragua in Revolution*, p. 96.

79. Nicaraguan sociologist Marvin Ortega, cited in B. Wright, "Pluralism and Vanguardism in the Nicaraguan Revolution," *Latin American Perspectives*, vol. 17, no. 3 (1990), p. 42.

80. J. L. Coraggio, "Economics and Politics in the Transition to Socialism: Reflections on the Nicaraguan Experience," in R. Fagen, C. D. Deere, and J. L. Coraggio, eds., *Transition and Development: Problems of Third World Socialism* (New York: Monthly Review, 1986), p. 97. Bayardo Arce, one of the leaders of perhaps the most radical faction, the Prolonged Popular War tendency (GPP), and the FSLN party director (1979–1990), defined the "four principles" of the FSLN's project as "a mixed economy, political pluralism, genuine nonalignment, and participatory democracy." IHCA (Central American Historical Institution), "Toward a New Constitution," *envío*, vol. 4, no. 53 (November 1985). Miguel D'Escoto, former foreign minister (1979–1990) and a Maryknoll priest, identified with the moderate Terceristas, identified "four fundamental pillars" of Sandinista thought: nationalism, democratic aspiration, the Christian element, and aspiration to social justice. See M. D'Escoto, "Nicaragua: Unfinished Canvas," *Sojourners*, March 1983. Jaime Wheelock, former minister of agriculture (1979–1990) and one of the leaders of the Proletarian tendency, argued that from the start, the FSLN had "included in our program a call for elections, and we maintain this position": J. Wheelock, *El gran desafío: entrevista por Marta Harnecker* (Managua: Editorial Nueva Nicaragua, 1983), p. 78.

81. On 20 July 1979, the Junta of the Government of National Reconstruction (JGRN) promulgated the "Fundamental Statute of the Republic of Nicaragua," which, along with the "Fundamental Statute on the Rights and Guarantees of the Nicaraguan People," issued a month later, served as Nicaragua's constitution until 1987. According to the "Fundamental Statute of the Republic of Nicaragua" (FBIS-LAM 1979, p. 11), "as soon as conditions of national reconstruction permit, general elections will be held for the National Assembly . . . in conformity with the new electoral law, which will be promulgated in due time." This commitment was strengthened by the previously mentioned 1979 elections held for the local Municipal Governments of Reconstruction.

82. For an excellent brief discussion of this viewpoint among the FSLN leadership, see Gilbert, *Sandinistas*, pp. 34–36. Other good reviews of Sandinista attitudes toward democracy are Jonas and Stein, "The Construction of Democracy in Nicaragua"; Wright, "Pluralism and Vanguardism in the Nicaraguan Revolution"; and Reding, "The Evolution of Governmental Institutions."

83. H. Ortega, "FSLN: Statement on the Electoral Process," in R. Leiken and B. Rubin, eds., *The Central American Crisis Reader* (New York: Summit Books, 1987), p. 227.

84. Booth and Walker pointed out that despite the (at least initial) scorn of national elections, which had been used in the past to legitimize the old dictatorship, local elections were held throughout the country immediately after the political victory. See Booth and Walker, *Understanding Central America*, p. 67.

85. This is evident in a series of speeches collected in B. Marcus, ed., *Nicaragua: The Sandinista People's Revolution: Speeches by Sandinista Leaders* (New York: Pathfinder, 1985). See, in particular, T. Borge, "This Is a Revolution of the Working People," p. 173; S. Ramírez, "Our Promises Were Made to the Poorest of Our Country," p. 191; and D. Ortega, "We Are a Very Small Country Confronting a Truly Colossal Force," p. 196, and "The Sandinista People's Revolution Is an Irreversible Political Reality," p. 210.

86. According to Reding, Carlos Tunnerman, Nicaragua's former ambassador to the United States, explained that Nicaragua wanted to adopt Western ideas about pluralism and the electoral system with socialism's idea that wealth must be spread around. See A. Reding, "Under Construction: Nicaragua's New Polity," in P. Rosset and J. Vandermeer, eds., *Nicaragua: Unfinished Revolution* (New York: Grove, 1986), p. 346. This view was echoed by Carlos Fernando Chamorro, editor of the FSLN newspaper *Barricada*, who noted that "if we have a mixed economy, we must have a political system that corresponds to that; we want to institutionalize dissent and opposition" (J. Lobel, "The

Meaning of Democracy: Representative and Participatory Democracy in the New Nicaraguan Constitution," *University of Pittsburgh Law Review*, vol. 49, no. 3 [1988], p. 84,
cited in Jonas and Stein, "The Construction of Democracy in Nicaragua," p. 14). According to former foreign minister Miguel D'Escoto, the FSLN's commitment was not
just to pro forma democracy: "We are talking about real participation. We are quite
aware that democracy entails social democracy, economic democracy, political democracy, and many rights, such as the right to work, to a family wage, to learn, to read, to
write—all those different rights that provide us with an opportunity to participate and
not be manipulated": D'Escoto, "Nicaragua: Unfinished Canvas." As Humberto Ortega
had before him, D'Escoto's argument made it clear that democracy would be defined by
more than elections.

87. Pastor, *Condemned to Repetition*, p. 307.

88. Ibid.

89. The Council of State was Nicaragua's interim legislative body. It had an FSLN
majority but included opposition parties and representatives of social groups. For more
on this and the other branches of the JGRN, see Booth, *The End and the Beginning*, pp.
29–43.

90. LASA, "The Electoral Process in Nicaragua," p. i. Specifically, according to
LASA, it was modeled after "key components of the French, Italian, Austrian, and
Swedish electoral systems" (p. 29).

91. Ibid., p. 12.

92. Beyond its legislative powers, the National Assembly was also directed to draft
a new constitution for the country. In its function as constitutional convention, the assembly was designated to define its own powers as well as those of the executive
branch.

93. This information, as well as that which follows, was drawn from LASA, "The
Electoral Process in Nicaragua," pp. 12–13. The assembly elections would be based on a
proportional representation model. The country was divided into nine multimember
geographical districts, with the number of delegates per region apportioned by population. Rather than voting for individuals, voters would choose a predetermined, party-
specific slate of candidates whose position on the slate was set by the party. According
to LASA, this was "likely to strengthen internal control and discipline within all the existing political parties." Given the tradition in most of Latin America of political parties
serving as little more than vehicles for personal ambition, this was presumably aimed at
creating parties not solely built on one individual. The choice of proportional representation was widely interpreted as a commitment to encourage pluralism; LASA, for
example, stressed that the kind of proportional representation system chosen "tilts
the National Assembly toward political pluralism, by assuring the representation of a
wider range of interest and opinions within the electorate than would be achieved under a U.S. style single-member district system" (p. 12). Others saw it as a ploy to frag-
ment the opposition. The election was to be overseen by the Supreme Electoral Council
(CSE). The CSE was assigned the tasks of establishing the voter registry and setting the
electoral calendar, both to be carried out in consultation with the National Council of
Political Parties, composed of one representative from each of the legally recognized
parties, and charged with overseeing the election campaigns and conducting the actual
balloting. The CSE was given the status of a fourth, autonomous branch of government
with the authority to make decisions free of governmental influence.

94. R. Gutman, *Banana Republic: The Making of American Policy in Nicaragua 1981–
1987* (New York: Simon and Schuster, 1988), p. 239; H. Sklar, *Washington's War on Nicaragua* (Boston: South End, 1988), p. 192.

95. At the center of these efforts in the United States was the Office of Public Diplomacy for Latin America and the Caribbean. Specific efforts included pamphlets prepared for selected members of the media and Congress, the manipulation of the media via nongovernment foreign policy experts, and putting pressure on U.S. allies, foreign labor leaders, and foreign journalists to condemn the elections. See R. Borosage and P. Kornbluh, "Behind Reagan's Propaganda Blitz," *Nation,* 13 April 1985. The short-lived Office of Public Diplomacy (1983–1987) was a true Washington hybrid. Authorized by President Reagan in National Security Directive 77 (NSDD 77), "Management of Public Diplomacy Relative to National Security," the Office of Public Diplomacy was run by the National Security Council (NSC), housed in the State Department, and staffed by the Defense Department, the Agency for International Development (AID), and the U.S. Information Agency (USIA). See P. Kornbluh, "Nicaragua," in P. Schraeder, ed., *Intervention in the 1980s: U.S. Foreign Policy in the Third World* (Boulder: Lynne Rienner, 1989), p. 245; Sklar, *Washington's War on Nicaragua,* p. 245. The Orwellian term *public diplomacy* referred to the Reagan administration's decision to conduct psychological warfare operations *in the United States,* the type of operation, according to one senior U.S. official, "the military conducts to influence a population in a denied or enemy territory" (ibid.). Priority was placed on "overt and covert propaganda, pressure on the media, and illegal lobbying tactics to manipulate public opinion" (Kornbluh, "Nicaragua," p. 246). A 1987 General Accounting Office investigation concluded that the Office of Public Diplomacy had sought to manipulate both the media and the public primarily through the planting of stories in the press and the ghost writing of "op-ed" pieces (p. 246; Sklar, *Washington's War on Nicaragua,* p. 247). Based on the violation of the restriction that bars the use of federal funds for publicity or propaganda purposes not authorized by the Congress, the U.S. Congress ordered the Office of Public Diplomacy for Latin America and the Caribbean shut in 1987.

96. Cruz first became affiliated with the FSLN when he left the Inter-American Development Bank to become a member of *Los Doce,* the Group of Twelve. The Group of Twelve was composed of prominent business people, lawyers, priests, and educators who in October 1977 announced their opposition to Somoza and support for the FSLN. Immediately after political victory Cruz was named president of the Central Bank. Later he served briefly in the JGRN and after that as Nicaragua's ambassador to the United States. Upon leaving that post, he returned to the Inter-American Development Bank. The CD coalition was a varied but conservative group centered around the Superior Council of Private Enterprise (COSEP), a very conservative national business organization. Nominated at the instigation of the United States, Cruz returned to Nicaragua and promptly announced that he would abstain from the elections unless the government complied with the CD's previously released "nine points" (LASA, "The Electoral Process in Nicaragua," p. 19). In December 1983 the CD had published nine points that they characterized as requirements for "authentic elections." See Democratic Coordinator, "Election Program," in Leiken and Rubin, *The Central American Crisis Reader,* pp. 284–288. The government accepted all the demands related to the election itself—abolition of press censorship, access to state-owned mass media, and suspension of the emergency restrictions on freedom of assembly, political mobilization, and union activity imposed in March 1982. More controversial were demands that the FSLN separate itself from its involvement with state institutions, repeal certain laws pertaining to private property, and open negotiations with the contras. Three days after his return, Cruz announced that the CD would boycott the election but that he would continue as a candidate. Negotiations aimed at resolving the CD's participation culminated in talks between Cruz and Bayardo Arce at a meeting of the Socialist International in Rio de

Janeiro, which produced a provisional pact. The CD dropped its call for contra talks and the government agreed to all of the CD demands, including postponing the election until January 1985. (This information is all from LASA, "The Electoral Process in Nicaragua," pp. 19–20.) What happened next remains unclear: Speculation centers on hardliners on both sides, but the pact was not finalized (see p. 20, or Gutman, *Banana Diplomacy*, pp. 247–253, on these negotiations). Even if Cruz and the CD had wanted to run, the contra leadership and the United States never intended that they do so (LASA, "The Electoral Process in Nicaragua," pp. 19, 29; Gutman, *Banana Diplomacy*, pp. 232–235; Jonas and Stein, "The Construction of Democracy in Nicaragua," p. 19). See also note 100.

97. LASA, "Electoral Democracy Under International Pressure," p. 8.

98. Gutman, *Banana Diplomacy*, p. 241.

99. Cited by Sklar, *Washington's War on Nicaragua*, p. 193. Sklar cited M. Cook, "The Reluctant Candidate," *Nation*, 13 October 1984.

100. This role for Cruz and the CD has been widely confirmed by high-ranking U.S. officials in both the United States and Nicaragua. See, for example, Booth, *The End and the Beginning*, p. 217; D. Gilbert, "Nicaragua," in M. Blachman, W. LeoGrande, and K. Sharpe, eds., *Confronting Revolution: Security Through Diplomacy in Central America* (New York: Pantheon), p. 111; R. Gutman, "Nicaraguan Turning Point: How the 1984 Vote Was Sabotaged," *Nation*, vol. 245 (7 May 1988); Gutman, *Banana Diplomacy*, pp. 235–255; Jonas and Stein, "The Construction of Democracy in Nicaragua," p. 19; Pastor, *Condemned to Repetition*, p. 248. U.S. efforts also included pressure on the candidates of the three moderate parties in the race not to participate (Gutman, "Nicaraguan Turning Point," and *Banana Diplomacy*, p. 253; Jonas and Stein, p. 19; LASA, "The Electoral Process in Nicaragua," pp. 30–31; J. Oakes, "'Fraud' in Nicaragua," *New York Times*, 15 November 1984; Pastor, *Condemned to Repetition*, p. 250; Sklar, *Washington's War on Nicaragua*, pp. 198–200; T. Walker, *Reagan Versus the Sandinistas: The Undeclared War on Nicaragua* (Boulder: Westview, 1987). After refusing considerable financial incentives, Democratic Conservative party (PCD) candidate Clemente Guido and Popular Social Christian party (PPSC) candidate Mauricio Díaz both chose to remain in the race (Sklar, *Washington's War on Nicaragua*, p. 198). The United States was more successful with the man widely seen as the number two candidate in the election, former JGRN minister of labor and Liberal Independent party (PLI) candidate Virgilio Godoy. Two weeks before the election and the morning after meeting with the U.S. ambassador, Godoy withdrew from the election (LASA, "The Electoral Process in Nicaragua," p. 30). The PLI repudiated Godoy's move, remained in the race, and ran third. Since all presidential candidates who gained over 1 percent of the vote were seated in the assembly, Godoy received a seat.

101. Gutman, "Nicaraguan Turning Point," p. 645. As the U.S. stalking-horse, Cruz was supposed to disrupt and discredit the election, a role he has since claimed to regret. See Pastor, *Condemned to Repetition*, p. 250; W. Smith, "Lies About Nicargua," *Foreign Policy*, no. 67 (1987), p. 93. By 1988 Cruz was taking pains to disassociate himself from his former colleagues, considering his affiliation with them "the biggest mistake I have ever made in my life": A. Cruz, *Harvard Law Bulletin*, vol. 39, no. 3 (Spring 1988), p. 25. Nonetheless, in 1984 Cruz and his colleagues in the opposition performed their role admirably.

102. It seems particularly noteworthy that the opposition parties that participated—all of which had registered serious complaints during the course of the campaign—agreed that overall the election was open and fair. See Sklar, *Washington's War on Nicaragua*, pp. 206–209. Sklar included comments by some of the prominent domestic opposition leaders—specifically Mauricio Díaz of the PPSC, Rafael Cordova Rivas of

the PCD, and Eduardo Coronado of PLI. PPSC candidate Mauricio Díaz went as far as to state that the elections proved "that it was possible to initiate the construction of a Western-style, democratic electoral system within a revolutionary process" (p. 206). Díaz expressed similar sentiments in CAHI, *Update,* 17 July 1986. This view was echoed by the international observers as well. Teams of observers from the British Houses of Commons and Lords, the Irish parliament, the Dutch government, the Socialist International (which was not particularly supportive of the revolution in Nicaragua), and the Latin American Studies Association all agreed "that the elections had been clean, competitive, and meaningful": LASA, "Electoral Democracy Under International Pressure," p. 9. Americas Watch noted that the "debate on major social and political questions . . . [was] robust, outspoken, even strident" and described the election as "a model of probity and fairness": Americas Watch, *Human Rights in Nicaragua: Reagan, Rhetoric and Reality* (New York: Americas Watch, 1985), p. 3. Even former members of the U.S. Congress and U.S. diplomatic corps appraised the election as a significant step that was reasonably well done under the circumstances. See Smith, "Lies About Nicaragua," p. 93. The United States condemned the elections as a fraud, a dramatic contrast with the enthusiastic U.S. endorsement of the 1984 elections in neighboring El Salvador, which were conspicuously less open and considerably less fair than those in Nicaragua. Many people who compared the two elections were much more impressed with those in Nicaragua. The British Liberal party's report on the Nicaraguan elections, for example, described them as "far superior to El Salvador's of the same year": Jonas and Stein, "The Construction of Democracy in Nicaragua," p. 17.

103. LASA, "The Electoral Process in Nicaragua," p. i.

104. If the election had been run in the manner of a U.S.-style winner-take-all, the FSLN would have been awarded ninety of the ninety-six seats.

105. The three center and right parties polled 29.2 percent (twenty-nine assembly seats), well over a quarter of the total vote. The PCD, heirs to the tradition of the Nicaraguan Conservative party, received 14 percent (fourteen seats). Despite the absence of its presidential candidate (see note 100), the PLI, which had splintered off from the elder Somoza's Nationalist Liberal party (PLN) as a progressive antidictatorial force, received 9.6 percent (nine seats). The PPSC, which had split from the PSC in 1976 because its members wanted to advocate armed struggle against the Somoza regime, received 5.6 percent (six seats). The three small parties to the left of the FSLN fared considerably worse, polling only 3.9 percent (six assembly seats) of the vote among them. The Nicaraguan Socialist party (PSN), founded in 1944 as an orthodox, Moscow-oriented Communist party, received 1.4 percent (two seats). The Communist Party of Nicaragua (PCdeN), a 1966 PSN offshoot, received 1.5 percent (two seats). The Marxist-Leninist Popular Action Movement (MAP-ML), representing a quasi-Maoist perspective in Nicaragua, received 1 percent (two seats).

106. Close, *Nicaragua,* p. 137.

107. Ibid.

108. The FSLN, Vickers noted, "was not immune to the influence of the dominant political culture . . . traditional politics colored every stage": G. Vickers, "A Spider's Web," *NACLA Report on the Americas,* vol. 24, no. 1 (June 1990), p. 20. In particular, Vickers later suggested, at least at the ministerial level there was an inclination toward the old personalistic, caudillo style of leadership (p. 22). See Gilbert, *Sandinistas,* p. 47, on this same point. A propensity for traditional Nicaraguan politics may be even more likely under the new government. O'Kane pointed out that the "new government carries with it the legacy of Nicaragua's traditional elite: 100 years of internecine warfare, accommodation with an occupying U.S. army, pacts with the Somoza dictatorship, *and a semi-feudal political style based on personal patronage and family bonds*": T. O'Kane, "The

New Old Order," *NACLA Report on the Americas,* vol. 24, no. 1 (June 1990), p. 29 (emphasis added). To take but one small example, Violeta Chamórro is the fifth Chamorro to serve as president of Nicaragua in the past hundred years. See M. Linfield, "Human Rights," in Walker, *Revolution and Counterrevolution in Nicaragua,* p. 279. Those interested in the myriad connections between and among Nicaragua's "old aristocracy" and the FSLN should consult S. Stone, *The Heritage of the Conquistadors: Ruling Classes in Central America from Conquest to the Sandinistas* (Lincoln: University of Nebraska Press, 1990), pp. 37–40.

109. Jonas and Stein, "The Construction of Democracy in Nicaragua," p. 11.

110. LASA, "Electoral Democracy Under International Pressure," p. 1.

111. Historically, the majority of the population has had little direct impact on decisions made by the revolutionary leadership.

112. Gilbert, *Sandinistas,* p. 3.

113. The FSLN remained largely true to its self-consciously chosen vanguardist role and kept party membership minimal. See M. Massing, "Who Are the Sandinistas?" *New York Review of Books,* vol. 35, no. 8 (1988), p. 53, or Gilbert, *Sandinistas,* p. 52.

114. Eckstein argued this is particularly true for governments that are democratically elected and thereby seek to maintain the status quo. See S. Eckstein, "Power and Popular Protest in Latin America," in S. Eckstein, ed., *Power and Popular Protest: Latin American Social Movements* (Berkeley: University of California Press, 1989), p. 41.

115. No effort was made to stop the emergence of non-FSLN-affiliated organizations. Many new organizations did form and many old ones were rejuvenated and resurrected in the aftermath of the political victory.

116. Interview. León, Nicaragua (1989).

117. J. Heine, "Introduction: *A Revolution Aborted,*" in J. Heine, ed., *A Revolution Aborted: The Lessons of Grenada* (Pittsburgh: University of Pittsburgh Press, 1990), p. 3. In the Caribbean, Heine argued, the Grenadian revolution "stands only after the Haitian Revolution of 1804 and the Cuban Revolution of 1959 in the scope and degree of change brought to political institutions (albeit obviously on a much smaller scale)." In a similar vein, Ambursley suggested that the revolutionary process "represented the highest level of class struggle attained in the English-speaking Caribbean since the tumultuous slave uprisings of the seventeenth and eighteenth centuries": F. Ambursley, "Grenada: The New Jewel Revolution," in F. Ambursley and R. Cohen, eds., *Crisis in the Caribbean* (New York: Monthly Review, 1983), p. 191.

118. G. Lewis, *Grenada: The Jewel Despoiled* (Baltimore: Johns Hopkins University Press, 1987), p. 2.

119. Cited in C. Sunshine, *The Caribbean: Survival, Struggle, and Sovereignty* (Boston: South End, 1988), p. 168.

120. A quick sampling finds no mention of the Grenadian revolution in J. DeFronzo, *Revolutions and Revolutionary Movements* (Boulder: Westview, 1991); Goldstone, Gurr, and Moshiri, *Revolutions of the Late Twentieth Century;* Q. Kim, ed., *Revolutions in the Third World* (Leiden: E. J. Brill, 1991); T. Greene, *Comparative Revolutionary Movements,* 3d ed. (Englewood Cliffs: Prentice-Hall, 1990); M. Kimmel, *Revolution: A Sociological Interpretation* (Philadelphia: Temple University Press, 1990); B. Schutz and R. Slater, *Revolution and Political Change in the Third World* (Boulder: Lynne Rienner, 1990); J. Dunn, *Modern Revolutions,* 2d ed. (Cambridge: Cambridge University Press, 1989); J. Goodwin and T. Skocpol, "Explaining Revolutions in the Third World," *Politics and Society,* vol. 17, no. 4 (1989); or Porter and Teich, *Revolution in History.* Grenada is mentioned in P. Calvert, *Revolution and Counterrevolution* (Minneapolis: University of Minnesota Press, 1990), and in the volume edited by T. Boswell, *Revolution in the World System* (New York: Greenwood, 1989), but no reference is made to the revolution: The

former has one reference to the U.S. invasion and one to U.S. destabilization; the latter has three references to the invasion (two in an interview with former U.S. president Jimmy Carter). Nor does the Grenadian revolution seem to appear in recent work related to the study of revolution, such as T. Wickham-Crowley, *Guerrillas and Revolution in Latin America: A Comparative Study of Insurgents and Regimes Since 1956* (Princeton: Princeton University Press, 1992), or assessments of social movments, such as S. Eckstein, *Power and Popular Protest,* or A. Escobar and S. Alvarez, *The Making of Social Movements in Latin America: Identity, Strategy, and Democracy* (Boulder: Westview, 1992)—although this may well be due to Grenada's non-Latino heritage.

121. Heine, *A Revolution Aborted.*

122. Cited in Lewis, *Grenada,* p. 35.

123. See, for example, J. Heine, "The Hero and the Apparatchik: Charismatic Leadership, Political Management, and Crisis in Revolutionary Grenada," in Heine, *A Revolution Aborted;* S. Clark, "The Second Assassination of Maurice Bishop," *New International,* no. 6 (1987); Lewis, *Grenada;* K. Schoenhals, "Grenada: The Birth and Death of a Revolution," in K. Schoenhals and R. Melanson, *Revolution and Intervention in Grenada: The New Jewel Movement, The United States, and the Caribbean* (Boulder: Westview, 1985). Heine offered probably the most nuanced discussion of the complex personal relationship that existed between the two men; Clark presented a fascinating account of their political relationship.

124. See, for example, L. Whitehead, "Democracy and Socialism: Reflections on the Grenada Experience," in Heine, *A Revolution Aborted,* or P. Henry, "Socialism and Cultural Transformation in Grenada," in ibid.

125. See, for example, J. Mandle, *Big Revolution Small Country: The Rise and Fall of the Grenada Revolution* (Lanham: North-South Publishing, 1985); T. Thorndike, *Grenada: Politics, Economics, and Society* (Boulder: Lynne Rienner, 1985); and A. Payne, P. Sutton, and T. Thorndike, *Grenada: Revolution and Invasion* (New York: St. Martin's, 1984).

126. Visionary and organizational leadership are discussed at length in Chapter 3.

127. As noted earlier, the Grenadian case fits rather uncomfortably into the designation assigned to it here, as illustrative of no institutionalization and no consolidation. Several scholars have argued that institutionalization was relatively far along at the time of the coup d'état and subsequent U.S. invasion. See, for example, Heine, "Introduction," p. 15; "The Hero and the Apparatchik," p. 247. Writing while the revolution was still under way, that is, prior to the U.S. invasion, Ambursley, "Grenada," p. 211, made a similar argument. The consensus, however, seems to be that institutionalization failed. See, for example, Payne, Sutton, and Thorndike, *Grenada,* pp. 35–39; Mandle, *Big Revolution Small Country,* pp. 18, 102; and Thorndike, *Grenada,* p. 68. There was also evidence that some degree of consolidation had occurred, especially if one interpreted popular reaction to the Coard faction's coup d'état and the rescue of Bishop from house arrest as indications of popular efforts to protect and defend the revolution.

128. See, for example, Heine, "Introduction," p. 8; M. Kurlansky, *A Continent of Islands: Searching for the Caribbean Destiny* (Reading: Addison-Wesley, 1992), p. 290; Lewis, *Grenada,* pp. 5–6; Thorndike, *Grenada,* pp. 4–7.

129. Not to mention neopatrimonial. Grantley Adams's son Tom was later prime minister of Barbados, Norman Manley's son Michael was later prime minister of Jamaica, and Antigua is run by two sons of Vere Bird, Sr.

130. Lewis, *Grenada,* p. 2.

131. Almost all accounts of Grenada concur that Gairy's stature among the Grenadian working class can be described as "heroic," at least for a time. See C. Sunshine, *Grenada: The Peaceful Revolution* (Washington, D.C.: EPICA, 1982), p. 37; F. Amburlsey and J. Dunkerley, *Grenada: Whose Freedom* (London: Latin American Bureau, 1984),

p. 20; Payne, Sutton, and Thorndike, *Grenada*, p. 7; Thorndike, *Grenada*, pp. 32–40; Lewis, *Grenada*, p. 12; Heine, "Introduction," p. 21. This heroism, Ambursley and Dunkerley suggested, was built on Gairy's manipulation of his image: "his peasant origins, trade union power, and populist style" (*Grenada*, p. 20). Virtually all these authors cited the in-depth study of Gairy and Gairyism circa 1962 in A. W. Singham's fascinating account of the politics of colonialism, *The Hero and the Crowd in a Colonial Polity* (New Haven: Yale University Press, 1968). Ambursley argued that the depiction of Gairy as a charismatic "hero" with immense "crowd" appeal ignored Gairy's rather dramatic fluctuations in electoral support between 1951 and 1967, the reasons why he had to resort to election rigging and repression to maintain his rule, and why he was so easily overthrown (Ambursley, "Grenada," p. 192). Nonetheless, Singham, who presaged Gairy's dictatorial excesses, provided an argument helpful to understanding the complex relationship between leaders who led the Eastern Caribbean nations to statehood and the population in the Eastern Caribbean.

132. The links with General Pak Chung Hee and the Duvalier regime were noted in H. O'Shaughnessy, *Grenada: An Eyewitness Account of the U.S. Invasion and the Caribbean History That Provoked It* (New York: Dodd, Mead, 1984), pp. 69–70. The connection with Somoza was noted by K. Boodhoo, "Violence and Militarization in the eastern Caribbean: The Case of Grenada," in A. Young and D. Phillips, eds., *Militarization in the Non-Hispanic Caribbean* (Boulder: Lynne Rienner, 1985), p. 71.

133. Boodhoo suggested that "the 1977 military agreement with General Augusto Pinochet of Chile, which called for the training of Grenadians in Chile and arms transfers, clearly indicated Gairy's future direction" (Boodhoo, "Violence and Militarization in the Eastern Caribbean," p. 71). On these links, see also O'Shaughnessy, *Grenada*, pp. 69–70, who noted the Chileans claim that their support for Gairy in Grenada would serve to counter Cuban aid to Jamaica.

134. Thorndike, *Grenada*, p. 39.

135. A number of people noted the introduction of this practice. See, for example, Sunshine, *Grenada*, p. 50. Lewis concluded that toward the end, Gairy's "unspeakable atrocities" constituted "a veritable reign of terror": Lewis, *Grenada*, p. 37.

136. Mandle referred to this as "the plantation economy": Mandle, *Big Revolution Small Country*, pp. 5–8.

137. Lewis, *Grenada*, p. 25.

138. Gairy's "traditional" opposition was from the Grenada National party (GNP), which represented the country's middle class, the Chamber of Commerce, employers, remnants of the colonial aristocracy, and the elite. The GNP held office from 1957 to 1961 and 1962 to 1967. With politics similar to those of Gairy and his organization, the Grenada United Labor party (GULP), Lewis pointed out, the GNP supported private ownership of property, an ongoing relationship with Britain, the endorsement of the social status quo, and the acceptance of elitism in politics (Lewis, *Grenada*, p. 16).

139. T. Thorndike, "People's Power in Theory and Practice," in Heine, *A Revolution Aborted*, p. 29. Jamaica's Trevor Munroe, according to Thorndike, was the only open "Marxist-Leninist"; Maurice Bishop, he suggested, was one of the reformers. Elsewhere, Thorndike suggested that nonetheless, "Marxist theories predominated" and cited the influence of Munroe (Thorndike, *Grenada*, p. 24). Although Munroe was undoubtedly influential, the independent black Marxism of Trinidad's C.L.R. James was probably more important. James conceived of direct democracy via a network of local citizens' assemblies; he saw the struggle of blacks as distinct from, albeit related to, the socialist struggle of Marxist parties. Lewis, *Grenada*, p. 25, referred to James's perspective as "Marxist populism." An excellent brief discussion of the populist black power movement in the Caribbean can be found in Sunshine, *The Caribbean*, pp. 58–61. Walter

Rodney, Trevor Munroe, and Clive Thomas are some of the people most commonly associated with this movement, which influenced the struggle of most of the subsequent leftists in the region.

140. MAP resulted from the unification of two smaller groups, the Movement for the Advancement of Community Effort (MACE), formed by Bishop, his law partner, and others to focus on political education, and the similarly focused Committee of Concerned Citizens (CCC).

141. See, for descriptions, Thorndike, *Grenada*, p. 42; "People's Power in Theory and Practice," p. 31; and Payne, Sutton, and Thorndike, *Grenada*, p. 9.

142. See O'Shaughnessy, *Grenada*, p. 46, or Ambursley and Dunkerley, *Grenada*, p. 23.

143. Although, as Ambursley and Dunkerley, *Grenada*, p. 24, pointed out, the word *socialism* is not even mentioned in the document. Thorndike, *Grenada*, p. 43, nonetheless, described the early NJM as "uncompromisingly socialist in general outlook," albeit not consciously Marxist.

144. Thorndike, "People's Power in Theory and Practice," p. 32. Perhaps the most important of these was the National Unity Council, a coalition of middle-class groups such as the Chamber of Commerce, trade unions, and churches, popularly known as the "Committee of 22."

145. Clark, "The Second Assassination of Maurice Bishop," p. 22; Heine, "The Hero and the Apparatchik," p. 222. According to Heine, Coard also was sent to London in 1973 to discuss plans for Grenadian independence on behalf of the opposition. The information here on Coard is drawn largely from the two sources in this note.

146. Heine, "The Hero and the Apparatchik," p. 223.

147. Ambursley and Dunkerley, for example, argued that "Coard played a leading role in drawing the party [the NJM] towards official communism": Ambursley and Dunkerley, *Grenada*, p. 27. Thorndike, *Grenada*, p. 50, made a similar point. Although it came to be dominated by Coard, OREL was founded in 1975 by a group of Grenadian secondary school students who considered themselves Marxist-Leninists. Coard, according to Heine, was "their intellectual guru and mentor": Heine, "The Hero and the Apparatchik," p. 223. On Coard's early role within OREL, see also Thorndike, *Grenada*, p. 50, and Clark, "The Second Assassination of Maurice Bishop," p. 22.

148. The first and last quotes are from Clark, "The Second Assassination of Maurice Bishop," p. 22. The self-description is from Thorndike, *Grenada*, p. 50.

149. Gairy was traveling to New York to lobby the Use of Outer Space Committee of the United Nations (UN) on the need for a UN agency to investigate UFOs and other cosmic phenomena, one of his particular interests, from an observation center in Grenada. On Gairy's decision to dispose of the NJM leadership, see O'Shaughnessy, *Grenada*, p. 78; Thorndike, *Grenada*, p. 54; and Lewis, *Grenada*, p. 78. On what Heine, "Introduction," p. 13, described as Gairy's "grotesque efforts" at the UN, see also O'Shaughnessy, *Grenada*, p. 77; Thorndike, *Grenada*, p. 54.

150. Coup d'état was the designation of O'Shaughnessy, *Grenada*, p. 77; Payne, Sutton, and Thorndike, *Grenada*, p. 13; and Lewis, *Grenada*, p. 77. Ambursley and Dunkerley opted for the notion that it was "in a strict sense . . . less a revolution than a popular coup." Thorndike, *Grenada*, p. 54, termed it an insurrection, which resonated with Clark's description of it as an "armed uprising": Clark, "The Second Assassination of Maurice Bishop," p. 23. Mandle, *Big Revolution Small Country*, pp. 16–17, and Schoenhals, "Grenada," p. 33, dubbed it a revolution, an argument made most compellingly by Heine, who suggested that it was a mistake to understand the NJM's seizure of power as "a Blanquist coup de main led by a small group of conspirators." Rather, Heine contended, this "was simply the culmination of six years of political struggle in which

Bishop and his colleagues had effectively managed to generate a considerable amount of support": Heine, "Introduction," p. 14. The argument here is that the entire process is most usefully understood as a revolutionary process, albeit one that failed to result in a social revolution.

151. See Thorndike, *Grenada*, p. 55, who described the population's reaction as "an island-wide carnival." Ambursley and Dunkerley, *Grenada*, p. 30; Mandle, *Big Revolution Small Country*, p. 18; and O'Shaughnessy, *Grenada*, p. 79, all concurred.

152. These assessments are, respectively, from Thorndike, *Grenada*, p. 32; Mandle, *Big Revolution Small Country*, p. 22; and Lewis, *Grenada*, p. 25.

153. A number of authors suggested that if the NJM had held elections, it would have won handily. See, for example, Schoenhals, "Grenada," p. 33; Thorndike, *Grenada*, p. 560; or Whitehead, "Democracy and Socialism," p. 309.

154. To some extent, according to Sunshine, *The Caribbean*, p. 103, this was realized. She noted that "at the monthly meetings of the grassroots councils, Grenadians debated local, national, and international issues in a format somewhat like that of a New England town meeting. Most major legislation underwent critique by these councils and by the NWO, the NYO, and the trade unions. In this experimental process, the mass organizations would discuss proposed legislation and send back recommendations to the government, which would take their suggestions into account before passing the law in final form. The national budgets for both 1982 and 1983 went through this procedure." Sunshine pointed out that this process was possible because of Grenada's "micro-society." Nonetheless, she conceded that this system of "popular democracy" was also deceptive, since not all the leaders were equally committed to such a process and reality often reflected decisions made by a handful of officials in the capital. "The fulcrum of power," Thorndike pointed out, "clearly and unambiguously lay with the Central Committee": Thorndike, *Grenada*, p. 90. Bishop, Sunshine suggested, was the champion of the process of participatory democracy. See Sunshine, *The Caribbean*, p. 103.

155. Ambursley and Dunkerley, *Grenada*, p. 37; Thorndike, *Grenada*, p. 89; "People's Power in Theory and Practice," p. 41; Sunshine, *The Caribbean*, p. 103. Heine described this innovative political structure as "one of the most important experiments in grass roots democracy to have taken place in the Caribbean": Heine, "Introduction," p. 16. As will be discussed, the experiment seems to have failed.

156. This, as indicated in note 127, was argued by Payne, Sutton, and Thorndike, *Grenada*, pp. 35–39; Mandle, *Big Revolution Small Country*, pp. 18, 102; and Thorndike, *Grenada*, p. 68. Heine claimed that the revolution was in fact poised to institutionalize at the time it self-destructed/was overthrown. See Heine, "Introduction," p. 15; "The Hero and the Apparatchik," p. 247.

157. Heine, "The Hero and the Apparatchik," p. 247. It is plausible to speculate that Coard was also fearful that the elections, which seemed increasingly likely, would further serve to strengthen Bishop.

158. Thorndike, *Grenada*, p. 68.

159. Heine argued that "blaming the failure of the revolution on its lack of institutionalization is a non sequitur." To wit, he said that "the timing of the Coard faction's bid for power was designed to avoid the institutionalization and consolidation of Maurice Bishop's rule. . . . In some sense, the revolution failed *because* it was about to institutionalize itself" (emphasis in the original): Heine, "The Hero and the Apparatchik," p. 247. This is a compelling point, but it would seem to support my contention that the revolutionary process was not institutionalized at the time the social revolutionary process ended.

160. David Lewis, cited in Lewis, *Grenada*, p. 33.

161. Payne, Sutton, and Thorndike, *Grenada*, p. 34.

162. M. Bishop, "Maurice Bishop Speaks to U.S. Working People," in B. Marcus and M. Taber, eds., *Maurice Bishop Speaks: The Grenada Revolution 1979–1983* (New York: Pathfinder, 1983), p. 294.

163. Mandle, *Big Revolution Small Country*, pp. 53–56. The information that follows is also from Mandle.

164. Ibid., p. 74.

165. See also Payne, Sutton, and Thorndike, *Grenada*, p. 105.

166. Sunshine, *The Caribbean*, pp. 101–102.

167. In seeking a theory that would allow precapitalist states to begin the transition to socialism without the obligatory capitalist stage, several Soviet scholars in the mid-1970s advanced the notion of a "non-capitalist path" to constructing socialism. See R. Ulyanovsky, *Socialism and the Newly Independent Nations* (Moscow: Progress Publishers, 1974); I. Andreyev, *The Non-Capitalist Way* (Moscow: Progress Publishers, 1974); and V. Solodivonikov and V. Bogoslovsky, *Non-Capitalist Dvevelopment: An Historical Outline* (Moscow: Progress Publishers, 1975). The "non-capitalist path" consisted of three stages: "decolonization and the 'shaping' of the noncapitalist way; national-democratic transformations; and socialist society" (Thorndike, *Grenada*, pp. 19–20). The national-democratic stage was the critical period when contradictions between socialism and capitalism and their proponents were greatest. For more on this, see Thorndike, *Grenada*, pp. 20–22; "People's Power in Theory and Practice," p. 35; or Mandle, *Big Revolution Small Country*, pp. 48–53.

168. See Thorndike, "People's Power in Theory and Practice," p. 37, and Sunshine, *The Caribbean*, p. 101.

169. Heine, "Introduction," p. 17. As Heine pointed out, this was dramatically different from the treatment these two organizations accorded similar efforts in Jamaica and Chile.

170. As Thorndike noted, the "backwardness of Grenadian society was . . . a constantly reiterated theme": Thorndike, "People's Power in Theory and Practice," p. 38.

171. Ambursley, "Grenada," p. 211; Mandle, *Big Revolution Small Country*, p. 59; Sunshine, *The Caribbean*, p. 103.

172. Thorndike, "People's Power in Theory and Practice," p. 44. Moreover, he noted, there were 94 candidates for membership and an additional 180 applicants.

173. Heine took note of the popular slogan "B is for Bishop and Betterment, C for Coard and Communism." He also related the stoning of Coard and his wife on their way to their trial for the murder of Bishop. See Heine, "The Hero and the Apparatchik," p. 237.

174. See, for example, Clark, "The Second Assassination of Maurice Bishop," passim; Lewis, *Grenada*, pp. 68–70; or Heine, "The Hero and the Apparatchik," p. 239.

175. Coard's Stalinist inclinations were one of the central theses of Clark, who rendered Coard as an unrepentant Stalinist within the party. See Clark, "The Second Assassination of Maurice Bishop." Coard's Stalinist tendencies were also mentioned by Thorndike, *Grenada*, p. 184; Lewis, *Grenada*, p. 80; and Heine, "The Hero and the Apparatchik," p. 235. Interpretation of Coard as a Stalinist is rooted in his propensity for strong measures against opponents, harsh discipline, his ritualistic—and often suspect—invocation of Lenin to justify abuses, and his conspiratorial disposition. Heine did argue that "reductionist portraits of a dyed-in-the-wool Stalinist lack credibility when applied to a minister of finance whose economic policy was marked by an extraordinary degree of pragmatism and accommodation to market forces" (p. 236).

Ambursley and Dunkerley, however, suggested that the pragmatism and flexibility Coard demonstrated in handling of the economy were not evident when it came to the party or political strategy. See Ambursley and Dunkerley, *Grenada*, p. 56.

176. See Heine, "The Hero and the Apparatchik."

177. Ibid., p. 233.

178. Ibid., pp. 235–236.

179. Ibid., pp. 237–243. Equally intriguing was Heine's analysis of Bishop's failure to respond to the increasingly obvious challenge that was posed by Coard (ibid., pp. 243–246).

180. See, for example, Heine, "Introduction," p. 3, or Ambursley, "Grenada," p. 191. Lewis rejected this argument, saying that in comparative terms Grenada's socialism "as far as it went in four brief years, would have to be placed more in the British-Scandinavian camp than any other." He went on to suggest that "the Grenada model was more 'social-welfarism' than socialism proper, not unlike the policies of the left-wing Michael Manley government in Jamaica in 1972–1980": Lewis, *Grenada*, pp. 28–29. Stone provided an interesting comparative study of Grenada and other roughly contemporaneous efforts to establish socialism in the Eastern Caribbean, Jamaica under the democratically elected Manley government (1972–1980) and Guyana under the quasi-police state of Forbes Burnham (1964–1975, but particularly the late 1970s and early 1980s). See C. Stone, "Whither Caribbean Socialism: Grenada, Jamaica, and Guyana in Perspective," in Heine, *A Revolution Aborted*. One critical difference, noted by Heine, "Introduction," p. 16, was that Jamaica and Guyana remained within the framework of the Westminster system the British left behind—the Grenadians rejected this system out of hand. A potentially interesting but, I believe, unexplored comparison might be with Suriname's socialist experimentation in the early 1980s.

181. Lewis, *Grenada*, p. 2.

182. Ibid., p. 190.

183. R. Darnton, "What Was Revolutionary About the French Revolution?" *New York Review of Books*, vol. 35 (19 January 1989).

184. One trace, discovered by Kurlansky, is a continued reverence for the martyred Bishop, combined with an apparent fear of mentioning him by name. See Kurlansky, *A Continent of Islands*, p. 293–294.

## CHAPTER THREE

1. As has been suggested, this has not stopped many scholars from presenting revolutions as such. See, e.g., T. Skocpol, *States and Social Revolution* (Cambridge: Cambridge University Press, 1979).

2. M. Rejai and K. Philips, *Loyalists and Revolutionaries: Political Leaders Compared* (New York: Praeger, 1988), p. 3.

3. A succinct overview of that research can be found in ibid., pp. 3–6.

4. R. D. Hopper, "The Revolutionary Process: A Frame of Reference for the Study of Revolutionary Movements," *Social Forces*, vol. 28, no. 3 (1950), and E. Hoffer, *The True Believer: Thoughts on the Nature of Mass Movements* (New York: Harper, 1951), are examples of the speculative analyses.

5. H. Lasswell and D. Lerner, eds., *World Revolutionary Elites* (Cambridge: MIT Press, 1965), and E. V. Wolfenstein, *The Revolutionary Personality* (Princeton: Princeton University Press, 1967), are examples of the empirical analyses.

6. See, for example, Y. Dror, "Visionary Political Leadership: On Imposing a Risky Requisite," *International Political Science Review*, vol. 9, no. 1 (1988); J. Migdal, "Vision

and Practice: The Leader, the State, and the Transformation of Society," *International Political Science Review*, vol. 9, no. 1 (1988); J. Blondel, *Government Ministers in the Contemporary World* (Beverly Hills: Sage, 1985); R. Tucker, *Politics and Leadership* (Columbia: University of Missouri Press, 1981); and the series of studies by M. Rejai and K. Phillips: *Leaders of Revolution* (Beverly Hills: Sage, 1979); *World Revolutionary Leaders* (New Brunswick: Rutgers, 1983); and *Loyalists and Revolutionaries*.

7. The most important exception to this is the work of Rejai and Phillips: *Leaders of Revolution; World Revolutionary Leaders;* and *Loyalists and Revolutionaries*.

8. Wolfenstein, *The Revolutionary Personality;* Rejai and Phillips: *Leaders of Revolution; World Revolutionary Leaders;* and *Loyalists and Revolutionaries*. For a critical evaluation of theory and research in the study of revolutionary personnel see M. Rejai, "Theory and Research in the Study of Revolutionary Personnel," in T. R. Gurr, ed., *Handbook of Political Conflict: Theory and Research* (New York: Free Press, 1980).

9. However, Kris Thalhammer argued persuasively that the analysis of personality traits might help explain why some people "react to revolutionary opportunities while others do not, or why some are visionary while others are organizational" (personal conversation, 1992).

10. It is interesting to note that Rejai and Phillips, two of the leading scholars of revolutionary leaders, suggested that "real" revolutionary leadership ceases to exist in what is construed here as the final phase of the social revolutionary process; "real" revolutionary leaders are those active *"during* and perhaps immediately *before* the revolution, but not necessarily *after* the success or failure of the revolution" (emphasis in the original). Their intention is to "distinguish the 'real' revolutionary from the dilettante, the propagandist, the pamphleteer": Rejai and Phillips, *Leaders of Revolution*, p. 13. I suspect this is rooted in Rejai and Phillips reliance on Rejai's earlier work on political or civil revolution as opposed to the focus here on social revolution. See M. Rejai, *The Comparative Study of Revolutionary Strategy* (New York: McKay, 1977), pp. 1–12. Rejai and Phillips summarized Rejai's definition of political revolution as *"illegal mass violence aimed at the overthrow of a political regime as a step toward overall societal change"* (emphasis in the original): Rejai and Phillips, *Leaders of Revolution*, pp. 12–13. This was subsequently refined to "the mass violent overthrow of a political regime in the interest of broad societal change": Rejai and Phillips, *Loyalists and Leaders*, p. xiv, n. Given the inclusion of "broad societal change," it strikes me as peculiar that Rejai implied that revolutionary leaders somehow disappeared after what has been defined here as political victory. Certainly in the four cases under consideration here, all the leaders who were important *"during* and perhaps immediately *before"*—Lechín, Paz, and Siles in Bolivia, the Castro brothers, Cienfuegos, and Guevara in Cuba, Bishop and Coard in Grenada, and the nine commandantes in Nicaragua—remained important, in fact critical, leaders after the political victory.

11. C. Brinton, *Anatomy of Revolution* (New York: Vintage, 1965), pp. 107–119.

12. Hopper, "The Revolutionary Process," pp. 270–279.

13. Hoffer, *The True Believer*, pp. 129–151.

14. H. Eckstein, *Internal War: Problems and Approaches* (New York: Free Press, 1964), p. 26.

15. Rejai and Phillips, *Leaders of Revolution*, pp. 131–139. More recently, Rejai and Phillips generated a set of hypotheses and propositions about revolutionary leaders. See Rejai and Phillips, *Loyalists and Revolutionaries*. In this project, the third in their ongoing analysis of revolutionary leadership, they explored the differences between political leaders who are "revolutionaries" and those who are "loyalists." Revolutionaries are those who risk their lives "by playing a prominent, active, and continuing role throughout the revolutionary process" (p. xiv). See note 10 above on their notion

of "throughout the revolutionary process." Loyalists are "the counterpart of a revolutionary in a key political (elective) or governmental (appointive) position" (ibid.). Revolutionaries are distinguished by their positive and optimistic views of the population and their powerful visions of social justice and the need to "right wrongs"(p. 112). There is, however, a significant degree to which revolutionary leaders are similar to nonrevolutionary leaders; this is, Greene noted, one of the "best-documented ironies of revolutionary movements": T. Greene, *Comparative Revolutionary Movements*, 3d ed. (Englewood Cliffs: Prentice-Hall, 1990), pp. 41–42. The inverse of this, clearly, is that revolutionary leaders are largely dissimilar from those in whose name they claim to struggle. One implication of this, Greene noted, is "obvious and dramatic: the great mass of those who would be liberated are unable to liberate themselves" (p. 42). Greene's point is well taken and reinforced across the cases here; none of the primary revolutionary leaders—Lechín, Paz, and Siles in Bolivia, the Castro brothers, Cienfuegos, and Guevara in Cuba, Bishop and Coard in Grenada, and Borge, the Ortega brothers, and Wheelock in Nicaragua—would be readily identified with the majority of the population they purported to represent.

16. Greene, *Comparative Revolutionary Movements*, p. 55.

17. This roughly corresponds with Brinton's idealist or formulator, Hopper's agitator or prophet, Hoffer's "men of words," or Eckstein's ideologues or demagogues. It does not correspond with the categories created by Rejai and Phillips.

18. This category, roughly, parallels Brinton's propagandist or organizer, Hopper's administrator-executive, Hoffer's "practical men of action," or Eckstein's organizers or administrators. It does not correspond with the categories created by Rejai and Phillips.

19. It is worth noting that in the four cases considered here, the category of quixotic idealist—or in its more negative incarnation, doctrinaire mandarin—appears clearly only in the case of Grenada's Bernard Coard.

20. It is interesting to note that Rejai and Phillips's lists of those with exceptional verbal skills—people "particularly skillful at fashioning and propagating revolutionary ideologies"—and those with "special organizational skills" have some overlap. Eight of the thirty-one revolutionaries are on both lists. These eight people include the five listed here—Castro, Ho, Lenin, Mao, and Trotsky—plus Samuel Adams (United States), Ben Bella (Algeria), and John Pym (England). See Rejai and Phillips, *Loyalists and Revolutionaries*, p. 114. In terms of this project, the United States and England had political revolutions; Algeria might be construed as having had a political revolution; however, it was most clearly a war of national independence/anticolonial war of liberation. Certainly none of these people has enjoyed the stature accorded to the other five revolutionary leaders on the list.

21. The case of Leon Trotsky is illustrative. Trotsky's stature as one of the leaders of the Russian revolution is second only to Lenin's; if Lenin was "the mastermind," Trotsky "was the active agent": P. Johnson, *Modern Times: The World from the Twenties to the Eighties* (New York: Harper and Row, 1983), p. 63. Trotsky's talents were extraordinary: "a brilliant orator, a first-rate organizer in his tenure as Commissar of War, and a Marxist theoretician of first rank": R. Alexander, *Trotskyism in Latin America* (Stanford: Hoover Institute Press, 1973), p. 4. Trotsky's vision, dynamism, and charisma were essential in the early part of the Russian revolution; he has been described in this period as an "extraordinary public speaker" who "dazzled the working classes of St. Petersburg" with his oratory; as a result, Trotsky played the key role in bringing the critical Petrograd military garrison over to the side of the revolutionaries. See, respectively, E. Wilson, *To the Finland Station: A Study in the Writing and Acting of History* (New York: Doubleday, 1940), p. 421, and J. Billington, *Fire in the Minds of Men: Origins of the Revolutionary Faith* (New York: Basic Books, 1980), p. 468. According to Wilson, Trotsky

"could handle the grim Marxist logic with a freer and more sweeping hand so as to make an instrument for persuasion and wield the knife of the Marxist irony for purposes of public exhibition, when he would flay the officials alive and, turning their skins inside out, display the ignominious carcasses concealed by their assurances and promises; he could dip down and raise a laugh from the peasant at the core of every Russian proletarian by hitting off something with a proverb or fable from the Ukrainian countryside of his youth; he could point epigrams with a swiftness and a cleanness that woke the wonder of the cleverest intellectuals; and he could throw wide the horizons of the mind to a vision of that dignity and liberty that every man among them there should enjoy. Between the vision and the horrible carcasses that stood in the way of their attaining it, the audience would be lashed to fury": Wilson, *To the Finland Station*, p. 421. Trotsky's organizational skills proved equally crucial early on in maximizing popular support for the October 1917 Bolshevik coup; the coordination "was essentially Trotsky's task": W. Rosenberg and M. Young, *Transforming Russia and China: Revolutionary Struggle in the Twentieth Century* (New York: Oxford University Press, 1982), p. 54. On Trotsky's role as the leading organizer of the 1917 Bolshevik seizure of power, see I. Deutscher, *The Prophet Armed: Trotsky: 1879–1921* (New York: Vintage Books, 1954), or B. Wolfe, *Three Who Made History: A Biographical History*, 4th ed., rev. (New York: Dell, 1964). Later, Trotsky's pragmatism and ability to maneuver and compromise were central to the creation of the Red Army and the subsequent direction—as well as exhortation and encouragement—of that army in battle against both the White Army and the invading Allied armed forces. The scholarly consensus on Trotsky's handling of the Red Army from 1918 to 1920 is summed up in Rosenberg and Young's description of his "remarkable leadership": Rosenberg and Young, *Transforming Russia and China*, p. 63. Throughout all three phases of the social revolutionary process, Trotsky demonstrated his skills as both a visionary and an organizational leader. Trotsky proved less adept at organizing in the context of internal party politics, where he was badly outmaneuvered by Joseph Stalin. Although the reasons for this are complex and multifaceted, one popular interpretation has been that Stalin relished the detail and minutiae of running the government on a day-to-day basis, a process with which Trotsky was far less intrigued.

22. To take an example, military leadership is often of critical importance during the insurrection and political victory. Huber Matos (Cuba), and Edén Pastora (Nicaragua) were important military figures who, to varying degrees, proved ill suited for the transformation phase. Historically such people have rarely been part of what might be considered the vanguard.

23. D. Gilbert, *Sandinistas: The Party and the Revolution* (New York: Basil Blackwell, 1988), p. viii. This is significant. Most other forms of political change involve efforts to at least marginalize and preferably neutralize the population.

24. Ibid., p. 33.

25. This paragraph is largely drawn from Lenin's classic statement of the role of the vanguard, *What Is to Be Done?* (New York: International Publishers, 1986). See in particular the discussion "Can a Newspaper Be a Collective Orgainser" [sic] (pp. 156–166), where Lenin drew the analogy with bricklaying as well as an interesting notion of the party as temporary scaffolding that is erected to assist in the construction of a permanent building and then torn down and disposed of after the edifice is complete. See also the section entitled "The Working Class as Vanguard Fighter for Democracy" (pp. 78–93). F. Moshiri, "Revolutionary Conflict Theory in an Evolutionary Perspective," in J. Goldstone, T. R. Gurr, and F. Moshiri, eds., *Revolutions of the Late Twentieth Century* (Boulder: Westview, 1991), p. 10, suggested that the vanguard notion comes directly from Marx and Engels, citing specifically the *Communist Manifesto*: "The communists,

therefore, are on the one hand, practically, the most advanced and resolute section of the working class parties of every country, that section which pushes forward all the others; on the other hand, they have over the great mass of the proletariat the advantage of clearly understanding the line of march, the conditions, and the ultimate general results of the proletarian movement": K. Marx and F. Engels, "The Communist Manifesto," in R. Tucker, ed., *The Marx-Engels Reader,* 2d ed. (New York: Norton, 1978), p. 494; also cited in Moshiri. Further evidence of this position by Marx and Engels can be found in a roughly contemporaneous piece, K. Marx and F. Engels, "Address of the Central Committee to the Communist League," in ibid., pp. 501–511.

26. L. Trotsky, *History of the Russian Revolution* (Ann Arbor: University of Michigan Press, 1957), p. xix.

27. A. Gramsci, *Selections from the Prison Notebooks,* Q. Hoare and G. N. Smith, eds. (New York: International Publishers, 1971), p. 418.

28. Interview, Poneloya, Nicaragua (June 1989).

29. Randall, *Sandino's Daughters: Testimonies of Nicaraguan Women in Struggle* (Vancouver: New Star Books, 1981), p. 53.

30. S. Wolin, *Politics and Vision* (Boston: Little, Brown, 1960), p. 436. This is cited in M. Keren, "Introduction," *International Political Science Review,* vol. 9, no. 1 (1988), p. 1. Keren pointed out that although every "leader endowed with vision may be called 'visionary' . . . vision alone is . . . no guarantee of effective social transformation." Of greater interest, therefore, are those Kern dubbed "visionary realists, those leaders who, while endowed with a vision, also possess a good sense of political reality" (ibid.).

31. Dror described visionary political leadership as "functionally useful and perhaps necessary during accelerated change": Dror, "Visionary Political Leadership," p. 9.

32. J. Heine, "The Hero and the Apparatchik: Charismatic Leadership, Political Management, and Crisis in Revolutionary Grenada," in J. Heine, ed., *A Revolution Aborted: The Lessons of Grenada* (Pittsburgh: University of Pittsburgh Press, 1990), p. 247.

33. Ibid.

34. This paragraph is drawn from Weber. See H. Gerth and C. Wright Mills, *From Max Weber: Essays in Sociology* (New York: Oxford University Press, 1946), pp. 245–252.

35. From 1868 to 1898 the Cubans waged an almost continuous struggle for independence, a struggle truncated by the U.S. entry into the Cuban War of Independence on the side of the Cubans.

36. On the decision to burn the sugarcane, see C. Judson, *Cuba and the Revolutionary Myth: The Political Education of the Cuban Rebel Army, 1953–1963* (Boulder: Westview, 1984), p. 179, or C. Judson, "Continuity and Evolution of Revolutionary Symbolism in *Verde Olivo,*" in S. Halebsky and J. Kirk, eds., *Cuba: Twenty-Five Years of Revolution, 1959–1984* (New York: Praeger, 1985), pp. 235–236. Both of these pieces are excellent sources on the importance of Cuban revolutionary mythology as well as the places of Guevara and Cienfuegos in that mythology.

37. J. P. Sartre, *Sartre on Cuba* (New York: Ballentine Books, 1961), p. 51.

38. E. Guevara, "Notes on Man and Socialism in Cuba," *Che Guevara Speaks* (New York: Pathfinder Press, 1967), p. 136.

39. Ibid.

40. E. Guevara, "To His Children," *Che Guevara and the Cuban Revolution: Writings and Speeches of Ernesto Che Guevara* (New York: Pathfinder Press, 1987), p. 371.

41. On the similarity of Guevara's and Castro's views, see D. Hodges, *Intellectual Foundations of the Nicaraguan Revolution* (Austin: University of Texas Press, 1986), p. 175. The Castro quotes here, cited in ibid. (p. 174), are from two speeches. See F.

Castro, "The Second Declaration of Havana" (4 February 1962), and "Speech" (13 March 1967), in M. Kenner and J. Petras, eds., *Fidel Castro Speaks* (New York: Grove Press, 1969), pp. 104, 131.

42. Quoted in Hodges, *Intellectual Foundations of the Nicaraguan Revolution*, p. 175.

43. C. Franqui, *Diary of the Cuban Revolution* (New York: Viking Press, 1980), p. 504.

44. Several people have suggested this. See, for example, M. Massing, "Who Are the Sandinistas?" *New York Review of Books*, vol. 35, no. 8 (1988), p. 53. Hodges argued that despite "adherents in virtually every Latin American country," Guevara's ideology found its home in Nicaragua, married to "the written and unwritten legacies of a great folk hero and national redeemer," Augusto Sandino. See Hodges, *Intellectual Foundations of the Nicaraguan Revolution*, pp. 172–173.

45. This was clearly an issue in Grenada; see in particular Heine, "The Hero and the Apparatchik." These concerns hover around the edges of any meaningful discussion of Castro.

46. Gilbert, *Sandinistas*, p. 47.

47. The other three cases offer varying contrasts to this. Bolivia's leadership may be usefully thought of as a false collective leadership—consensus, compacts, and consistency were largely transitory. With respect to Cuba, it is difficult to talk about any meaningful collective leadership, especially once Guevara left. Nonetheless, it is perhaps possible to talk about some sort of quasi-collective leadership during the insurrection. Grenada would appear to be a clear case of failed collective leadership, particularly since the polarization between the two principal leaders resulted in the collapse of the social revolutionary process.

48. Gilbert, *Sandinistas*, p. 47.

49. T. Borge, "This Is a Revolution of the Working People," in B. Marcus, ed., *Nicaragua: The Sandinista People's Revolution: Speeches by Sandinista Leaders* (New York: Pathfinder Press, 1985), p. 38.

50. Borge's wife was killed, and he was unmercifully tortured. Hodges pointed out that Borge was beaten until he screamed, he was locked in a cell lined with ice, and he had electric prods used on him. When, according to Hodges, Somoza decided to drive him insane by treating him like an animal, Borge was subjected to "nine months in chains and completely covered by a hood; nine months completely naked and cold; nine months on a diet of crumbs." When he was released, Hodges noted, "he was skin and bones and too weak to stand": Hodges, *Intellectual Foundations of the Nicaraguan Revolution*, p. 266. Kinzer also described the "serious and sustained torture . . . [and] inhuman brutality" Borge suffered. See S. Kinzer, *Blood of Brothers: Life and War in Nicaragua* (New York: Putnam, 1991), p. 180.

51. Given their shared history and knowledge, Borge's famous words to his torturers, "I told them: 'I am going to get back at you; now comes the hour of my revenge, and my revenge is that we are not going to harm a single hair on your heads,'" spoke that much more powerfully to the population in the aftermath of political victory. See T. Borge, "On Human Rights in Nicaragua," in T. Borge, C. Fonseca, D. Ortega, H. Ortega, and J. Wheelock, *Sandinistas Speak* (New York: Pathfinder Press, 1982), pp. 87–88. Despite a profound commitment to avoid physical torture, Borge was apparently not averse to psychological torture. See Kinzer, for example, who argued that although "Borge had decreed an end to the old-style forms of torture that had been used in Latin America for generations, and which he himself had suffered . . . he had implanted a much less bloody though arguably more effective system of coercive pressures." Kinzer continued that instead of having "prisoners kicked and beaten, tortured with electric prods, or burned with cigarette butts, he [Borge] had them sealed into poorly ventilated

dark closets, where heat was intense and inmates lost their sense of time. Confinement was interrupted at odd intervals for long, draining interrogations and for threats against either the inmate or the inmate's family": Kinzer, *Blood of Brothers*, p. 181.

52. Gilbert, *Sandinistas*, p. 43.

53. Ibid., p. 47.

54. I first heard this point made by August Nimtz in 1985. Massing, "Who Are the Sandinistas?" p. 59, quoted an anonymous diplomat to this effect.

55. Some have suggested that this was due, in part, to the role played by his brother Humberto. It certainly was the case that Humberto penned many of the Tercerista positions. As head of the army, Humberto was also strongly positioned behind his brother. It is interesting to note that in choosing the traditional Latin American stronghold of power—the head of the army—Humberto was able to retain his position in the new government.

56. This is thought to be the basis for Trotsky's dictum that revolutions are the "mad inspiration of history": L. Trotsky, *My Life* (New York: Pathfinder Press, 1930), p. 20. The MNR in Bolivia was equally unprepared for the direction of events during the struggle for political power, and the Monimbó and Matagalpa uprisings in 1978 similarly caught Nicaragua's FSLN trailing behind the population.

57. L. Sargent, *Contemporary Political Ideologies* (New York: Dorsey Press, 1987), p. 2.

58. See, for example, Gramsci, *Selections from the Prison Notebooks*, p. 78.

59. U.S. troops first intervened in Nicaragua in 1909. From 1912 to 1933, "with the exception of a short period in the mid-1920s, the United States maintained an occupation force in Nicaragua," according to J. Booth and T. Walker, *Understanding Central America* (Boulder: Westview, 1989), p. 29.

60. Gilbert, *Sandinistas*, p. 155.

61. Hodges, *Intellectual Foundations of the Nicaraguan Revolution*, is the definitive work on Sandino's thought. Hodges uncovered its complexity, teasing out the various strands that had long been obscured. (Hodges continued this exploration, with some interesting results, in *Sandino's Communism: Spiritual Politics in the Twenty-First Century* [Austin: University of Texas Press, 1992].) For two different but highly illuminating views of the use and interpretation of Sandino's thought by the FSLN, compare Hodges and Gilbert, *Sandinistas*. Hodges discerned a significant FSLN "debt to Sandino for his political assessments of Nicaraguan reality, revolutionary strategy, and ideology of liberation" (*Intellectual Foundations of the Nicaraguan Revolution*, p. 161). Gilbert, in contrast, argued that the FSLN found "little in Sandino's thought that they could incorporate into the party's emerging ideology. Instead of Sandino's ideas, the Sandinistas adopted their hero's symbols, his image, and his myth" (*Sandinistas*, p. 22).

62. V. Tirado, "Karl Marx: The International Workers' Movement's Greatest Fighter and Thinker," in B. Marcus, ed., *Nicaragua: The Sandinista People's Revolution* (New York: Pathfinder Press, 1985), p. 105. Victor Tirado, one of the few surviving members from the FSLN's earliest years, argued that Fonseca "rescued" Sandino's ideas from obscurity, revised them, and used them to train a new revolutionary vanguard. Tirado's argument is in Hodges, *Intellectual Foundations of the Nicaraguan Revolution*, pp. 164–165. Gilbert, *Sandinistas*, p. 20, made a similar point, although he diminished the importance of Sandino in the FSLN's ideology (p. 22). The Sandinista leadership, according to Gilbert, had and continued to evince strong emotional and in some cases personal identification with Sandino (ibid.). He noted, for example, that the Ortegas' father fought with Sandino. Gilbert argued that the example of Sandino may have "helped wean the early Sandinistas from a dogmatic Marxism they were already outgrowing" (ibid.). This was consistent with Tirado's view that "through Marxism we came to know Sandino, our history, and our roots" and in turn then read Marx "with Nicaraguan eyes": Tirado,

"Karl Marx," p. 105. The critical judgment, Tirado argued, was the development of an explicitly nationalist ideology (Hodges, *Intellectual Foundations of the Nicaraguan Revolution*, p. 165). As a consequence, Fonseca laid the base for Sandinismo, which could be extended and adapted later when the revolutionaries incorporated liberal and Christian perspectives into their social revolutionary ideology. Others "found" Sandino through their heroes or mentors. Omar Cabezas, for instance, claimed to have discovered Sandino not through Marx but through Guevara. See O. Cabezas, *Fire from the Mountain: The Making of a Sandinista* (New York: Crown Books, 1985), p. 12. One young Nicaraguan told me that he had discovered Sandino through Borge; another told me that she "came to" Sandino via Jesus Christ.

63. S. Ramírez, "Interview," in W. Gentile, *Nicaragua* (New York: W. W. Norton, 1989), p. 129.

64. T. Walker, *Nicaragua: The First Five Years* (New York: Praeger, 1985), p. 24. The eclectic nature of the ideology was reiterated in other scholars' views of Sandinismo. Hodges characterized Sandinismo as "a composite of the national and patriotic values of Sandino and of the ethical recasting of Marxism-Leninism in the light of the philosophical humanism of the young Marx." Sandinismo "shares," according to Hodges, aspects of other ideologies, notably liberalism's "belief in basic human rights," albeit interpreted somewhat differently, "new" Christianity's "belief in the ultimate redemption of the poor and oppressed," and the "Marxist philosophical tradition cult of a new socialist man": Hodges, *Intellectual Foundations of the Nicaraguan Revolution*, p. 288. Ruchwarger defined Sandinismo as "a complex mixture of nationalism, anti-imperialism, Marxism, liberation theology, and classical liberalism": G. Ruchwarger, *People in Power: Forging a Grassroots Democracy in Nicaragua* (South Hadley: Bergin and Garvey, 1987), p. 74. Close similarly described Sandinismo as a "blend of Sandino's anti-imperialist revolutionary nationalism, Christian moral values, liberal concerns about human rights, Nicaraguan patriotism, and Marxism—both orthodox Marxism-Leninism and the more voluntaristic latinate version": D. Close, *Nicaragua: Politics, Economics, and Society* (London: Pinter, 1988), p. 110. Serra invoked comparable elements to identify Sandinismo as the union of "revolutionary christianity, historical materialism, and the thought of Sandino": L. Serra, "Ideology, Religion and the Class Struggle in the Nicaraguan Revolution," in R. Harris and C. M. Vilas, eds., *Nicaragua: A Revolution Under Siege* (London: Zed, 1985), p. 166.

65. J. Booth, *The End and the Beginning: The Nicaraguan Revolution*, 2d ed. (Boulder: Westview, 1985), pp. 146–147; D. Slater, "Socialism, Democracy, and the Territorial Imperative: Elements for a Comparison of the Cuban and Nicaraguan Experiences," *Antipode*, vol. 18, no. 2 (1986), p. 178; T. Walker, *Reagan Versus the Sandinistas: The Undeclared War on Nicaragua* (Boulder: Westview, 1987), pp. 3–4; D. Close, *Nicaragua*, p. 110.

66. This discussion draws on S. Jonas and N. Stein, "The Construction of Democracy in Nicaragua," *Latin American Perspectives*, vol. 17, no. 3 (1990), pp. 13–14. Jonas and Stein argued that pluralism was rooted in three sources: (1) "the desire to overcome the centuries-old legacies of repression and lack of experience in democratic politics"; (2) "the evolution of the FSLN itself during the last years of the insurrection, specifically, its development into the coalition of three tendencies which made victory possible"; and (3) "ideological pluralism." To these three, Jonas and Stein added a "more structural basis for pluralism in the Nicaraguan Revolution . . . the Sandinistas had to carry out a program of national reconstruction." I have done little more than rearrange and merge their list and perhaps push a bit further their notion of the FSLN's internal pluralism. Bruce Wright called my attention to the discussions of Sandinista pluralism in R. Burbach and O. Núñez, *Fire in the Americas* (London: Verso, 1987), and J. Wheelock, *El gran desafío: entrevista por Marta Harnecker* (Managua: Editorial Nueva Nicaragua,

1983), they are also cited in Wright's interesting article on pluralism and vanguardism in the revolution. See B. Wright, "Pluralism and Vanguardism in the Nicaraguan Revolution," *Latin American Perspectives*, vol. 17, no. 3 (1990), p. 41.

67. Jonas and Stein, "The Construction of Democracy in Nicaragua," p. 14.

68. Burbach and Núñez, *Fire in the Americas*, p. 56. These included Marxists, Maoists, Trotskyites, and their variants.

69. Wheelock, *El gran desafío*, p. 73.

70. Gilbert, *Sandinistas*, p. 8. Hodges, *Intellectual Foundations of the Nicaraguan Revolution*, p. 234, described the GPP as "the heirs of the FSLN's original rural organization." After political victory this faction focused on the Guevarist notion of the "new person."

71. Gilbert, *Sandinistas*, p. 8. Prior to political victory, this group stressed organizing and propagandizing in poor neighborhoods and factories and emphasized urban guerrilla tactics. For more on the Proletarian tendency, see Hodges, *Intellectual Foundations of the Nicaraguan Revolution*, pp. 233–239.

72. Gilbert, *Sandinistas*, p. 8.

73. A good discussion of the Terceristas is in Hodges, *Intellectual Foundations of the Nicaraguan Revolution*, pp. 239–245.

74. Gilbert, *Sandinistas*, pp. 8–9.

75. This process of negotiation, compromise, and unification explains (in part), why the Terceristas' more pragmatic approach assumed such a central role in the social revolutionary process. It also accounts for some of the confusion (both domestically and internationally) about the FSLN's exact views at the time of political victory and in the earliest years of the transformation process.

76. H. Sklar, *Washington's War on Nicaragua* (Boston: South End Press, 1988), p. 36.

77. Hodges, *Intellectual Foundations of the Nicaraguan Revolution*, pp. 116–121.

78. A. Sandino, *El pensamiento vivo*, 2d ed., selected and with an introduction and notes by Sergio Ramírez (Managua: Editorial Nueva Nicaragua, 1981), pp. 183–184; this is cited in Gilbert, *Sandinistas*, p. 22. Sandino's writings as edited by Ramírez have been translated into English, with some additional editing, by R. Conrad under the title *Sandino: The Testimony of a Nicaraguan Patriot, 1921–1934* (Princeton: Princeton University Press, 1990).

79. In 1985 directorate member Bayardo Arce described Sandinismo as "a political project . . . where 70 percent of the economy is in private hands, where you have 12 legally existing political parties, where all religion is freely operating, where you have radios and newspapers that freely operate pro and con": D. English, "We Are Sandinistas: Conversations with Nicaragua's Embattled Leaders," *Mother Jones*, vol. 10 (August-September 1985), p. 22.

80. R. Harris and C. Vilas, *Nicaragua: A Revolution Under Siege* (London: Zed, 1985), p. 1. This is completely in character since concepts such as "national," "popular," and "democratic" have figured far more prominently in the words and actions of the leadership than either "Marxist-Leninist" or "communist." See Slater, "Socialism, Democracy, and the Territorial Imperative," p. 163.

81. Interview. León, Nicaragua (1989). This was echoed by an older man who at one time had worked as a veterinarian on one of Somoza's ranches, who also noted: "We believe in Sandinismo. The Sandinistas are more or less honorable people, quite unlike Somoza." Interview. León, Nicaragua (1989).

82. Ramírez, "Interview," p. 130.

83. G. Rudé, *Ideology and Popular Protest* (New York: Pantheon, 1980), p. 28. This entire paragraph is drawn from there.

84. Rudé suggested, as an example, that "among the 'inherent' beliefs of one generation, and forming part of its basic culture, are many beliefs that were originally derived from outside by an earlier one" (ibid.).

85. S. Huntington, *Political Order in Changing Societies* (New Haven: Yale University Press, 1968), p. 461.

86. Gilbert, *Sandinistas*, p. 41. The translation of *consigna* is my own.

87. This point was made to me by John Dunn in a conversation at the University of Minnesota, Minneapolis (1991).

88. Hoffer, *The True Believer*, p. 146.

89. Hopper, "The Revolutionary Process," pp. 278–279.

90. Information on the three is largely from J. Dunkerley, *Rebellion in the Veins: Political Struggle in Bolivia 1952–1982* (London: Verso, 1984), pp. 40–44.

91. See ibid., pp. 50–53.

92. This draws on one of the best brief descriptions of Raúl Castro's efforts: Judson, *Cuba and the Revolutionary Myth*, pp. 139–149.

93. Heine, "The Hero and the Apparatchik," pp. 224–225 (Heine's is perhaps the most detailed personal analysis of Coard). Probably the most thorough political analysis of Coard is S. Clark, "The Second Assassination of Maurice Bishop," *New International*, no. 6 (1987).

94. Heine, "The Hero and the Apparatchik," p. 224.

95. Gilbert, *Sandinistas*, p. 43.

96. Ibid.

97. Huntington, *Political Order in Changing Societies*, p. 266.

98. Rejai, *The Comparative Study of Revolutionary Strategy*, p. 26. Rejai referred to these two as "conditions" and "manipulables."

99. There are several good references. The best is Gilbert's essential *Sandinistas*, which is the only large-scale comprehensive study of the FSLN to date. Good brief overviews may be found in the volumes edited by T. Walker: *Nicaragua in Revolution* (New York: Praeger, 1982); *Nicaragua: The First Five Years* (New York: Praeger, 1985); and *Reagan Versus the Sandinistas: The Undeclared War on Nicaragua* (Boulder: Westview, 1987). D. Nolan, *The Ideology of the Sandinistas and the Nicaraguan Revolution* (Coral Gables: Institute of International Studies, 1984), outlined the FSLN's ideology, based on oral and written records. Part 2 of Hodges's invaluable text on Sandino, *Intellectual Foundations of the Nicaraguan Revolution*, is an insightful investigation into the lineage and formation of the FSLN's ideology. For the perspective of some key participants, see Cabezas's entertaining autobiography, *Fire from the Mountain*; M. Edelman's interview with Dora María Telléz, in *NACLA Report on the Americas*, vol. 20, no. 5 (1986), and Randall's interview with her in *Sandino's Daughters*; and the key speeches and documents available in Borge et al., *Sandinistas Speak*, and Marcus, *Nicaragua*. The classic statement of the FSLN remains their 1969 "The Historic Program of the FSLN," in Borge et al., *Sandinistas Speak*.

100. Although it would be a mistake to overstate any similarities between the FSLN's eighteen-year struggle in "the wilderness" and the early Christian martyrs, there is a tradition among Latin American revolutionaries of casting their struggle in exactly those terms (see Chapter 4, note 144). This is certainly how the FSLN saw itself. The FSLN leaders were all raised in the Catholic church, most were altar boys, and several, including Borge and Daniel Ortega, are said to have considered the priesthood. As will be discussed in Chapter 4, this invocation of religious themes resurfaced in Violeta Chamorro's 1990 presidential campaign.

101. Massing, "Who Are the Sandinistas?" p. 53.

102. Gilbert, *Sandinistas*, p. 52.

103. Opposition to the Somoza regime by wealthy and middle-class Nicaraguans increased dramatically in the aftermath of the 1972 earthquake that destroyed downtown Managua. The bourgeoisie watched first in amazement and then in anger as Somoza pocketed the millions of dollars of international aid that came pouring into the country.

104. Nicaraguan sociologist Marvin Ortega, "Sandinismo y revolución: posibilidades de una experiencia plualista de izquierda en la revolución" (mimeo cited in B. Wright, "Pluralism and Vanguardism in the Nicaraguan Revolution," p. 42). Wright explicitly addressed the relationship between vanguardism and pluralism in the Nicaraguan revolutionary process. It is interesting to note that the FSLN was the *only* leftist party in Nicaragua that did not call for a "dictatorship of the proletariat." This, according to Massing, led "Soviet bloc officials" to decide that the members of the FSLN were "romantic adventurers with little real understanding of Marxist theory" and East Europeans to brand their style "socialism in the tropics," meant to connote "a frenetic, seat-of-the-pants brand of Marxism": Massing, "Who Are the Sandinistas?" p. 52.

105. A. Guillermoprieto, "Letter from Managua," *New Yorker*, 26 March 1990, p. 83.

106. Even in the Junta of the Government of National Reconstruction (JGRN), where the FSLN held a three-to-two majority, all decisions were made on the basis of consensus rather than voting. The Council of State, which likewise had a FSLN majority, had a similar practice. Nor did the FSLN reconfigure itself as a political party. In fact, membership estimates from the early post–political victory period range from 3,000 to 5,000. Although there was a strong party organization led by party professionals, membership, according to Gilbert, was limited to those who were invited to join *after* qualifying through a lengthy program of apprenticeship that stressed community service and self-abnegation. See Gilbert, *Sandinistas*, p. 52. Gilbert estimated that there were 16,000 to 50,000 activists—less than 1 percent of the country's population. Massing, in "Who Are the Sandinistas?" put membership at 24,000 in 1988; LASA estimated it at 30,000 in its postelection report. See LASA, "Electoral Democracy Under International Pressure," Report of the Latin America Studies Association Commission to Observe the 1990 Election (Pittsburgh: LASA, 1990), p. 15.

107. Gilbert, *Sandinistas*, pp. 43–45. Not surprisingly, these factions mirror to some extent the visionary (ideological) and organizational (pragmatic) types of leadership that were discussed at length in Chapter 3.

108. Ibid., p. 45.

109. Ibid.

110. Ibid.

111. Gilbert argued that the positions of Carrión and Núñez were not clear (ibid.), but by 1989 the two were definitely aligned with the pragmatist position.

112. Interview. Poneloya, Nicaragua (1989).

113. There is a famous maxim, variously attributed, that more or less says, "The hills/mountains don't breed democrats."

114. This "internationalization" is exacerbated when the social revolution is combined with a war of national independence. Angola and Mozambique involved the dissolution of Portugal's empire, NATO interests, South Africa, other African countries, and the United States.

115. Rejai, *The Comparative Study of Revolutionary Strategy*, p. 44.

116. Migdal, "Vision and Practice," p. 28.

117. Ibid., p. 30.

118. Nicaraguan politics has always been internationalized. From its earliest postindependence experience with the Central American Union through today, Nicaraguan politics has rarely, if ever, been solely about Nicaragua. Although the nature of the U.S. role in Nicaragua is extensive, few have matched the Somoza regime(s) as U.S.-oriented creatures. The entire dynasty was built on U.S. power and access to that power gained in exchange for services rendered. The litany of services rendered to the United States by the Somozas is impressive. In 1954 Nicaragua provided a staging base for the U.S. overthrow of the Guatemalan government, a favor repeated in 1961 when the United

States needed training areas, staging areas, ports, and airfields for the invasion of Cuba. In 1965 Nicaragua contributed troops to the U.S. invasion of the Dominican Republic and offered to send more to fight the war in Southeast Asia (J. Booth and T. Walker, *Understanding Central America* [Boulder: Westview, 1989], p. 31). Under the Somoza regime the United States had no stauncher ally in the UN or the Organization of American States (OAS) than Nicaragua. It is hardly surprising that even the Carter administration, which had actively sought to alter the U.S. traditional posture in Latin America, felt obliged to help the Somoza regime in its final days. After all, both the first and last Somoza were popularly known as "the last Marine" and the first Somoza was allegedly the subject of Franklin Roosevelt's (in)famous phrase, "He may be a sonofabitch, but he's our sonofabitch," a remark that Somoza treated as a badge of honor. (Many people cite this phrase; for a recent example, see S. Ramírez, "Nicaragua: Confession of Love," *This Magazine*, vol. 24, no. 8 [1991], p. 25.) As with other "badges of honor" he wore, however, Somoza may have created this one himself. It is not entirely clear that Roosevelt ever said it or that it was even said about Somoza. Thomas, for example, attributed the remark to William Wieland, director of the Office of Caribbean and Mexican Affairs for the U.S. State Department, who said, "I know Batista is considered by many as a son of a bitch . . . but American interests come first . . . at least he is our son of a bitch": H. Thomas, *Cuba: The Pursuit of Freedom* (New York: Harper and Row, 1971), p. 977. I was recently assured by a colleague that John Foster Dulles, U.S. secretary of state during the Eisenhower administration, made this remark about the dictator of the Dominican Republic, Rafael Trujillo. Regardless of the original subject, all three men provide an excellent fit with the comment. For most of Nicaragua's history and at least since 1855, the country's internal politics have been intimately tied to the United States. Nicaragua is not unique in this. The legacy of the Monroe Doctrine and U.S. notions of manifest destiny generated a sordid history for the United States in Latin America, particularly in Central America and the Caribbean between 1898 and 1934. When, under the auspices of Franklin Roosevelt's Good Neighbor Policy, the United States turned its attention briefly elsewhere, it left behind a system set up to its liking. (For an excellent discussion of the "setting up [of] the system," by the United States, see W. LaFeber, *Inevitable Revolutions: The United States in Central America*, 2d ed. [New York: Norton, 1984]). The return of the United States to an activist policy in Latin America in 1948 (beginning with Costa Rica's civil war) was marked by intervention or prevention of perceived revolutionary threats: British Guiana, 1952–1964; Bolivia, 1964; Brazil, 1964; Guatemala, 1954; Cuba, 1961; Dominican Republic, 1965; Jamaica, 1972–1980; Chile, 1973; Grenada, 1983; El Salvador since 1980; and Peru since the mid-1980s. U.S. policy in this regard remains in place.

119. Guevara, "Notes on Man and Socialism in Cuba," p. 129.

120. Gilbert, *Sandinistas*, p. 47.

121. The role of dead visionary leaders in Nicaragua was significant also. It is discussed in Chapter 2.

## CHAPTER FOUR

1. P. Kornbluh, "U.S. Role in the Counterrevolution," in T. Walker, ed., *Revolution and Counterrevolution in Nicaragua* (Boulder: Westview, 1991), p. 344. The figure of 30,865 that he cited is from the Nicaraguan Ministry of the President.

2. M. Cooper, "Soaring Prices, Plunging Hopes," *Village Voice*, 25 July 1989.

3. Kornbluh cited official Nicaraguan statistics that placed "property destruction from CIA/contra attacks" at $221.6 million and production losses at $984.5 million. He

added estimates from Nicaraguan economists that placed "monetary losses due to the trade embargo at $254 million and the loss of development potential from the war at $2.5 billion": Kornbluh, "U.S. Role in the Counterrevolution," p. 245. For any country such numbers are significant; for a poor country they are devastating.

4. See the discussion in Chapter 1 concerning the difficulties of ascertaining precisely when consolidation is "complete."

5. This discussion relies heavily on interviews and fieldwork during the winter of 1988–1989 and the summer of 1989. My research was based in and around the state of León, dominated by the city of León, Nicaragua's second-largest city. The importance of the interviews was twofold: Interpreted according to my theoretical approach, they allowed me to ascertain the importance of the variables identified and therefore to discern support for or opposition to the revolutionary project through word and action. The people interviewed were located with what Berteaux dubbed the "snowball sampling" strategy. See D. Bertaux, *Biography and Society: The Life History Approach in the Social Sciences* (Beverly Hills: Sage, 1981). Broadly, the questions asked fell into five categories: support for or opposition to the government; types of activism; economic situation before and after the revolution; geographic location before and after the revolution; and attitudes about trust, opportunity, and the future. In general, the interviews were "structured" and "open-ended." I interviewed fifty people: eighteen women and thirty-two men. The ages ranged from eighteen to eighty-three, with the greatest number, thirty-four, between eighteen and thirty-nine. All but one person had some schooling, and twenty-six had degrees ranging from high school to advanced. Among the fifty there were ten professionals, nine government workers, seven businesspeople, seven workers, seven students, four teachers, three homemakers, two entertainers, and one large landowner. Half of the people interviewed belonged to organized groups with the largest number, ten, being members of the Sandinista Youth. Four people identified themselves as active members of opposition parties. Forty considered themselves to have been involved in some form of popular protest or demonstration, including ten who had participated in antigovernment protests or demonstrations in the preceding few months. Although these numbers are undoubtedly on the high side—and reflect possibly a bit of exaggeration by those interviewed—they nonetheless show that participation came to be seen as a positive attribute by Nicaraguans, regardless of whether it was for or against the government. This is especially noteworthy in a country where participation was historically, at the very least, strongly discouraged. Moreover, this participation seems to run across a relatively broad spectrum of Nicaraguan society, ranging from the poorest to the most affluent. Finally, the interviewees were decidedly weighted toward urban backgrounds: Thirty-six lived in urban settings (populations of 20,000+) prior to political victory, and forty-six did at the time that they were interviewed.

6. Virtually everyone I spoke with discussed the economy, particularly how bad it was, and made some reference to either their or other people's current versus previous economic status. This was consistently invoked by people as one of the key determinants of their support or the support of others. Less often, but still with some frequency, people implied that their support or the support of others was related in part to their geographic location, particularly the proximity to the contra war. In both cases these were clearly relevant categories for people and appeared to be critical factors in determining support, or lack thereof, for the consolidation process.

7. F. Castro, *Granma*, Weekly Review (15 December 1968), p. 3.

8. J. Collins, D. Coursen, and D. Drukker, "20–20 Hindsight: The Anatomy of the FSLN Defeat," *Nicaragua Through Our Eyes: The Bulletin of US Citizens Living in Nicaragua*, vol. 5, no. 1 (1990), p. 3; LASA, "Electoral Democracy Under International Pres-

sure," Report of the Latin America Studies Association Commission to Observe the 1990 Election (Pittsburgh: LASA, 1990), p. 19; J. Riccardi, "The Nicaraguan Mixed Economy: From Revolution to Stabilization," *Against the Current*, no. 25 (1990), p. 39.

9. The figure of 33,600 percent was provided by Alejandro Martinez, the minister of planning and budget from mid-1988 to February 1990 and the minister of foreign trade and commerce from 1979 to 1988 (A. Martinez, public presentation, University of Minnesota, Minneapolis [May 1990]). Estimates have ranged from 20,000 to 36,000 percent: H. Vanden and T. Walker stated that inflation "finally exceeded 20,000 percent" in 1988 ("U.S. Foreign Relations with Nicaragua During the Reagan Years," paper read at the meeting of American Political Science Association, 31 August—3 September 1989, p. 16); D. Close pegged it at exactly 21,742 percent ("The Nicaraguan Revolution: Toward the Next Ten Years," *Canadian Dimension*, no. 7/8, 1989, p. 10); whereas M. Cooper cited 25,000 percent ("Soaring Prices, Plunging Hopes," p. 29); *Envío* said the inflation "topped 30,000 percent" ("Economy," *envío*, vol. 8, no. 96 [July 1989], p. 8); and W. Gasparini and D. Dye placed the figure at 36,000 percent ("Growing Pains: Sandinista Nicaragua's Difficult First Decade," *In These Times*, 19 July 1989, p. 12). Riccardi, citing the "annual 1988 estimate from the Ministry of Planning and Budget" (of which Martinez was minister), also put the rate at 36,000. See J. Riccardi, "Economic Policy," in Walker, *Revolution and Counterrevolution in Nicaragua*, p. 265. In a note, he pointed out that estimates varied widely, and he included one that computed the rate at 11,500—by far the lowest number.

10. The centerpiece, as it were, of these layoffs were the estimated 35,000 state employees fired in the first half of 1989 in what was euphemistically termed *compactación* (compacting).

11. LASA, "Electoral Democracy Under International Pressure," p. 19.

12. Martinez, public presentation.

13. C. Vilas, "What Went Wrong," *NACLA Report on the Americas*, vol. 24, no. 1 (1990), p. 12.

14. In these interviews, as well as general conversation, Nicaraguans employed a rough assessment of their economic status as well as that of others. Initial reactions to a question posed about their current economic situation were dominated by responses such as "hard," "bad," and "very hard." Other responses included "suffering," "terrible," "disaster," "crazy," and, in one instance, "ha!" Only three of the people I interviewed described their current economic situation as "good"; only one of them indicated no displeasure with the current economic situation.

15. Fifty percent of those interviewed had urban or rural working-class backgrounds. Eight percent had "elite" backgrounds. When describing their economic situation prior to the revolution, people used terms such as "hard," "bad," "poor," or "good" or phrases such as "we had nothing," "we had a little/enough," or "we had a lot."

16. It is interesting to note these responses roughly concurred with some of the findings of a 1988 poll conducted by ITZTANI-INOP, an independent Nicaraguan research firm, and those of a 1989 poll by Univision, the leading Spanish-language television network in the United States. The ITZTANI-INOP poll found that 74 percent of the people interviewed said their economic situation had worsened in the past year. See ITZTANI-INOP, "La opinión políticada los managuas," *Encuentro*, no. 35 (1988), p. 127. At the same time, however, 58 percent rated the government's economic performance as fair or better. Similarly, the Univision poll found that 61 percent felt that their quality of life had been higher before the revolution; 15 percent were undecided. See "Update: Media Watch: Nicaragua's Poll Wars," *envío*, vol. 9, no. 103 (1990), p. 15. Once again, however, the majority of those polled, 57 percent, felt that President Ortega was doing a good job.

This appears to further suggest the importance of people's relative position as the appropriate measure when one considers people's perceptions of their economic situation.

17. Interview. León, Nicaragua (1988).

18. Interview. León, Nicaragua (1989).

19. Interview. León, Nicaragua (1989).

20. Interview. León, Nicaragua (1989).

21. Interview. León, Nicaragua (1989).

22. Interview. León, Nicaragua (1989).

23. It is interesting to note that in summer 1989 there were far more responses categorized as "more or less the same" and far fewer responses categorized as "better off than before" than in winter 1988–1989.

24. A 1989 poll conducted by the U.S. firm Greenberg-Lake found that 47 percent of the people polled felt that the United States was directly or indirectly responsible for Nicaragua's economic problems; 36 percent blamed the government. See "Update: Media Watch: Nicaragua's Poll Wars," p. 16. The 1989 Univision poll cited earlier found that 57 percent of those polled believed that the United States was responsible for Nicaragua's problems—a figure that jumped rather strikingly to 73 percent in the northern part of the country, where the impact of the long-running contra war has been the greatest (ibid., p. 15). The degree of frustration brought on by this is evident in the 1988 ITZTANI poll that found that almost three-quarters of those polled were critical of the government's handling of the economy. See ITZTANI-INOP, "La opinión políticada los managuas," p. 126.

25. Interview. León, Nicaragua (1988).

26. Interview. León, Nicaragua (1989).

27. One woman, shaking her finger in my face and speaking with evident frustration, loudly told me: "Don't you understand! They hate you! Look at the national anthem! They want to kill you!" (Interview. León, Nicaragua [1989]).

28. Interview. León, Nicaragua (1988).

29. Interview. León, Nicaragua (1988).

30. Interview. León, Nicaragua (1988).

31. Although the figure 35,000 was widely reported, some put the figure at 34,000.

32. The notion of geographic distinctions has cropped up often in popular accounts of Nicaragua since the revolution began. See, for example, A. Levie, *Nicaragua: The People Speak* (South Hadley: Bergin and Garvey, 1985), or P. Davis, *Where Is Nicaragua?* (New York: Simon and Schuster, 1987).

33. D. Slater, "Socialism, Democracy, and the Territorial Imperative: Elements for a Comparison of the Cuban and Nicaraguan Experiences," *Antipode,* vol. 18, no. 2 (1986), p. 174.

34. Although the rural peasantry nurtured the revolutionaries for at least seventeen years and the revolutionaries themselves tended to focus on the "heroic guerrillas in the mountains," as Massey pointed out, it was the urban poor who did much of the fighting and dying toward the end of the insurrectionary process. See D. Massey, *Nicaragua* (Philadelphia: Open University Press, 1987), pp. 20–21.

35. Although this reflects in part the long-standing relationship between the FSLN and the campesinos, another explanation for this may be that the expectations of those in the urban areas have not been met in full. In contrast, the comparatively lower expectations of many of those in the rural areas may well have been surpassed. A separate issue is that there is an increasingly urban population. The war and the economic conditions resulted in people heading for the cities, particularly Managua and León. Both are said to have at least doubled in population since 1979.

36. Almost everyone had some story to tell about people they knew or, more commonly, had heard about, whose support was determined by where they lived before or after the revolution. Yet neither of these factors seemed to be particularly important in determining personal support for the vast majority of those interviewed. It may be that interviews conducted in the contra front, perhaps in a city like Esteli, would be more useful in assessing this factor.

37. Interview. León, Nicaragua (1989).

38. Interview. León, Nicaragua (1989). The New Year's Message is Nicaragua's equivalent of the U.S. president's annual State of the Union address.

39. Interview. León, Nicaragua (1989).

40. Interview. León, Nicaragua (1989).

41. Interview. León, Nicaragua (1989).

42. Interview. León, Nicaragua (1989).

43. Interview. León, Nicaragua (1989). This is a variation on the maxim cited in the notes to Chapter 3 to the effect that the mountains do not breed democracy.

44. Interview. León, Nicaragua (1989).

45. Interview. León, Nicaragua (1988).

46. This is supported by several of the polls that were conducted in Nicaragua during the 1989 preelection period. A September–October 1989 ITZTANI-INOP poll found that 75 percent of those polled felt that the elections would be free and honest; only 9 percent felt that they would not. See "Update: Media Watch: Nicaragua's Poll Wars," p. 14. An October 1989 CID-Gallup poll found that 77 percent of those polled felt that there would be honest elections (ibid., p. 15). The 1989 Greenberg-Lake poll cited in note 24 found that 72 percent of those polled felt that the elections would be honest; 7 percent felt that they would not and 11 percent were undecided (ibid.). This certainly suggests some level of trust had emerged between the government and the population.

47. Interview. León, Nicaragua (1989).

48. Interview. Nagarote, Nicaragua (1989).

49. Interview. León, Nicaragua (1989).

50. Interview. León, Nicaragua (1989).

51. Interview. León, Nicaragua (1989).

52. Interview. León, Nicaragua (1988).

53. Interview. Chichigalpa, Nicaragua (1989).

54. Interview. León, Nicaragua (1989).

55. Interview. León, Nicaragua (1989).

56. Interview. León, Nicaragua (1988).

57. Interview. León, Nicaragua (1989).

58. Interview. León, Nicaragua (1989).

59. Interview. León, Nicaragua (1989).

60. T. Wickham-Crowley, "Winners, Losers, and Also-Rans: Toward a Comparative Sociology of Latin American Guerrilla Movements," in S. Eckstein, ed., *Power and Popular Protest: Latin American Social Movements* (Berkeley: University of California Press, 1989), p. 156.

61. Interview. León, Nicaragua (1989).

62. Indirect attacks began even prior to political victory, and planning for direct attacks was concurrent with it. As early as 1977 the Carter administration was engaged in efforts to forestall a FSLN victory; in 1978 Carter authorized Central Intelligence Agency (CIA) support for "democratic elements" in Nicaraguan society (*Newsweek*, 8 November 1982). During Somoza's waning days in office, the United States and elements of the Nicaraguan elite offered "Somocismo sin Somoza" ("Somozaism" without

Somoza) and tried to cobble together a government that would exclude the FSLN and rely on a "cleansed" National Guard. Simultaneously the Carter administration was seeking to alter the composition of the provisional government junta that had been announced in Costa Rica on 16 June 1979, which included non-FSLN elements. Interestingly, the resistance to U.S. interference in the junta's composition, according to Robert Pastor, former director of Latin American and Caribbean affairs on the National Security Council in the Carter administration, came from the JGRN's "moderates," Alfonso Robelo and Violeta Chamorro, a stance Daniel Ortega recalled with pride in his speech on the revolution's tenth anniversary. See, respectively, R. Pastor, *Condemned to Repetition: The United States and Nicaragua* (Princeton: Princeton University Press, 1987), p. 168, and D. Ortega, "Ortega Praises Revolution on Anniversary," FBIS-LAM (20 July 1989), p. 41. For the perspective of the Carter administration on these events in general, see Pastor. Interpretations of the same events and processes that are less generous to the Carter administration can be found in H. Sklar, *Washington's War on Nicaragua* (Boston: South End, 1988), pp. 7–56, and W. LeoGrande, "The United States and the Nicaraguan Revolution," in T. Walker, ed., *Nicaragua in Revolution* (New York: Praeger, 1982), pp. 63–77. Even as Somoza fell, the United States was laying the foundation for its future policy. On the same day that the revolutionaries achieved political victory, according to Dickey, the U.S. government sent a DC-8 jet disguised as a Red Cross relief plane— in violation of international agreements—into Managua to evacuate some of the remaining leadership of the hated National Guard. Over the next several days U.S. "operatives" airlifted remnants of Somoza's U.S.-created praetorian guard to Miami to prepare for the battle to oust the new government of Nicaragua. See C. Dickey, *With the Contras* (New York: Simon and Schuster, 1986), pp. 51–55. Official codification of this policy came within six months of the political victory, when Carter signed a "presidential finding" authorizing the CIA to begin providing approximately $1 million to anti-Sandinista elements in and out of the victorious coalition. See E. Chamorro, "Confessions of a 'Contra,'" *New Republic*, 5 August 1985; *Los Angeles Times*, 3 March 1985; R. Woodward, *Veil: The Secret Wars of the CIA, 1981–1987* (New York: Pocket Books, 1987), p. 111.

63. *Washington Post*, 8 May 1983. The public birth of the contras came in March 1981 when *Parade Magazine* reported that Nicaraguan exiles were training at private military camps in Florida and elsewhere in the United States. See E. Adams, "Exiles Rehearse for the Day They Hope Will Come," *Parade Magazine*, 15 March 1981, pp. 4–6. Two days later the story was picked up by the *New York Times*. On 23 November long-term support for the contras was sanctioned by National Security Decision Directive 17 (NSDD-17), which included the decision to "work primarily through non-Americans [sic] . . . but in some circumstances CIA might (possibly using U.S. personnel) take unilateral paramilitary action" (*Washington Post*, 8 May 1983). The "non-Americans" included Argentines, who had agreed to arm and train the contras (*Los Angeles Times*, 3 March 1985), "unilaterally controlled Latin assets" (UCLAs)—contract operatives drawn from Bolivia, Chile, Ecuador, El Salvador, and Honduras (P. Kornbluh, "The Covert War," in T. Walker, ed., *Reagan Versus the Sandinistas: The Undeclared War on Nicaragua* [Boulder: Westview, 1987], p. 29), and the CIA's usual ragtag mercenary army of Cuban exiles, Taiwanese, "Rhodesians," and Southeast Asians. In December, Reagan signed a "presidential finding" authorizing further covert activities (*Washington Post*, 8 May 1983). Ten days prior to the signing of NSDD-17, Secretary of State Alexander Haig was asked at a hearing of the U.S. House of Representatives Foreign Affairs Committee whether he could assure the committee that the United States was not and would not be involved in either direct or indirect attempts to overthrow or destabilize the Nicaraguan government. His response was succinct: "No, I would not give you

such an assurance": J. Goshko, "Haig Won't Rule out Anti-Nicaraguan Action," *Washington Post*, 13 November 1981.

64. These denials became all the more important when the U.S. Congress voted unanimously on 22 December 1982 to bar the use of U.S. funds "for the purpose of overthrowing the government of Nicaragua" (the first Boland Amendment). In an attempt to forestall further congressional cutoffs, on 27 April 1983, Reagan assured a joint session of Congress that he did not seek to overthrow the government of Nicaragua. The text of the president's remarks was in the *Washington Post*, 28 March 1983, p. A12. Almost a year later, with further restrictions still an important issue in the Congress, according to Smith, Reagan wrote Senator Howard Baker (4 April 1984) to assure him not only that he was not trying to destabilize or overthrow the Nicaraguan government but also that he did not seek "to impose or compel any particular form of government there": W. Smith, "Lies About Nicaragua," *Foreign Policy*, no. 67 (1987), p. 88. Perhaps as a result, great effort was expended to give the appearance that the activities of these Nicaraguan "freedom fighters" were purely homegrown. To handle awkward questions, according to Sklar, the operation was presented as an already existing Argentine operation to train the contras (Sklar, *Washington's War on Nicaragua*, p. 100; The U.S. paid Argentina $50 million for this "service"). Behind the pretense, however, the United States was busy; the contra leaders were often told which actions were to be taken on their behalf—on some occasions after the fact, as they were being handed the press release to read in which they were taking credit for the action. See L. Cockburn, *Out of Control: The Story of the Reagan Administration's Secret War in Nicaragua, the Illegal Arms Pipeline, and the Contra Drug Connection* (New York: Atlantic Monthly Press, 1987), pp. 2, 10–11; Kornbluh, "The Covert War," pp. 25–31; Sklar, *Washington's War on Nicaragua*, pp. 149–155. At the same time that the Reagan administration was denying that the United States sought the overthrow of the Nicaraguan government, the CIA was assuring the contras not only that such an overthrow was their joint mission but also that they would do so soon (Cockburn, *Out of Control*, p. 10; Dickey, *With the Contras*, pp. 112, 156–158; R. Gutman, *Banana Republic: The Making of American Policy in Nicaragua 1981–1987* [New York: Simon and Schuster, 1988]; *New Republic*, 5 August 1985; *New York Times*, 7 December 1982).

65. Smith, "Lies About Nicaragua," p. 88. The emphasis on the primacy of the goal is mine. In early 1985 Reagan, who likened the contras to the "founding fathers" of the United States, admitted at a 21 February press conference that his goal in Nicaragua was "to remove [the government] in the sense of its present structure." Pressed as to whether that would necessarily entail the overthrow of the Nicaraguan government, Reagan responded, "Not if the present government would turn around and . . . say 'uncle'" (Smith, "Lies About Nicaragua," p. 88). Amid increasingly open discussion of the U.S. efforts to overthrow the government of Nicaragua, confirmation came from two high-level, unimpeachable sources. In February 1986, White House spokesperson Larry Speakes was asked if the purpose of U.S. policy was to overthrow the Nicaraguan government. Speakes responded, "Yes, to be absolutely frank" (*Los Angeles Times*, 19 February 1986). A few months later, White House Chief of Staff Donald Regan was equally candid on NBC's "Meet the Press." Asked about the Nicaraguan government, Regan responded, "We have to get rid of it in some way or another. . . . What we want to do is to try and help those who are trying to overthrow that communist government": *Washington Post National Weekly*, 28 July 1986, p. 9, and *New Yorker*, 7 July 1986, p. 64.

66. Jonas and Stein argued that although the contra army—created, funded, trained, and directed by the United States—was anticipated to be a central component of the Reagan administration's effort to overthrow the government of Nicaragua, the United States was prepared to "settle" for simply making Nicaragua a memorable object lesson

for the rest of the Third World. See S. Jonas and N. Stein, "The Construction of Democracy in Nicaragua," *Latin American Perspectives*, vol. 17, no. 3 (1990), p. 23. Jonas and Stein cited a Pentagon official who explained that "2,000 hard-core guys could keep the pressure on the Nicaraguan government, force them to use their economic resources for the military, and prevent them from solving their economic problems" (ibid.). The United States, in fact, supported considerably more than 2,000 troops. By 1983 there were 15,000 contra troops in Honduras alone, according to D. Gilbert, "Nicaragua," in M. Blachman, W. LeoGrande, and K. Sharpe, eds., *Confronting Revolution: Security Through Diplomacy in Central America* (New York: Pantheon, 1986), p. 103. There were more troops with the Democratic Revolutionary Alliance (ARDE) in Costa Rica as well as two small indigenous armed movements on the Atlantic Coast. All received substantial U.S. aid.

67. LASA, "Electoral Democracy Under International Pressure," p. 5.

68. The preferred method, according to Jonas and Stein, was to try to provoke government "crackdowns" on the opposition. See Jonas and Stein, "The Construction of Democracy in Nicaragua," p. 24. In support of this they cited contra leader Enrique Bermúdez's 1986 explanation that the contra military attacks were designed, not to foster democratic reforms, but to "heighten repression" (ibid.). An almost peculiar yet constant sidelight of the effort to discredit the Nicaraguan government was administration efforts to link Nicaragua with what the U.S. government apparently considered the "outlaws" of the world: the Soviets prior to their Gorbachev-led transformation from "the evil empire," the Cubans, the Libyans, the North Koreans, the late Ayatollah Khomeini in Iran, and "South American drug dealers." See the discussion of the U.S. Office of Public Diplomacy in Chapter 2, note 95.

69. Hundreds of millions of dollars and a massive effort, however, were not producing quite the example that the Reagan administration had sought. Besides accruing some international sympathy in the face of the all-out U.S. attack—much as the Cubans had twenty years before—the revolution continued apace. As a result, Jonas and Stein argued, the United States "viewed the [1984] Nicaraguan election, Constitution, and political process in general as a 'threat' *not because they were insufficiently democratic, but because they were too democratic,* hence too attractive to other countries": Jonas and Stein, "The Construction of Democracy in Nicaragua," p. 24 (emphasis in original).

70. For more on the violation of U.S. and international law, see J. Hackel and D. Siegel, *In Contempt of Congress: The Reagan Record on Central America* (Washington, D.C.: Institute for Policy Studies, 1985), pp. 128–136. Domestically, there continued to be serious questions about the role of George Bush, then vice president (*Washington Post,* 10 June 1990; M. Byrne, "Illuminating Notations from the Scandal's Chief Operative," *In These Times,* 20 June 1990); and the role of many of the major failed savings and loan institutions in the CIA's contra-supply network (see P. Brewton, series on the Savings and Loan Scandal and the CIA, *Houston Post,* 6 February; 18 February; 21 February; 2 March; 11 March 1990). Internationally, there continued to be fallout from the U.S. protection of CIA operative John Hull, whose extradition was sought by Costa Rica. Hull was charged by the Costa Ricans with international drug trafficking, violation of the neutrality laws, and involvement in the 1984 murder of eight people in the CIA's failed attempt to assassinate Edén Pastora—a former FSLN hero who had gone into exile but was refusing to work with either the CIA or the U.S.-backed contras—and blame it on the Nicaraguan government (J. Bleifuss, "In Short," *In These Times,* 14 February 1990; N. Wax and M. Hardesty, "Drug Trade: Farmer John's Homegrown Connection," *Zeta Magazine,* April 1990).

71. Interview. Managua, Nicaragua (1989).

72. LASA, "Electoral Democracy Under International Pressure," p. 5; Smith, "Lies About Nicaragua," pp. 97–98.

73. Sklar, *Washington's War on Nicaragua,* pp. 300–308; Smith, "Lies About Nicaragua," p. 98. A National Security Council background paper exulted, "We have trumped the latest Nicaraguan/Mexican efforts to rush signature of an unsatisfactory Contadora agreement" (Sklar, *Washington's War on Nicaragua,* p. 304; Hackel and Siegel, *In Contempt of Congress,* p. 22).

74. J. Booth and T. Walker, *Understanding Central America* (Boulder: Westview, 1989), p. 137.

75. Ibid.

76. Ibid. Walker learned about the inner workings of the commission from a diplomat involved in the CIVS (pp. 179–180, n. 9).

77. These accords also played a central role in the temporary defeat of further U.S. military aid to the contras in the U.S. Congress.

78. This compliance, as well as the noncompliance of Nicaragua's neighbors, was recognized by the CIVS (Jonas and Stein, "The Construction of Democracy in Nicaragua," p. 25; Booth and Walker, *Understanding Central America,* p. 137) and the Latin American Studies Association Commission on Compliance with the Central American Peace Accord (LASA, "Extraordinary Opportunities . . . and New Risks," Report of the Latin American Studies Association Commission on Compliance with the Central American Peace Accord [Pittsburgh: LASA, 1988]). Even the *New York Times,* whose coverage of Nicaragua may be best characterized as considerably less than sympathetic, hailed the behavior of the Nicaraguan government in moving to put in place the accords. For more on the *New York Times's* stance on Nicaragua, see, e.g., N. Chomsky, "All the News That Fits," *Utne Reader,* no. 14 (1986), p. 56, and "U.S. Polity and Society: The Lessons of Nicaragua," in Walker, *Reagan Versus the Sandinistas;* E. Herman, "Lemoynespeak," *Zeta Magazine,* May 1988; Sklar, *Washington's War on Nicaragua,* pp. 67–69, 204–206; and J. Spence,"The U.S. Media: Covering (Over) Nicaragua," in Walker, ibid.

79. Booth and Walker argued that the Reagan administration's successful manipulation of the media and public opinion created a situation where "the Sandinistas found themselves to be in the curious position of having to take a major step beyond the [Esquipulas] accord in order not to appear to the U.S. public and Congress (then being pressed for more aid to the contras) to be in fundamental violation of that agreement": Booth and Walker, *Understanding Central America,* p. 138.

80. Operating rules and locations were to be jointly decided upon and the humanitarian aid was to be channeled through mutually agreed-upon neutral, i.e., non-U.S., organizations. See "Sapoá—A New Benchmark," *envío,* vol. 7, no. 83 (1988). Verification would be handled by Nicaraguan Cardinal Miguel Obando y Bravo and the OAS.

81. Booth and Walker, *Understanding Central America,* p. 138.

82. Cooper, "Soaring Prices, Plunging Hopes"; Collins, Coursen, and Drukker, "20–20 Hindsight," p. 3; Vilas, "What Went Wrong," pp. 12–13.

83. Vilas, "What Went Wrong," pp. 12–13.

84. Ibid.

85. Ibid. Vilas related that in April 1989 cotton "magnates" were awarded large subsidies that they had not requested while at the same time cotton worker's demands for a raise to a minimum wage that would cover basic foodstuffs were turned down. Worse, Vilas noted, when those hardest hit by the austerity measures reacted and demanded higher wages, the government responded with angry accusations, branding people as antirevolutionary and pawns of the United States. One state employee told a reporter that the FSLN was going too far to woo the opposition, "and that's a mistake for two reasons. First, because the Sandinistas don't yet understand that no matter what they do or say, the private sector doesn't want to *work* with them, it wants to *get rid* of them! And the second mistake is the Sandinistas thinking the Nicaraguan people will automatically understand. . . . They want to have people pull together to improve the econ-

omy? Fine. But you don't do that by letting the private sector piss all over you and then ask the poor to sacrifice. You do it by kicking the rich in the ass. People risk no longer knowing what they are fighting for, or no longer caring about the revolution, but instead just struggling to eat": Cooper, "Soaring Prices, Plunging Hopes," pp. 24–25 (emphases in original); also cited in H. Sklar, "Many Nicaragua Voters Cry Uncle," *Zeta Magazine*, vol. 13, no. 4 (April 1990), p. 17.

86. The arrogance was discussed with me by Father Miguel Gabaldon during an interview in Minneapolis, Minnesota, in 1989. The view that the FSLN's leadership was uninterested in "bad news" was noted in Collins, Coursen, and Drukker, "20–20 Hindsight," pp. 3–4, and A. Guillermoprieto, "Letter from Managua," *New Yorker*, 26 March 1990, pp. 88–89.

87. Quoted in Jonas and Stein, "The Construction of Democracy in Nicaragua," p. 31.

88. Martinez, public presentation.

89. LASA, "Electoral Democracy Under International Pressure," p. 19.

90. This was not lost on the FSLN. It recognized the importance of the economy and understood that things had not improved for the majority and might even have worsened. Yet the FSLN was equally convinced that the people would not hold it responsible for their dire straits. In fact, as Vilas pointed out, the "belief that an adjustment program could meet with popular acquiescence turned out to be a technocratic fantasy that cost the revolution dearly": Vilas, "What Went Wrong," p. 13. In any country an election in the aftermath of an austerity program such as the one introduced in Nicaragua would threaten the tenure of the incumbents. The government believed, however, that it could defy this logic by blaming the economic crisis on the war and the embargo and directing the focus of the campaign to other issues.

91. Nevertheless, as LASA pointed out, the United States was able to minimize the concessions made by the Nicaraguans and to keep world attention, and the concomitant pressure, focused almost solely on Nicaragua rather than Central America as a whole. See LASA, "Electoral Democracy Under International Pressure," p. 9.

92. See ibid., pp. 9–10. This was a further attempt to discourage the proliferation of small parties. Specifically, the rules governing the legislative elections were rewritten to favor the larger parties. This clause, which was dropped in later negotiations, specified that a party could win a seat in the National Assembly only if it won more than 5 percent of the vote nationwide. The logic—common in one form or another in most Western democracies—was to encourage the formation of true political parties rather than small personalistic vehicles. This continued efforts introduced in the laws for the 1984 elections.

93. LASA, "Electoral Democracy Under International Pressure," p. 10.

94. Ibid.

95. Ibid. Even after August, the United States continued to act through the opposition parties and the other Central American states to demand changes in what were the region's most liberal electoral laws.

96. "Setting the Rules of the Game: Nicaragua's Reformed Electoral Law," *envío*, vol. 8, no 95 (1989), p. 29. In Costa Rica, Venezuela, and Guatemala parties receiving less than 4–5 percent of the vote are ineligible for public funding. In the United States, public funds are granted on the basis of the preceding election results, according to which parties are classified as majority (over 25 percent), minority (5–25 percent), or new (under 5 percent). In Nicaragua, however, the United States and the opposition demanded that public funds be divided equally; if this were done in the United States, the Communist Party U.S.A. and its perennial presidential candidate, Gus Hall, would receive the same amount as that year's Republican or Democratic nominee.

97. Ibid., p. 33.

98. Many countries, including the United States, prohibit foreign funding of political parties. Yet under intense U.S. pressure and the implicit threat of the primary opposition party's boycotting another election, the Nicaraguan government agreed to the legalization of foreign funding of the political campaigns. According to the law, donations of material aid were duty free. Cash donations had to be reported, and 50 percent of the amount received had to be turned over to the Electoral Council's fund, which was being used to defray the administrative costs of the election.

99. The NED was created by the Reagan administration in 1983 as a bipartisan organization dedicated to "promoting democracy abroad." The NED's 1985 annual report is more specific about its mission: "planning, coordinating and implementing international political activities in support of U.S. policies and interests relative to national security." See W. Robinson, "U.S. Overt Intervention: Nicaragua's Electoral Coup," *Covert Action Information Bulletin,* no. 34 (Summer 1990), p. 9. Operating through an array of subsidiary and related organizations, the NED has been most active in Afghanistan, Chile, Eastern Europe, Nicaragua, the Philippines, Poland, South Africa, and the former Soviet Union. See H. Sklar, "Dollars Don't Buy Democracy," *Nicaraguan Perspectives,* 18 (1990), or the report by the Council on Hemispheric Affairs and the Inter-Hemispheric Education Resource Center, "National Endowment for Democracy (NED): A Foreign Policy Branch Gone Awry" (Albuquerque: Resource Center, 1990). In Nicaragua the funds were designated to support civic education, poll-watcher training, voter registration, a contingency fund, and support for some election observers. Another $3 million-plus of NED money, according to Sharkey, was received by various offshoots of the UNO: the Institute for Electoral Promotion and Training (IPCE); the Council of Trade Union Unification (CUS) (Sharkey noted that from 1984 to 1988 CUS also received $500,000 from the Free Trade Union Institute, the AFL-CIO conduit for NED moneys); Vía Cívica; the Center for Youth Formation; and the Nicaraguan Woman's Movement. *La Prensa,* the newspaper owned by the UNO's presidential candidate, received $470,000 from the NED for the election. See J. Sharkey, "Nicaragua: Anatomy of an Election," *Common Cause,* vol. 16, no. 3 (1990), pp. 25–28. The UNO and its affiliates also received hundreds of thousands of dollars in private donations from U.S. citizens.

100. LASA, "Electoral Democracy Under International Pressure," pp. 25–26.

101. Ibid., p. 24; Sharkey, "Nicaragua: Anatomy of an Election," p. 24.

102. LASA, "Electoral Democracy Under International Pressure," p. 26.

103. Collins, Coursen, and Drukker, "20–20 Hindsight," p. 3.

104. F. Goldman, "Daniel, Dona Violeta, Democracy: On the Campaign Trail in Nicaragua," *Harper's* (February 1990), p. 78.

105. The PSOC was the personal vehicle of Fernando Agüero, a former leader of the Nicaraguan Conservative party who had ties to Somoza.

106. "Navigating the Electoral Map," *envío,* vol. 8, no. 99 (1989), p. 13. These four parties included the Social Christian party (PSC), which for the 1990 election created an alliance with one of its offshoots, the Popular Social Christian party (PPSC), and the north Atlantic Coast–based Organization of the Nations of the Motherland (YATAMA), and three microparties: the Democratic Conservative party (PCD), the Central American Unionist party (PUCA), and the National Unity Liberal party (PLIUN). The PPSC, which had been part of the governing coalition immediately after the political victory, ended up split between the alliance of the PCS and the PPSC and the UNO.

107. LASA, "Electoral Democracy Under International Pressure," p. 18.

108. The PRT, Trotskyites affiliated with the International Workers League and the Fourth International, felt it was time for an "authentic revolution," which would

eradicate the FSLN's economic program ("Navigating the Electoral Map," p. 13). MAP-ML charged that to date the revolution had "betrayed socialism and the workers" in pursuit "of staying in power and maintaining a privileged standard of living that separates its leaders from the Nicaraguan masses": "Ideologies in Conflict: Platforms of Four Nicaraguan Political Parties," *envío*, vol. 8, no. 101 (1989), p. 37.

109. Three of the parties discussed here—the PCD (14 percent), PPSC (5.6 percent), and MAP-ML (1 percent)—accounted for over 20 percent of that vote. The three other opposition parties that ran in the 1984 election, PLI (9.6 percent), PCdeN (1.5 percent), and PSN (1.3 percent), were part of the UNO in 1990.

110. These figures were bolstered, respectively, by the 1.2 percent received by the MUR's Hassán and the 1.6 percent National Assembly vote tallied by the PSC slate.

111. Although the president of the National Endowment for Democracy (NED) assured the U.S. Senate Foreign Relations Committee that the NED funds were designed to ensure that opposition parties would become an "enduring force in Nicaraguan society and the guarantor of pluralism," the only one of the nine opposition parties to receive NED funds was the UNO. An NED official later explained that "if Congress had wanted money to go to other parties, it should have said so." See Sharkey, "Nicaragua: Anatomy of an Election," p. 24.

112. LASA, "Electoral Democracy Under International Pressure," p. 18.

113. Ibid., p. 41. *Continuismo* was defined by LASA as "a self-perpetuating hold on power." Wiarda and Kline similarly defined it as "the prolonging of one's term in office beyond its constitutional limits": H. Wiarda and H. Kline, "Government Machinary and the Role of the State," in *Latin America Politics and Development,* 3d ed. (Boulder: Westview, 1990), p. 85.

114. Vilas, "What Went Wrong," p. 15. Such concern, Vilas suggested, was heightened by the FSLN's decision to include numerous relatives of Sandinista leaders on their National Assembly slate.

115. LASA, "Electoral Democracy Under International Pressure," p. 20.

116. Ibid.

117. These ranged from baseball caps and T-shirts to "articles of clothing, toys for the children, emblems, toiletries, etc": Vilas, "What Went Wrong," p. 14.

118. This description is drawn primarily from LASA, "Electoral Democracy Under International Pressure," p. 21, as well as various descriptions including L. Bensky, "Campaigning with the Sandinistas: Everything Will Be Better?" *Nation*, vol. 250, no. 9 (1990), p. 303; Goldman, "Daniel, Dona Violeta, Democracy," pp. 74–75; Guillermoprieto, "Letter from Managua," pp. 88–89; J. Preston, "The Defeat of the Sandinistas," *New York Review of Books*, vol. 37, no. 6 (1990), p. 27; and Vilas, "What Went Wrong," pp. 14–15. Goldman described a similar scenario at an appearance by Ortega's running mate, Ramírez ("Daniel, Dona Violeta, Democracy," pp. 71–72).

119. LASA, "Electoral Democracy Under International Pressure," p. 21.

120. Ibid.

121. Guillermoprieto, for example, noted the assumption "that the Sandinistas' spiritual link with the people was so strong that it could override any temporary romance with the opposition": Guillermoprieto, "Letter from Managua," p. 89.

122. Ibid., p. 88.

123. See also Collins, Coursen, and Drukker, who argued that the FSLN "apparently failed to understand that the time in which a majority of the population saw it as a vanguard had passed. By continuing to act as a vanguard party, complete with a vertical structure and a largely secret decision-making process, the FSLN separated itself from the general population": Collins, Coursen, and Drukker, "20–20 Hindsight," p. 3.

124. Goldman, "Daniel, Dona Violeta, Democracy," p. 71. "Muchachos" is an affectionate nickname for the "boys" who lead the FSLN.

125. A political alignment would likely have resulted in at least four factions: the Far Right (Neo-Liberal party [PALI], National Action party [PAN], Democratic Party of National Confidence [PDCN], Constitutionalist Liberal Party [PLC], and National Conservative party [PNC]); the Right ([National Conservative Action party [ANC] and Popular Conservative Alliance party [PAPC]); the Center (PLI, MDN, Central American Integrationist party [PIAC], and Social Democratic party [PSD]); and the Left (PPSC, PSN, and PCdeN). Vilas, "What Went Wrong," p. 16, identified six "broad ideological currents" that made up the UNO: parties from the old Conservative party, those that grew out of the old Liberal party, social democrats, social Christians, Communists, and the Central American integrationists. *Envío* categorized the makeup as conservatives, liberals, social Christians, social democrats, and Marxists (split into Communists and socialists). See "Ideologies in Conflict," p. 28.

126. The PAN, the PDCN, PLC, and the PNC. The rightist party was the PAPC.

127. The leftist parties were the PPSC dissidents and Nicaragua's two pre–political victory leftist parties, the PSN, founded in 1944, and its 1967 offshoot, the PCdeN.

128. The far-right PALI, the rightist ANC, and three centrist parties, the MDN, the PIAC, and the PSD.

129. It was a point of great pride, according to a former member of COSEP (Interview. León, Nicaragua 1989), that members had not left the country or joined the contras, although they strongly supported the contras' efforts. As we have seen, COSEP was an integral part of the CD in 1984 and thus boycotted the election.

130. Blue and white are the colors of the Nicaraguan flag.

131. The PLI and PSN had been founded in 1944, the PCdeN in 1967, and the PPSC in 1976. The PLC (1967) and MDN (1978) are the only other coalition partners that existed prior to 1979. In contrast, seven of the other parties have been in existence since only 1984.

132. For an interesting discussion of Godoy's role in the National Assembly, see A. Reding, "Under Construction: Nicaragua's New Polity," in P. Rosset and J. Vandermeer, eds., *Nicaragua: Unfinished Revolution* (New York: Grove, 1986).

133. The PALI, the MDN, and the PSD all apparently bore "stigmas" of which the others were leery. The PALI's blemish lay in its creation and domination by former Somoza allies. The MDN and the PSD were stained by their contra connections. In both cases their most important leaders—the MDN's Robelo and the PSD's Alfredo César and Pedro Joaquín Chamorro, Jr.—had left Nicaragua and joined the contra political directorate. Neither the ANC nor the PIAC, lacking party structure, had acquired legal status as parties prior to the election.

134. "Navigating the Electoral Map," p. 11; LASA, "Electoral Democracy Under International Pressure," p. 17.

135. It is interesting to note that it was apparently threats by the PSN and PCdeN to quit that assured Godoy of the vice-presidential slot over Bolaños. It was, O'Kane pointed out, hard enough for them to accept a ticket headed by one of Nicaragua's most powerful families—adding the leader of the country's most reactionary elements would apparently be too much. See T. O'Kane, "The New Old Order," *NACLA Report on the Americas*, vol. 24, no. 1 (1990), p. 39, n. 9.

136. "Navigating the Electoral Map," p. 12. Godoy was undoubtedly acceptable to the United States, whose last-minute request that he drop out of the 1984 presidential campaign he had heeded. Godoy's selection prompted two days of COSEP-directed attacks on him that accused him of being a "Marxist" in the pay of the FSLN. To placate COSEP, members were awarded a disproportionate number of slots on the UNO's National Assembly slate. For example, LASA noted that Godoy's PLI "received only five positions on the UNO assembly slate—equal in number to the much smaller PNC, PDCN, and the PLC—in spite of its much larger base and electoral success in 1984":

LASA, "Electoral Democracy Under International Pressure," p. 17, n. 39. The preference for the small COSEP-affiliated parties was also noted by O'Kane, who pointed out that some brand-new parties such as PALI "were offered as many slots as parties with considerable political weight, such as the Popular Social Christian party (PPSC), one of the best organized in the country with its own newspaper and foundation": O'Kane, "The New Old Order," p. 31.

137. "Ideologies in Conflict," p. 24.

138. V. Chamorro, News Conference, *La Prensa* FBIS-LAM (14 September 1989), p. 1.

139. Ibid., p. 12.

140. For an excellent discussion of Chamorro's "team" and CORDENIC, see O'Kane, "The New Old Order."

141. Ibid., p. 29.

142. If the allusion to the Virgin Mary seems extreme, consider that on more than one occasion during the campaign Chamorro was hailed as *La Santa* (the Saint) by people (several observers reported this to me; see also O'Kane, "The New Old Order," p. 29). Dressed all in white and confined for much of the campaign to a wheelchair because of her chronic osteoporosis, Chamorro, according to one reporter, would appear in white vehicles "stretching her hands out to the crowd like a prelate": J. Preston, "Chamorro, Familial Conciliator, Faces a Wider Task," *Washington Post,* 27 February 1990, p. A16. O'Kane noted that "Chamorro was paraded in rallies and marches in much the same way that the Virgin Mary is carried in religious processions throughout Latin America" ("The New Old Order," p. 28). On several occasions, O'Kane continued, all pretense of subtlety was abandoned and Chamorro was introduced at rallies as Nicaragua's "Maria" (Mary), the "white dove of peace" (ibid.). Nicaragua's Cardinal Obando y Bravo was often in evidence and her audience with the pope widely covered.

The mix of revolution and religion is no surprise; liberation theology, for example, was an important element of Sandinismo. More important, there is a long tradition in Latin America of mixing the two. When Sandino was assassinated, his father noted that "those who are redeemers are always crucified": G. Selser, *Sandino, general de hombres libres* (Mexico City: Diógenes, 1979), pp. 288–289. In Cuba one of the great symbols of the revolution is the "Legend of the 12," the twelve people who, along with Fidel Castro, are supposed to have been the only ones to survive the landing of the *Granma* in the 1956 invasion (the actual number was closer to twenty; cf. R. Bonachea and M. San Martin, *The Cuban Insurrection 1952–1959* [New Brunswick: Transaction Press, 1974], pp. 88–89. Bonachea and San Martin also discussed the various other numbers given for the survivors, from seven to nineteen, that the principals cited at various times.). Castro began the voyage with the promise that "we will be free or we will be martyrs": E. Guevara, "Episodes of the Revolutionary War: The Revolution Begins," *Che Guevara and the Cuban Revolution: Writings and Speeches of Ernesto Che Guevara* (New York: Pathfinder, 1987), p. 36. "The 12" are used to symbolize determination, commitment, and sacrifice. Later, Guevara wrote to Castro that "one thing is clear, the 26th of July [the guerrilla movement], the Sierra Maestra, and you are three separate entities and only one God": C. Franqui, *Diary of the Cuban Revolution* (New York: Viking, 1980), p. 271. The proliferation of Christ-like pictures of Guevara himself in the years after his death further attested to the mingling of the revolutionary and the religious in Latin America.

143. Chamorro, News Conference, p. 12. The effort of the FSLN (which included two of her children and one of her brothers-in-law) to divest Chamorro of her husband's surname was an ill-conceived attempt to disassociate her from Pedro Joaquín's martyrdom and almost certainly a tactical error. If anything, it served to remind people of the reverence they felt for her husband and made the FSLN look mean spirited.

144. V. Chamorro, Campaign Speech, Radio Católica. FBIS-LAM (19 December 1989).

145. V. Chamorro, Final Campaign Speech, Managua Radio Corporation. FBIS-LAM (20 February 1990).

146. Ortega, "Ortega Praises Revolution on Anniversary," p. 41.

147. Goldman argued that "men like Reagan and Bush" began "not surprisingly, if ironically . . . to care about free, fair elections in Nicaragua in the summer of 1979 . . . ; *ironically*, because it was the political space opened that summer by the revolution . . . that for the first time made it possible to talk about free and fair Nicaraguan elections and, more important, the establishment of a true and progressive democracy": Goldman, "Daniel, Dona Violeta, Democracy," p. 70.

148. D. Durenberger, "Congratulations to the Nicaraguan People," *Congressional Record—Senate*, vol. S1563 (26 February 1990).

149. The 1990 Nicaraguan election was perhaps the most intensely observed in history. The UN and OAS sent hundreds of observers, who were present throughout the process. On election day, commissions from virtually every Western European parliament, representatives of the election offices from every Latin American and most Caribbean nations, and a wide array of international delegations including the Council of Freely-Elected Heads of State (former U.S. president Carter's organization), the European Parliament, Freedom House, the Latin American Studies Association, and a myriad of other groups contributed to the more than one thousand observers who were present. None of the major monitoring groups judged the election process to be anything less than fair, open, and honest.

150. Sklar, "Many Nicaragua Voters Cry Uncle," p. 18.

151. M. D'Escoto, "There Was Fraud, But the Revolution Won," *Barricada Internacional*, vol. 10, no. 314 (21 April 1990), p. 18; Martinez, public presentation; C. Peters, "Letter from Managua," *Zeta Magazine*, April 1990.

152. Martinez, public presentation. Martinez is the former minister of both budget and planning (1988–1990) and of foreign trade and commerce (1979–1988).

153. T. Wickham-Crowley suggested that the 1973 midterm elections in Chile represented another such case. In fact, Salvador Allende's Popular Unity party (UP) received almost 50 percent of the vote in the April 1971 local/municipal elections and 43 percent in the March 1973 midterm congressional elections—the first time a "Chilean president had ever been able to increase his support in a midterm congressional election": Thomas Skidmore and Peter Smith, *Modern Latin America*, 3d ed. (New York: Oxford University Press, 1992), p. 137. The figures are from pp. 136–137. I am uncomfortable about describing the longtime political functionaries of the UP as revolutionaries—I would be inclined to call them reformists—and it seems pertinent to me that they, having been elected in the first place, would not be loath to put themselves before the public again. I know of nothing that would call into question the UP's commitment to democratic electoral procedures. In contrast, to the best of my knowledge, no revolutionary movement that came to power via armed insurrection had, prior to the FSLN, ever held popular elections in which the opposition was allowed to participate freely.

154. A. Cruz, "Nicaragua: The Sandinista Regime at a Strategic Watershed," *Strategic Review*, Spring 1984, p. 11.

155. Berman argued that "Nicaraguans who voted against the party" were "in their own minds . . . defending the revolution—against the Sandinistas": P. Berman, "Who Lost Nicaragua? A Response to William M. LeoGrande," *Tikkun*, vol. 5, no. 3 (1990), p. 17.

156. The split is serious. The UNO Right tried to remove Chamorro from the ticket even before the election when she was on a trip outside of the country. Largely because

of U.S. pressure, that effort failed. Many people believe that the UNO's right wing has coup plans and that it is behind the steady stream of death threats that Chamorro receives.

157. Preston, "The Defeat of the Sandinistas," p. 28.


## CHAPTER FIVE

1. J. Dunn, *Modern Revolutions*, 2d ed. (Cambridge: Cambridge University, 1989), p. 226. John Dunn, in a 1991 conversation with me, stressed the importance of this idea.

2. To take one example, Hodges explained that Alberto Bayo, a loyalist Spanish Air Force officer forced into exile after the destruction of the Spanish Republic in 1939 by the fascist forces, hooked up with and trained surviving Sandinistas in the 1940s in Costa Rica. Bayo subsequently trained Castro's Cuban exiles in Mexico, where his "star" student was Ché Guevara. In Cuba, Bayo and Guevara helped train a new generation of Nicaraguan exiles, passing on to them lessons from Spain, Sandino, Guevara's 1954 experiences watching the destruction of democracy in Guatemala, and the ill-fated Caribbean Legion. The latter was a collection of progressive fighters in the region dedicated to overthrowing Central American and Caribbean dictators. Bayo specifically trained the expeditionary forces that sailed against the first Somoza in 1948 and the Dominican Republic's Trujillo in 1949. See D. Hodges, *Intellectual Foundations of the Nicaraguan Revolution* (Austin: University of Texas Press, 1986), pp. 167–172. For more on the Caribbean Legion, see C. Ameringer, *The Democratic Left in Exile: The Antidictatorial Struggle in the Caribbean, 1945–1959* (Coral Gables: University of Miami Press, 1974).

3. Not everyone would describe these four cases as socialist. Stone pointed out, for example, that some "Marxist commentators . . . have challenged the claims to genuine socialist practice by the Manley regime in Jamaica in the 1970s and by Guyana under the late Forbes Burnham": C. Stone, "Whither Caribbean Socialism: Grenada, Jamaica, and Guyana in Perspective," in J. Heine, ed., *A Revolution Aborted: The Lessons of Grenada* (Pittsburgh: University of Pittsburgh Press, 1990), p. 291. Howe similarly noted that the Jamaican socialists have "especially in Marxist eyes, only rather dubious socialist credentials": S. Howe, "Manley Vices, Socialist Virtues," *New Statesman and Society*, vol. 2, no. 35, p. 23. The title of the Latin American Bureau's book about Guyana is *Guyana: The Fraudulent Revolution* (London: Latin American Bureau, 1984). Sunshine has characterized the Surinamese as "reluctant revolutionaries": C. Sunshine, *The Caribbean: Survival, Struggle, and Sovereignty* (Boston: South End, 1988), p. 181.

4. This last apparently refers to Scandinavian-style social democracy.

5. Ironically, in both cases, the effort to distort and/or destroy democracy came in large part from the bastion of democracy, the United States. Henry Kissinger, national security adviser to (and later secretary of state for) U.S. President Richard Nixon, declared after the 1970 election of longtime Chilean Senate leader and three-time presidential candidate Salvador Allende, "I don't see why we need to stand by and watch a country go Communist due to the irresponsibility of its own people" (this remark is cited in a number of places, most recently, M. McClintock, *Instruments of Terror: U.S. Guerrilla Warfare, Counter-Insurgency, Counter-Terrorism* [New York: Pantheon, 1992], p. 419). U.S. efforts to instigate a coup d'état in Chile have been well documented; see, e.g., W. Blum, *The CIA: A Forgotten History, U.S. Global Interventions Since World War 2* (London: Zed, 1986), pp. 232–243; S. Hersh, *The Price of Power* (New York: Summit, 1983), pp. 258–296; and J. Prados, *President's Secret Wars* (New York: William Morrow, 1986), pp. 315–322. The U.S. efforts to destabilize economically the government of Michael Manley in Jamaica are equally well documented: see, e.g., Blum, *The CIA*,

pp. 299–304. In both cases the United States and its local allies were successful: In 1973 the Chilean military overthrew the government and instituted a brutal seventeen-year military dictatorship; the Jamaicans fared somewhat better after the socialists were unseated in the 1980 election to be replaced by a conservative government. H. Sklar, *Washington's War on Nicaragua* (Boston: South End, 1988), pp. 390–391, and others have referred to 1980 as an "electoral coup."

6. S. Amin, "The Issue of Democracy in the Contemporary Third World," *Socialism and Democracy*, no. 12 (1991), p. 95. Amin also noted (ibid.) that "Western democracy has no social dimension."

7. Chile's Socialist party is the second strongest political force within the country's ruling Democratic Coalition alliance; party leader Senator Riccardo Núñez said, "Socialism is not dead, but it is ever stronger in the conscience of the exploited and the humiliated and of those who, despite the obstacles, are striving for a better world": *Latin American Regional Report: Southern Cone Report* RS–91–10 (25 December 1991), p. 3.

8. R. Borosage and S. Landau, "Lonely Manley," *Mother Jones*, vol. 16 (March–April 1991), p. 29.

9. Other interesting cases that speak to the continued power of socialism in Latin America and the Caribbean include the Worker's party in Brazil, which almost won the 1989 election and seems poised to do very well in the next election; the role of Uruguay's former urban guerrillas, the Tupamaros, in that country's opposition coalition, the Broad Front (FA); and the October 1992 election of longtime Marxist Cheddi Jagan in Guyana.

10. The FMLN is named for Augustín Farabundo Martí, described by Booth and Walker as "a charismatic Marxist intellectual," who briefly fought alongside Sandino in Nicaragua before returning to El Salvador to organize peasant uprisings against the government; he was tortured and killed by the Salvadoran government in 1932. See J. Booth and T. Walker, *Understanding Central America* (Boulder: Westview, 1989), p. 33. The Peruvian social revolutionaries popularly known as Sendero Luminoso (the Shining Path) grew out of a variety of splits within Peru's Communists and dubbed themselves the Peruvian Communist Party–Shining Path (PCP-SL); the latter term came from the subtitle of their party newspaper, "By the shining path of Comrade José Carlos Mariátegui": H. Dietz, "Peru's Sendero Luminoso as a Revolutionary Movement," *Journal of Political and Military Sociology*, no. 18 (1990), p. 126; D. Poole and G. Renique, "The New Chroniclers of Peru: US Senderologists and the 'Shining Path' of Peasant Rebellion," *Bulletin of Latin American Research*, vol. 10, no. 2 (1991), pp. 141–142. According to Luís Arce Borja, editor of *El Diario*, a newspaper sympathetic to the PCP-SL, "Sendero Luminoso is a pejorative term, used by the foreign and bourgeois press; the correct name is Communist Party of Peru, PCP": A. Fokkema, "There Is No Other Way: An Interview With Luís Arce Borja," *NACLA Report on the Americas*, vol. 24, no. 4 (1990/1991), p. 23.

11. There are many excellent pieces on the revolutionary process in El Salvador. Particularly useful are T. S. Montgomery, *Revolution in El Salvador: Origins and Evolution* (Boulder: Westview, 1982); J. Dunkerley, *The Long War: Dictatorship and Rebellion in El Salvador* (London: Verso, 1982); *Power in the Isthmus: A Political History of Modern Central America* (London: Verso, 1988); M. McClintock, *The American Connection*, Vol. 1: *State Terror and Popular Resistence in El Salvador* (London: Zed, 1985); T. Barry, *El Salvador: A Country Guide* (Albuquerque: Inter-Hemispheric Resource Center, 1990); and Americas Watch, *El Salvador's Decade of Terror: Human Rights Since the Assassination of Archbishop Romero* (New Haven: Yale University Press, 1991). Good brief overviews are Booth and Walker, *Understanding Central America*, and J. Dunkerley, "El Salvador,

1930–89," *Political Suicide in Latin America and Other Essays* (London: Verso, 1992). Insight into the FMLN-FDR and its thinking is available in two pieces by leader J. Villalobos, "A Democratic Revolution for El Salvador," *Foreign Policy*, no. 74 (1989), and "Popular Insurrection: Desire or Reality?" *Latin American Perspectives*, vol. 16, no. 3 (1989); and in S. Miles and B. Ostertag, "FMLN New Thinking," *NACLA Report on the Americas*, vol. 23, no. 3 (1989). Tina Rosenberg offered some interesting insights into the Far Right in her chapter, "The Laboratory," in *Children of Cain: Violence and the Violent in Latin America* (New York: William Morrow, 1991).

12. Booth and Walker, *Understanding Central America*, p. 85. Long and Smyth cited El Salvador's Roman Catholic Human Rights Office, which claimed that most Salvadoran dead were killed in "deliberate assassination campaigns carried out by government security forces, elite U.S.-trained battalions, and military death squads": T. Long and F. Smyth, "How the FMLN Won the Peace," *Village Voice*, vol. 37, no. 7 (1992), p. 19. Perhaps the most comprehensive assessment of the death and destruction in El Salvador was offered by Americas Watch, *El Salvador's Decade of Terror.* The figure of 75,000 is from Long and Smyth ("How the FMLN Won the Peace," p. 19). Booth and Walker, writing three years earlier, put the total at 70,000 (*Understanding Central America*, p. 85).

13. Booth and Walker, *Understanding Central America*, p. 35.

14. Mexico and France both recognized the FMLN-FDR as a "belligerent force": Booth and Walker, *Understanding Central America*, p. 81; Dunkerley assigned it "belligerent status": Dunkerley, *Power in the Isthmus*, p. 385; according to Americas Watch, it was a "representative political force": Americas Watch, *El Salvador's Decade of Terror*, p. 10.

15. Wickham-Crowley highlighted some important differences between the FMLN-FDR and the FSLN, most important, that the FMLN-FDR was never as multiclass or broad based as the FSLN. See T. Wickham-Crowley, *Guerrillas and Revolution in Latin America: A Comparative Study of Insurgents and Regimes Since 1956* (Princeton: Princeton University Press, 1992), pp. 285–287. The MNR and NJM were probably most akin to the FDR, since all three were composed of opposition politicians of various stripes. The FMLN probably resembled more M-26 in structure, although M-26 could not be characterized as Marxist.

16. M. Davis, "What Brought El Salvador's FMLN to a New Kind of Power," *Cross-Roads*, no. 19 (1992), p. 12. Davis pointed out that the Salvadorans have not only looked within their own hemisphere. He noted that there was a vague connection with "Eastern European Communism" and that inspiration was drawn from other Third World "anti-imperialist" struggles (p. 13).

17. Dunkerley, *Power in the Isthmus*, pp. 407–408.

18. This period did, however, see the near-demise of the FMLN-FDR. As Wickham-Crowley pointed out, a number of the important FDR figures decided to participate in the 1988 and 1989 elections despite misgivings and even outright opposition by the FMLN leadership. The new party that was formed, the Democratic Convergence (CD), even criticized the FMLN's use of violence.

19. N. Svarzman, "Salvadorans Achieve Peace," *Times of the Americas*, 8 January 1992, p. 1. It is also worth noting that, according to Long and Smyth, the late Roberto D'Aubisson, widely credited as the man who began and oversaw much of the government and quasi-government terror, had predicted when the far-right ARENA party was elected in 1989 that it would be able to negotiate a settlement with the FMLN-FDR. See Long and Smyth, "How the FMLN Won the Peace," p. 20.

20. The Handal quote is from R. Gomez, "Peace Agreement: Interview With Shafik Handal of the FMLN," *Latin American News Update: Monthly Foreign Press Digest*, vol. 8,

no. 2 (1992), p. 21; the details are from J. Melendez, "Writing the History of the Peace," *Latin American News Update: Monthly Foreign Press Digest*, vol. 8, no. 2 (1992), p. 23.

21. Long and Smyth, "How the FMLN Won the Peace," p. 22; Davis, "What Brought El Salvador's FMLN to a New Kind of Power," p. 18; and D. Dye, "The Peace Accords in a Nutshell," *In These Times*, vol. 16, no. 18 (1992), p. 8. As Dye put it, "Though the accords also contain social and economic planks, they don't by themselves achieve the social justice goals sought by the FMLN. By ending gross repression, they open up space in the political arena for the left to press for reform by peaceful means for the first time in Salvadoran history" (ibid.).

22. The term *negotiated revolution* has been invoked by both the UN secretary general (Davis, "What Brought El Salvador's FMLN to a New Kind of Power," p. 12) and FMLN leader Ferman Cienfuegos (Long and Smyth, "How the FMLN Won the Peace," p. 19); Shafik Handal is source of the lament about what could have been (Gomez, "Peace Agreement").

23. On the origins of the name, see note 10.

24. Poole and Renique, in "The New Chroniclers of Peru," convincingly, if harshly, challenged many of the assumptions that have dominated the first ten years of study, including both the character of Sendero and whether it is either enigmatic or mysterious at all. Recent Peruvian works did suggest that early interpretations of Sendero may have missed a great deal; see in particular the reviews by O. Starn, "New Literature on Peru's Sendero Luminoso," *Latin American Research Review*, vol. 27, no. 2 (1992), and D. Lehmann, "The Shining Path to Terror," *Times Literary Supplement*, 26 July 1991.

25. C. Degregori, "A Dwarf Star," *NACLA Report on the Americas*, vol. 24, no. 4 (1990/1991), p. 11.

26. On the degree to which Sendero actually follows Mariátegui's thought, see A. Wheat, "Shining Path's 'Fourth Sword' Ideology," *Journal of Political and Military Sociology*, no. 18 (1990). On Mariátegui in general, see H. Vanden, *National Marxism in Latin America: José Carlos Mariátegui's Thought and Politics* (Boulder: Lynne Rienner, 1986).

27. The Túpac Amaru Revolutionary Movement (MRTA). As Rosenberg pointed out, the MRTA "reveres Ché Guevara . . . publishes intellectual tracts, seeks to form alliances with left-wing groups, sends its troops out to do the necessary political drudgery of organizing, and tries to ingratiate itself with the poor sectors of Peru": T. Rosenberg, "Dialectic," *Children of Cain*, p. 151. For the *Senderistas*, Rosenberg noted, the MRTA were simply more bourgeois revisionists. One Senderista interviewed by Puertas explained that the MRTA "is the principal enemy of the revolution and there will ultimately have to be a confrontation with them": L. Puertas, "Senderista," *New Internationalist*, no. 197 (1989), p. 10.

28. R. Kirk, "Shining Path's War on Hope: Murder in a Shantytown," *Nation*, vol. 254, no. 12 (1992); Degregori, "A Dwarf Star," p. 13. The phrase "heighten the contradictions" refers to the notion that the way to hasten the conflict of opposing forces or interests or even ideas is to exacerbate the tension between them. One avenue for this, as suggested in the text, is to wipe out any middle ground so that only the polar opposites remain and, in the the case of Peru, people are forced to chose one side or the other.

29. This suggests at least some of the elements of pragmatism that characterized the other cases we have studied. Wickham-Crowley noted two "minor exceptions": Sendero "formed a 'tactical alliance' in late 1985 with . . . the Túpac Amaru Revolutionary Movement; and it had ties to the Peruvian Peasants' Confederation of Apurímac": Wickham-Crowley, *Guerrillas and Revolutionaries*, p. 403, n. 138.

30. Dietz, "Peru's Sendero Luminoso as a Revolutionary Movement," p. 136. In Dietz's estimation, "Global actors have thus had only minimal or no influence on Sendero, aside from rhetorical ideological statements of support, and the reverse is true as well: Sendero has not had, nor has it sought to have, influence on other revolutionary movements" (p. 137).

31. N. Manrique, "Time of Fear," *NACLA Report on the Americas*, vol. 24, no. 4 (1990/1991), p. 29.

32. The description of the Soviets and the lament about the Cultural Revolution pulling up short are from Rosenberg, "Dialectic," p. 150; the remark about the Chinese is from P. Symmes, "Out to Lunch with Sendero," *American Spectator*, vol. 24, no. 12 (1991), p. 27.

33. Dietz, "Peru's Sendero Luminoso as a Revolutionary Movement," p. 132.

34. Castro as a traitor is from Wickham-Crowley, *Guerrillas and Revolution*, p. 298; as revisionist servant, from Symmes, "Out to Lunch with Sendero," p. 27; the Guevara reference is from Rosenberg, "Dialectic," p. 151.

35. Fokkema, "There Is No Other Way," p. 25; Rosenberg, "Dialectic," p. 150.

36. As one Senderista explained to Rosenberg: "When Deng Xiaoping began to exhibit counter-revolutionary tendencies, he was sent to care for pigs to proletarize him. And look what happened. If he had been liquidated, he wouldn't have caused all these problems. Mao was only the head of the party, while others headed the state and the military. We've learned from that. The party has to control everything. Absolutely everything": Rosenberg, "Dialectic," p. 150. Deng Xiaoping was perhaps Sendero's favorite target. In 1980 the Sendero hung dead dogs from traffic lights and lampposts throughout Lima with placards proclaiming, "Deng Xiaoping, sonofabitch." Renique reported one discussion where Deng Xiaoping was regularly referred to as an "infected pustule": J. Renique, "The Revolution Behind Bars," *NACLA Report on the Americas*, vol. 24, no. 4 (1990/1991), pp. 17–18.

37. Starn, "New Literature on Peru's Sendero Luminoso," pp. 220–221. According to Symmes, however, some feel that the Khmer Rouge fell short. Although they had "the right techniques, they simply lacked an effective Communist party to carry the revolution to its end": Symmes, "Out to Lunch with Sendero," p. 27. This echoed the comment about the failure of the Cultural Revolution in note 36.

38. G. Gorriti, "The War of the Philosopher-King: The Strange Career of the Shining Path," *New Republic*, vol. 202, no. 25 (1990), p. 18.

39. Ibid.

40. Degregori, "A Dwarf Star," p. 12. The other observer was Kirk, "Shining Path's War on Hope," p. 412.

41. Manrique, "Time of Fear," p. 36.

42. Americas Watch, *Peru Under Fire: Human Rights Since the Return to Democracy* (New Haven: Yale University Press, 1992), pp. 59, 64. Emphasis in the original.

43. Cited in Starn, "New Literature on Peru's Sendero Luminoso," p. 219.

44. Ibid. In support of this, Starn cited Guzmán's vision of himself as a "revolutionary Moses" leading his followers across "a river of blood" into the promised land: "People of Peru, . . . today your finest children, flesh of your flesh, steel of your steel . . . have unleashed the redwind and the flaming banner of rebellion . . . the children of your powerful womb offer you their armed actions and their lives." Earlier in his article, Starn cited Guzmán as well, telling his followers that their "armed struggle has begun. . . . The invincible flames of the revolution will glow, turning to lead and steel. . . . There will be a great rupture and we will be the makers of the new dawn. . . . We shall convert the black fire into red and the red into pure light" (p. 212).

45. Cited in Americas Watch, *Peru Under Fire*, p. 58. Victor Smith, a British sociol-

ogist and "Senderologist" noted that after dispensing revolutionary justice, Sendero tries "to reorganize agricultural production, distributing livestock between rich and poor peasants. And they instruct farmers to cut back food production to the level needed to sustain the family and feed the guerilla army. The aim is to starve the towns and heighten urban dissatisfaction. Sendero then appoints its own supporters to positions of authority, selecting cadres to direct production and distribution, organize party cells and choose recruits for the guerilla army": V. Smith, "A Shining Path of Blood," *New Internationalist*, no. 197 (1989), p. 9.

46. Manrique, "Time of Fear," pp. 33–34, described how people are executed and "Draconian punishments" meted out for drinking and adultery. According to Smith, "Sendero always follows the same procedure when it enters a new area. All the landlords, medium-scale merchants and State representatives, like district governors or justices of the peace, are either killed or ordered to leave or resign their posts. Criminals are hauled up before 'people's' courts. . . . Many are summarily executed in bloody fashion": Smith, "A Shining Path of Blood," p. 9. Gorriti argued that Sendero's control is often "superficial and to some degree enforced by terror—but the state does not have continuity." Cited in Americas Watch, *Peru Under Fire*, p. 58.

47. Wheat argued that Sendero recognizes that "few Peruvians desire a government modelled after the Gang of Four and China's Cultural Revolution": Wheat, "Shining Path's 'Fourth Sword' Ideology," p. 51. The result, he contended, is that "Sendero emphasizes the evils of the current political system rather than detailing its own plans for Peru's future." Wheat also cited Berg, who argued that it was in Sendero's interest to "keep its program obscure and vague, because then peasants can continue to sympathize with its actions while basically remaining opposed to ideas of collectivization and revolution": R. Berg, "Sendero Luminoso and the Peasantry of Andahuaylas," *Journal of Interamerican Studies and World Affairs*, vol. 28, no. 4 (1986/1987), p. 193. Degregori, "A Dwarf Star," p. 16, suggested that some see the "revolution as a means for social mobility."

48. Lehmann, "The Shining Path to Terror." Americas Watch, *Peru Under Fire*, pp. 13–20, documented the government's slaughter; it was a recurring theme throughout the book. Americas Watch put the overall death toll since 1980 at 18,000 dead and another 3,500 "disappeared" by the government and therefore presumed dead (p. 142).

49. Americas Watch argued that "Sendero is, in fact, omnipresent in Peru": Americas Watch, *Peru Under Fire*, p. 62.

50. Degregori, "A Dwarf Star," p. 16, clearly thought that Sendero had reached its limits, an attitude shared by other Peruvian observers such as Gorriti, "The War of the Philosopher-King," p. 21, and Manrique, "A Time of Fear," pp. 37–38. Non-Peruvians seem to agree. See, e.g., Starn, "New Literature on Peru's Sendero Luminoso," p. 224; Lehmann, "The Shining Path to Terror," p. 10; Dietz, "Peru's Sendero Luminoso as a Revolutionary Movement," p. 124; and Smith, "A Shining Path of Blood," p. 9. None of these people ruled out an eventual victory for Sendero, but they clearly think it improbable. The real threat, Manrique warned with eerie prescience, was "a military coup or the de facto militarization of the state, which would destroy the popular organizations, the Left, and the democratic progress achieved at the grass roots in recent decades." A 1991 Peruvian novel, he continued, "entitled 'Attila's Colts: The 1992 Coup in Peru' lays out the implications of such a development: Sendero is defeated at the cost of 600,000 lives, the elimination of all democratic organizations, and a dictatorship lasting 25 years. What makes the book so disturbing is that it seems absolutely credible, given where Peru stands today, especially since the military admitted in November [1990] to having prepared contingency plans for just such a scenario. (The military's plans assumed that the dictatorship would last only 15 or 20 years.) Such a catastrophe is not, of

course, the only way out; the book could well have been written as a way of exorcising the possibility of a coup. Perhaps if we look over the brink of the abyss we will find a way to avoid falling into it": Manrique, "A Time of Fear," pp. 37–38. As of this writing, the April 1992 coup is more than a year old.

51. P. Andreas, "Fujimori's Coup," *Nation*, vol. 254, no. 16 (1992), p. 545. T. Moore, "War Odds Shorten After Peruvian Coup," *Guardian*, 1992, and J. Goldman, "Peru's Coup Reveals Fault Lines in Latin America," *In These Times*, vol. 16, no. 20 (1992) also argued that the coup served to legitimate Sendero Luminoso.

52. J. Domínguez and C. Mitchell, "The Roads Not Taken: Institutionalization and Political Participation in Cuba and Bolivia," *Comparative Politics*, vol. 9, no. 2 (1977); T. Wickham-Crowley, "The Rise and Sometimes Fall of Guerrilla Governments in Latin America," in *Exploring Revolution: Essays on Latin American Insurgency and Revolutionary Theory* (Armonk: M. E. Sharpe, 1991).

53. R. Darnton, "What Was Revolutionary About the French Revolution?" *New York Review of Books*, vol. 35 (19 January 1989), p. 20.

# Selected Bibliography

Alvarez, F. A. 1988. "Transition Before the Transition." *Latin American Perspectives*, vol. 15, no. 1.

Ambursley, F. 1983. "Grenada: The New Jewel Revolution." In F. Ambursley and R. Cohen, eds., *Crisis in the Caribbean*. New York: Monthly Review.

Ambursley, F., and J. Dunkerley. 1984. *Grenada: Whose Freedom*. London: Latin American Bureau.

Americas Watch. 1985. *Human Rights in Nicaragua: Reagan, Rhetoric and Reality*. New York: Americas Watch.

———. 1991. *El Salvador's Decade of Terror: Human Rights Since the Assassination of Archbishop Romero*. New Haven: Yale University Press.

———. 1992. *Peru Under Fire: Human Rights Since the Return to Democracy*. New Haven: Yale University Press.

Amin, S. 1991. "The Issue of Democracy in the Contemporary Third World." *Socialism and Democracy*, no. 12.

Arendt, H. 1965. *On Revolution*. New York: Penguin.

Aya, R. 1979. "Theories of Revolution Reconsidered." *Theory and Society*, vol. 8, no. 1.

———. 1984. "Popular Intervention in Revolutionary Situations." In C. Bright and S. Harding, eds., *Statemaking and Social Movements: Essays in History and Theory*. Ann Arbor: University of Michigan Press.

Azicri, M. 1988. *Cuba: Politics, Economics, and Society*. London: Pinter.

———. 1990. "Twenty-six Years of Cuban Revolutionary Politics: An Appraisal." In S. Jonas and N. Stein, eds., *Democracy in Latin America: Visions and Reality*. New York: Bergin and Garvey.

———. 1990. "The Cuban Rectification: Safeguarding the Revolution While Building the Future." In Halebsky and Kirk, *Transformation and Struggle*.

Bengelsdorf, C. 1990. "The Matter of Democracy in Cuba: Snapshots of Three Moments." In Halebsky and Kirk, *Transformation and Struggle*.

Bishop, M. 1983. "Maurice Bishop Speaks to U.S. Working People." In B. Marcus and M. Taber, eds., *Maurice Bishop Speaks: The Grenada Revolution 1979–83*. New York: Pathfinder.

Black, G. 1981. *Triumph of the People: The Sandinista Revolution in Nicaragua*. London: Zed.

Blum, W. 1986. *The CIA: A Forgotten History, U.S. Global Interventions Since World War 2*. London: Zed.

Bonachea, R., and M. San Martin. 1974. *The Cuban Insurrection 1952–1959*. New Brunswick: Transaction Press.

Bonachea, R., and N. Valdés, eds. 1972. *Cuba in Revolution*. New York: Anchor Books.

Booth, J. 1985. "The National Government System." In Walker, *Nicaragua: The First Five Years*.
———. 1985. *The End and the Beginning: The Nicaraguan Revolution*, 2d ed. Boulder: Westview.
Booth, J., and M. Seligson, eds. 1989. *Elections and Democracy in Central America*. Chapel Hill: University of North Carolina Press.
Booth, J., and T. Walker. 1989. *Understanding Central America*. Boulder: Westview.
Borge, T. 1982. "On Human Rights in Nicaragua." In Borge et al., *Sandinistas Speak*.
———. 1985. "This Is a Revolution of the Working People." In Marcus, *Nicaragua*.
Borge, T., C. Fonseca, D. Ortega, H. Ortega, and J. Wheelock. 1982. *Sandinistas Speak*. New York: Pathfinder.
Boswell, T., ed. 1989. *Revolution in the World System*. New York: Greenwood.
Brinton, C. 1965. *Anatomy of Revolution*. New York: Vintage.
Burbach, R., and O. Núñez. 1987. *Fire in the Americas*. London: Verso.
Cabezas, O. 1985. *Fire from the Mountain: The Making of a Sandinista*. New York: Crown Books.
Camjeo, P., and P. Murphy, eds. 1979. *The Nicaraguan Revolution*. New York: Pathfinder.
Castro, F. 1962. *Fidel Castro Denounces Bureaucratization and Sectarianism*. New York: Pioneer Publishers.
———. 1968. *Granma*. Weekly Review (15 December).
———. 1969. "The Second Declaration of Havana" (4 February 1962). In M. Kenner and J. Petras, eds., *Fidel Castro Speaks*. New York: Grove.
———. 1969. "Speech" (13 March 1967). In M. Kenner and J. Petras, eds., *Fidel Castro Speaks*. New York: Grove.
———. 1987. "Important Problems for the Whole of International Revolutionary Thought." *New International*, no. 6.
———. 1989. "Che's Ideas Are Absolutely Relevant Today." In C. Tablada, *Che Guevara: Economics and Politics in the Transition to Socialism*. Sydney: Pathfinder/Pacific and Asia.
———. 1989. "Thirty Years of the Cuban Revolution." *In Defense of Socialism: Four Speeches on the 30th Anniversary of the Cuban Revolution*. New York: Pathfinder.
Chamorro, V. 1989. News Conference. *La Prensa*, 14 September. FBIS-LAM.
———. 1989. Campaign Speech. Radio Católica (19 December). FBIS-LAM.
———. 1990. Campaign Speech. Radio Católica (23 January). FBIS-LAM.
———. 1990. Final Campaign Speech. Managua Radio Corporation (20 February). FBIS-LAM.
Clark, S. 1987. "The Second Assassination of Maurice Bishop." *New International*, no. 6.
Close, D. 1988. *Nicaragua: Politics, Economics, and Society*. London: Pinter.
Cook, M. 1990. "Nicaragua: UNO: One Is Not Enough," *NACLA Report on the Americas*, vol. 23, no. 5.
Coraggio, J. L. 1986. "Economics and Politics in the Transition to Socialism: Reflections on the Nicaraguan Experience." In Fagen, Deere, and Coraggio, *Transition and Development*.
Cruz, A. 1984. "Nicaragua: The Sandinista Regime at a Strategic Watershed." *Strategic Review*, Spring.
———. 1988. *Harvard Law Bulletin*, vol. 39, no. 3.
Darnton, R. 1989. "What Was Revolutionary About the French Revolution?" *New York Review of Books*, vol. 35, no. 19.
Davies, J. 1962. "Toward a Theory of Revolution." *American Sociological Review*, vol. 27, no. 1.
DeFronzo, J. 1991. *Revolutions and Revolutionary Movements*. Boulder: Westview.

Degregori, C. 1990/1991. "A Dwarf Star." *NACLA Report on the Americas,* vol. 24, no. 4.

del Aguila, J. 1988. *Cuba: Dilemmas of a Revolution.* Boulder: Westview.

Denardo, J. 1985. *Power in Numbers.* Princeton: Princeton University Press.

D'Escoto, M. 1983. "Nicaragua: Unfinished Canvas." *Sojourners,* March.

Diamond, L., J. Linz, and S. M. Lipset, eds. 1989. *Democracy in Developing Countries,* Vol. 4: *Latin America.* Boulder: Lynne Rienner.

Dickey, C. 1986. *With the Contras.* New York: Simon and Schuster.

Dietz, H. 1990. "Peru's Sendero Luminoso as a Revolutionary Movement." *Journal of Political and Military Sociology,* no. 18.

Dix, R. 1984. "Why Revolutions Succeed and Fail." *Polity,* vol. 16, no. 3.

Dixon, M. 1985. *Nicaragua Under Siege.* San Francisco: Synthesis.

Domínguez, J. 1987. "Political Change: Central America, South America, and the Caribbean." In M. Weiner and S. Huntington, eds., *Understanding Development.* Boston: Little, Brown.

Domínguez, J., and C. Mitchell. 1977. "The Roads Not Taken: Institutionalization and Political Participation in Cuba and Bolivia." *Comparative Politics,* vol. 9, no. 2.

Dror, Y. 1988. "Visionary Political Leadership: On Imposing a Risky Requisite." *International Political Science Review,* vol. 9, no. 1.

Dunkerley, J. 1982. *The Long War: Dictatorship and Rebellion in El Salvador.* London: Verso.

———. 1984. *Rebellion in the Veins: Political Struggle in Bolivia 1952–1982.* London: Verso.

———. 1988. *Power in the Isthmus: A Political History of Modern Central America.* London: Verso.

———. 1992. "El Salvador, 1930–89." *Political Suicide in Latin America and Other Essays.* London: Verso.

Dunn, J. 1989. *Modern Revolutions,* 2d ed. Cambridge: Cambridge University Press.

Eckstein, H. 1964. *Internal War: Problems and Approaches.* New York: Free Press.

———. 1965. "On the Etiology of Internal Wars." *History and Theory,* vol. 4, no. 2.

Eckstein, S. 1982. "The Impact of Revolution on Social Welfare in Latin America." *Theory and Society,* vol. 11, no. 1.

———. 1983. "Transformation of a 'Revolution from Below': Bolivia and International Capital." *Comparative Studies in Society and History,* vol. 25, no. 1.

———. 1983. "Revolution and Redistribution in Latin America." In C. McClintock and A. F. Lowenthal, eds., *The Peruvian Experiment Reconsidered.* Princeton: Princeton University Press.

———. 1985. "Revolutions and the Restructuring of National Economies." *Comparative Politics,* vol. 17, no. 4.

———. 1989. "Power and Popular Protest in Latin America." In S. Eckstein, *Power and Popular Protest.*

Eckstein, S., ed. 1989. *Power and Popular Protest: Latin American Social Movements.* Berkeley: University of California Press.

Edelman, M. 1986. "Dora Maria Telléz." *NACLA Report on the Americas,* vol. 20, no. 5.

Eisenstadt, S. N. 1978. *Revolutions and the Transformation of Societies.* New York: Free Press.

Fagen, R. 1964. "Charismatic Authority and the Leadership of Fidel Castro." *Western Political Quarterly,* vol. 18.

———. 1969. *The Transformation of Political Culture in Cuba.* Stanford: Stanford University Press.

———. 1972. "Continuities in Cuban Revolutionary Politics." *Monthly Review,* vol. 23, no. 11.

————. 1986. "The Politics of Transition." In Fagen, Deere, and Coraggio, *Transition and Development*.

Fagen, R., C. D. Deere, and J. L. Coraggio, eds. 1986. *Transition and Development: Problems of Third World Socialism*. New York: Monthly Review.

Finley, M. I. 1986. "Revolution in Antiquity." In Porter and Teich, *Revolution in History*.

Fitzgerald, F. 1990. *Managing Socialism: From Old Cadres to New Professionals in Revolutionary Cuba*. New York: Praeger.

Fitzgerald, F., and J. Petras. 1988. "Confusion About the Transition to Socialism." *Latin American Perspectives*, vol. 15, no. 1.

Franqui, C. 1980. *Diary of the Cuban Revolution*. New York: Viking.

FSLN. 1986. "The Historic Program of the FSLN." In Borge et al., *Sandinistas Speak*.

Gamarra, E., and J. Malloy. 1990. "Bolivia: Revolution and Reaction." In Wiarda and Kline, *Latin American Politics and Development*.

Gilbert, D. 1986. "Nicaragua." In M. Blachman, W. LeoGrande, and K. Sharpe, eds., *Confronting Revolution: Security Through Diplomacy in Central America*. New York: Pantheon.

————. 1988. *Sandinistas: The Party and the Revolution*. New York: Basil Blackwell.

Goldfrank, W. 1979. "Theories of Revolution and Revolution Without Theory: The Case of Mexico." *Theory and Society*, vol. 7, no. 1-2.

Goldstone, J. 1980. "Theories of Revolution: The Third Generation." *World Politics*, vol. 23, no. 3.

————. 1991. *Revolution and Rebellion in the Early Modern World*. Berkeley: University of California Press.

Goldstone, J., T. R. Gurr, and F. Moshiri, eds. 1991. *Revolutions of the Late Twentieth Century*. Boulder: Westview.

Goodrich, C. 1971. "Bolivia in Time of Revolution." In Malloy and Thorn, *Beyond the Revolution*.

Goodwin, J., and T. Skocpol. 1989. "Explaining Revolutions in the Third World." *Politics and Society*, vol. 17, no. 4.

Gramsci, A. 1971. *Selections from the Prison Notebooks*, Q. Hoare and G. N. Smith, eds. New York: International Publishers.

Greene, T. 1990. *Comparative Revolutionary Movements*, 3d ed. Englewood Cliffs: Prentice-Hall.

Grynspan, D. 1991. "Nicaragua: A New Model for Popular Revolution in Latin America." In Goldstone, Gurr, and Moshiri, *Revolutions of the Late Twentieth Century*.

Guevara, E. 1967. *Che Guevara Speaks*. New York: Pathfinder.

————. 1968. *Venceremos: The Speeches and Writings of Che Guevara*. New York: Simon and Schuster.

————. 1987. *Che Guevara and the Cuban Revolution: Writings and Speeches of Ernesto Che Guevara*. New York: Pathfinder.

Guillermoprieto, A. 1990. "Letter from Managua." *New Yorker*, 26 March.

Gurr, T. R. 1970. *Why Men Rebel*. Princeton: Princeton University Press.

Gutman, R. 1988. *Banana Republic: The Making of American Policy in Nicaragua 1981–1987*. New York: Simon and Schuster.

Habel, J. 1991. *Cuba: The Revolution in Peril*. London: Verso.

Hagopian, M. 1974. *The Phenomena of Revolution*. New York: Dodd, Mead.

Halebsky, S., and J. Kirk, eds. 1990. *Transformation and Struggle: Cuba Faces the 1990s*. New York: Praeger.

Halperin, M. 1981. *The Taming of Fidel Castro*. Berkeley: University of California Press.

Harris, R. L. 1988. "Marxism and the Transition to Socialism in Latin America." *Latin American Perspectives*, vol. 15, no. 1.

Harris, R. L., and C. M. Vilas, eds. 1985. *Nicaragua: A Revolution Under Siege.* London: Zed.

Haugaard, L. 1991. "In and Out of Power: Dilemmas for Grassroots Organizing in Nicaragua." *Socialism and Democracy,* vol. 7, no. 3.

Heine, J., ed. 1990. *A Revolution Aborted: The Lessons of Grenada.* Pittsburgh: University of Pittsburgh Press.

Henry, P. 1990. "Socialism and Cultural Transformation in Grenada." In Heine, *A Revolution Aborted.*

Hobsbawm, E. 1986. "Revolution." In Porter and Teich, *Revolution in History.*

Hodges, D. 1986. *Intellectual Foundations of the Nicaraguan Revolution.* Austin: University of Texas Press.

Hoffer, E. 1951. *The True Believer: Thoughts on the Nature of Mass Movements.* New York: Harper.

Hopper, R. D. 1950. "The Revolutionary Process: A Frame of Reference for the Study of Revolutionary Movements." *Social Forces,* vol. 28, no. 3.

Huntington, S. 1968. *Political Order in Changing Societies.* New Haven: Yale University Press.

ITZTANI. 1988. "La opinión políticada los managuas." *Encuentro,* vol. 35 (September-December).

Jonas, S. 1989. "Elections and Transition: The Nicaraguan and Guatemalan Cases." In Booth and Seligson, *Elections and Democracy in Central America.*

Jonas, S., and N. Stein. 1990. "The Construction of Democracy in Nicaragua." *Latin American Perspectives,* vol. 17, no. 3.

Judson, C. 1984. *Cuba and the Revolutionary Myth: The Political Education of the Cuban Rebel Army, 1953–1963.* Boulder: Westview.

———. 1985. "Continuity and Evolution of Revolutionary Symbolism in *Verde Olivo.*" In S. Halebsky and J. Kirk, eds., *Cuba: Twenty-Five Years of Revolution, 1959–1984.* New York: Praeger.

Kelly, J., and H. Klein. 1982. *Revolution and the Rebirth of Inequality: A Theory Applied to the National Revolution in Bolivia.* Berkeley: University of California Press.

Keren, M. 1988. "Introduction." *International Political Science Review,* vol. 9, no. 1.

Kimmel, M. 1990. *Revolution: A Sociological Interpretation.* Philadelphia: Temple University Press.

Kinzer, S. 1991. *Blood of Brothers: Life and War in Nicaragua.* New York: Putnam.

Kirchheimer, O. 1965. "Confining Conditions and Revolutionary Breakthroughs." *American Political Science Review,* vol. 59, no. 4.

Klein, H. 1982. *Bolivia: Evolution of a Multi-Ethnic Society.* New York: Oxford University Press.

Knight, A. 1990. "Social Revolution: A Latin American Perspective." *Bulletin of Latin American Research,* vol. 9, no. 2.

Kochanek, S. 1973. "Perspectives on the Study of Revolution and Social Change." *Comparative Politics,* vol. 5, no. 3.

Kornbluh, P. 1987. "The Covert War." In Walker, *Reagan Versus the Sandinistas.*

———. 1989. "Nicaragua." In P. Schraeder, ed., *Intervention in the 1980s: U.S. Foreign Policy in the Third World.* Boulder: Lynne Rienner.

———. 1991. "U.S. Role in the Counterrevolution." In Walker, *Revolution and Counterrevolution in Nicaragua.*

Kornbluh, P., and R. Parry. 1988. "Iran-Contra's Untold Story." *Foreign Policy,* no. 72.

Kurlansky, M. 1992. *A Continent of Islands: Searching for the Caribbean Destiny.* Reading: Addison-Wesley.

La Ramée, P., and E. Polakoff. 1990. "Transformation of the CDSs and the Breakdown of Grassroots Democracy in Revolutionary Nicaragua." *New Political Science,* no. 18/19.

Lacayo, H.E. Sergio. 1989. "Consolidating Democracy Under Fire." In J. M. Kirk and G. W. Schuyler, eds., *Central America: Democracy, Development, and Change*. New York: Praeger.

LaFeber, W. 1984. *Inevitable Revolutions: The United States in Central America*, 2d ed. New York: Norton.

LASA. 1984. "The Electoral Process in Nicaragua: Domestic and International Influences." Report of the Latin American Studies Association Delegation to Observe the Nicaraguan General Election of November 4, 1984. Austin: LASA.

———. 1988. "Extraordinary Opportunities ... and New Risks." Report of the Latin American Studies Association Commission on Compliance with the Central American Peace Accord. Pittsburgh: LASA.

———. 1990. "Electoral Democracy Under International Pressure." Report of the Latin American Studies Association Commission to Observe the 1990 Election. Pittsburgh: LASA.

Lenin, V. I. 1986. *What Is to Be Done?* New York: International Publishers.

LeoGrande, W. 1978. "Mass Political Participation in Socialist Cuba." In J. Booth and M. Seligson, eds., *Political Participation in Latin America*, Vol. 1: *Citizen and State*. New York: Holmes and Meier.

———. 1979. "Party Development in Revolutionary Cuba." *Journal of Interamerican Studies and World Affairs*, vol. 21, no. 4.

———. 1982. "The United States and the Nicaraguan Revolution." In Walker, *Nicaragua in Revolution*.

Levine, D. 1978. "Venezuela Since 1958: The Consolidation of Democracy." In J. Linz and A. Stepan, eds., *The Breakdown of Democratic Regimes: Latin America*. Baltimore: Johns Hopkins University Press.

Lewis, G. 1987. *Grenada: The Jewel Despoiled*. Baltimore: Johns Hopkins University Press.

Lijphart, A. 1990. "Size, Pluralism and the Westminster Model of Democracy: Implications for the Eastern Caribbean." In Heine, *A Revolution Aborted*.

Linz, J. 1978. *The Breakdown of Democratic Regimes: Crisis, Breakdown and Equilibrium*. Baltimore: Johns Hopkins University Press.

Malloy, J. 1970. *Bolivia: The Uncompleted Revolution*. Pittsburgh: University of Pittsburgh Press.

———. 1971. "Revolutionary Politics." In Malloy and Thorn, *Beyond the Revolution*.

Malloy, J., and E. Gamarra. 1988. *Revolution and Reaction: Bolivia 1964–1985*. New Brunswick: Transaction.

Malloy, J., and R. Thorn, eds. 1971. *Beyond the Revolution: Bolivia Since 1952*. Pittsburgh: University of Pittsburgh Press.

Mandle, J. 1985. *Big Revolution Small Country: The Rise and Fall of the Grenada Revolution*. Lanham: North-South Publishing.

Manrique, N. 1990/1991. "Time of Fear." *NACLA Report on the Americas*, vol. 24, no. 4.

Maravell, J. M., and J. Santamaría. 1986. "Political Change in Spain and the Prospects for Democracy." In G. O'Donnell, P. C. Schmitter, and L. Whitehead, eds., *Transitions From Authoritarian Rule: Southern Europe*. Baltimore: Johns Hopkins University Press.

Marchetti, P. 1986. "War, Popular Participation, and Transition to Socialism: The Case of Nicaragua." In Fagen, Deere, and Coraggio, *Transition and Development*.

Marcus, B., ed. 1985. *Nicaragua: The Sandinista People's Revolution: Speeches by Sandinista Leaders*. New York: Pathfinder Press.

Martínez Heredia, F. 1991. "Cuban Socialism: Prospects and Challenge." *Latin American Perspectives*, vol. 18, no. 2.

Marx, K. 1978. "The Eighteenth Brumaire of Louis Bonaparte." In Tucker, *The Marx-Engels Reader*.

Marx, K., and F. Engels. 1978. "Address of the Central Committee to the Communist League." In Tucker, *The Marx-Engels Reader*.

———. 1978. "The Communist Manifesto." In Tucker, *The Marx-Engels Reader*.

Massing, M. 1988. "Who Are the Sandinistas?" *New York Review of Books*, vol. 35, no. 8.

Migdal, J. 1974. *Peasants, Politics, and Revolution: Pressures Toward Political and Social Change in the Third World*. Princeton: Princeton University Press.

———. 1985. "A Model of State-Society Relations." In H. Wiarda, ed., *New Directions in Comparative Politics*. Boulder: Westview Press.

———. 1988. "Vision and Practice: The Leader, the State, and the Transformation of Society." *International Political Science Review*, vol. 9, no. 1.

———. 1989. *Strong Societies and Weak States: State-Society Relations and State Capabilities in the Third World*. Princeton: Princeton University Press.

Miles, S., and B. Ostertag. 1989. "FMLN New Thinking." *NACLA Report on the Americas*, vol. 23, no. 3.

Montgomery, T. 1982. *Revolution in El Salvador: Origins and Evolution*. Boulder: Westview.

Moore, B. 1966. *Social Origins of Dictatorship and Democracy*. Boston: Beacon Press.

Moshiri, F. 1991. "Revolutionary Conflict Theory in an Evolutionary Perspective." In Goldstone, Gurr, and Moshiri, *Revolutions of the Late Twentieth Century*.

Nimtz, A. 1992. "Marxism: An Interpretative Essay." In *The Oxford Companion to Politics of the World*. Oxford: Oxford University Press.

Nolan, D. 1984. *The Ideology of the Sandinistas and the Nicaraguan Revolution*. Coral Gables: Institute of International Studies.

O'Donnell, G., and P. C. Schmitter. 1986. *Transitions from Authoritarian Rule: Tentative Conclusions About Uncertain Democracies*. Baltimore: Johns Hopkins University Press.

O'Donnell, G., P. C. Schmitter, and L. Whitehead, eds. 1986. *Transitions from Authoritarian Rule: Comparative Perspectives*. Baltimore: Johns Hopkins University Press.

———. 1986. *Transitions from Authoritarian Rule: Latin America*. Baltimore: Johns Hopkins University Press.

———. 1986. *Transitions from Authoritarian Rule: Prospects for Democracy*. Baltimore: Johns Hopkins University Press.

O'Kane, T. 1990. "The New Old Order." *NACLA Report on the Americas*, vol. 24, no. 1.

O'Shaughnessy, H. 1984. *Grenada: An Eyewitness Account of the U.S. Invasion and the Caribbean History That Provoked It*. New York: Dodd, Mead.

Ortega, D. 1985. "We Are a Very Small Country Confronting a Truly Colossal Force." In Marcus, *Nicaragua: The Sandinista People's Revolution*.

———. 1985. "The Sandinista People's Revolution Is an Irreversible Political Reality." In Marcus, *Nicaragua: The Sandinista People's Revolution*.

———. 1989. "Ortega Praises Revolution on Anniversary" (20 July). FBIS-LAM.

Ortega, H. 1982. "Nicaragua—The Strategy of Political Victory." In Borge et al., *Sandinistas Speak*.

———. 1987. "FSLN: Statement on the Electoral Process." In R. and B. Rubin, eds., *The Central American Crisis Reader*. New York: Summit Books.

Paige, J. 1975. *Agrarian Revolution: Social Movements and Export Agriculture in the Underdeveloped World*. New York: Free Press.

Pastor, R. 1987. *Condemned to Repetition: The United States and Nicaragua*. Princeton: Princeton University Press.

Payne, A., P. Sutton, and T. Thorndike. 1984. *Grenada: Revolution and Invasion*. New York: St. Martin's.

Peeler, J. 1989. "Democracy and Elections in Central America: Autumn of the Oligarchs?" In Booth and Seligson, *Elections and Democracy in Central America.*

Pérez, L., Jr. 1988. *Cuba: Between Reform and Revolution.* New York: Oxford University Press.

———. 1990. *Cuba and the United States: Ties of Singular Intimacy.* Athens: University of Georgia Press.

Pérez-Stable, M. 1990. "Socialism and Democracy: Some Thoughts After 30 Years of Revolution in Cuba." In Halebsky and Kirk, *Transformation and Struggle.*

Petras, J. F., and F. T. Fitzgerald. 1988. "Authoritarianism and Democracy in the Transition to Socialism." *Latin American Perspectives,* vol. 15, no. 1.

Poole, D., and G. Renique. 1991. "The New Chroniclers of Peru: US Senderologists and the 'Shining Path' of Peasant Rebellion." *Bulletin of Latin American Research,* vol. 10, no. 2.

Porter, R., and M. Teich, eds. 1986. *Revolution in History.* Cambridge: Cambridge University Press.

Prevost, G. 1991. "The FSLN as Ruling Party." In Walker, *Revolution and Counterrevolution in Nicaragua.*

Rabkin, R. 1991. *Cuban Politics: The Revolutionary Experiment.* New York: Praeger.

Ramírez, S. 1985. "Our Promises Were Made to the Poorest of Our Country." In Marcus, *Nicaragua: The Sandinista People's Revolution.*

———. 1989. "Interview." In W. Gentile, *Nicaragua.* New York: W. W. Norton.

———. 1991. "Nicaragua: Confession of Love." *This Magazine,* vol. 24, no. 8.

Randall, M. 1981. *Sandino's Daughters: Testimonies of Nicaraguan Women in Struggle.* Vancouver: New Star Books.

Reding, A. 1986. "Under Construction: Nicaragua's New Polity." In P. Rosset and J. Vandermeer, eds., *Nicaragua: Unfinished Revolution.* New York: Grove.

———. 1991. "The Evolution of Governmental Institutions." In Walker, *Revolution and Counterrevolution in Nicaragua.*

Rejai, M. 1977. *The Comparative Study of Revolutionary Strategy.* New York: McKay.

Rejai, M., and K. Phillips. 1979. *Leaders of Revolution.* Beverly Hills: Sage.

———. 1983. *World Revolutionary Leaders.* New Brunswick: Rutgers.

———. 1988. *Loyalists and Revolutionaries: Political Leaders Compared.* New York: Praeger.

Renique, J. 1990/1991. "The Revolution Behind Bars." *NACLA Report on the Americas,* vol. 24, no. 4.

Robinson, W. 1990. "U.S. Overt Intervention: Nicaragua's Electoral Coup," *Covert Action Information Bulletin,* no. 34 (Summer).

———. 1990. "Nicaragua: The Making of a 'Democratic' Opposition," *NACLA Report on the Americas,* vol. 23, no. 5.

Robinson, W., and David MacMichael. 1990. "NED Overt Action: Intervention in Nicaragua's Election." *Covert Action Information Bulletin,* no. 33 (Winter).

Rosenberg, T. 1991. *Children of Cain: Violence and the Violent in Latin America.* New York: William Morrow.

Rosenberg, W., and M. Young. 1982. *Transforming Russia and China: Revolutionary Struggle in the Twentieth Century.* New York: Oxford University Press.

Roxborough, I. 1989. "Theories of Revolution: The Evidence from Latin America." *LSE Quarterly,* vol. 3, no. 2.

Ruccio, D. F. 1988. "State, Class, and Transition in Nicaragua." *Latin American Perspectives,* vol. 15, no. 2.

Ruchwarger, G. 1987. *People in Power: Forging a Grassroots Democracy in Nicaragua.* South Hadley: Bergin and Garvey.

Rudé, G. 1980. *Ideology and Popular Protest.* New York: Pantheon.

Sandino, A. 1981. *El pensamiento vivo*, 2d ed. Selected and with an introduction and notes by Sergio Ramírez. Managua: Editorial Nueva Nicaragua.

Schoenhals, K. 1985. "Grenada: The Birth and Death of a Revolution." In K. Schoenhals and R. Melanson, *Revolution and Intervention in Grenada: The New Jewel Movement, The United States, and the Caribbean*. Boulder: Westview.

Schutz, B., and R. Slater. 1990. *Revolution and Political Change in the Third World*. Boulder: Lynne Rienner.

Scott, J. 1976. *The Moral Economy of the Peasant*. New Haven: Yale University Press.

———. 1985. *Weapons of the Weak: Everyday Forms of Peasant Resistance*. New Haven: Yale University Press.

Searle, C., ed. 1984. *In Nobody's Backyard: Maurice Bishop's Speeches 1979–1983: A Memorial Volume*. London: Zed.

Selser, G. 1979. *Sandino: general de hombres libres*. Mexico City: Diógenes.

Serra, L. 1982. "The Sandinista Mass Organizations." In Walker, *Nicaragua in Revolution*.

———. 1985. "Ideology, Religion and the Class Struggle in the Nicaraguan Revolution." In Harris and Vilas, *Nicaragua: A Revolution Under Siege*.

———. 1991. "The Grass-Roots Organizations." In Walker, *Revolution and Counterrevolution in Nicaragua*.

Sewell, W. 1985. "Ideologues and Social Revolution: Reflections on the French Case." *Journal of Modern History*, vol. 57, no. 1.

Sklar, H. 1988. *Washington's War on Nicaragua*. Boston: South End.

———. 1990. "Many Nicaragua Voters Cry Uncle." *Zeta Magazine*, vol. 13, no. 4.

———. 1990. "Dollars Don't Buy Democracy." *Nicaraguan Perspectives*, no. 18.

Skocpol, T. 1976. "From France, Russia, China: A Structural Analysis of Social Revolutions." *Comparative Studies in Society and History*, vol. 18, no. 2.

———. 1979. *States and Social Revolution*. Cambridge: Cambridge University Press.

———. 1982. "What Makes Peasants Revolutionary?" *Comparative Politics*, vol. 14, no. 3.

———. 1982. "Rentier State and Shi'a Islam in the Iranian Revolution." *Theory and Society*, vol. 11, no. 3.

———. 1985. "Cultural Idioms and Political Ideologues in the Revolutionary Reconstruction of State Power: A Rejoinder to Sewell." *Journal of Modern History*, vol. 57, no. 1.

———. 1988. "Social Revolutions and Mass Military Mobilizations." *World Politics*, vol. 42, no. 2.

Slater, D. 1986. "Socialism, Democracy, and the Territorial Imperative: Elements for a Comparison of the Cuban and Nicaraguan Experiences." *Antipode*, vol. 18, no. 2.

Smith, W. 1987. "Lies About Nicargua." *Foreign Policy*, no. 67.

Stahler-Sholk, R. 1987. "Building Democracy in Nicaragua." In G. Lopez and M. Sthol, eds., *Liberalization and Redemocratization in Latin America*. New York: Greenwood.

Stepan, A. 1978. *The State and Society: Peru in Comparative Perspective*. Princeton: Princeton University Press.

Stone, C. 1990. "Whither Caribbean Socialism: Grenada, Jamaica, and Guyana in Perspective." In Heine, *A Revolution Aborted*.

Sunshine, C. 1982. *Grenada: The Peaceful Revolution*. Washington, D.C.: EPICA.

———. 1988. *The Caribbean: Survival, Struggle, and Sovereignty*. Boston: South End.

Thomas, H. 1971. *Cuba: The Pursuit of Freedom*. New York: Harper and Row.

Thomas, H., G. Fauriol, and J. Weiss. 1984. *The Cuban Revolution, 25 Years Later*. Boulder: Westview.

Thorn, R. 1971. "The Economic Transformation." In Malloy and Thorn, *Beyond the Revolution*.

Thorndike, T. 1985. *Grenada: Politics, Economics, and Society.* Boulder: Lynne Rienner.
————. 1990. "People's Power in Theory and Practice." In Heine, *A Revolution Aborted.*
Tilly, C. 1975. "Revolutions and Collective Violence." In F. Greenstein and N. Polsby, eds., *The Handbook of Political Science.* Reading: Addison-Wesley.
————. 1978. *From Mobilization to Revolution.* New York: Random House.
Tirado, V. 1985. "Karl Marx: The International Workers' Movement's Greatest Fighter and Thinker." In Marcus, *Nicaragua: The Sandinista People's Revolution.*
Trimberger, E. K. 1978. *Revolution from Above.* New Brunswick: Transaction.
Trotsky, L. 1930. *My Life.* New York: Pathfinder Press.
————. 1957. *History of the Russian Revolution.* Ann Arbor: University of Michigan Press.
Tucker, R. 1966. "The Marxian Revolutionary Idea." In C. Friedrich, ed., *Revolution.* New York: Atherton.
Tucker, R., ed. 1978. *The Marx-Engels Reader,* 2d ed. New York: Norton.
Vanden, H. 1982. "Ideology of the Nicaraguan Revolution." *Monthly Review,* vol. 34, no. 2.
————. 1986. *National Marxism in Latin America: José Carlos Mariátegui's Thought and Politics.* Boulder: Lynne Rienner.
Vickers, G. 1990. "A Spider's Web." *NACLA Report on the Americas,* vol. 24, no. 1.
Vilas, C. 1990. "What Went Wrong." *NACLA Report on the Americas,* vol. 24, no. 1.
Villalobos, J. 1989. "A Democratic Revolution for El Salvador." *Foreign Policy,* no. 74.
————. 1989. "Popular Insurrection: Desire or Reality?" *Latin American Perspectives,* vol. 16, no. 3.
Walker, T. 1991. *Nicaragua: The Land of Sandino,* 3d ed. Boulder: Westview.
Walker, T., ed. 1982. *Nicaragua in Revolution.* New York: Praeger.
————. 1985. *Nicaragua: The First Five Years.* New York: Praeger.
————. 1987. *Reagan Versus the Sandinistas: The Undeclared War on Nicaragua.* Boulder: Westview.
————. 1991. *Revolution and Counterrevolution in Nicaragua.* Boulder: Westview.
Walton, J. 1984. *Reluctant Rebels: Comparative Studies of Revolution and Underdevelopment.* New York: Columbia University Press.
Weber, M. 1946. "The Sociology of Charismatic Authority." In H. H. Gerth and C. W. Mills, eds., *From Max Weber: Essays in Sociology.* New York: Oxford University Press.
Wheat, A. 1990. "Shining Path's 'Fourth Sword' Ideology." *Journal of Political and Military Sociology,* no. 18.
Wheelock Román, J. 1983. *El gran desafío: entrevista por Marta Harnecker.* Managua: Editorial Nueva Nicaragua.
Wiarda, H., and H. Kline. 1990. "Government Machinery and the Role of the State." In Wiarda and Kline, eds., *Latin America Politics and Development.*
Wiarda, H., and H. Kline, eds. 1990. *Latin America Politics and Development,* 3d ed. Boulder: Westview.
Wickham-Crowley, T. 1989. "Winners, Losers, and Also-Rans: Toward a Comparative Sociology of Latin American Guerrilla Movements." In S. Eckstein, *Power and Popular Protest.*
————. 1991. *Exploring Revolution: Essays on Latin American Insurgency and Revolutionary Theory.* Armonk: M. E. Sharpe.
————. 1992. *Guerrillas and Revolution in Latin America: A Comparative Study of Insurgents and Regimes Since 1956.* Princeton: Princeton University Press.
Wolf, E. 1969. *Peasant Wars of the Twentieth Century.* New York: Harper and Row.
Wolin, S. 1960. *Politics and Vision.* Boston: Little, Brown.
Wright, B. 1990. "Pluralism and Vanguardism in the Nicaraguan Revolution." *Latin American Perspectives,* vol. 17, no. 3.
Wright, T. 1991. *Latin America in the Era of the Cuban Revolution.* New York: Praeger.

# Acronyms

| | |
|---|---|
| AID | Agency for International Development |
| ARDE | Democratic Revolutionary Alliance |
| ANC | National Conservative Action party |
| CCC | Committee of Concerned Citizens |
| CD | Democratic Convergence |
| CD | Democratic Coordinating Committee |
| CDC | Community Development Committee |
| CDR | Committee for the Defense of the Revolution |
| CDS | Sandinista Defense Committee |
| CIA | Central Intelligence Agency |
| CIVS | International Commission of Verification and Security |
| COB | Bolivian Workers Confederation |
| COMIBOL | Bolivian Mining Corporation |
| CORDENIC | Commission on the Recuperation and Development of Nicaragua |
| COSEP | Superior Council of Private Enterprise |
| CSE | Supreme Electoral Council |
| CUS | Council of Trade Union Unification |
| FDN | Nicaraguan Democratic Force |
| FDR | Revolutionary Democratic Front |
| FSLN | Sandinista National Liberation Front |
| FMLN | Farabundo Martí National Liberation Front |
| FMLN-FDR | Farabundo Martí National Liberation Front–Revolutionary Democratic Front |
| GNP | Grenada National party |
| GPP | Prolonged Popular War tendency |
| GULP | Grenadian United Labor party |
| IPCE | Institute for Electoral Promotion and Training |
| JEWEL | Joint Endeavour for Welfare, Education, and Liberation |
| JGRN | Junta of the Government of National Reconstruction |
| LASA | Latin American Studies Association |
| M-26-7 | 26th of July Movement |
| MACE | Movement for the Advancement of Community Effort |
| MAP | Movement for the Assemblies of the People |
| MAP-ML | Marxist-Leninist Popular Action Movement |
| MDN | Nicaraguan Democratic Movement |
| MNR | National Revolutionary Movement |
| MRTA | Túpac Amaru Revolutionary Movement |

| | |
|---|---|
| MUR | Movement for Revolutionary Unity |
| NED | National Endowment for Democracy |
| NJM | New Jewel Movement |
| NSC | National Security Council |
| NWO | National Women's Organization |
| NYO | National Youth Organization |
| OAS | Organization of American States |
| OREL | Organization for Research, Education, and Liberation |
| ORI | Integrated Revolutionary Organization |
| PALI | Neo-Liberal party |
| PAN | National Action party |
| PAPC | Popular Conservative Alliance party |
| PCD | Democratic Conservative party |
| PCdeN | Communist Party of Nicaragua |
| PCP-SL | Peruvian Communist party–Shining Path |
| PDCN | Democratic Party of National Confidence |
| PIAC | Central American Integrationist party |
| PLC | Constitutionalist Liberal party |
| PLI | Liberal Independent party |
| PLIUN | National Unity Liberal party |
| PLN | Nationalist Liberal party |
| PNC | National Conservative party |
| PPSC | Popular Social Christian party |
| PRG | Provisional Revolutionary Government (later, People's Revolutionary Government) |
| PRI | Institutionalized Revolutionary party |
| PRT | Revolutionary Workers party |
| PSC | Social Christian party |
| PSD | Social Democratic party |
| PSN | Nicaraguan Socialist party |
| PSOC | Social Conservatism party |
| PSP | Popular Socialist party |
| PUCA | Central American Unionist party |
| PURS | United Party of the Socialist Revolution |
| SMP | Popular Military Service |
| UCLA | unilaterally controlled Latin assets |
| UDEL | Democratic Union of Liberation |
| UN | United Nations |
| UNO | National Opposition Union |
| UP | Popular Unity party |
| USIA | U.S. Information Agency |
| YATAMA | Organization of the Nations of the Motherland |

# About the Book and Author

In contrast to previous studies that have been centered on the institutionalization of revolution in Latin America and the Caribbean, *Modern Latin American Revolutions* introduces the concept of consolidation of the revolutionary process—the efforts of revolutionary leaders to transform society and the acceptance by a significant majority of the population of the core of the social revolutionary project. As a result, the spotlight is on people, not structures, and transformation, not simply revolutionary transition.

This book focuses on the cases of Bolivia, Cuba, Nicaragua, and Grenada, assessing the extent to which each revolution was both institutionalized and consolidated. Dr. Selbin argues that there is a strong link between organizational leadership and the institutionalization process on the one hand, and visionary leadership and the consolidation process on the other. Particular attention is given to the ongoing revolutionary process in Nicaragua, with an emphasis on the implication and ramifications of the 1990 electoral process. A final chapter includes brief analyses of the still unfolding revolutionary processes in El Salvador and Peru.

Eric Selbin is assistant professor of political science at Southwestern University in Texas.

# Index